Available Servers - QLLC, JONES_DM

Use acctinfo for normal log-on

Group Name SQL server Group

Transact-SQL

Transact-SQL

William C. Amo

IDG Books Worldwide, Inc.
An International Data Group Company

Foster City, CA ◆ Chicago, IL ◆ Indianapolis, IN ◆ New York, NY

Transact-SQL

Published by
IDG Books Worldwide, Inc.
An International Data Group Company
919 E. Hillsdale Blvd., Suite 400
Foster City, CA 94404
www.idgbooks.com (IDG Books Worldwide Web site)

Library of Congress Catalog Card Number: 98-72472
ISBN: 0-7645-8048-5
Printed in the United States of America

10 9 8 7 6 5 4 3 2

1B/RY/QZ/ZY/FC

Distributed in the United States by IDG Books Worldwide, Inc.

Distributed by Macmillan Canada for Canada; by Transworld Publishers Limited in the United Kingdom; by IDG Norge Books for Norway; by IDG Sweden Books for Sweden; by Woodslane Pty. Ltd. for Australia; by Woodslane (NZ) Ltd. for New Zealand; by Addison Wesley Longman Singapore Pte Ltd. for Singapore, Malaysia, Thailand, Indonesia, and Korea; by Norma Comunicaciones S.A. for Colombia; by Intersoft for South Africa; by International Thomson Publishing for Germany, Austria, and Switzerland; by Toppan Company Ltd. for Japan; by Distribuidora Cuspide for Argentina; by Livraria Cultura for Brazil; by Ediciencia S.A. for Ecuador; by Ediciones ZETA S.C.R. Ltda. for Peru; by WS Computer Publishing Corporation, Inc., for the Philippines; by Unalis Corporation for Taiwan; by Contemporanea de Ediciones for Venezuela; by Computer Book & Magazine Store for Puerto Rico; by Express Computer Distributors for the Caribbean and West Indies. Authorized Sales Agent: Anthony Rudkin Associates for the Middle East and North Africa.

For general information on IDG Books Worldwide's books in the U.S., please call our Consumer Customer Service department at 800-762-2974. For reseller information, including discounts and premium sales, please call our Reseller Customer Service department at 800-434-3422.

For information on where to purchase IDG Books Worldwide's books outside the U.S., please contact our International Sales department at 650-655-3200 or fax 650-655-3297.

For information on foreign language translations, please contact our Foreign & Subsidiary Rights department at 650-655-3021 or fax 650-655-3281.

For sales inquiries and special prices for bulk quantities, please contact our Sales department at 650-655-3200 or write to the address above.

For information on using IDG Books Worldwide's books in the classroom or for ordering examination copies, please contact our Educational Sales department at 800-434-2086 or fax 317-596-5499.

For press review copies, author interviews, or other publicity information, please contact our Public Relations department at 650-655-3000 or fax 650-655-3299.

For authorization to photocopy items for corporate, personal, or educational use, please contact Copyright Clearance Center, 222 Rosewood Drive, Danvers, MA 01923, or fax 978-750-4470.

is a trademark under exclusive
license to IDG Books Worldwide, Inc.,
from International Data Group, Inc.

ABOUT IDG BOOKS WORLDWIDE

Welcome to the world of IDG Books Worldwide.

IDG Books Worldwide, Inc., is a subsidiary of International Data Group, the world's largest publisher of computer-related information and the leading global provider of information services on information technology. IDG was founded more than 25 years ago and now employs more than 8,500 people worldwide. IDG publishes more than 275 computer publications in over 75 countries (see listing below). More than 90 million people read one or more IDG publications each month.

Launched in 1990, IDG Books Worldwide is today the #1 publisher of best-selling computer books in the United States. We are proud to have received eight awards from the Computer Press Association in recognition of editorial excellence and three from *Computer Currents'* First Annual Readers' Choice Awards. Our best-selling *...For Dummies*® series has more than 50 million copies in print with translations in 38 languages. IDG Books Worldwide, through a joint venture with IDG's Hi-Tech Beijing, became the first U.S. publisher to publish a computer book in the People's Republic of China. In record time, IDG Books Worldwide has become the first choice for millions of readers around the world who want to learn how to better manage their businesses.

Our mission is simple: Every one of our books is designed to bring extra value and skill-building instructions to the reader. Our books are written by experts who understand and care about our readers. The knowledge base of our editorial staff comes from years of experience in publishing, education, and journalism — experience we use to produce books for the '90s. In short, we care about books, so we attract the best people. We devote special attention to details such as audience, interior design, use of icons, and illustrations. And because we use an efficient process of authoring, editing, and desktop publishing our books electronically, we can spend more time ensuring superior content and spend less time on the technicalities of making books.

You can count on our commitment to deliver high-quality books at competitive prices on topics you want to read about. At IDG Books Worldwide, we continue in the IDG tradition of delivering quality for more than 25 years. You'll find no better book on a subject than one from IDG Books Worldwide.

John Kilcullen
John Kilcullen
CEO
IDG Books Worldwide, Inc.

Steven Berkowitz
Steven Berkowitz
President and Publisher
IDG Books Worldwide, Inc.

WINNER

Eighth Annual Computer Press Awards ≥1992

WINNER

Ninth Annual Computer Press Awards ≥1993

Tenth Annual Computer Press Awards ≥1994

WINNER

WINNER

Eleventh Annual Computer Press Awards ≥1995

IDG Books Worldwide, Inc., is a subsidiary of International Data Group, the world's largest publisher of computer-related information and the leading global provider of information services on information technology. International Data Group publishes over 275 computer publications in over 75 countries. More than 90 million people read one or more International Data Group publications each month. International Data Group's publications include: **ARGENTINA:** Buyer's Guide, Computerworld Argentina, PC World Argentina; **AUSTRALIA:** Australian Macworld, Australian PC World, Australian Reseller News, Computerworld, IT Casebook, Network World, Publish, Webmaster; **AUSTRIA:** Computerwelt Osterreich, Networks Austria, PC Tip Austria; **BANGLADESH:** PC World Bangladesh; **BELARUS:** PC World Belarus; **BELGIUM:** Data News; **BRAZIL:** Annuário de Informática, Computerworld, Connections, Macworld, PC Player, PC World, Publish, Reseller News, Supergamepower; **BULGARIA:** Computerworld Bulgaria, Network World Bulgaria, PC & MacWorld Bulgaria; **CANADA:** CIO Canada, Client/Server World, ComputerWorld Canada, InfoWorld Canada, NetworkWorld Canada, WebWorld; **CHILE:** Computerworld Chile, PC World Chile; **COLOMBIA:** Computerworld Colombia, PC World Colombia; **COSTA RICA:** PC World Centro America; **THE CZECH AND SLOVAK REPUBLICS:** Computerworld Czechoslovakia, Macworld Czech Republic, PC World Czechoslovakia; **DENMARK:** Communications World Danmark, Computerworld Danmark, Macworld Danmark, PC World Danmark, Techworld Denmark; **DOMINICAN REPUBLIC:** PC World Republica Dominicana; **ECUADOR:** PC World Ecuador; **EGYPT:** Computerworld Middle East, PC World Middle East; **EL SALVADOR:** PC World Centro America; **FINLAND:** MikroPC, Tietoverkko, Tietoviikko; **FRANCE:** Distributique, Hebdo, Info PC, Le Monde Informatique, Macworld, Reseaux & Telecoms, WebMaster France; **GERMANY:** Computer Partner, Computerwoche, Computerwoche Extra, Computerwoche FOCUS, Global Online, Macwelt, PC Welt; **GREECE:** Amiga Computing, GamePro Greece, Multimedia World; **GUATEMALA:** PC World Centro America; **HONDURAS:** PC World Centro America; **HONG KONG:** Computerworld Hong Kong, PC World Hong Kong, Publish in Asia; **HUNGARY:** ABCD CD-ROM, Computerworld Szamitastechnika, Internetto online Magazine, PC World Hungary, PC-X Magazin Hungary; **ICELAND:** Tolvuheimur PC World Island; **INDIA:** Information Communications World, Information Systems Computerworld, PC World India, Publish in Asia; **INDONESIA:** InfoKomputer PC World, Komputek Computerworld, Publish in Asia; **IRELAND:** ComputerScope, PC Live!; **ISRAEL:** Macworld Israel, People & Computers/Computerworld; **ITALY:** Computerworld Italia, Macworld Italia, Networking Italia, PC World Italia; **JAPAN:** DTP World, Macworld Japan, Nikkei Personal Computing, OS/2 World Japan, SunWorld Japan, Windows NT World, Windows World Japan; **KENYA:** PC World East African; **KOREA:** Hi-Tech Information, Macworld Korea, PC World Korea; **MACEDONIA:** PC World Macedonia; **MALAYSIA:** Computerworld Malaysia, PC World Malaysia, Publish in Asia; **MALTA:** PC World Malta; **MEXICO:** Computerworld Mexico, PC World Mexico; **MYANMAR:** PC World Myanmar; **NETHERLANDS:** Computer! Totaal, LAN Internetworking Magazine, LAN World Buyers Guide, Macworld Netherlands, Net, WebWereld; **NEW ZEALAND:** Absolute Beginners Guide and Plain & Simple Series, Computer Buyer, Computer Industry Directory, Computerworld New Zealand, MTB, Network World, PC World New Zealand; **NICARAGUA:** PC World Centro America; **NORWAY:** Computerworld Norge, CW Rapport, Datamagasinet, Financial Rapport, Kursguide Norge, Macworld Norge, Multimediaworld Norge, PC World Ekspress Norge, PC World Nettverk, PC World Norge, PC World ProduktGuide Norge; **PAKISTAN:** Computerworld Pakistan; **PANAMA:** PC World Panama; **PEOPLE'S REPUBLIC OF CHINA:** China Computer Users, China Computerworld, China InfoWorld, China Telecom World Weekly, Computer & Communication, Electronic Design China, Electronics Today, Electronics Weekly, Game Software, PC World China, Popular Computer Week, Software Weekly, Software World, Telecom World; **PERU:** Computerworld Peru, PC World Profesional Peru, PC World SoHo Peru; **PHILIPPINES:** Click!, Computerworld Philippines, PC World Philippines, Publish in Asia; **POLAND:** Computerworld Poland, Computerworld Special Report Poland, Cyber, Macworld Poland, Networld Poland, PC World Komputer; **PORTUGAL:** Cerebro/PC World, Computerworld/Correio Informático, Dealer World Portugal, Mac*In/PC*In Portugal, Multimedia World; **PUERTO RICO:** PC World Puerto Rico; **ROMANIA:** Computerworld Romania, PC World Romania, Telecom Romania; **RUSSIA:** Computerworld Russia, Mir PK, Publish, Seti; **SINGAPORE:** Computerworld Singapore, PC World Singapore, Publish in Asia; **SLOVENIA:** Monitor; **SOUTH AFRICA:** Computing SA, Network World SA, Software World SA; **SPAIN:** Communicaciones World España, Computerworld España, Dealer World España, Macworld España, PC World España; **SRI LANKA:** Infolink PC World; **SWEDEN:** CAP&Design, Computer Sweden, Corporate Computing Sweden, Internetworld Sweden, it.branschen, Macworld Sweden, MaxiData Sweden, MikroDatorn, Nätverk & Kommunikation, PC World Sweden, PCaktiv, Windows World Sweden; **SWITZERLAND:** Computerworld Schweiz, Macworld Schweiz, PCtip; **TAIWAN:** Computerworld Taiwan, Macworld Taiwan, NEW ViSiON/Publish, PC World Taiwan, Windows World Taiwan; **THAILAND:** Publish in Asia, Thai Computerworld; **TURKEY:** Computerworld Turkiye, Macworld Turkiye, Network World Turkiye, PC World Turkiye; **UKRAINE:** Computerworld Kiev, Multimedia World Ukraine, PC World Ukraine; **UNITED KINGDOM:** Acorn User UK, Amiga Action UK, Amiga Computing UK, Apple Talk UK, Computing, Macworld, Parents and Computers UK, PC Advisor, PC Home, PSX Pro, The WEB; **UNITED STATES:** Cable in the Classroom, CIO Magazine, Computerworld, DOS World, Federal Computer Week, GamePro Magazine, InfoWorld, I-Way, Macworld, Network World, PC Games, PC World, Publish, Video Event, THE WEB Magazine, and WebMaster; online webzines: JavaWorld, NetscapeWorld, and SunWorld Online; **URUGUAY:** InfoWorld Uruguay; **VENEZUELA:** Computerworld Venezuela, PC World Venezuela; and **VIETNAM:** PC World Vietnam.   5/7/98

Credits

ACQUISITIONS EDITOR
John Osborn

DEVELOPMENT EDITOR
Barbra Guerra

TECHNICAL EDITOR
David M. Williams

COPY EDITORS
Dennis Weaver
Anne Friedman

PROJECT COORDINATOR
Susan Parini

COVER COORDINATOR
Cyndra Robbins

COVER DESIGN
© mike parsons design

**GRAPHICS AND PRODUCTION
SPECIALISTS**
Jude Levinson
Mary Penn
Sue DeFloria

QUALITY CONTROL SPECIALISTS
Mick Arellano
Mark Schumann

PROOFREADER
Arielle Carole Mennelle

INDEXER
C² Editorial Services

About the Author

William Amo has over 20 years of experience developing databases and database applications from mainframe to desktop. He has developed numerous Microsoft Access applications and has coauthored *Access for Windows 95 Secrets* and *Access 97 Secrets*, both from IDG Books Worldwide.

Bill has done extensive SQL Server development since Version 4.2 and specializes in client/server component development in database systems. He is currently developing database solutions with C++, Access 97, and SQL Server 6.5 for a leading actuarial consulting firm in Connecticut.

Bill holds a Bachelor of Arts degree in computer science from the State University of New York at Potsdam and a Master of Science degree in computer science from Rensselaer Polytechnic Institute.

First on my list and in my life is my lovely wife Marianne whose love and support has guided this book to completion. You are my life forever.

For my daughter Kirsten and her family — Bill, Willy, and Zachary — for supporting this effort and the good times you all gave me when I needed a break.

For my son Dean and his lovely wife Jennifer, for their support and for keeping my computers running throughout this project.

I dedicate this work to my family and thank you all for the constant joy you give me.

Preface

My purpose in writing *Transact-SQL* is to present a clear and concise explanation of the fundamentals of Microsoft Transact-SQL as implemented in Microsoft SQL Server 7.

Intended Audience

The book is intended for the beginning to intermediate SQL Server database application developers as a handy reference to Transact-SQL. It will also provide Microsoft Visual C++ developers with an introduction to working with SQL Server 7 databases using a variety of application programming interfaces, such as DB-Library, ODBC, and ActiveX Data Objects.

Microsoft SQL Server 7 is an excellent database environment for supporting applications of all sizes from the desktop to the enterprise. A command of the Transact-SQL language is a must for working in this environment, and this book helps you achieve that goal quickly and completely.

Organization of the Book

Part I contains three chapters that introduce you to the SQL Server programming environment – the basics of Transact-SQL statements, expressions, operators, literals, and functions. You see how to build a database, define tables and views, and build constraints and indexes. And, you learn about SQL Server security and how to define logins and roles and establish permissions.

In Part II you explore the depths of SQL Server queries, how to use GROUP BY clauses, joins, unions, and distributed queries to external data sources. In Chapter 15 specifically, you explore stored and extended stored procedures and see how triggers can be built to perform custom processing when a given event takes place in the database.

Part III contains hands-on chapters. The samples presented here illustrate the use of code common in many database applications. In Chapter 18, you learn how to access SQL Server using DB-Library. In Chapter 19, you see how an OBDC application works. The latest database access technology, ActiveX Data Objects, is explored in Chapter 20. At the end of Part III, in Chapter 21, you learn about Open Data Services and see an example of an extended stored procedure that can be used as is to provide a custom application log file. In addition, this example gives you the basics of how an extended stored procedure is implemented, which will enable you to create custom procedures for your own applications.

I have included a number of appendixes that I believe will help you in your work with SQL Server. Some of these appendixes provide detailed reference material while others only provide an overview, in which case you will need to refer to the SQL Server Books Online to acquire the detail. Nonetheless, the appendixes are useful as a quick reference in your day-to-day work.

CD-ROM Content

At the back of the book, you'll find a CD-ROM containing the samples from the book, the scripts used to build the sample mutual fund account database, the program source for Part III programs, and other scripts.

Explanation of Icons Used

Throughout this book, you will encounter various icons intended to focus your attention on specific points.

Where you see the Cross Reference icon, you are directed to other chapters or sections of a chapter for further information on the topic.

Experience is a good teacher, so I've pointed out potential problem areas using the Warning icon.

The CD-ROM icon tells you that the content of this book's CD-ROM is applicable to the topic at hand.

Acknowledgments

I thank Cary Prague, my longtime friend and coauthor of the two *Access Secrets* books we did a short while ago, for getting me started in this business of writing books. He has given me some valuable tips from his many years of experience and success. I value his friendship greatly, as I do his many opinions.

I thank Linne Landgraf for her applying her expertise and excellent work on all of the graphics in the book, and for the many hours she put into editing each chapter. I thank her, too, for the work she did putting the appendixes together. Without her efforts, the book would have been much longer in the making.

I thank John Osborn, Senior Acquisitions Editor at IDG Books Worldwide, for giving me the opportunity to write this book and for pushing it through to market on time. I also thank Barbra Guerra, Development Editor at IDG Books Worldwide, and Dennis Weaver, Copy Editor, for their excellent work on editing the content. They are true professionals I hope to work with again in the future.

Contents at a Glance

Contents

Appendixes

Part I

SQL Server Programming Environment

Chapter 1

Introduction to the SQL Server Programming Environment

IN THIS CHAPTER

- ◆ Learn about the components that make up a SQL Server installation
- ◆ Overview of objects contained in a database
- ◆ See what utilities ship with SQL Server 7.0
- ◆ Find out about licensing modes and how they impact the programmer
- ◆ Learn about character sets and sort orders
- ◆ Explore database interfaces that connect your application to a SQL Server database

A SQL SERVER DATABASE application comes into the world through the joint efforts of people in the roles of systems analysts, database administrators, system administrators, programmers, and project managers. These people are responsible for translating a business problem into a technical solution.

The development of the technical solution involves:

- ◆ the design of a database (to include the tables and their columns)
- ◆ a set of stored procedures for processing portions of the application at the server
- ◆ establishing table constraints and relationships among the tables
- ◆ establishing users, roles, and permissions
- ◆ setting up a maintenance plan to include backup and recovery procedures

◆ the selection of a database interface for client applications

◆ the development of the client application software that will use the
database

The list is actually much longer than this, but I think you can see the magnitude
of the effort.

The database interface is the client application's gateway to the database and
primarily involves two components. The first component is the call-level interface
(CLI) and the second component is the language used on that interface.

A database application uses the CLI to retrieve a set of rows from the database
and work with the data contained in those rows. The application may need to visit
the retrieved rows multiple times, scrolling forward and backward through the
result set to inspect each row before taking some other action.

I use the term *call-level interface* here to mean any method or technology to
enable an application to access a database and work with the data and
other objects contained in it. In many cases, especially in the samples illustrated in Part III of this book, the database access technology uses an application programming interface (API) such as DB-Library. The SQL standard
definition of a call-level interface is best represented by ODBC.

Additionally, a database application will use the CLI to change data in the database, add new rows, and delete rows no longer needed.

No matter what processing the application needs to undertake, the CLI is the
means of communicating with the database. The CLI is the conduit through which
the program's database service requests pass to SQL Server and returned results
pass back to the program.

Requests for database services that the program passes to SQL Server need to be
specified in a language that SQL Server understands. The language is the second
component of the database interface and describes what we need SQL Server to do.
With this language, we express what actions SQL Server is to take, whether it is to
retrieve a set of rows, add rows, delete rows, or perform some other database task.

In the SQL Server environment, the language we use is called *Transact-SQL*, and
that language is the primary subject of this book. In Part III, we'll explore a few CLI
options to give you a sense of what's available and how those options are used.

The following sections present a brief overview of the SQL Server programming
environment and the components that enable a database application to function.

Components of the SQL Server Environment

The SQL Server environment in which you implement your application is comprised, in part, of a set of operating system services installed on a machine designated as the database server. These services are responsible for managing the SQL Server installation and for the processing of various data requests from clients.

Figure 1-1 illustrates a conceptual overview of the SQL Server environment and some of the objects you will be concerned with in your programming projects.

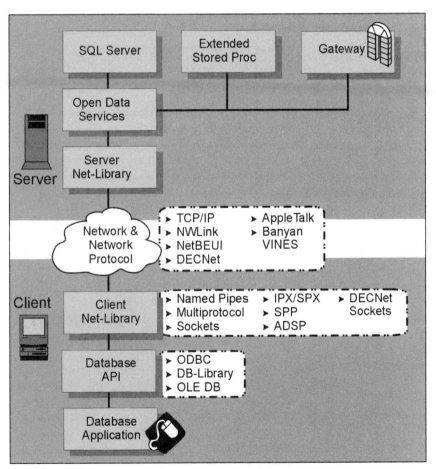

Figure 1-1: Conceptual view of the components that make up the SQL Server environment

The objects that SQL Server manages in a database extend well beyond the tables where the data is stored. To ensure that the integrity of the data is maintained, we need to establish rules for data entering the database and default values for data items that are not provided by a user of the database when entering data. Also, we must ensure that relationships established between tables in the database are always valid.

In addition to data concerns, we will need to store objects that are involved in processing and retrieving data, such as views and stored procedures, and with event mechanisms called triggers.

SQL Server

Requests for data services and the results of those requests are sent over a network connection between the client machine and SQL Server on the database server machine. Requests for data can come from SQL Server client tools installed on the client or from any SQL Server application, such as those explored in Part III of this book. Data requests can also come from procedures executing on other SQL Server installations.

SQL Server can be considered as a collection of Windows NT services, support DLLs, database objects, and stored procedures that are used to manage data in a multiuser environment.

In addition to Windows NT, SQL Server 7 can be hosted on Windows 95 or later. This book addresses SQL Server 7 running on a Windows NT 4 server only. Although there are architectural differences in the operating systems and the manner in which SQL Server is supported, the Transact-SQL covered in this book should behave the same on all platforms.

A major component of this collection is the SQL Server query processor. The processor is responsible for translating Transact-SQL statements into a plan of execution that will yield the desired results in an efficient manner.

As an example of this process, consider a query that is to select Account Number (acct_no), Account Name (acct_lastname), ZipCode (zip), and Home Phone Number (home_phone) from the Accounts table in the mutual fund accounts database (see Appendix B for the structure of this database). Instead of selecting these columns from all rows in the table, we'll select only those rows where state = "CT" and ZipCode is in the range 06100 to 06300.

Say we have three indexes defined on the Accounts table. The first index indexes the values in the zip column. The second index indexes values in the state column and the third index indexes values in both the state and zip columns together.

When we submit the query to SQL Server, how will SQL Server go about building the result set? What options does the query processor have? Let's take a look.

1. Scan through each row in the table and check the `zip` column and the `state` column against our selection criteria. This is what it would do if there were no usable indexes available.

2. Choose the `state` index, select all the "CT" rows contained in this index, and visit each one of these rows to check the `zip` against our criteria.

3. Choose the `zip` index and select rows in our `zip` range of 06100 to 06300, then visit each of these rows and check for `state` equal to "CT."

4. Select the `state` index, scan for "CT" entries, select the `zip` index and scan for 06100 to 06300 entries, then select data rows where the index data addresses match.

5. Choose the index containing both `state` and `zip` values and check these entries for a match against our selection criteria. This would be the most likely plan for the processor to choose. We'll come back to this example later in the book and find out if the query processor lives up to our expectations.

You can see from this scenario that the query processor's job isn't all that simple. For any given query submitted for execution, there could exist more than one way to retrieve the results. The one chosen is the least-cost method according to the query optimizer's internal algorithms and statistics on the data at the time of query compilation.

The query processor has two distinct phases for each query it looks at. The process of parsing Transact-SQL statements into a normalized format is called *resolution* and the process of building a *plan* of execution is called *compilation.*

When you create a stored procedure, for example, SQL Server will examine the Transact-SQL statements in the procedure for proper syntax and convert the procedure to a normalized form that is then stored in the `sysprocedures` system table.

When the procedure is executed, SQL Server reads the normalized form from `sysprocedures` and processes it through the resolution phase. During resolution, the existence of objects referenced by the procedure is checked as well as data type compatibility between referenced column types and procedure variables.

Once resolution is completed successfully, the current database statistics are used to evaluate how the query or queries in the procedure will be carried out. The outcome of this process is a *plan* of execution that is then cached in the procedure cache for the current and subsequent execution requests.

What are some of the statistics SQL Server looks at when developing a plan? The number of rows of data in the referenced tables is one factor the optimizer considers. Another factor is the existence of usable indexes and the distribution of keys in those indexes. To effectively use any indexes that might exist, the optimizer needs to evaluate the Transact-SQL statement for `WHERE` conditions, `GROUP BY`, `ORDER BY`, and other clauses that may impact how a query can be run.

It is important that database statistics be kept up-to-date in order for the optimizer to do its job correctly. In Chapter 14, you'll learn about the UPDATE STATISTICS statement that updates statistics on the distribution of keys in an index.

Databases and Database Objects

A SQL Server database is an allocation of two or more operating system files. At a minimum, one file is used for storage of database objects and another file is used to record a log of database activity. Objects are stored on an initial primary file and may overflow to one or more secondary files. SQL Server reads and writes to these files in 8KB blocks, called *pages*.

The pages that make up a file are numbered sequentially from zero on the first page of the file. To locate a page in the database, SQL Server uses a file ID to designate the file where the page is stored and a page number to designate the page within the file.

The database files grow and shrink as needed to store the objects in the database. You'll see how these files are allocated and learn about file groups when you read about the CREATE DATABASE statement in Chapter 5.

The objects stored in a database are tables, indexes, stored procedures, triggers, rules, permissions, views, defaults, and user-defined data types.

Table 1-1 presents an overview of the objects that can be stored in a SQL Server database.

TABLE 1-1 SQL SERVER DATABASE OBJECTS

Database Object	Description
Table	Used to store the data pertaining to entities of interest to the database application for which the database was created. The entities are represented by rows (or records) in the table. The common attributes of the entities are represented by columns (or fields) of the table.

Database Object	Description
Index	Used to enhance the performance of accessing the rows of a table. Each index entry is composed of one or more key values and a pointer to the row in the table containing those values. Indexes in SQL Server are either clustered or nonclustered.
Stored procedure	A named collection of Transact-SQL statements executed as a unit.
Trigger	A special stored procedure that is invoked when specified data in a table is modified.
Rule	A specification or statement as to the values that may be entered in a particular column of a table.
Permission	Authorization assigned to a user or group that allows that user or group to execute some statement or access some object.
View	A virtual table defined by columns from one or more base tables or from another view.
Default	A specified value to be entered by SQL Server into a column if the column value is not given at the time a row is inserted into a table.
User-defined data type	A type of data defined in terms of basic SQL Server data types. Once defined to SQL Server, this type may be used like any other data type.

Tables

A *table object* represents some entity of interest to the scope of the application. In the Fund Account Management application introduced in Chapter 4, we are interested in entities such as client accounts, the fund accounts held by our clients, the transactions applied to the fund accounts, and the statements issued to our clients on a regular basis.

Although there are other entities that could be represented within the domain of fund account management, the scope of this application only requires that these entities be present to support the intended purpose of the application. Design efforts will yield one or more table objects (tables) in our fund account database to store the data associated with these entities.

Tables are used to store the data for a specific entity. They are composed of rows (or records), which can store a maximum of 8,060 bytes of data (not counting text and image columns).

A table's rows are composed of columns; each one defined as some data type. In addition to data type, columns are given other attributes such as a name and constraints that define the allowable values and relationships with other tables. You'll learn more about columns in Chapter 5 when we cover the CREATE TABLE statement.

Indexes

To enhance the retrieval of data from a table, a database may contain one or more *index objects.* Indexes hold key values from one or more columns of a table and a pointer that points to data rows containing the key values.

The number of rows pointed to by any given key in an index depends on whether the index is a unique index or a nonunique index.

A *unique* index contains keys that will point to only one data row in a table. These indexes ensure that each row in the table contains unique values in the indexed columns. No two rows in the table will have the same values in the indexed columns.

Unique indexes are created on columns that are designated as a *primary key* for the table. The primary key is comprised of one or more columns whose values will uniquely identify a row in the table. For example, a social security number might be used as a primary key in a customer table where the customers are individuals.

Nonunique indexes will contain entries that may point to one or more rows for any given key value. These values are usually nonidentifiers for a row. They will generally be used for quick access to a small subset of the total row population in a table. An example of a nonunique key on a customer table would be the ZIP code in the customer's address. A given ZIP code may return one row, several rows, or hundreds of rows, depending on the distribution of zip code values in the table.

Choices of columns to index depend in part on the queries that the application will submit to SQL Server. Deciding on an index is a tradeoff between query activity and update activity on a table.

While indexes help to speed query execution, they also need to be updated whenever the indexed columns change values and when rows are added or deleted. Heavy update activity on indexes can be detrimental to the performance of the update operation. Which is more important in the application, the speed of the query or the speed of the update?

The answer depends on the application and will often have an impact on how the database is designed and how your application program will use the database. Index usage needs to be considered carefully in all aspects of your Transact-SQL programming.

Indexes are implemented using a data structure called a B-tree. The *root-level* page of the index tree holds ranges of index values. Each range entry in this page points to other pages at a lower level in the tree. The lower-level pages each store a more constrictive range of values until the bottom level of the tree, called the *leaf level,* is reached.

Leaf-level pages hold the key values and pointers to the rows in the table containing these values or, as in the case of a clustered index, the rows themselves. The leaf page architecture depends on the type of index and can be nonclustered or clustered.

- ◆ *Nonclustered* indexes impose a logical ordering of a table's rows according to the sort order of the index entries. The order of the physical rows in the table is not affected by a nonclustered index.

- ◆ *Clustered* indexes impose a physical ordering of the table's rows. The leaf pages of a clustered index hold the actual data pages of the table rather than a pointer to the data pages residing somewhere else on disk.

Because of the physical ordering of rows imposed by the clustered index, you can only have one clustered index per table. Primary key constraints defined for a table result in a clustered index being created for the primary key if no index type is specified for the key *and* a clustered index does not already exist on the table.

Primary key constraints are discussed further in Chapter 5.

Pointer entries in a nonclustered index will point to the location of the corresponding table rows if no clustered index is present. If a clustered index is present on a table, the nonclustered index entries point to a clustering key in the clustered index. The reason for pointing into a clustered index instead of into data rows is to enhance the performance of the system when index page splits occur.

How is performance enhanced over prior versions of SQL Server? In prior versions, when a row key was inserted into an index page that caused the page to become full, SQL Server needed to split the full page into two pages. Keys would be moved from the page being split into the new page such that both pages could take on more entries.

When this split occurred in a clustered index, the actual data rows were taking part in the move from one page to another page. Since any nonclustered index pointed to these rows being moved on disk, the nonclustered index also had to be updated to reflect the new location of the data rows. Hence, a page split meant more overhead maintenance on indexes when nonclustered indexes were present.

In SQL Server 7, nonclustered index entries no longer point into data pages when a clustered index is present, but instead point to clustering keys in the clustered index. With this architecture, the nonclustered index doesn't require maintenance when an index page split occurs since the clustering key the nonclustered index points to remains constant no matter where it resides. The clustering key is then used by a nonclustered index lookup to locate the data row residing in the clustered index leaf pages.

So, with SQL Server 7, cluster index page splits never cause nonclustered index maintenance other than to insert a new clustering key for new rows. This activity can still cause page splits in the nonclustered index itself, however, when its pages run out of space for a new key.

Stored Procedures

Another database object you will be using heavily in your application work is the *stored procedure.*

A stored procedure is a collection of one or more Transact-SQL statements compiled as a unit. A procedure can incorporate actions against a database, variable declarations, and control-of-flow statements to implement application logic that is executed at the server.

Stored procedures can be created to accept multiple arguments and to return output values and return values, in addition to multiple result sets from SELECT statements within the procedure.

Procedures are compiled at create time and stored in the sysprocedures system table with the text of the procedure stored in the syscomments table. When first executed, the procedure is retrieved, resolved against referenced objects, and generates a plan that is cached in the procedure cache for the current and subsequent executions.

Since referenced objects in the procedure are not resolved until execution time, you can create procedures that reference objects that don't exist at procedure create time but will exist at procedure runtime.

SQL Server ships with a number of stored procedures you'll find useful. These stored procedures are organized into the following categories and are listed in the Appendix F:

- ◆ Catalog Stored Procedures provide information about databases and the SQL Server installation. These procedures also play a role in ODBC applications.

- ◆ Extended stored procedures extend the functionality of SQL Server by enabling a DLL function to be called in the same manner as a stored procedure is called. These procedures also implement e-mail capabilities from within SQL Server.

- ◆ Replication stored procedures implement replication operations.

- ◆ SQL Server agent stored procedures are used to manage the scheduling of activities.

- ◆ System stored procedures can be used for various data management tasks in any database.

Implementing portions of your application as server-side procedures can improve overall application performance, reduce network traffic, and simplify application maintenance.

In Chapter 15, you'll learn how to write your own stored procedures.

Network Components

Transact-SQL statements submitted from a client machine to a SQL Server for processing need to be routed through the network components of both the client and server machines before SQL Server can do its job.

The network components, as shown in Figure 1-1, consist of a Net-Library, an interprocess communication mechanism (IPC), a network protocol, a network interface card (NIC), and the physical network.

An application's SQL request passes through a client API, such as DB-Library or ODBC. It is then routed through a Net-Library to some IPC mechanism that communicates the request over the network using some network protocol.

On connection to SQL Server, the client API will determine which Net-Library to load based on the client configuration. Once loaded, the Net-Library handles the API requests and passes them to a lower-level process, the IPC mechanism.

The IPC mechanism used is specific to the Net-Library loaded and the network protocol. Some of the popular Net-Libraries and IPCs are listed in Table 1-2.

TABLE 1-2 NET-LIBRARIES AND INTERPROCESS COMMUNICATION PROTOCOLS
USED TO COMMUNICATE WITH SQL SERVER

Net-Library	IPC Mechanism	Comments
Named Pipes	NetBEUI or TCP/IP	SQL Server listens for named pipe connections on pipe `\\.\pipe\sql\query` by default.
TCP/IP Sockets	Windows sockets	Default port is 1433.
NWLink	IPX/SPX	SQL Server is registered on the Novell network through a Novell Bindery service name. Default service name is the name of the server computer.
Multiprotocol	TCP/IP, IPX/SPX, Named Pipes	Allows the use of integrated security and supports encryption.

Continued

TABLE 1-2 NET-LIBRARIES AND INTERPROCESS COMMUNICATION PROTOCOLS
          USED TO COMMUNICATE WITH SQL SERVER *(Continued)*

Net-Library	IPC Mechanism	Comments
Banyan VINES	Sequenced Packet Protocol (SPP)	Requires the entry of a StreetTalk service name.
AppleTalk	ADSP	Enables connections from Apple Macintosh-based clients. Requires the entry of an AppleTalk service object name.

As you can see in Figure 1-1, the same network components are found on the server side of a request. SQL Server installs Named Pipes as the default Net-Library/IPC but enables other Net-Libraries to be installed as well. All installed protocols can be used by SQL Server simultaneously to communicate with client machines.

The SQL statements routed to SQL Server, as well as any results from SQL Server to the client, are packaged into a data stream called *Tabular Data Stream* (TDS) which in turn is wrapped by the IPC protocol for transmission across the network.

Fortunately, all of the work done at the network level is transparent to the application programmer. Thanks to the client API, a buffer is set up between the application and the network that enables the application to concentrate on application tasks and ignore the complexities of communicating across a network.

Client Libraries

To support programs that talk to SQL Server, you will need to install one or more of the client-side libraries, such as ODBC or DB-Library, and do some configuration of these libraries before your program can communicate with SQL Server. These application programming interface (API) libraries are the program's link to the database — what I referred to earlier as the call-level interface, or CLI.

Part III of this book illustrates programs using various client API libraries to talk to SQL Server. The language of these libraries is well known to the program side, while the other side of the library has the task of communicating with a given Net-Library.

ODBC, for example, exposes a set of API functions that an application program can use to carry out the database processing that the application needs to do. Some of this processing involves establishing a connection with SQL Server, submitting Transact-SQL statements, and processing the results. Other API functions deal with local program/API housekeeping and are not transmitted to the network.

The choice of a client library is up to you. The factors that will play a role in that choice are your knowledge of the various APIs, the application programming language you are using, your perception of an API's future, your installation's standards, and performance implications.

Prior to ODBC, DB-Library and C were the popular kids on the block. When ODBC arrived, there were a few immediate takers but questions of performance were plentiful. Just about every magazine that catered to programming documented the issue of DB-Library's performance versus that of ODBC.

As ODBC evolved and became better understood, the popularity of DB-Library (and C) started to wane. A huge boon to this movement was object-oriented mechanisms such as Data Access Objects (DAO) to aid in the task of communicating with ODBC. There is still a hefty following of DB-Library today, however, and that group strongly believes in the performance of DB-Library.

The new arrival is OLE DB. With the advent of COM and OLE, the "componentization" of application architectures – including the operating system – is now in vogue. This trend was sure to engulf database access APIs sooner or later. OLE DB is the answer and, as shown in Part III, looks promising.

Client Applications

The client database application is a set of one or more programs designed to solve some problem. These programs are written in a language such as C, C++, Visual Basic, Java, and so forth, and access SQL Server through one of the client libraries.

Transact-SQL is used by these applications either in the form of strings containing SQL statements, by referencing stored procedures, or a combination of these. The performance of the application depends quite strongly on how well the database is tuned for the SQL statements the application will use. For this reason, all processing against SQL Server needs to be carefully considered and steps need to be taken to ensure that SQL Server and the application are optimally tuned.

The Transact-SQL Language

Transact-SQL (T-SQL) is the extended SQL language used by SQL Server to manage relational data. T-SQL is based on the American National Standards Institute (ANSI) SQL-92 standard and extends it to provide an enhanced language for manipulating SQL Server objects. The T-SQL language has been changed significantly by SQL Server 7.0.

T-SQL statements can be organized into three categories: Data Definition Language, Data Manipulation Language, and Data Control Language.

Data Definition Language (DDL) statements are used for defining (creating and altering) SQL Server objects. You'll read about DDL in Chapter 5 and use it to create tables, indexes, stored procedures, triggers, and views for your applications.

SQL Server 7, unlike earlier versions, allows procedures, triggers, and views to be altered without the need to drop and redefine them. This capability preserves the permissions on these objects, making redefinition of permissions unnecessary when altering these objects.

The data manipulation category (DML) is introduced in Chapter 6 and includes statements used to retrieve and maintain data stored in a database's tables. You'll use statements such as SELECT to retrieve a set of rows from one or more tables, UPDATE to modify rows, DELETE to remove rows from a table, and INSERT to add new rows to a table. All these are Data Manipulation Language statements.

Statements in the last category are covered in Chapter 15, where you'll explore stored procedures. Control statements are used to express some logic or algorithm that the SQL query processor is to execute. Data Control Language (DCL) statements are much like statements found in common programming languages and include statements such as IF . . . ELSE, BEGIN . . . END, WHILE, GOTO, RETURN, and PRINT.

T-SQL includes a rich set of functions that can greatly enhance the power of your procedures. SQL Server 7.0 has added new string functions such as SUB-STRING, LEN, and REPLACE, and several other functions in the categories of security and object information.

Functions are presented by category in Chapter 7.

Licensing Modes and Connections

SQL Server requires licenses to run the server and for each client that accesses SQL Server. When SQL Server is installed, the administrator is given a choice between two client licensing modes: *Per Seat* and *Per Server*. The choice will have an impact on how your applications should manage connections.

Per Seat Licensing Mode

With this mode, a separate Client Access License is required for each computer that will connect to a SQL Server. The license agreement allows client applications, or any client access for that matter, including Microsoft client utility access, to connect to any SQL Server.

Per Seat is a good choice for installations where clients will access more than one SQL Server.

Per Server Licensing Mode

This mode assigns a Client Access License to a specific SQL Server. A concurrent client connection to the server is allowed for each of the licenses assigned.

Your applications running under this mode will need to manage connections carefully. You will most likely want to, or be forced to, close connections when they are not in use. The most popular scenario with this licensing mode is to open a connection, do what you have to do with it (and be quick about it), and then close it. This practice frees up a connection count at the server for someone else to use.

The longer you hold a connection open, either some other user will either be denied access or more client licenses will have to be purchased to meet the demand. This is one reason why administrators are interested in what your application will be doing with the database.

Node-based Client Access

As of SQL Server 6.0, you can use node-based access with either client-licensing mode.

Node-based access enables SQL Server to detect multiple connections from a single machine and count those connections against a single client license.

This capability lightens the connection management burden on your application, however, you should still be prudent with connections due to the 40KB per connection memory overhead.

Character Sets and Sort Orders

A *character set,* also known as a *code page,* is a collection of symbols. These symbols include letters of the alphabet (uppercase and lowercase), numbers, and special characters. There are 256 symbols in a character set. The first 128 symbols are the same in all character sets, while the last 128 symbols vary from character set to character set. SQL Server installs character set ISO 8859-1 (code page 1252) by default or the character set in use by the SQL Server 6.5 installation being upgraded.

Character sets are important in that they determine how SQL Server compares characters in your Transact-SQL expressions and which characters SQL Server recognizes as valid data.

SQL Server's default sort order is dictionary order, case-insensitive. This means that a select query containing a WHERE condition of State = "CT" will return rows with State equal to "CT" and State equal to "ct" since case is ignored.

If this select query were to contain an ORDER BY clause, the default sort order provides no guarantee that "ct" will appear before "CT" or vice versa.

You should be sure that both server and clients are set up with the same character set and sort order.

SQL Server Tools

The tools that ship with SQL Server are useful for tasks such as testing a client connection to a SQL Server, testing Transact-SQL statements, and even managing SQL Server objects.

In addition to installing utilities, the setup installs files that support application development. These files include the .h and .lib files necessary for developing DB-Library, ODBC, ODS, and OLE DB applications.

The 32-bit client utility options listed in Table 1-3 are briefly summarized in this section and discussed in more detail in Chapter 2.

TABLE 1–3 THE CLIENT TOOLS OPTIONS

Utility	Description
BCP	Bulk copy utility used to copy data between a SQL Server database and flat operating system files.
SQL Enterprise Manager	Used to administer SQL Servers and their objects such as devices, databases, tables, and so forth.
SQL Server Profiler	Used to monitor database activity.
SQL Client Configuration Utility	Configures a client for DB-Library connections.
SQL Server Query Analyzer	Used to run Transact-SQL commands and procedures. You may also view query plans and SQL Server statistics with this utility.
makepipe and readpipe	Tests Named Pipes connections to SQL Server.

Bulk Copy Program

You can use the bulk copy program (BCP) to copy data from a database table to an external file or load data into a table from an external file.

The utility is a command-line utility that accepts a string of arguments to specify how the utility should process the data.

BCP is a good tool to load tables for testing or production when you have the data in operating system files from an external source or exported from another SQL Server.

SQL Server Enterprise Manager

This utility is a graphical user interface that can be used to manage one or more SQL Server installations across the enterprise.

Enterprise Manager can be used to create databases and their objects, users and user permissions, schedule tasks such as backup jobs and launch other utilities such as the Query Analyzer.

Database administrators will generally use this utility to manage the installation because all administration functions are available in this one utility.

SQL Server Profiler

The SQL Server Profiler is especially helpful to analyze SQL Server database activity generated from your application or from stored procedures and scripts executed from another utility.

This utility monitors the database activity in real time and can be logged to an external file. A review of this log or the real-time trace can then be used to tune your application for optimal performance prior to releasing it to your end users.

SQL Server Query Analyzer

The Query Analyzer can be used to test Transact-SQL statements and procedures for proper operation. The Analyzer provides options for viewing the SQL Server query optimizer plan that gives you an indication as to how SQL Server will satisfy your data request. This information provides more insights into how to tune your application.

Exploring Database Application Interfaces

The SQL standard defines a Call-Level Interface (CLI) that an application can use to work with a SQL database.

A CLI is a set of functions that can be called from within an application to connect to and work with a SQL relational database.

ODBC 3.5 is a CLI that is becoming more and more popular in the industry.

TIP I strongly recommend that you learn how to use ODBC 3.5 functions for interfacing to SQL Server. This library will undoubtedly surpass DB-Library as the CLI of choice and become very useful to those who know how to use it effectively.

Even as we progress to COM object technology for database access, ODBC will continue to provide a low-level interface to SQL Server.

Other library options are addressed in Part III of this book, as an overview to what's available today for accessing SQL Server. The sample applications found in Part III only begin to touch the surface of what can be done with the technology, but give you enough of a foundation to research the technology further on your own.

DB-Library

DB-Library is a 32-bit database API that provides a set of functions an application program can use to establish a connection with a database, execute Transact-SQL statements, and process result sets.

Although DB-Library is still used as the interface for some of the SQL Server utilities explored in Chapter 2, ODBC and OLE DB are quickly replacing DB-Library as the interface of choice. DB-Library has not been enhanced for SQL Server 7.0. Some functionality, especially that which deals with Unicode data, is not supported in DB-Library. Nonetheless, DB-Library is still a powerful interface for many applications.

XREF Chapter 18 will develop a sample DB-Library application implemented in C++. There is a version of DB-Library for Visual Basic programmers, but in keeping with the C++ theme, it will not be illustrated in this book.

Open Database Connectivity

Open database connectivity (ODBC) is a specification that defines an interface enabling an application to access heterogeneous data sources using a common set of API functions.

The conceptual view of the ODBC architecture includes a driver manager, a set of drivers (each specific to a particular database), and a set of user-defined data sources, as shown in Figure 1-2.

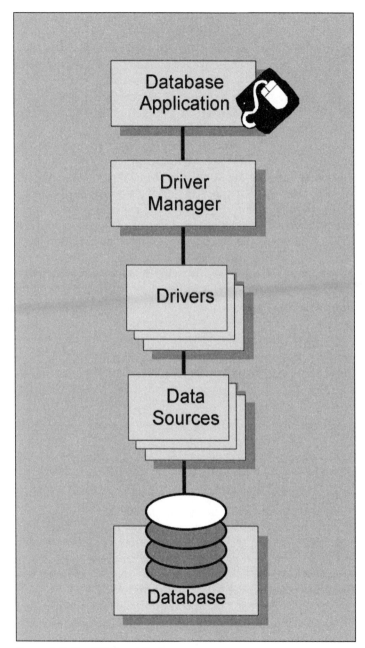

Figure 1-2: The ODBC architecture

The driver manager component of this architecture is responsible for fielding a database request from an application and loading the proper driver corresponding to the information specified in the data source named by the application. The manager processes some ODBC function calls itself while passing others to the driver for processing.

SQL Server provides a driver that can be installed on the client machine and used to communicate with SQL Server. This driver passes Transact-SQL from the application to a SQL Server database specified in the data source and is enhanced to meet the specifications of ODBC 3.5. Results from SQL Server are processed by the SQL Server driver and forwarded to the application when requested.

A user-defined data source specifies the SQL Server installation and database to connect to. Certain network information can also be supplied here. Data sources can easily be created and modified using the ODBC Administrator located in the Windows Control Panel. An application can also provide the data source information internally, and therefore would not require an external data source to be defined.

SQL Server 7 ships with an ODBC 3.5 driver. This driver supports new functionality for bulk copy and several other new capabilities, all of which are covered in the Microsoft ODBC 3.5 SDK.

In Chapter 19, you'll see how a data source is created with the ODBC Administrator and used in an ODBC application.

OLE DB and ActiveX Data Objects

The latest database interface option, OLE DB, is recommended if you are developing COM objects in your application and require access to a database.

In the world of OLE DB, there are providers and consumers. A *provider* provides some sort of service such as access to specialized data structures or a set of complex procedures. The *consumer* is the requestor and user of these services.

OLE DB is a specification that describes how the provider should expose its services to consumers and how consumers can work with the results.

In terms of SQL Server database access, a provider (the OLE DB provider that ships with SQL Server) provides an interface for client applications (the consumers) to access SQL Server databases.

With an understanding of the OLE DB specification, you can develop your own customized provider that can be used throughout your organization. Such a provider might implement business rules for your organization on top of the standard OLE DB interface required by all OLE DB providers.

ActiveX Data Objects (ADO) is a set of COM objects that sits between your application and the OLE DB provider. These objects can be used by your application to interact with SQL Server instead of handling calls directly to the OLE DB provider.

ADO presents your application with a simple model of a SQL Server database by exposing COM objects such as a `Connection`, `Recordset`, `Field`, `Command`, `Parameter`, and `Error`, as shown in Figure 1-3.

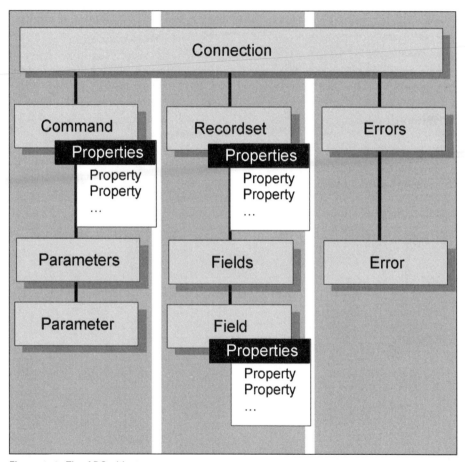

Figure 1-3: The ADO objects

Chapter 20 discusses ADO and the OLE DB specification in more detail and illustrates a program that uses ADO for database access.

Extending SQL Server with Open Data Services

Open Data Services (ODS) is an application programming interface that resides on the server. The Open Data Services API enables you to write server-side programs that can be called by a client application in the same way that SQL Server can be called. Additionally, you can write server-side programs that can be called from SQL Server directly, and actually extend SQL Server functionality.

ODS programs running on the server can be connected to and queried just as you do SQL Server itself. These programs are known as *ODS servers* and can provide your applications with server-based access to a SQL Server database or some other server-side service.

Extended stored procedures are ODS programs that can be called from within SQL Server procedures or directly from a client, just as you call SQL Server's extended stored procedures.

Using ODS, you could provide a gateway to another application in your organization in which data is shared or events are processed. For example, the addition of a transaction in a mutual fund accounting system could trigger an event to a customer tracking system. The customer tracking system could be based on any file system at all, because the ODS extended stored procedure can provide customized handling of the interface between the mutual fund SQL Server application and the customer tracking application.

ODS handles all network communication with clients and uses remote procedure calls to communicate with other servers.

A sample ODS extended stored procedure is illustrated in Chapter 21.

The Book's Sample Programs

The sample applications in Part III are written in Visual C++ 5.0 and developed with the Microsoft Developer Studio Enterprise Edition.

All code presented in Part III is found on the CD at the back of the book. The CD directory structure follows the chapter structure for ease of locating the samples.

In addition to the sample programs, the CD contains Transact-SQL scripts illustrating the Transact-SQL discussed in Part II of the book.

Summary

This chapter has presented an overview of the SQL Server environment and the components found in this environment.

You learned about the makeup of a SQL Server database and about the Transact-SQL statement categories used to create and manipulate database objects.

SQL Server ships with several utilities that make not only the database administrator's job easier but also the programmer's job as well, especially when it comes to testing and tuning your application.

Although seemingly minor topics for the programmer, character sets, sort orders, and licensing modes can impact a SQL Server database application's operation. You learned what these items are all about and why they are important.

Finally, you discovered what database interface options are available to your application and learned what they consisted of. In Part III, you'll get to sample these interface libraries firsthand.

Chapter 2

Using the SQL Server Tools

IN THIS CHAPTER

- ◆ Find out what utilities are available with SQL Server and how they are used
- ◆ Learn how to create a database with Enterprise Manager
- ◆ Use Enterprise Manager to create tables in a database
- ◆ Use Enterprise Manager table properties to add indexes and constraints to tables
- ◆ Discover how to create T-SQL scripts with the Enterprise Manager
- ◆ Explore the Bulk Copy Program (BCP) to import/export SQL Server data
- ◆ Learn how to create a BCP Format file
- ◆ Execute queries and view the SQL Server plan of execution with the Query Analyzer
- ◆ Learn how to configure and test SQL Server network connections

THE SQL SERVER client installation contains a number of tools you'll find useful in your development efforts. Some of these tools will help you in testing and tuning your applications while others are helpful in the day-to-day operation and maintenance of a SQL Server installation.

Files necessary for ODBC and DB-Library application development are also installed when you run the client installation.

The following tools are available for installation:

SQL Server Enterprise Manager – This utility is a Microsoft Management Console application used to manage SQL Server installations throughout the enterprise. Administrative functions for managing users, databases, and database objects are available in this utility through a graphical user interface.

Other tools such as the SQL Server Query Analyzer and SQL Server Profiler can be launched from within the Enterprise Manager.

SQL Server Profiler – The Profiler is used to monitor certain SQL Server activities. Using this utility you can monitor resource usage for applications, monitor overall system performance, monitor SQL Server access, and collect information helpful for tuning your applications.

SQL Server Query Analyzer – The Analyzer can be used to execute queries against SQL Server and to view the plans for those queries produced by the query optimizer. Viewing the optimizer's plans for query execution can be a tremendous benefit to you in your efforts to tune your database application.

Client Diagnostic Utilities – The SQL Server Client Configuration utility is used to display the version of DB-Library installed on a client machine and to set up SQL Server connection information. Two other utilities useful for testing named pipes connections to SQL Server are the makepipe and readpipe programs.

MS DTC client support – Microsoft Distributed Transaction Coordinator (MS DTC) coordinates transactions across Microsoft Windows-based systems in a network. This transaction manager service enables SQL Server to update data residing on multiple SQL Server installations. We'll explore transactions in Chapter 16.

Development files – Files needed for C/C++ application development, such as include (*.h) files and library (*.lib) files, are installed with the client setup to enable the development of OLE DB, ODBC, DB-Library, ODS, DMO, ESQL, and MS DTC. These files are installed in the `\<sql server directory>\DevTools\Include` and the `\<sql server directory>\DevTools\Lib` directories where `<sql server directory>` is the directory you chose during SQL Server setup of the client tools. If you accepted the default installation directory, the SQL Server directory will be named Mssql7.

Sample files – You may also install sample programs for ODBC, DB-Library, ODS, DMO, ESQL, and OLEDB, to help you get started in developing with these database interfaces. These files are installed into folders in the `\<sql server directory>\DevTools\Samples` directory.

In the sections that follow, we'll take a brief tour of the SQL Server Enterprise Manager, the BCP utility, the SQL Server Query Analyzer, the Client Configuration utility and the makepipe/readpipe utilities. You can find more information on the tools in the SQL Server Books Online.

Using SQL Server Enterprise Manager

The SQL Server Enterprise Manager is a Microsoft Management Console version 1.0. The Management Console provides a common framework for Microsoft BackOffice products. Consoles load programs known as *snap-ins* that perform the functionality specific to the product while the console functionality provides a consistent look and feel for the user interface.

The SQL Server Enterprise Manager.MSC is a console file containing a number of snap-ins and windows to enable you to manage one or more SQL Server installations in your organization.

A console can provide one or more windows. A window contains two panes. The left-hand pane is called the *scope pane.* The scope pane displays a tree view of all the objects in the application namespace.

The right-hand pane is called the *results pane.* The results pane is used to display a list of the objects contained in an object selected in the scope pane, or it may display information about the selected object in the form of a Web page or some other document format.

Touring the Enterprise Manager

Let's take a brief tour of Enterprise Manager and then use it to create the fund accounts management sample database and one of its tables. We'll be working with this database throughout the book. (See Chapter 4 for a discussion of the FundAccts database.) Launch SQL Server Enterprise Manager from the Programs/Microsoft SQL Server folder on the Windows taskbar.

Microsoft Management Console version 1.0 displays it's banner and then opens the SQL Server Enterprise Manager.MSC console file and displays the console root.

Expand the Microsoft SQL Servers folder to view the SQL Server groups and servers. If there are no servers displayed, you will need to register a server by right-clicking on the Microsoft SQL Servers folder and choosing Register SQL Server from the pop-up menu. This will launch the Register SQL Server Wizard. Follow the steps in the wizard to register a server with the Enterprise Manager.

Next, expand a server to view the objects managed by that server. You should see objects such as SQL Server Agent, SQL Mail, Logins, Databases, and so on, as shown in Figure 2-1.

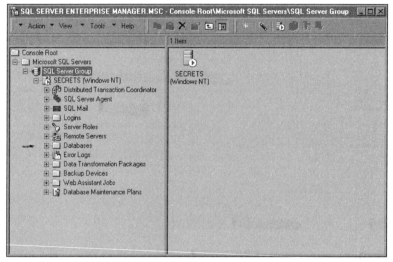

Figure 2-1: The SQL Server Enterprise Manager console showing the objects managed by a server

Expand the Databases folder to view the databases defined for this server and then expand the Master Database folder.

Viewing the Master Database

The server registration for the server you are viewing must be set up to enable the system databases and objects to be displayed. If you don't see the Master database in the Databases folder, perform the following steps:

1. Right-click the server entry you want to view.

2. Select "Edit SQL Server Registration ..." from the pop-up menu.

3. In the "Registered SQL Server Properties" page, check the "Show system databases and system objects" check box.

4. Click OK to dismiss the Properties page and you should see the Master database listed under the Databases folder.

Under the Master Database folder, you see a collection of folders representing the objects stored in the Master database. Here, you'll find objects such as Stored Procedures, Tables, Database Roles, Database Users, SQL Server Views, and Rules.

Click the Stored Procedures folder to view the procedures in the Results pane. We'll be exploring a few of these stored procedures throughout the rest of this book, starting with Chapter 3 when we use some of the procedures that deal with SQL Server database security.

To change the view of the Results pane, you can select the desired view from the View menu or from the View selection on the pop-up menu that results from right-clicking in the Results pane. You can choose from Large, Small, List, and Detail views.

Right-click one of the procedures listed in the Results pane and select Properties from the pop-up menu. This will display the Stored Procedure Properties dialog, as shown in Figure 2-2.

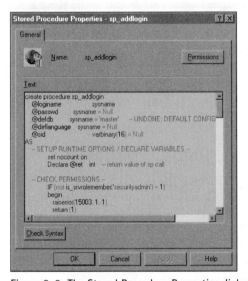

Figure 2-2: The Stored Procedure Properties dialog

The Stored Procedure Properties dialog displays the definition of the selected stored procedure. The dialog allows you to check the syntax of the displayed procedure by clicking the Check Syntax button.

This dialog is good for copying code from one procedure to paste into another procedure or to discover how a particular technique is implemented in a procedure.

We'll write some stored procedures for the FundAccs database in Chapter 15.

Next, click the Logins folder under the SQL Server object and view the defined logins listed in the Results pane. The Type column in Detail view indicates whether the login is a Standard SQL Server user, an NT Group, or an NT User.

Chapter 3 explains what these types mean and how to define logins with these types.

Enterprise Manager also hosts a number of wizards that can help guide you through the process of creating or managing various SQL Server objects. The wizards are available by clicking the Run a Wizard toolbar button. Although these wizards may not always yield robust results, they can be used to create a starting point. The Stored Procedures Wizard, for example, only creates stored procedures for INSERT, DELETE and UPDATE actions on your database tables.

Creating the Fund Accounts Sample Database

Let's put on a database administrator's hat for a moment and build our Fund Accounts sample database and one of the tables, the Accounts table, where we'll store information on client accounts. We'll load data into this table later in this chapter when we discuss using the BCP utility.

To start off, select a SQL Server installation where you can define the sample database. Generally in an enterprise, you'll have one or more SQL Servers earmarked for production systems and one or more servers for testing. The testing servers enable you to define databases and test applications without hindering the performance of critical production systems.

In previous versions of SQL Server, setting up testing servers and enabling developers to create databases on demand was usually somewhat of a political nightmare. With SQL Server 7's scalability from Windows 95 machines to the high-end NT server platforms, establishing test servers and development are much more viable.

Use these steps to create the FundAccts database:

1. Select the Databases folder and then click Add a new button on the toolbar or choose New Database from the pop-up menu in the Results pane.

2. In the Database Properties dialog, enter **FundAccts** in the Name text box on the General tab. This is the name by which the sample database will be known to SQL Server. The other options shown in Figure 2-3, such as Initial size, File growth, and so on are defaults.

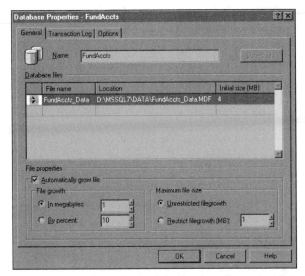

Figure 2-3: The General tab of the Database Properties dialog

Notice the default file name of FundAccts_Data.MDF. This is the physical operating system file that will be used to store the database objects.

3. Now click the Transaction Log tab and look at the file allocation properties for the transaction log (see Figure 2-4). This is the physical operating system file where SQL Server will log change activity against the FundAccts database to enable recovery. Here again, the defaults were accepted.

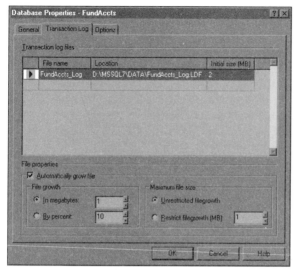

Figure 2-4: The Transaction Log tab of the Database Properties dialog

4. The Options tab shown in Figure 2-5 displays the various options you can specify for the database. You can change these at any time. To prepare for our BCP utility exercise coming up later in this chapter, check the Select Into/Bulk Copy check box.

not on this dialog box anymore.

1, create the database

2. right-click on new db icon in results pane.

Click "Properties"

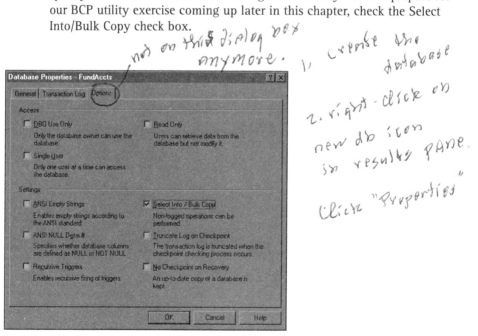

Figure 2-5: The Options tab of the Database Properties dialog

5. Click the OK button to create the FundAccts database. You should see the database listed in the Databases folder along with the Master database and any others that may have already existed.

6. Expand the FundAccts database folder and then click the Tables folder. The Results pane will display all the tables contained in the database we just created. Assuming you are still displaying system objects in the server registration, you should see a rather long list of tables. Since we haven't yet defined any tables in the database, where did these tables come from? The answer is the Model database.

   The Model database is used by SQL Server as a template database. When new databases are created, SQL Server copies the Model database and its objects to the newly created database. The tables you see are used by SQL Server to manage the database.

7. To compare the Model database tables to our FundAccts database tables, right-click the Model database folder and choose New window from here from the pop-up menu. This will create a new console window listing the Model database objects.

8. Click the Tables folder to display the tables in the Model database and then tile the windows horizontally to see both the Model database tables and FundAccts database tables. You'll find all the Model tables contained in the FundAccts database.

Some organizations may modify the Model database to contain certain custom tables and other objects to be included in all databases created in the organization. Table names beginning with sys are generally reserved for SQL Server system tables.

Creating the Accounts Table

Let's add our own Accounts table to the FundAccts database with the following steps:

1. With the FundAccts Tables listed in the Results pane, click the Add a new toolbar button. ✳ or Action Menu bar

2. Enter the name **Accounts** in the Table Name text box and then enter the column definitions into the Console window, as shown in Figure 2-6.

3. When you save the table definition, Enterprise Manager prompts you to save the script file containing the T-SQL statements used to create the table. The script file for the Accounts table is shown in Figure 2-7. Not True

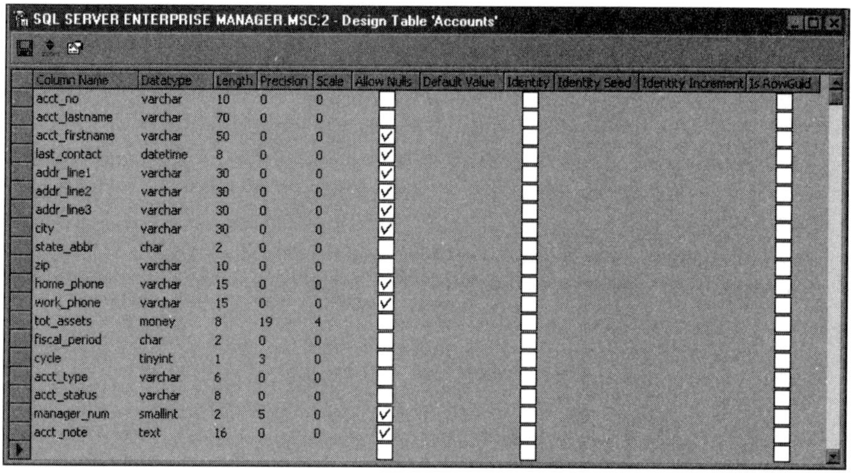

Column Name	Datatype	Length	Precision	Scale	Allow Nulls	Default Value	Identity	Identity Seed	Identity Increment	Is RowGuid
acct_no	varchar	10	0	0						
acct_lastname	varchar	70	0	0						
acct_firstname	varchar	50	0	0	✓					
last_contact	datetime	8	0	0	✓					
addr_line1	varchar	30	0	0	✓					
addr_line2	varchar	30	0	0	✓					
addr_line3	varchar	30	0	0	✓					
city	varchar	30	0	0	✓					
state_abbr	char	2	0	0						
zip	varchar	10	0	0						
home_phone	varchar	15	0	0	✓					
work_phone	varchar	15	0	0	✓					
tot_assets	money	8	19	4						
fiscal_period	char	2	0	0						
cycle	tinyint	1	3	0						
acct_type	varchar	6	0	0						
acct_status	varchar	8	0	0						
manager_num	smallint	2	5	0	✓					
acct_note	text	16	0	0	✓					

Figure 2-6: The Accounts table Properties dialog

```
BEGIN TRANSACTION
SET QUOTED_IDENTIFIER ON
GO
SET TRANSACTION ISOLATION LEVEL SERIALIZABLE
GO
COMMIT
BEGIN TRANSACTION
CREATE TABLE dbo.Accounts
        (
        acct_no varchar(10) NOT NULL,
        acct_lastname varchar(70) NOT NULL,
        acct_firstname varchar(50) NULL,
        last_contact datetime NULL,
        addr_line1 varchar(30) NULL,
        addr_line2 varchar(30) NULL,
        addr_line3 varchar(30) NULL,
        city varchar(30) NULL,
        state_abbr char(2) NOT NULL,
        zip varchar(10) NOT NULL,
        home_phone varchar(15) NULL,
        work_phone varchar(15) NULL,
        tot_assets money NOT NULL,
        fiscal_period char(2) NOT NULL,
        cycle tinyint NOT NULL,
        acct_type varchar(6) NOT NULL,
        acct_status varchar(8) NOT NULL,
        manager_num smallint NULL,
        acct_note text NULL
        ) ON [default]
GO
COMMIT
```

Figure 2-7: The script file generated for the Accounts table

TIP

It's good practice to save the generated scripts created when you build tables and other objects in Enterprise Manager so that you have a file that can be executed to re-create the object at a later date, if necessary.

You can generate scripts for many of your database objects using the Generate SQL Scripts dialog. In just a moment, we'll use this dialog to generate a script for the Accounts table.

Creating a Column Constraint

Here, we'll create a column constraint on the `acct_type` column so that the only values SQL Server will allow in the column are 'Tax' and 'Nontax'. We do this by creating a CHECK constraint.

XREF

In Chapter 5, we explore constraints that can be placed on tables to limit the values a column can accept.

1. Right-click the Accounts table and choose Design Table from the pop-up menu. A Console window will be displayed showing the table's columns as you entered them when you created the table.

2. Click the Properties button on the toolbar to display the Properties sheet for the table, as shown in Figure 2-8. Here, you can set table and column check constraints.

3. Click the New button in the CHECK constraints for table and columns frame and then enter the following expression in the Constraint expression text box:

```
([acct_type] = 'Tax' or [acct_type] = 'Nontax')
```

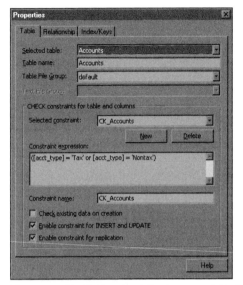

Figure 2-8: The Table tab of the Accounts table Properties sheet

4. Check the Enable constraint for INSERT and UPDATE check box.

5. While you're here, select the Index/Keys tab and create an index for the Accounts table. Click New and then choose the acct_no column in the Column name list box.

6. Check the Create as CLUSTERED check box and the Create UNIQUE check box and Constraint radio button. These choices will create a Unique constraint on the acct_no column and a clustered index on that column.

In Chapter 5, we explore the creation of indexes via T-SQL statements. There, you will learn a little more about the options you've just chosen.

7. Close the Properties page and save the changes you've just made before exiting the Table Design window. You now have a UNIQUE index on the acct_no and a CHECK constraint on the acct_type column.

Generating a SQL Script File

To see how our work up to now would look in a T-SQL statement, let's generate a
SQL script file for the Accounts table.

[handwritten: Select FundAcct database under folder 'Databases']

1. ~~Right-click the Accounts table~~ and select Generate SQL Scripts from the *[handwritten: results pane]*
~~Task menu~~. The Generate SQL Scripts dialog will be displayed, as shown
in Figure 2-9.

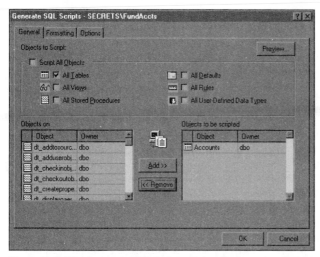

Figure 2-9: The Generate SQL Scripts dialog that can be used to generate script files for most
of your database objects

[handwritten: Click Preview]

2. When generating scripts for tables, check the Script PRIMARY and
FOREIGN Keys check box on the Options tab to include these constraints
in the generated script. You won't see any primary or foreign keys in the
generated script since we haven't defined them yet. We'll do that next.

[handwritten: Click OK]

[handwritten: C:\MSSQL7\Binn to save]

Declaring Referential Integrity

Let's find out how we can define relationships between tables and how to specify
primary and foreign keys. These are the basic ingredients for referential integrity, as
you'll see in Chapter 5.

1. Create the Fund Accounts Statements table as defined in Appendix B. Follow the same steps we took in creating the Accounts table above.

2. After you have finished creating the Statements table and saved it, click the Database Diagrams folder under the FundAccts database. In the Results pane, click the New toolbar button to create a new database diagram. You'll see a blank Console window displayed.

3. Arrange the two windows so that you can see the FundAccts tables and the new Database Diagram window at the same time. Click the Accounts table and drag it to the Database Diagram window and drop it. Do the same with the Statements table. Now you can bring the Database Diagram window into full view so we can work with it.

4. To create the primary key for the Accounts table, highlight the acct_no column, right-click, and select Set Primary Key from the pop-up menu.

5. To set the primary key for the Statements table, highlight both the acct_no and stmt_date columns and click Set Primary Key. A small Key icon will appear in the primary key columns as you set the keys.

   Now let's create a relationship between the Accounts table and the Statements table on the acct_no column.

6. Highlight the Accounts.acct_no column and drag it to the Statements.acct_no column and drop it. This will display the Create Relationship dialog showing the Accounts table as the primary key table and the Statements table as the foreign key table. The suggested name of the relationship is FK_Statements_Accounts. Dismiss the Create Relationship dialog to set the Statements.acct_no as a foreign key referencing the Accounts.acct_no column. Right-click the Accounts table diagram and select Properties to display the Table Properties page. The Relationship tab of the Properties page should look like that shown in Figure 2-10.

Now we can put some data into our Accounts table so we have something to work with when we explore the SQL Server Query Analyzer.

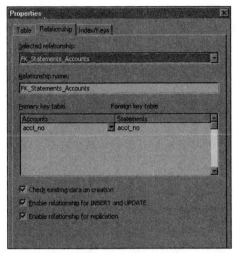

Figure 2-10: The Relationship tab of the Accounts Table Properties page after creating a relationship between the Accounts table and the Statements table

Exploring the BCP Utility

The BCP utility located in the `<sqlserverdirectory>\Binn` directory is used to import and export data into and out of SQL Server tables.

 Another method of importing and exporting data in SQL Server 7.0 uses a feature called Data Transformation Services (DTS). DTS can be used to import, export, and transform data between a variety of data sources. You can use the DTS Wizard to build reusable DTS packages that can be stored in SQL Server. This wizard can be started from Enterprise Manager or a command prompt. See Appendix L for a description of these services and an example of using the DTS Wizard.

BCP is an excellent tool for loading test data into a database or to import production data extracted from another application. The data we'll be loading into the Accounts table was exported from a Microsoft Access 2.0 database into a tab-delimited file named accounts.dat.

 You'll find this file on the CD that accompanies this book, in the Chapter 2 directory.

In order to load data into the Accounts table without logging the inserts, be sure to check the Select Into/Bulk Copy check box in the FundAccts database properties before running BCP (see Figure 2-4). It is also a good idea to drop indexes on the Accounts table before loading and then rebuild the indexes after loading is complete. On small tables such as those you find in the sample database, the performance increase from this practice won't be noticeable, but for large table loads, BCP will run much faster without index maintenance.

In order to copy data, BCP needs to know how to locate and interpret the column values in the input file. To help in this effort, we can supply a format file that instructs BCP on the location and data type of each column to be loaded into the Accounts table. The format file we'll use is also found on the CD in the Chapter 2 directory and is named accounts.fmt.

Using a Format File

To create a format file, you could use any ASCII editor and enter the column specifications manually; however, there is a better way.

When executing BCP with command line arguments specifying a table name, an output file, and the *format* directional indicator, BCP will create a format file for you. Each column in the table is represented in the resulting file. You can control the data types that will appear in the format file by using the flags /c to write char types to the output, /n to write native SQL Server types and /6 to write native SQL Server 6.0 or 6.5 types. A sample command line to produce the accounts.fmt format file follows:

```
bcp FundAccts..Accounts format d:\data\accounts.dat
/fd:\data\accounts.fmt /Usa /Ssecrets /ed:\data\bcperr.txt /c
```

The resulting accounts.fmt format file is shown in Figure 2-11. This file can be used in loading the Accounts table, provided our data file, accounts.dat, holds the data as specified in the format file.

```
7.0
19
1    SQLCHAR    0    10    "\t"     1     acct_no
2    SQLCHAR    0    70    "\t"     2     acct_lastname
3    SQLCHAR    0    50    "\t"     3     acct_firstname
4    SQLCHAR    0    30    "\t"     4     last_contact
5    SQLCHAR    0    30    "\t"     5     addr_line1
6    SQLCHAR    0    30    "\t"     6     addr_line2
7    SQLCHAR    0    30    "\t"     7     addr_line3
8    SQLCHAR    0    30    "\t"     8     city
9    SQLCHAR    0    2     "\t"     9     state_abbr
10   SQLCHAR    0    10    "\t"     10    zip
11   SQLCHAR    0    15    "\t"     11    home_phone
12   SQLCHAR    0    15    "\t"     12    work_phone
13   SQLCHAR    0    41    "\t"     13    tot_assets
14   SQLCHAR    0    2     "\t"     14    fiscal_period
15   SQLCHAR    0    1     "\t"     15    cycle
16   SQLCHAR    0    6     "\t"     16    acct_type
17   SQLCHAR    0    8     "\t"     17    acct_status
18   SQLCHAR    0    7     "\t"     18    manager_num
19   SQLCHAR    0    0     "\r\n"   19    acct_note
```

Figure 2-11: The accounts.fmt file used to load the Accounts table

The first line indicates the SQL Server version number. The second line of the file indicates the number of format records (column specifications) in the file. The records that follow provide BCP with instructions on how to interpret the input data file in accounts.dat. Let's take a closer look at the record for the acct_no column:

```
1   SQLCHAR    0   10   "\t"   1    acct_no
```

The leftmost 1 is the position of the column in a row in the data file. The data type of the column in the data file is specified as SQLCHAR, a SQL Server CHAR data type. In ASCII files, this is the type you will want to use. If you are using native format data files instead of ASCII files, you can use any of the data types shown in Table 2-1.

TABLE 2-1 THE DATA TYPE SPECIFIERS USED IN THE BCP FORMAT FILE

SQL Server Data Type	BCP Type Specifier
binary	SQLBINARY
bit	SQLBIT
char	SQLCHAR
datetime	SQLDATETIME

Continued

TABLE 2-1 THE DATA TYPE SPECIFIERS USED IN THE BCP FORMAT FILE *(Continued)*

SQL Server Data Type	BCP Type Specifier
decimal	SQLDECIMAL
float	SQLFLT8
image	SQLBINARY
int	SQLINT
money	SQLMONEY
nchar	SQLNCHAR
ntext	SQLNCHAR
numeric	SQLNUMERIC
nvarchar	SQLNCHAR
real	SQLFLT4
smalldatetime	SQLDATETIM4
smallint	SQLSMALLINT
smallmoney	SQLMONEY4
text	SQLCHAR
timestamp	SQLBINARY
tinyint	SQLTINYINT
uniqueidentifier	SQLUNIQUEID
varbinary	SQLBINARY
varchar	SQLCHAR

The 0 following the data type indicates the prefix length. This value can be 0, 1, 2, or 4 depending on the type of data being copied. The prefix length is used by BCP to indicate the length of the field when copying data to a file in native format.

The value 10 is the maximum number of characters to store the data of the type specified. The acct_no column is 10 characters long, so this is the maximum specified to BCP.

The \t indicates a tab delimiter follows the column data in the input file. Other common delimiters are as follows:

```
\n      newline
\r      carriage return
","     comma
```

Following the column delimiter is the server column order of 1. This is the column's position in the SQL Server table. In the Accounts table, the acct_no column was the first column we specified when we created the table, so we enter a 1 in the format file for this column.

If you do not want a column to receive any data, set the server column order to 0 and BCP will skip the column.

The last item specified on the first format line is the name of the SQL Server table column. This item can be anything you wish since BCP does not use it to map table columns to data file. You do need to specify something, however, so it might as well be the column name to make it easy for humans to map.

The rest of the columns are interpreted the same as line one. Now let's use this format file to load data into the Accounts table.

Executing the BCP Utility

If you are loading large data files or extracting from large tables, it is best to execute BCP on the server machine. This will eliminate the network traffic incurred by transfer of rows between the client and the server. For the purposes of our tiny accounts.dat sample, you can run BCP on a client machine.

Open a Command window, switch to the <sql server directory>\Binn directory and enter the following command line, substituting your own target paths where output and input files are stored:

```
bcp FundAccts..Accounts in d:\data\accounts.dat
/fd:\data\accounts.fmt /Usa /Ssecrets /ed:\data\bcperr.txt
```

The first argument in the command line is the name of the database and table BCP should copy to. The server name of the SQL Server machine BCP will connect to is Secrets as denoted by the /S flag. The direction of copy is from an operating system file named accounts.dat located in the d:\data\ directory to the Accounts table located in the FundAccts database.

The direction of copy is indicated by in after the table name. To copy data from a SQL Server table to an operating system file, use out as the direction of copy. The flag /U indicates the user to connect to SQL Server with — in this case, the default system administrator (sa) and the flag /e points to an error log for BCP error messages. The flags that can be used on the command line are listed in Table 2-2.

TABLE 2-2 BCP COMMAND-LINE FLAGS

Flag	Description
/m maxerrors	maxerrors is the maximum number of errors allowed before bcp cancels. Defaults to 10.
/f formatfile	formatfile is full path to the format file bcp will use to copy data.
/e errfile	errfile is full path to the file bcp will write errors into.
/F firstrow	firstrow is the number of the first row to be copied.
/L lastrow	lastrow is the number of the last row to be copied.
/b batchsize	batchsize is the number of rows to include in one batch. Defaults to all rows.
/n	Use data types from table.
/c	Use char as the data type, \t as the field separator and \n as the row delimiter.
/6	Use SQL Server 6.0 or 6.5 data types
/E	Identity values are present in input file.
/t field_term	field_term is the field terminator.
/r row_term	row_term is the row terminator.
/i inputfile	inputfile is the name of the redirected input file.
/o outputfile	outputfile is the name of the redirected output file.
/U login_id	login_id is the login used to connect to SQL Server.
/P password	password to be used with login_id. If none supplied, BCP will prompt when making connection.
/S servername	servername is the name of the SQL Server computer on the network.
/v	Displays the BCP version number.
/a packet_size	packet_size is the size of the network packet in bytes. Default is 4,096. Range is 512 to 65,535.
/T	Uses a trusted connection to connect to SQL Server.
/q	Used when quoted identifiers are being used.

When you execute the command line, BCP prompts you for the `sa` password. If this is still the default password, just hit the Enter key to pass a `null` password. Most likely, you will use your own login ID instead of `sa`.

In the Chapter 2 directory on the CD that accompanies this book, you'll find other samples of BCP format files that show how to skip columns in the input data file and how to specify data files that are missing columns.

Now that we've explored the BCP utility and loaded some data into the Accounts table, let's take a look at some of the other tools available to us.

We'll first query out some of the data we just loaded using the SQL Server Query Analyzer. If you still have Enterprise Manager open, you can launch the Query Analyzer by selecting it from the Tools menu. If you don't have Enterprise Manager open, launch it from the Windows taskbar.

Exploring the SQL Server Query Analyzer

The SQL Server Query Analyzer provides a graphical way to query SQL Server, analyze the execution plan of a query, and view statistical information about an executed query.

When you first open the Query Analyzer, you are prompted for a SQL Server to connect to and a login ID and password. Enter your SQL Server login ID and password or click the Use the Windows NT Authentication radio button to use your NT login account.

After connection to SQL Server is established, the Query window is displayed as shown in Figure 2-12.

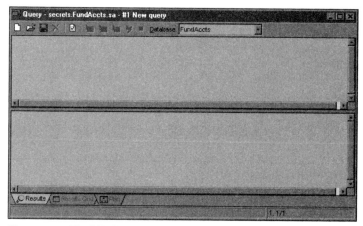

Figure 2-12: The SQL Server Query Analyzer's Query window

You can make multiple connections to SQL Server using another login (or the same login for that matter), which will bring up another Query window for each connection. This is often useful for testing the behavior of Transact-SQL and stored procedures under different logins with different permissions.

Running a Query

In the Database drop-down list at the top of the window, select the FundAccts database. Enter the following query in the top Query pane:

```
SELECT acct_no,acct_type,tot_assets FROM Accounts
```

Before executing this query, choose Set Options from the Query menu and then click the Format tab. In the Result output format drop-down list, select Tab Delimited and click the OK button to dismiss the Options dialog. This formats the Results pane with tab-delimited columns. You can also choose Column Aligned, Comma Separated (CSV), and Other Delimiter (of your own choice) formats.

Execute the query by clicking the Execute Query toolbar button and view the results in the Results pane at the bottom of the window.

To view the results in a grid, click the Execute Query Into Grid toolbar button and view the results on the Results Grid tab.

If you enter multiple query statements in the Query pane and execute them, the Query Analyzer will display the results from all queries. To execute a selected query, highlight the query you want to execute by dragging the mouse over the query statement and then click the Execute Query button. This will cause the Query Analyzer to execute the highlighted query only.

You can save your queries to a file and reload them later for execution. Click the Query pane and choose Save or Save As... from the File menu. The default extension for query files is .sql. Likewise, you can save the query results to a .rpt file.

To change the default extensions, choose Configure from the File menu and set the appropriate extensions.

Viewing the Query Analysis Information

Click the Display Execution Plan toolbar button to view the query plan for the currently selected query on the Plan tab.

Position the mouse over the FundAccts.Accounts icon to display the plan information pop-up as shown in Figure 2-13.

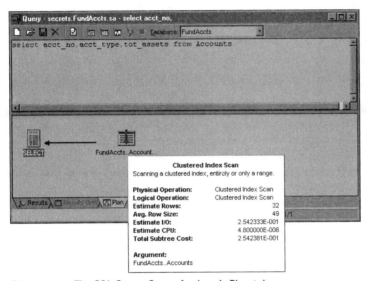

Figure 2-13: The SQL Server Query Analyzer's Plan tab

The items in this display are equivalent to the SET SHOWPLAN_ALL output discussed in Chapter 4. Learning to interpret this information will enable you to write queries that perform optimally.

In the case of this simple query, the SQL Server optimizer chose to use the clustered index we created on the acct_no column to return our results.

To display the compile-and-execute statistics for the query, select Set Options... from the Query menu and then check the Show Stats Time check box on the Execution tab.

When you execute the query, you'll see a statistics display at the end of the results that looks similar to this:

```
SQL Server Execution Times:
   cpu time = 16 ms.  elapsed time = 0 ms.
SQL Server Parse and Compile Time:
   cpu time = 0 ms.
```

Spend some time experimenting with various queries, using the query plan and execution statistics to gain a good understanding of this tool. It will be invaluable to you in your application development.

Using the SQL Client Configuration Utility

The Client Configuration utility is used to set default net libraries for connection with a SQL Server installation and to choose date/time and currency formats for DB-Library.

The default network protocol for client/server connections is Named Pipes. To select another protocol, open the SQL Server Client Configuration utility from the SQL Server program group and click the General tab.

On the General tab, select the desired protocol from the Default Network protocol drop-down list. If you don't see the protocol you want in the list, it means that protocol is not installed on your machine. To install another network protocol, go into the Control Panel and select the Network icon.

The SQL Server client installation installs the current versions of the Microsoft client Net-Libraries. The SQL Client Configuration utility can be used to check the version numbers of these network libraries installed on your machine by selecting the Network Libraries tab. Here, you can view the protocol name, library name, version number of the library, date of the library, and file size.

Add a New Network Protocol

To set a connection to use a protocol other than the default or to set an alternate port number, click the Add button on the General tab.

Enter the name of the server you are using in your applications in the Server text box. In the Server Protocols frame, select a network protocol to use and enter the required parameters.

You are now ready to use the new default protocol or alternate protocol to make a connection with SQL Server.

Set DB-Library Options

On the DB-Library Options tab, you can view DB-Library version information and set a couple of options.

The Automatic ANSI to OEM conversion option enables character set conversion between different code pages being used on the client and server. If both client and server are using the same code page, then conversion is not necessary and this check box can be cleared. The default code page for SQL Server is 1252 (ANSI).

When the Use international settings check box is checked, DB-Library gets date, time, and currency format information from the operating system settings rather than from a parameter file.

On Windows NT and Windows 95, both of these check boxes are checked by default.

Using the makepipe and readpipe Programs

If you are experiencing connection problems in your application using the default NamedPipes protocol, you can use the `makepipe` and `readpipe` utilities to test the connection between your client machine and the SQL Server machine.

In a Command window on the server machine you wish to connect to, change to the `<sqlserver directory>\Binn` directory and enter the command below:

```
makepipe
```

To specify a wait time between reads and writes on the pipe, use the `/w` flag and enter a wait time in seconds.

If you want to test a pipe other than the default `pipename`, use the `/p` flag and specify the `pipename` after it.

Testing a Connection

To initiate and test a connection to the `makepipe` server you just started on the server machine, enter the command below:

```
readpipe /Sservername /Dstring
```

The `/Sservername` designates the server where `makepipe` is running. The `/D` flag specifies a string of characters to feed into the pipe connection.

The flags you can use for `readpipe` are listed in Table 2-3.

TABLE 2-3 READPIPE FLAGS

Flag	Description
/n	Specifies the number of iterations to run in the test.
/q	Causes a polling for incoming data on the pipe.
/w	Specifies the wait time to pause while polling. Default is zero seconds.
/t	Requests Transact-SQL named pipes.
/p	Specify an alternate pipe name.
/D	Specify string of characters to feed into the pipe.
/h	Displays usage information.

Viewing the Results

If I enter the following readpipe after starting makepipe on the Secrets server machine,

```
readpipe /Ssecrets /Dmytest
```

I should see the response below in the server machine makepipe window:

```
Making PIPE:\\.\pipe\abc
read to write delay (seconds):0
Waiting for Client to Connect...
Waiting for client to send...  1
Data Read:
mytest
Waiting for client to send...  2
Pipe closed
Waiting for Client to Connect...
```

The first three lines were displayed after entering the makepipe command. The first line tells me the default pipe name is being tested and the second line tells me the default delay is being used between reads and writes. The third line indicates the makepipe server is ready for a readpipe connection.

After I enter the above readpipe on the client, lines 4 through 9 appear in the makepipe window. This indicates that makepipe read the connection and transmission of the string mytest I entered on the client and the closepipe command issued by readpipe. Makepipe then went back to waiting for another connection.

My client readpipe window displays the following response:

```
SvrName:\\secrets
PIPE    :\\secrets\pipe\abc
DATA    :mytest
Data Sent: 1 :mytest
Data Read: 1 :mytest
```

The client response indicates that the string was successfully transmitted and received to and from makepipe running on the Secrets server.

When your tests are complete, return to the server makepipe session and press Ctrl+Break to stop execution of makepipe.

Summary

In this chapter, you've learned what SQL Server tools are available for your application development and you've explored some of these tools to get a feel for what features the tools provide.

The SQL Server Enterprise Manager was used to view various system objects in a SQL Server installation, and you learned how to create a database and table. You also saw how to set constraints and indexes on a database table.

In the BCP section, you explored how to use a BCP format file to import data into a SQL Server table and to export data from a table to a file. You also learned about the various flags that can be specified on the BCP command line.

In the SQL Server Query Analyzer, you learned how to enter query statements, and view and save the results of executing those statements. You learned how to turn on I/O statistics for a query and how to view the query processor's execution plan for the query.

Finally, you explored the Client Configuration utility for setting up a default network protocol other than named-pipes and to establish an alternate protocol for connection to SQL Server. To test a named-pipe connection between a client machine and server machine, you learned how to initiate and interpret the makepipe and readpipe programs.

Chapter 3

Understanding SQL Server Security

IN THIS CHAPTER

- ◆ Understand the SQL Server security modes
- ◆ Learn how to manage users and logins with system stored procedures
- ◆ Explore SQL Server roles and permissions

PRIOR TO DEVELOPING a SQL Server application, you should have an understanding of SQL Server's security mechanisms.

This chapter presents a brief overview of SQL Server 7.0 security and how you can work with it using a few stored procedures and Transact-SQL statements.

Using the material presented in this chapter, you will be able to add users and groups to your database, grant them access to SQL Server, give them permissions to use database objects, and remove permissions and access rights when no longer needed.

An Overview of SQL Server Security

The basic premise on which you build your database security should be to "give users only what is necessary to do their job."

SQL Server security provides the architecture and tools to enable you to manage your security plan based on this premise.

Conceptually, SQL Server security consists of one or more users, the authentication of those users, permissions, and validation of permissions for users attempting to perform some operation against a SQL Server object. Figure 3-1 shows the relationships between NT and SQL Server for a given security plan.

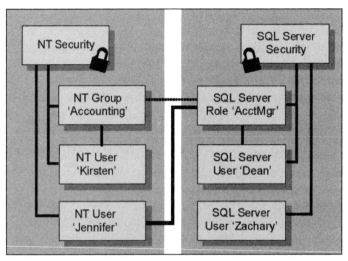

Figure 3-1: Conceptual view of a SQL Server security plan

In Figure 3-1, the NT group 'Accounting' with its member 'Kirsten' is trusted by SQL Server. SQL Server contains two users, 'Zachary' and 'Dean,' not known to NT and it contains a role called 'AcctMgr' containing 'Dean' and an NT user 'Jennifer' as members.

Let's take a look at how this type of security plan can be established and how SQL Server goes about authenticating a user attempting to make a connection with SQL Server. There are two modes available for this process.

Security Modes

SQL Server can use one of two security modes when authenticating a login user. These modes are Windows NT Authentication mode and SQL Server Authentication mode.

SQL Server Authentication mode allows users to connect through their Windows NT user account name or through a username established only within SQL Server.

Windows NT Authentication mode allows users to connect only through their Windows NT account.

Authentication is the process of identifying a user and either granting access or revoking access depending on the user's rights as entered in the security system. In the case of Windows NT authentication, SQL Server is trusting NT to properly authenticate the user attempting to make the connection.

After authenticating a user connection, SQL Server checks the user account for the right to access the database the user is attempting to use. If a security account exists for the database and it matches the login user, access is granted; otherwise, the user is denied access with an error message.

After granting a connection to a database, the user is free to send Transact-SQL statements to SQL Server for execution. As SQL Server receives these Transact-SQL statements, permission to execute the statement and permission to access the database object are checked against statement permissions and object permissions. If either permission is not validated for the user, the statement is not executed and an error message is returned.

Users and Groups

As you can see from the overview of SQL Server's security modes, some identity is needed for the purpose of granting access rights and permissions. The identity to which these rights and permissions are assigned can be an individual user or a group of users.

If you have more than one user with the same access needs, you can define a group, place the users into the group as members, and assign the rights to the group rather than to all individual users. In this case, the authentication and permission validation process is applied against the group instead of the user.

A user is granted access to a database if either a group containing the user has the proper access rights or the individual user has the access rights.

Logins

A user that is to be granted access to SQL Server requires a login account.

If NT authentication is being used, the user attempting to log in is trusted by SQL Server as having been properly authenticated by NT.

If SQL Server authentication is being used, then the user attempting to log in must have a SQL Server login account established within SQL Server and SQL Server performs the authentication process against this account.

Roles

Users in an organization are most likely associated with certain roles in that organization. Users might be internal auditors, for example, or they might be an account manager and an auditor.

People with the same roles most likely do the same types of work and require the same types of database access. You can establish a role in a database and give permissions to it according to the data access needs of the role. Once established, you can then add users to the role and all users inherit the permissions assigned to the role.

You can also assign members into one of SQL Server's predefined roles. These are roles set up based on generic database activities such as administrator, data reader, and data writer.

Permissions

Permissions assigned to roles, individual users, and groups are of two types: statement permissions and object permissions.

Statement permissions grant a user the right to execute specified Transact-SQL statements against a database. For example, a user could be granted the right to create procedures but not create tables.

Object permissions grant a user the right to access a database object such as a table or view, or to execute a stored procedure.

Managing Users and Logins

A user is added to SQL Server as an NT user in the form of `NT DomainName\NT UserName` or as a SQL Server user account. This identity needs to be established so that a connection can be authenticated by SQL Server or authenticated by NT and trusted by SQL Server.

Beyond the authentication, the identity is required to grant access to a database and to grant permissions for database object access and statement execution. These permissions can be assigned in several ways, as you'll see later in this chapter.

Establishing Users and Logins

Our first order of business is to establish a user in SQL Server and grant that user the right to connect to SQL Server.

Although you can use the facilities in SQL Server Enterprise Manager to establish users, this book will not cover this method. Instead, we will use SQL Server's system stored procedures executed through the SQL Query Analyzer.

Adding Users with Stored Procedures

To create a login that will be authenticated by SQL Server, you can use the `sp_addlogin` stored procedure.

Using `sp_addlogin`, we can grant a user named Dean the right to log in to SQL Server as shown below:

```
sp_addlogin Dean, password, FundAccts
```

Executing this procedure successfully adds Dean to the syslogins table in the master database and enables him to log in to SQL Server.

After logging in to SQL Server, Dean will be connected to the `FundAccts` database as noted by the third argument to `sp_addlogin`. This alone, however, is not enough to grant him the right to use the `FundAccts` database. He will not be able to do anything with it.

If we wish to allow an NT user to log in, we would use the stored procedure sp_grantlogin to inform SQL Server that the user will be authenticated through NT:

```
sp_grantlogin 'Develop\Kirsten'
```

— NOTE single quote marks (handwritten annotation)

Develop is the name of the NT domain in which the user Kirsten is defined and will be authenticated. This procedure also enters the login name into the syslogins table in the master database.

Now, both Dean and Kirsten have the right to log in to SQL Server. If we don't specify a user name specifically using one of the above procedures, a user can still gain access to SQL Server using a *guest* account.

By setting up a guest account in a database, you allow unidentified users to access the database. The permissions associated with the guest account are granted to the guest user. You would normally either not establish a guest account in your database or not grant any permissions to it. How you handle guest logins is dependent on your application and it's data security requirements.

At this point, neither Dean nor Kirsten can do anything with a database. We need to grant them the right to use the FundAccts database. To do this, we use the sp_grantdbaccess stored procedure. Here's the script:

```
USE FundAccts
GO
sp_grantdbaccess Dean
GO
sp_grantdbaccess 'Develop\Kirsten','Kirsten'
```

This procedure adds the user to the sysusers system table in the FundAccts database and grants them the right to use the database.

Note that with the NT user, we have specified an alias in the second argument for use in this database. All permissions we will assign to this user can be assigned to the alias instead of to the fully qualified NT username.

To see a report listing the users and their associated roles within a database, you can execute the sp_helpuser procedure:

```
USE FundAccts
GO
sp_helpuser
```

You can use this procedure with a specific user account to list the user's roles and rights in the current database:

```
USE FundAccts
GO
sp_helpuser Dean
```

The DefDBName column in the resulting report lists the default database for the user listed in the UserName column.

To remove a security account from a database, use sp_revokedbaccess. This procedure removes the account from the current database and all permissions granted to the account:

```
USE FundAccts
GO
sp_revokedbaccess 'Develop\Kirsten'
```

There are times, of course, when you'll need to remove an NT login from SQL Server. If a user has left the organization or no longer requires access to SQL Server, you can use the sp_revokelogin procedure to remove the login rights. Pass the user's name as the first argument to remove the login rights for that user:

```
sp_revokelogin 'Kirsten'
```

This procedure is used to revoke an NT user login. Once completed, the user will no longer be able to log in to SQL Server using that login name. If they have another NT login name, belong to an NT group having login rights, or have a SQL Server login, they will still have access to SQL Server.

To revoke a SQL Server login, use the sp_droplogin procedure:

```
sp_droplogin Dean
```

If an NT user is to be denied login rights but not revoked from SQL Server, you can use the sp_denylogin procedure:

```
sp_denylogin 'Develop\Kirsten'
```

To activate the user login right, execute the sp_grantlogin procedure as you did when first adding the user.

Exploring Permissions and Roles

Establishing a user, granting that user the right to login to SQL Server, and granting a connection to a database is only the halfway point to enabling the user to do any useful work with a database.

What the user does in a database is governed by the permissions granted to the user. We need to set two kinds of permissions: object permissions and statement permissions.

Object permissions give a user the right to work with a table, view, or stored procedure. The FundAccts Transaction History table (see Appendix B for the structure of the FundAccts database) might need to be accessed by people entering transactions into an account and by account managers managing an account, but not necessarily by someone responsible for keeping fund prices up-to-date. People entering fund prices only require access to the Fund table. Setting permissions on the Transaction History table for account managers (or their roles, as you'll soon see) is an example of using object permissions.

When an account manager sends a Transact-SQL statement to SQL Server to insert a transaction into the Transaction History table, SQL Server validates the statement against the user's object permissions for the Transaction History table. If an INSERT statement is allowed for the user, the statement is processed. If INSERT is not permitted for the user, SQL Server rejects the statement and returns an error message.

Statement permissions cover statements such as CREATE TABLE, CREATE VIEW, CREATE DATABASE, CREATE PROCEDURE, CREATE DEFAULT, CREATE RULE, DUMP DATABASE, and DUMP TRANSACTION. These are normally granted to people with administrative or development responsibilities and not to application users.

Some permissions are implied. If the user attempting to access a table happens to be the owner of that table, then the user can do what he or she wants with the table. They have full permissions on objects they own.

Likewise, if a user is a member of the sysadmin group, they too have full permissions on the table, in addition to every other object in the database. These users are administrators and need to access all objects for the purpose of managing the database and the users accessing the database.

Instead of assigning permissions to individual users, we can establish roles in the database and assign permissions to the role. To grant the same permissions to users, we add the users as members of the role.

Our fund accounts management system has account managers to bring in client business and manage the client's portfolio, data entry clerks to enter client and fund transactions, and fund maintenance clerks to add new funds to the database and keep pricing information up-to-date.

We'll create these roles in the FundAccts database and add the employees to the appropriate roles. Each role will be granted only the permissions it needs to perform the duties of the role.

INTRODUCTION TO ROLES AND PERMISSIONS

SQL Server ships with fixed server and database roles already created. These roles have certain permissions assigned to them that you cannot assign to roles you create yourself.

The preassigned permissions in the *fixed server roles* are summarized in Table 3-1. These roles are used primarily by system administrators and database administrators. The permissions of these roles pertain to tasks needed to manage the overall SQL Server installation.

TABLE 3-1 THE SQL SERVER FIXED SERVER ROLES

Role	Permissions
dbcreator	Permitted to create and alter databases
diskadmin	Manages disk files for databases
processadmin	Manages processes running in SQL Server
serveradmin	Permitted to configure settings that apply to the server
setupadmin	Permitted to install replication and manage extended stored procedures
securityadmin	Manages server logins
sysadmin	Permitted to perform any SQL Server installation activity

In addition to server roles, SQL Server defines fixed database roles. The *fixed database roles* are present in each database within the installation and are assigned permissions as summarized in Table 3-2.

TABLE 3-2 THE SQL SERVER FIXED DATABASE ROLES

Role	Permissions
db_accessadmin	Permitted to add or remove users in the database
db_datareader	Permitted to see any data in all user-defined tables in the database
db_datawriter	Permitted to add, change, or delete data from all user-defined tables in the database
db_denydatareader	Denies permission to see any data in the database
db_denydatawriter	Denies permission to change any data in the database
db_ddladmin	Permitted to use DDL to add, modify, or drop objects in the database
db_securityadmin	Manages roles and SQL Server role members. Also manages the statement and object permissions in the database
db_dumpoperator	Permitted to back up the database

Role	Permissions
db_owner	Permitted to perform the activities of the db_accessadmin, db_datareader, db_datawriter, db_ddladmin, db_securityadmin, db_dumpoperator, and other maintenance and configuration tasks in the database

Unlike user-defined roles, you cannot change the permissions assigned to SQL Server fixed roles. Assigning users to these roles or removing users from them is about the only way you can control who gets the permissions associated with these roles.

There is a special type of role you can use for your SQL Server applications. *Application roles* can have permissions assigned to them, but they do not allow members to be assigned. A user is granted the role's permissions when they use your application and your application has designated the role to be used.

In the next section, we'll use more of SQL Server's system stored procedures to establish roles in the database and manage permissions and role memberships.

USING STORED PROCEDURES TO MANAGE ROLES

To create a user-defined role, we'll use the sp_addrole stored procedure.

```
sp_addrole 'AcctManager'
```

We now have a role named 'AcctManager' representing the permissions for account managers. Next we'll need to add members to this role:

```
sp_addrolemember 'AcctManager', Dean
sp_addrolemember 'AcctManager', Kirsten
```

The sp_addrolemember is only used to add members to user-defined roles. Next, we'll use another stored procedure to add members to fixed SQL Server roles:

```
sp_addsrvrolemember Bill, sysadmin
```

The above statement adds Bill as a member of the fixed server role named sysadmin. From Table 3-1, you can see that Bill now has system administration permissions to perform any task in the SQL Server installation.

To remove a role from the database, we need to remove all members from the role and then drop the role.

To remove a role's members from a SQL Server role, use the sp_dropsrvrole-member stored procedure. To remove members from a user-defined role, use sp_droprolemember:

```
sp_dropsrvrolemember Bill, sysadmin
GO
sp_droprolemember 'AcctManager', Dean
```

Once you've removed the members, the role can be dropped from the database with the `sp_droprole` stored procedure:

```
sp_droprole 'AcctManager'
```

To establish an application role, you use the `sp_addapprole` stored procedure:

```
sp_addapprole AcctBrowser, ba6848
```

The `sp_addapprole` procedure above establishes the application role 'AcctBrowser' in the database with the password 'ba6848'. In order to use this role, an application must set the role and provide the proper password.

Once activated for the application, the user of the application inherits the permissions granted to the role and loses the permissions granted to the user. This special role ensures that the application will have the rights to do what it was designed to do. The application must, however, authenticate the user for use of the application and the permissions it has.

To activate the application role permissions, an application can issue the `sp_setapprole` stored procedure:

```
sp_setapprole 'AcctBrowser', 'ba6848'
```

Once the application sets the role on behalf of the application user, the user's permissions granted through other roles or directly to the user will be temporarily disabled. In other words, SQL Server will only use the permissions granted to the application role when executing Transact-SQL statements for the application connection.

When the application disconnects from SQL Server, the application role is deactivated.

To drop the application role from the database, use `sp_dropapprole`.

```
sp_dropapprole 'AcctBrowser'
```

Now that we have an `AcctManager` role for the `FundAccts` database and we know how to add and remove users, we're ready to assign permissions to the role. To do that, we'll use the `GRANT` statement.

GRANTING PERMISSIONS WITH THE GRANT STATEMENT

The `GRANT` statement is used to assign a permission to a security account. The security account can be a Windows NT user, Windows NT group, SQL Server user, or SQL Server role.

Statement permissions can be assigned using GRANT to permit a user or role to execute these statements:

◆ CREATE DATABASE

◆ CREATE DEFAULT

◆ CREATE PROCEDURE

◆ CREATE RULE

◆ CREATE TABLE

◆ CREATE VIEW

◆ DUMP DATABASE

◆ DUMP TRANSACTION

Say our investment firm hires Zachary as a database developer to develop stored procedures to be used by the account managers. Zachary needs CREATE PROCEDURE permissions to do his job.

```
sp_addlogin Zachary, password, FundAccts
GO
GRANT CREATE PROCEDURE TO Zachary
```

Since Zachary will need to access the FundAccts tables in his stored procedures, we'll need to grant him the right to work with those tables. We won't grant him DELETE permissions however.

```
USE FundAccts
GO
GRANT INSERT, UPDATE, SELECT ON Accounts TO Zachary
```

When Zachary creates his stored procedures, he'll need to enable users and roles to execute them. Say he creates a procedure named SumAcct. To enable the AcctManager role to execute this procedure, Zachary would issue the following:

```
USE FundAccts
GO
GRANT EXECUTE ON SumAcct TO AcctManager
```

To grant object permissions for the Accounts table to the account managers, we use GRANT to assign all object permissions to the AcctManager role:

```
USE FundAccts
GO
GRANT ALL ON Accounts TO AcctManager
```

The above statement gives the AcctManager role the right to INSERT, UPDATE, SELECT, and DELETE from the Accounts table in the FundAccts database. We would use similar statements to grant access to the other tables and views of the FundAccts database.

The keyword in the GRANT statement that indicates the statement is granting object permissions and not statement permissions is the word ON. This keyword designates the object that is receiving the permission.

To list the permissions we've created thus far, execute the sp_helprotect stored procedure. The results are shown in Figure 3-2.

Owner	Object	Grantee	Grantor	ProtectType	Action	Column
dbo	Accounts	AcctManager	dbo	Grant	Delete	-
dbo	Accounts	AcctManager	dbo	Grant	Insert	-
dbo	Accounts	AcctManager	dbo	Grant	References	(All+New)
dbo	Accounts	AcctManager	dbo	Grant	Select	(All+New)
dbo	Accounts	AcctManager	dbo	Grant	Update	(All+New)
dbo	sysalternates	public	dbo	Grant	Select	(All)
dbo	syscolumns	public	dbo	Grant	Select	(All+New)
dbo	syscomments	public	dbo	Grant	Select	(All+New)
dbo	sysdepends	public	dbo	Grant	Select	(All+New)
dbo	sysfilegroups	public	dbo	Grant	Select	(All)
dbo	sysfiles	public	dbo	Grant	Select	(All)
dbo	sysindexes	public	dbo	Grant	Select	(All+New)
dbo	sysobjects	public	dbo	Grant	Select	(All+New)
dbo	syspermissions	public	dbo	Grant	Select	(All+New)
dbo	sysprotects	public	dbo	Grant	Select	(All+New)
dbo	sysreferences	public	dbo	Grant	Select	(All+New)
dbo	syssegments	public	dbo	Grant	Select	(All+New)
dbo	systypes	public	dbo	Grant	Select	(All+New)
dbo	sysusers	public	dbo	Grant	Select	(All+New)

Figure 3-2: Partial view of the sp_helprotect stored procedure output

Notice in Figure 3-2 that when we granted ALL permissions, a permission labeled REFERENCES was assigned to our AcctManager role.

The REFERENCES permission allows the grantee (user, group, or role) to refer to a table or column for which they don't have SELECT permissions. REFERENCES is used whenever the grantee changes a column containing a FOREIGN KEY constraint. Since SQL Server must check the value in the foreign key column against the table column it references, the user must have at least SELECT permissions on the referenced table column. If they don't have SELECT permissions, then REFERENCES must be granted to the user.

In addition to granting permissions to our user-defined role, we can grant permissions to two accounts inherited from the model database: the guest account and the public account.

Guest is used whenever a user logs into the database but doesn't have a login account established. If the guest account is present, then SQL Server will enable the user to log in under this guest account and will grant to the user whatever permissions have been assigned to the guest account. Generally, the guest account is either removed from the database or no permissions are assigned to it.

Public represents all users in the database. When you assign permissions to public, you are in fact assigning to all database users.

When users leave their position or leave the company, you'll need to remove them from the roles they have membership in as well as revoke any permissions granted directly to their security account. The next section deals with the task of denying user permissions.

DENY ACCESS WITH THE DENY STATEMENT

Let's say that at one time you granted Bill the permissions to INSERT, UPDATE, SELECT and DELETE on the Accounts table.

```
USE FundAccts
GO
GRANT ALL ON Accounts TO Bill
```

Now, due to a change in Bill's job, you need to deny Bill the right to make changes to Account records. He can, however, still read records from the table.

To deny Bill change permissions, use the DENY statement.

```
DENY INSERT, UPDATE, DELETE ON Accounts TO Bill
```

There is an interesting point about the DENY statement. If Bill is added to a role or group after the above DENY statement is executed, and the role or group is granted any of INSERT, UPDATE, or DELETE permissions, Bill will *not* receive those permissions. Reason? As a user, he has been directly denied those permissions. No matter where Bill ends up as a member, he will not have these permissions.

Technically there is a bigger rule at play here. Say you didn't execute the above DENY statement and that Bill is a member of a role that has ALL object permissions granted to it. Let's call this role Clerks.

If you now deny change permissions to Clerks, all members of Clerks, including Bill, will be denied change permission. Even though Bill himself has these change permissions, he will not be able to apply them.

The bigger rule at play? When SQL Server validates permissions and finds a conflict in the permissions between a member user and the role's permission assignments, the *most restrictive* permission is the one SQL Server uses. Since Bill himself has UPDATE permission on the Accounts table but is a member in a role that doesn't, he too is denied UPDATE permission.

REVOKING PERMISSIONS WITH THE REVOKE STATEMENT

Both the GRANT statement and the DENY statement insert entries into the sysprotects system table. The GRANT statement inserts a permission and the DENY statement inserts a permission denial. You can remove these entries using the REVOKE statement.

Had we denied Bill change permissions using the DENY statement in the previous section, we could remove the denied permissions using the following REVOKE statement:

```
REVOKE INSERT, UPDATE, DELETE ON Accounts FROM Bill
```

Use GRANT to reapply the permissions to Bill.

Summary

This chapter has presented an introduction to SQL Server security. As a Transact-SQL programmer, security is a topic you need to deal with in every project.

Every action in SQL Server is associated with a security account and passes through a validity check to determine if the security account has the right to invoke the action.

You've explored security accounts and how to create them. You learned how to use a Windows NT security account to grant a SQL Server login and to grant permissions.

Permissions are required to access SQL Server objects and execute statements. You saw here how to set up roles for your application and how to grant permissions to those roles.

You now have the basics of how SQL Server security works and how to manage it for your application.

Part II

The Transact-SQL Language

Chapter 4

Introduction to Transact-SQL

IN THIS CHAPTER

- ◆ Learn about the sample mutual fund account database
- ◆ Explore the elements of Transact-SQL statements
- ◆ Discover how to set environment options
- ◆ See how Transact-SQL statements can be batched together
- ◆ Find out how to execute a Transact-SQL string and a stored procedure that requires input parameters

THIS CHAPTER EXPLORES the basic elements of the Transact-SQL (T-SQL) language. The material here introduces the T-SQL language components, statements, and concepts that apply globally to T-SQL programming.

In the discussion of SQL Server Enterprise Manager in Chapter 2, you were given a glimpse of the sample database we'll be using to illustrate T-SQL programming. The following section provides more information on that sample database.

Introduction to the Mutual Fund Account Database

The sample database is one that might be used by a money management firm to store account information for mutual fund investors. The schema for this database is shown in Figure 4-1.

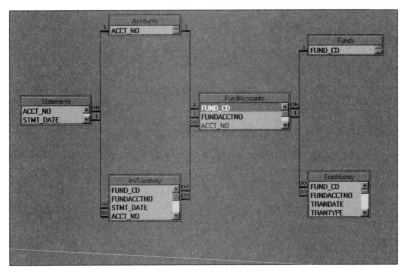

Figure 4-1: The mutual fund account sample database schema

This money management firm advises its clients as to where to invest their money and handles the purchasing, selling, and transfer of various mutual fund shares directly from the funds. The database is used to track their clients' portfolios.

The database, named FundAccts, contains six tables to store information on the individual investors, the mutual funds they are invested in, the transactions against their mutual fund accounts, and the value of their portfolio.

A client is established in the Accounts table and may invest in one or more mutual funds. These funds are recorded in the FundAccounts table and linked via foreign key to the investor accounts in the Accounts table. Each FundAccount record is linked to its associated fund record in the Funds table to identify the characteristics of the fund, such as name, address, phone numbers, and so forth.

A history of transactions against a client's fund accounts, such as buys, sells, dividend reinvestments, and so on are recorded in the TransHistory table. Each of these transaction history records is linked to its associated fund account record in the FundAccounts table through the foreign key FundAcctNo.

The Statements table is used to store information sent to clients on the quarterly statements. The statement table is linked to the InvSummary table by account number and statement date. Together, these two tables comprise an online record of a client's portfolio on the statement date.

The FundAccts database and the Accounts table were created in Chapter 2 to illustrate how a database and a table could be built with the SQL Server Enterprise Manager tool.

The remainder of the database objects will be created with T-SQL Data Definition Language (DDL) statements in Chapter 5. Before continuing that effort and learning how to get data into our database, let's explore the basic elements of a T-SQL statement.

Introduction to Transact-SQL Elements

Transact-SQL is the language by which you define and manipulate database objects and the data they contain. It is an enhanced version of the SQL-92 standard specifically for management of Microsoft SQL Server databases.

Each Transact-SQL statement contains a number of elements that when grouped together adhere to the syntactic rules of the SQL-92 grammar. Some elements in a statement are mandatory while others are optional. Transact-SQL adds keywords and extensions to the base grammar to enhance the language for SQL Server use.

Statements presented throughout the book will take a "practical use" approach and explain Transact-SQL as you would use it in practice, leaving the full linguistic features of the statements to the SQL Server Books Online if you need them.

The following statement element groups will be covered:

- Comments
- Literals
- Identifiers
- Expressions
- Keywords
- Operators

Comments

It's always good programming practice to document your code. This applies to Transact-SQL as well as it does to any other programming language. A good way to do that is to use comments in your code.

Comments are text strings that are ignored by the Transact-SQL query processor. Lines of text designated as comments are only for humans attempting to understand your code.

Transact-SQL allows you to introduce comments into your code in two ways. You can use the two-character sequence /* to begin a comment and the sequence */ to end the comment. These comment characters are useful if you want to add several lines of comments to your code. It is common to find comments that look like the following:

```
/*******************************************************************
This is a comment that takes multiple lines to explain what the code
is doing. Note that all lines between the comment character
delimiters are considered a comment and not processed by the query
processor.
*******************************************************************/
```

The other comment characters you can use are the -- character pair. These characters must appear in front of every comment line. They cannot be used to delimit a block of comments like the /*   */ comment characters can. If you want to use several lines in your comment and prefer the -- characters, then you must use the -- characters on each line of the comment block.

```
-- This is a comment that takes multiple lines to explain
-- what the code is doing. Note that all lines beginning
-- with two dashes are considered to be a comment line
-- and not processed by the query processor.
```

Literals

As you glance through the statement syntax reference in the appendix, you'll note that several Transact-SQL statements allow you to specify an expression or a search condition.

Both expressions and search conditions allow constants, also called *literals*, to be specified. For example, as you'll soon explore in the SELECT statement, you can enter a WHERE clause containing a search condition to limit the rows of data you want SQL Server to return. You may want to see only clients that have a NonTax account type:

```
SELECT acct_lastname, acct_firstname, acct_no
FROM Accounts
WHERE acct_type = 'NonTax'
```

In the above SELECT statement, the search condition in the WHERE clause contains a constant string literal to inform SQL Server that we only want to see accounts that have an acct_type with a value of 'NonTax'.

Although the literal in the SELECT statement is spelled with uppercase and lowercase characters, the default code-page installed is case insensitive. That means that rows containing acct_type values of 'NONTAX', 'nontax', 'nonTAX', and so on will all match the criteria of 'NonTax' and be returned by SQL Server.

Columns that have text or character data types must be compared to literals of the same type. Strings of characters are delimited by the single quote as shown in the above SELECT statement.

How would you specify a literal that contains a quote? To do this, you must specify two single quotes (which does not equal a single double quote) to inform the query processor that one quote is to be taken as a character and not the end of the literal. To select data where the account last name is equal to D'Arcy, you would use:

```
SELECT acct_firstname, acct_no, work_phone
FROM Accounts
WHERE acct_lastname = 'D''Arcy'
```

For columns that are a numeric data type, you can just enter the number without any delimiters.

```
SELECT acct_lastname, acct_firstname, acct_no
FROM Accounts
WHERE tot_assets > 100000
```

Here we are looking for accounts that have a total assets value greater than $100,000.

Identifiers

To be able to refer to a database object, we define names or identifiers for objects. Identifiers in SQL Server must adhere to certain rules.

An identifier can contain up to 128 characters. The first character of the identifier must be an alphabetic character, an underscore, the @ sign, or the # sign. Letters after the first may be letters, numbers or the # sign, @ sign, underscore or $ sign. No spaces are allowed within the identifier.

If an identifier begins with the @ sign, it denotes a local variable and those identifiers beginning with # signs denote temporary tables or procedures.

Since identifiers can be duplicated from object to object, we need some way to qualify a reference to an identifier.

For example, if we refer to the acct_no identifier, how do we know if the reference is intended for the Accounts table, the Statements table or some other object identifier called acct_no? To enable a specific reference, we can use database and owner qualifiers in front of the identifier like this:

```
FundAccts.dbo.Accounts.acct_no
```

This statement refers to the acct_no column of the Accounts table owned by the dbo in database FundAccts.

If the database and owner name is not significant for your reference, you can simply use:

```
Accounts.acct_no
```

In this case, SQL Server implies that the database is the current database and that the owner is the currently logged in user making the reference. If this is not the case, you will need to provide more qualification.

You may use keywords as identifiers by setting QUOTED_IDENTIFIER ON whenever you refer to an object using a keyword identifier. This is required since the keyword identifier must be delimited by either brackets [ ] or double quotes " ". See the Keywords section below for an example.

Expressions

A simple expression might be entered in a SELECT statement to retrieve a calculated value from a table.

In those Transact-SQL statements that allow expressions to be entered, you can enter a column name, a variable name, a function name, a literal constant, a CASE statement, a subquery (introduced in Chapter 9) or an operator specifying an operation with any of these elements.

```
SELECT acct_no, (tot_assets * .10) As Fee
FROM Accounts
```

The above SELECT statement selects the account number and 10% of the account's total assets from the Accounts table. The expression (tot_assets * .10) is asking the query processor to multiply the tot_assets column of each Accounts record by the numeric constant .10 and return the result in a column named Fee. You'll learn more about alias names for columns in Chapter 6. Note that this is an example of an operator * (multiplication operator) acting on a column expression (tot_assets) and a literal expression (.10).

Another common use of an operator in an expression is to select out a concatenation of a client's first name and last name together.

```
SELECT (acct_firstname + acct_lastname) As Client
FROM Accounts
```

The + symbol in the above statement is specifying that the two character type columns are to be concatenated together and returned as a single result column called Client. Let's expand this concatenation to include a literal constant.

```
SELECT (acct_firstname + acct_lastname) + ' From ' + city As
 Client_Name_City
FROM Accounts
```

The above statement is concatenating the string literal 'From' and the client's city to the end of the first name last name concatenation. The result may look something like this:

```
BillAmo From Wethersfield
```

When using a concatenation like this, remember to put a space on both sides of the string literal so you don't end up with results that look like this:

```
BillAmoFrom Wethersfield
```

or

```
BillAmo FromWethersfield
```

Notice that the `acct_firstname` and `acct_lastname` concatenation does not contain a space between them. This is because we didn't concatenate a space into the string.

Another method of assigning alias column names follows:

```
SELECT Client_Name_City  = (acct_firstname + ' ' + acct_lastname) +
 ' From ' + city
FROM Accounts
```

When you want to concatenate numeric columns, including dates, you will need to convert the column to a string. Conversions of data types can be accomplished by using the `CONVERT()` function:

```
SELECT (acct_firstname + ' ' + acct_lastname) + ' Has a current
 value of ' + CONVERT(varchar(15),tot_assets)
FROM Accounts
```

Later, we add some formatting to this converted value to make the result look better. For now, just remember the `CONVERT()` function is one you'll depend on quite often.

Creating columns in a query with numeric expressions, as we did above to calculate a fee, yield a numeric value. What is the data type of that value? The answer lies in the value of the data type codes used in the expression.

Each data type in SQL Server has a data type code, as shown in Table 4-1. Generally, data types in an expression with lower codes are converted to the types in the expression having higher codes.

There is an exception to this conversion behavior, however. When a money data type is used in an expression, the result is converted to money.

In the Fee expression, (`tot_assets` * `.10`), the data type of the result would be money since the `tot_assets` data type of money has a higher code than the decimal constant.

TABLE 4-1 PRECEDENCE OF SQL SERVER DATA TYPES

Name	Type Code
image	34
text	35
uniqueidentifier	36
varbinary	37
sysname	39
varchar	39
binary	45
timestamp	45
char	47
tinyint	48
bit	50
smallint	52
decimal	55
int	56
smalldatetime	58
real	59
money	60
datetime	61
float	62
numeric	63
smallmoney	122

Keywords

As you've probably noticed by now, Transact-SQL has a collection of elements that the SQL query processor applies a special meaning to. These elements are reserved keywords and are listed in Appendix E.

Transact-SQL keywords are words like SELECT, CREATE, TABLE, VIEW, and so on. I recommend these words be used only as keywords in Transact-SQL statements and not as identifiers for your database objects or the names of columns. Following this simple rule will reduce confusion and errors.

If for some reason you need to use a keyword as an identifier, here's an example of how to create a table with a name of VIEW.

Transact-SQL allows you to enclose a name within brackets. When you do, the name and its brackets become the full name of the object. For example, to use the keyword VIEW as a table name, you would create the table as:

```
SET QUOTED_IDENTIFIER ON
GO
CREATE TABLE [VIEW]
(   )
```

When using keywords in this fashion, you must ensure that QUOTED_IDENTIFIER is on whenever you want to refer to the object using quoted identifiers.

Operators

In the sample statements above, we used the + symbol for string concatenation and the * symbol for multiplication. These symbols are examples of operators in expressions.

Transact-SQL places operators into four categories:

◆ String Concatenation

◆ Arithmetic

◆ Comparison

◆ Bitwise Operation

STRING CONCATENATION

As you've already seen, string concatenation is accomplished with the + operator applied to two character type values.

String concatenation will come into use often, especially in business applications. This operator used in conjunction with the string functions explored in Chapter 7 is a very powerful combination you should become familiar with.

ARITHMETIC OPERATORS

Arithmetic operators are used in calculations such as addition, subtraction, multiplication, and division. The Fee calculation above was an example of a multiplication operator.

The arithmetic operator symbols are as follows:

* (Multiplication)

/ (Division)

- (Subtraction)

+ (Addition)

% (Modulo)

The arithmetic operators have a precedence level within an expression. Multiplication and division are carried out first, followed by modulo, subtraction, and addition. Operators within the same precedence level are applied in order left to right in the expression.

To change the order of this precedence, you can use parentheses. Placing parentheses around an expression places that expression at the top of the precedence order so that it is evaluated before the normal precedence hierarchy. Within the parentheses, however, the order of evaluation adheres to the normal precedence.

With normal precedence, the following expression yields 5:

```
4 * 2 - 3
```

With parentheses, the expression yields –4:

```
4 * (2 - 3)
```

COMPARISON OPERATORS

Comparison operators are used to compare two character, numeric, or date values and return a TRUE if they are equal and a FALSE otherwise.

You can use comparison operators in T-SQL WHERE or HAVING clauses or in the IF statement.

The > (greater than) operator tests for argument 1 being greater in value than argument 2:

```
IF Arg1 > Arg2
  --Arg1 is greater than Arg2
ELSE
  --Arg1 is not greater than Arg2
```

The < (less than) operator tests for argument 1 being less than argument 2:

```
IF Arg1 < Arg2
  --Arg1 is less than Arg2
ELSE
  --Arg1 is not less than Arg2
```

The = (equal) operator tests for equality between argument 1 and argument 2:

```
IF Arg1 = Arg2
  --Arg1 equals Arg2
ELSE
  --Arg1 does not equal Arg2
```

You may pair the equal operator with the less than or greater than operator to form a less-than-or-equal-to or a greater-than-or-equal-to comparison:

```
IF Arg1 <= Arg2
  --Arg1 is less than or equal to Arg2
ELSE
  --Arg1 is greater than Arg2

IF Arg1 >= Arg2
  --Arg1 is greater than or equal to Arg2
ELSE
  --Arg1 is less than Arg2
```

The <> (not equal) operator tests for argument 1 not equal to argument 2:

```
IF Arg1 <> Arg2
  --Arg1 is not equal to Arg2
ELSE
  --Arg1 is equal to Arg2
```

Keep in mind that comparison between character data types is dependent upon the sort order selected at installation time. For example, if you have Dictionary Order-case insensitive installed, then the following statement will yield TRUE:

```
IF 'A' = 'a'
```

If on the other hand you have selected Dictionary Order-case sensitive, then the above statement would yield FALSE.

BITWISE OPERATORS

Bitwise operators act on integer data types: int, smallint, and tinyint. These operators treat the integer value as a binary string of 1s and 0s.

The ~ (bitwise NOT) operator is a unary operator (acting on only one argument) that changes 1s to 0s and 0s to 1s. This operator may also be applied to the bit data type:

~1 = 0

~0 = 1

The | (bitwise OR) operator is a binary operator (acting on two arguments) whose result is 1 if either argument is 1 and 0 otherwise:

1 | 1 = 1

1 | 0 = 1

0 | 1 = 1

0 | 0 = 0

The & (bitwise AND) operator is a binary operator whose result is 1 if both arguments are 1s and 0 otherwise:

1 & 1 = 1

1 & 0 = 0

0 & 1 = 0

0 & 0 = 0

The ^ (bitwise Exclusive OR) operator is a binary operator that results in a 1 if argument 1 and argument 2 are different and results in 0 if both arguments are the same:

1 ^ 1 = 0

1 ^ 0 = 1

0 ^ 1 = 1

0 ^ 0 = 0

Using the SET Statements

The SET statements listed in Appendix C are used to modify the behavior of certain aspects of SQL Server. They either set a value for a given option or they enable/disable option settings.

This section will explore some SET statements you may find helpful in your programming tasks. They will give you a feel for what these settings can do. Refer to the appendix and to Microsoft SQL Server Books Online for a description of other SET statements.

The ANSI_DEFAULTS Option

This setting either enables or disables the ANSI options. The setting is in force for the duration of a work session, stored procedure, or trigger.

If enabled with SET ANSI_DEFAULTS ON, the options in Table 4-2 are enabled.

TABLE 4-2 OPTIONS SET ON BY SET ANSI_DEFAULTS ON

Option	Description
ANSI_NULLS	Forces equality and inequality comparisons with NULL values to return FALSE.
CURSOR_CLOSE_ON_COMMIT	Closes open cursors when a transaction is committed.
ANSI_NULL_DFLT_ON	Causes new columns in ALTER TABLE and CREATE TABLE statements to be designated as NULL if nullability is not specified. OFF by default.
IMPLICIT_TRANSACTIONS	Forces the statements FETCH, ALTER **TABLE**, DELETE, INSERT, CREATE, OPEN, GRANT, REVOKE, DROP, TRUNCATE TABLE, SELECT, and UPDATE to start a transaction if one isn't already started.
ANSI_PADDING	Defines how character data types are stored. The following uses show how the ANSI_PADDING behaves. Option is ON with ANSI_DEFAULTS ON.
ANSI_PADDING ON	char(*n*): Pad value with spaces to fill column to *n* characters. varchar(*n*): Store value as is, no padding spaces. varbinary(*n*): Store value as is, no padding zeros.

Continued

TABLE 4-2 **OPTIONS SET ON BY SET ANSI_DEFAULTS ON** *(Continued)*

Option	Description
ANSI_PADDING OFF	char(*n*): Trim trailing spaces from value, no padding with trailing spaces. varchar(*n*): Trim trailing spaces from value, no padding with trailing spaces. varbinary(*n*): Trim trailing zeros, no padding with zeros.
QUOTED_IDENTIFIER	Set ON by ANSI_DEFAULTS ON and allows identifiers to be delimited by double quotes and literals are required to be delimited by single quotes. When this option is OFF, identifiers cannot be quoted and are required to follow Transact-SQL rules for identifiers. Literals are allowed to be delimited by single or double quotes.
ANSI_WARNINGS	Generates a warning message when NULL values found in aggregate functions. Divide-by-zero and arithmetic overflow errors cause message and statement rollback. Updates and Inserts of values longer than column will allow are aborted.

The DATEFORMAT Option

This setting affects the order of date string parts when interpreting the string for assignment into a date data type.

The following example sets the datewrk variable to a literal string that is to be interpreted as year, month, day, and then month, day, year. If the date string is not entered in the format set by DateFormat, an error message results.

```
set dateformat ymd
go
declare @datewrk datetime
select @datewrk = '97/7/4'
select @datewrk
go

set dateformat mdy
go
declare @datewrk datetime
select @datewrk = '7/4/97'
select @datewrk
go
```

The results of the query is

```
1997-07-04 00:00:00.000
 (1 row(s) affected)
1997-07-04 00:00:00.000

 (1 row(s) affected)
```

Notice that the display of the @datewrk variable still adheres to the date format of the datetime data type and not the format set with SET DATEFORMAT.

The NOEXEC Option

When this option is set on with SET NOEXEC ON, subsequent queries are only compiled and not executed.

You can use this setting to check the syntax of a query without actually executing it. Any errors the query might contain are reported to you. This setting is helpful for checking batches and stored procedures before running them.

The SHOWPLAN_ALL Option

Another setting that causes the query to be compiled and not executed is the SHOWPLAN_ALL option. Unlike NOEXEC, however, SHOWPLAN_ALL does more than just compile the query.

Using SET SHOWPLAN_ALL ON compiles the query and reports information about how SQL Server will go about executing the query and returning the results.

The report contains a hierarchy of steps for each T-SQL statement that the SQL query processor will take to execute your query. Table 4-3 explains the report columns.

TABLE 4-3 COLUMNS FOUND IN THE SHOWPLAN_ALL REPORT

Item	Description
StmtText	The Transact-SQL statement or an execution step description.
QueryId	The number of the query in the current batch of statements.
NodeId	The ID of the node in the current query.
Parent	The ID of the parent step.

Continued

TABLE 4–3 COLUMNS FOUND IN THE SHOWPLAN_ALL REPORT *(Continued)*

Item	Description
LogicalOp	Used in PLAN_ROWS, this is the relational algebraic operator represented by this node.
PhysicalOp	The node's physical implementation algorithm: MergeJoin, NestedLoops, HashMatch, HashMatchTeam.
Argument	The name of the item used in the step.
EstimateRows	Used in PLAN_ROWS, this is the estimated number of rows output by this operator.
EstimateIO	Used in PLAN_ROWS, this is the estimated I/O cost for this operator.
EstimateCPU	Used in PLAN_ROWS, this is the estimated CPU cost for this operator.
Type	This will be the Transact-SQL statement type for the parent node, and for subnodes it will be PLAN_ROW.
TableScan	Sequential scan of the table named in the argument column. Table scans are used in queries where an index is not available or not appropriate for the query.
IndexScan	Scan the index named in the argument.
IndexSeek	Use an index to retrieve rows using an equality or range comparison with indexed column values.
ConstantScan	Act as a base table containing a single value.
EmptyScan	Act as a base table containing no rows.
Sort	Sort all input rows prior to producing any output rows.
Filter	Remove rows that do not meet the specified condition.
Spool	Store a copy of each row in an internal table.
Concatenation	Scan and return multiple sets of rows.
Sequence	Usually for index maintenance.
Distinct	Scan all input rows and remove duplicates. Output rows are returned only after all rows are processed.
FlowDistinct	Scan all input rows and remove duplicates. Output rows are returned as they are processed.

Item	Description
Join Operations	Pair a row from one of two inputs with a row from the other input and compare with the predicate. The output depends on the join type: Inner, Left Semi, Right Semi, Left Outer, Right Outer, Full Outer, Left Anti Semi, Right Anti Semi. See discussion of joins in Chapter 9.
Set Operations	Operate over two sets of inputs. IntersectAll, LeftDiff, LeftDiffAll, RightDiff, RightDiffAll, AntiDiff
Split	Split or copy a row to be processed as a DELETE followed by an INSERT operation in place of an UPDATE.
Collapse	Recombine split rows after the completion of an UPDATE.
Delay	Prepare the storage engine for the location of the next indexseek.
StartParallelism	Marks the start of a parallel operation.
PartitionParallelism	Mark the repartitioning step of a parallel operation.
EndParallelism	Marks the end of a parallel operation.
Assert	Validate referential integrity for a statement.
Stream Aggregate	Perform aggregation on a sorted input. Used for aggregate functions, as discussed in Chapter 7.
Locate	Return the corresponding row from a bookmark lookup.
LocateHint	Inform the storage engine that the row with the specified bookmark is likely to be requested in the future.
ClusteredUpdate	Perform a clustered index UPDATE.
Insert, Update, Delete	Apply the change to the table data.
IndexUpdate, IndexInsert, IndexDelete	Apply the change to the index entries.
Rank	Create a computed column containing the rank of the values in an existing table column.
Top	Process and return only the first *n* rows.
Segment	Split the output into segments. Used in conjunction with the TOP operation to return the top *n* rows from each segment.
ComputeScalar	The result of a computation is being added as a column in the current row.

An explanation of the values you might find in the PhysicalOp column in the plan output is given below:

MergeJoin	Perform a simultaneous pass over two sorted inputs.
NestedLoops	Perform a pass over the right input for each row in left input.
HashMatch	Hash the input values and compare with values in the hash table for matches.
HashMatchTeam	Multiple hashing operators working together on the same column or set of columns.

A related setting is the SET SHOWPLAN_TEXT ON. This setting provides an execution plan output that is intended to be more readable than SHOWPLAN_ALL but results in less information than SHOWPLAN_ALL.

SHOWPLAN_TEXT is used when you select the Show Query Plan check box in the Query Options dialog of the SQL Server Query Analyzer. The following SQL SELECT statement produces the results shown when SHOWPLAN_TEXT is set ON:

```
set showplan_text on
go
select acct_lastname,home_phone,tot_assets
from Accounts where state_abbr = 'CT'
go

StmtText
select acct_lastname,home_phone,tot_assets
from Accounts where state_abbr = 'CT'

(1 row(s) affected)

StmtText
  |--Clustered Index Scan(FundAccts..Accounts,
 Accounts.state_abbr=@1)

(1 row(s) affected)
```

Note that SHOWPLAN_TEXT tells you that the query will be satisfied by a scan of the clustered index. You don't get as much information as you do from SHOW-PLAN_ALL where some estimation of cost is reported. The choice, of course, depends on how much information you need to make your tuning decisions.

The STATISTICS IO Option

SET STATISTICS IO ON causes SQL Server to display the required disk activity for Transact-SQL statements.

The output report from this setting can be interpreted through the use of Table 4-4.

TABLE 4-4 ITEMS IN THE STATISTICS IO REPORT

Item	Description
Table	Name of the table
Scan count	Number of scans performed
Logical reads	Pages read from the data cache
Physical reads	Pages read from the disk
Read ahead reads	Pages placed into the cache

Batching SQL Statements

Although you can always submit Transact-SQL statements one at a time to SQL Server, you'll often find it helpful and maybe even necessary to submit a group of Transact-SQL statements. SQL Server refers to a group of statements submitted together as a *batch*.

Creating a Batch File

You can build a batch by editing an ASCII text file and including the Transact-SQL statements you want to execute. You may also edit your batch directly in the SQL Server Query Analyzer Query window and save the batch to an external file.

To use this batch file, insert a GO statement within the file where you want to terminate the batch. A GO statement is interpreted by SQL Server as an end-of-batch indicator. Any statements prior to the GO statement are considered part of the batch.

Since GO is the delimiter of the batch, you could include multiple batches in the same file, with each batch being delimited by a GO statement.

Exploring Multiple-Batch Files

We used a multiple-batch file above when we were looking at SET SHOWPLAN_TEXT. Here is another example of a Transact-SQL batch:

```
select Max(tot_assets) As maxasset into #assets from Accounts
select maxasset  as 'max assets 1' from #assets
go
select acct_no, tot_assets from Accounts
  where tot_assets = (select maxasset from #assets)
go
drop table #assets
```

The statements above the first GO statement select the maximum tot_assets value from the Accounts table and place it into a temporary table called #assets with a column name of maxasset. The value selected is then displayed to the results as max assets 1.

The second batch selects the acct_no and tot_assets columns from the Accounts table where the tot_assets value equals the maxasset column selected from the temporary table. These columns are displayed to the results.

The third batch uses a DROP TABLE statement that forces the temporary table #assets to be deleted immediately. A GO statement isn't necessary after the DROP statement since the end-of-file implies a batch delimiter.

The results of executing this multibatch file are shown below:

```
(1 row(s) affected)
max assets 1
-------------------
506296.0320

(1 row(s) affected)
acct_no    tot_assets
---------- -----------
1023        506296.0320

(1 row(s) affected)
```

Realize that this example does not require multiple batches to accomplish the results shown. The same results can be achieved from one batch containing one SELECT statement and no temporary table. Multiple batches were used here only to illustrate the technique.

The USE Statement

When batching Transact-SQL statements together, you may find it necessary to declare the database you intend to work with. To declare the intended database you wish to act on, specify the USE statement. USE changes the database context to the database you name:

```
USE FundAccts
--statements here apply to the FundAccts database.

USE Pubs
--statements here apply to the Pubs database
```

Any statements following the USE statement apply to the named database. This scope remains in effect until another USE statement is encountered or the database context is implicitly changed by SQL Server.

If a default database has been set up for your login ID and all of your work will be against that database, then you will not need to specify a USE statement. If, on the other hand, you are connected to some other database at login, or you need to use multiple databases in a batch, then the USE statement will be necessary.

All the standard security administration regarding the database you name in the USE statement applies, of course. If you don't have permission to access the database, the USE statement will fail.

Using the EXECUTE Statement

The EXECUTE keyword is not required to execute a stored procedure, but is required to execute a string containing Transact-SQL. For a procedure execution, EXECUTE is implied.

We have a stored procedure similar to the batch used above that selects the account number from the account having the largest tot_assets value. The procedure takes one parameter that designates a filter on acct_type. Using this parameter, we can obtain the largest tot_assets for any given acct_type such as Tax or NonTax.

In addition, the stored procedure, named BigAcct, returns a value indicating the account number having the biggest value or zero if failure (no accounts for the input type).

The BigAcct procedure is defined as follows:

```
create procedure BigAcct @type varchar(6),
  @acct varchar(10) OUTPUT,
  @outtot money OUTPUT AS

  declare @tot money
  declare @act varchar(10)

  select @tot = MAX(tot_assets)
    from Accounts where acct_type = @type

   select @act = acct_no
    from Accounts
    where acct_type = @type and tot_assets = @tot

  select @acct = @act,@outtot = @tot
```

Executing a Stored Procedure

We'll use EXECUTE to execute the procedure returning the procedure's OUTPUT values into local variables, which we display as the results at the end of the batch. Here's the batch:

```
DECLARE @bigtot money
DECLARE @bigacctno varchar(10)
EXECUTE BigAcct 'Tax',@acct = @bigacctno OUTPUT, @outtot = @bigtot OUTPUT
SELECT @bigacctno As Account,@bigtot As Assets,
    'Tax' As Type
```

After execution of the procedure, @bigacctno should contain the account number with the biggest tot_asset value for acct_type 'Tax' and the @bigtot variable should contain the biggest tot_asset:

```
Account     Assets              Type
-------     -----------         ----
1023        506296.0320         Tax

(1 row(s) affected)
```

Executing Strings

A string can be specified as an argument to the EXECUTE statement as long as the string parses to one or more valid executable Transact-SQL statements:

```
DECLARE @SQLStmt varchar(255)
DECLARE @type varchar(6)
SET @type = 'Tax'
SET @SQLStmt = "SELECT acct_no,tot_assets,acct_type
                FROM Accounts
                WHERE acct_type = '" + @type + "'"
EXECUTE (@SQLStmt)
```

The above set of statements retrieves all accounts and their tot_assets values for acct_type 'Tax' as a check against the return values from the BigAcct procedure.

The local variable @type was set to the literal 'Tax' in this batch to illustrate the concatenation of a string variable to a string literal (the SELECT statement). The single quotes inserted before and after the @type variable are necessary to yield a valid SQL statement that treats the value of @type ('Tax') as a literal string for comparison to acct_type. Without these quotes, the resultant statement would make 'Tax' appear as a column name and a syntax error would result.

The EXECUTE statement passes the entire Transact-SQL string contained in @SQLStmt to SQL Server for execution. A scan of the results verifies our BigAcct procedure.

Summary

We've learned about the sample mutual fund account database that we'll use through the book to illustrate the use of Transact-SQL statements. We looked at the tables contained in this sample database and the relationships the database is to define among those tables.

Next we looked at some of the basic elements of Transact-SQL statements. We learned about comments, expressions, literals, identifiers, keywords, and operators. Each of these elements will be used to build Transact-SQL statements as we proceed through the book.

We explored some SET statement options that are helpful in working with Transact-SQL and in tuning our stored procedures for better performance. We learned that understanding the query optimizer's plan output can go a long way to improving the performance of our Transact-SQL applications.

Finally, we saw how to create statement batches, how to designate the database we intend to work with in a batch or procedure with the USE statement, and how to execute procedures that may require parameters and strings that specify a valid Transact-SQL statement using the EXECUTE statement.

Chapter 5

Using the Data
Definition Language

IN THIS CHAPTER

- ◆ Learn about the SQL Server data types
- ◆ Discover how to build a database
- ◆ Explore database tables and indexes
- ◆ Learn about referential integrity and how to define it
- ◆ Learn about NULL data, constraints, and default values
- ◆ Change databases and tables with the ALTER statements

THE STATEMENTS COVERED in this chapter are used to create SQL Server objects and alter their definitions after creation. This group of statements is categorized as *Data Definition Language* (DDL). You'll learn about DDL here so that you can complete the rest of the mutual fund account sample database we started in Chapter 2. All table descriptions are found in the appendix.

Prior to storing and retrieving data from a SQL Server database, we have to define the database and its contained objects such as tables, indexes, views, users, and so on.

Before we get started, let's explore the data types we can use when we define or alter a table, declare a variable, or build a user-defined data type.

Exploring Data Types

Choosing the proper data type for a table column is one point in the database design where you have the opportunity to influence performance. The right choice will reduce data type conversions and help enhance the performance of the database application.

To help you decide which data type to use, we'll explore here each of the data types available in SQL Server. You can view the data types SQL Server supports by executing the systypes stored procedure:

```
SELECT * FROM systypes
```

Binary Data

SQL Server stores binary data using the data types `binary` and `varbinary`.

The binary data type is defined to be a fixed length for all rows while the varbinary type can vary in length from one row to the next.

To assign constants into binary data types, precede the value with `0x` followed by a hexadecimal string containing two hexadecimal characters for each byte of the specified length:

```
--Assign variable loopcount a value of 10
declare @loopcount Binary(4)
set @loopcount = 0x0000000A
select convert(int,@loopcount)
-----------
10
(1 row(s) affected)
```

With the `@loopcount` variable declaration above, an assignment of a hexadecimal string that is longer than the specified length will result in truncation of the assigned string. Assignment of a hexadecimal string shorter than the specified length results in padding the assigned value with `0x00` up to the specified length.

A maximum of 8,000 bytes can be declared for `binary` data types.

Character Data

The data types `char` and `varchar` are used to store character data up to 8,000 bytes in length. As with `binary` data, `varchar` columns can vary in length, up to some specified maximum less than or equal to 8,000 characters and `char` column lengths remain fixed at their specified length.

An assignment to a `char` variable or column that is shorter than the specified length would result in the variable or column being padded with spaces.

Constant data is assigned to character data types using single quotes around the value to be stored. To assign a string to the account lastname field, which we specified as `varchar(70)` in the Accounts table, you would code:

```
acct_lastname = 'some lastname'
```

To assign a value containing an apostrophe, use two single quotes as follows:

```
acct lastname = 'D''Arcy'
```

Date and Time Data

The date and time types include `datetime`, which uses 8 bytes of storage, and `smalldatetime`, which uses 4 bytes.

These data types also require single quotes around constant values being assigned.

Values for `datetime` data types use 4 bytes for the date portion and 4 bytes for the time. A negative value represents the number of days prior to January 1, 1900, while a positive value represents the number of days after January 1, 1900. This yields a range of dates from January 1, 1753 to December 31, 9999.

The 4-byte time portion specifies the number of milliseconds after midnight, accurate to 3.33 milliseconds.

If you assign a `date` value to a `datetime` data type, the time defaults to 12 midnight. Assigning only a time to a `datetime` data type will default the date to January 1, 1900:

```
--Assign accountdate  a value of 1/1/97 9AM
declare @accountdate datetime
set @accountdate = '1/1/97 9AM'
select convert(char,@accountdate ,100)
-----------------------------
Jan  1 1997  9:00AM
(1 row(s) affected)
```

The `smalldatetime` data type uses a 2-byte integer to store the number of days after January 1, 1900 and a 2-byte integer to store the number of minutes after midnight, accurate to a minute.

The date range for `smalldatetime` is from January 1, 1900 to June 6, 2079.

Integer Data

For storage of positive and negative whole numbers, you have three data types to choose from; `int`, `smallint`, and `tinyint`. Your choice from these three depends on the range of values you want to store.

The `int` type uses 4 bytes of storage and handles a range of values from -2,147,483,648 (-2^{31}) to +2,147,483,647 ($+2^{31} - 1$).

The `smallint` data type stores whole numbers in 2 bytes ranging from -32,768 (-2^{15}) through 32,767 ($+2^{15} - 1$).

The storage size of the `tinyint` type is 1 byte and stores values from 0 to 255.

Use the smallest storage size to accommodate the values you'll be storing in the column or variable.

Assignment of constant data to integer types doesn't require any delimiters. For example, the Accounts table contains a column named cycle that designates the print cycle an account belongs to for controlling the statement printing. To assign a value of 3 to an account cycle, which is defined as `tinyint`, you would simply code as follows:

```
cycle = 3
```

Exact Numeric Data

The exact numeric types, decimal and numeric, store an integer value to the left of the decimal point and a fractional value to the right of the decimal point. Both of these types are equivalent in their storage sizes and use.

The storage size depends on the maximum value to be stored within the range -10^{38} to $10^{38} - 1$. The storage used for these types depends on the specified precision and ranges from 2 bytes to 17 bytes.

These data types are specified with a precision and a scale. The precision denotes the number of places to the left of the decimal point and a scale to denote the total number of digits to the left and right of the decimal point. The scale specifies the number of places to the right of the decimal place and must be less than or equal to the precision.

Approximate Numeric Data

Approximate types in SQL Server are float and real. These data types store an approximation of an entered value due to the binary representation of floating point data. The value is precise for the specified precision but may vary when compared to other float values.

A float can be specified to have a mantissa from 1 to 53. This yields a range of positive values from approximately $2.23 * 10^{-308}$ to $1.79 * 10^{+308}$ and a range of negative values from approximately $-2.23 * 10^{-308}$ through $-1.79 * 10^{+308}$.

The storage size required for floats is 8 bytes if the precision is greater than 7, and 4 bytes otherwise.

Constants are assigned by using a decimal number followed optionally by the letter E followed by a positive or negative integer. The number after the E denotes an exponent of 10, which is multiplied by the value to the left of E.

An approximation of pi, for example, can be stored into a variable as follows:

```
--Assign variable pi a value of 3.14
Declare @pi float(5)
set @pi = 314159E-5
select @pi
-----------------------
3.1415901
(1 row(s) affected)
```

Specifying float without a precision yields a float(15) by default.

If you specify a mantissa from 1 to 24, SQL Server uses real as the data type. Real uses 4 bytes of storage and has a precision of 7 digits to store a range of positive values from approximately $1.18 * 10^{-38}$ through $3.40 * 10^{+38}$ and a range of negative values from $-1.18 * 10^{-38}$ through $-3.40 * 10^{+38}$.

Monetary Data

The data types money and smallmoney are used to store monetary values. The money data type is used often in the mutual fund sample database.

The money data type stores values ranging from -922,337,203,685,477.5807 through +922,337,203,685,477.5807 in 8 bytes of storage.

Smallmoney stores a range of values from -214,748.3648 through +214,748.3647 in 4 bytes of storage.

Both types are assigned constants using a dollar sign ($) followed by the value, which may include a decimal point. To specify a negative value, place a minus sign (-) after the dollar sign. Commas are not permitted.

```
--Assign variable temptotassets a value of $470,526.2757
Declare @temptotassets money
set @temptotassets = $470526.2757
select @temptotassets
select convert(char,@temptotassets,1)
--------------------
470526.2757
(1 row(s) affected)
---------------------      ----
                      470,526.28
(1 row(s) affected)
```

Notice in the results of the above example how the CONVERT() function caused the displayed value to be rounded to the nearest cent.

Text and Image Data

The data types text and image are used to store character and binary data whose size is greater than 8,000 bytes. The maximum size of text and image types is 2,147,483,647 bytes (2^{31} - 1).

Table columns defined as text or image data types actually store 16-byte pointers to the text and image data physically stored in another file. The file is organized as a tree structure in which each leaf node stores up to 8,072 bytes of data. When we explore text and image functions in Chapter 7, the pointer will be used with other functions for manipulating the text and image data.

The text data type can store any ASCII characters and the image data type can store any binary string. These types would be chosen if you needed to store items such as documents and pictures.

Assignment of constants into text adheres to the same rules as for char data types; that is, the constant must have surrounding single quotes.

The assignment of constants to image data types follows the rules of binary data types. You must prefix the constant hexadecimal string with 0x.

Special Data Types

This category includes the `timestamp`, `uniqueidentifier`, `bit`, and `user-defined` data types.

The `timestamp` type is either a `binary(8)` or `varbinary(8)` data type that holds a counter value unique to a database. It is not the same value as `datetime` or `smalldatetime` types and has no relation to system time.

Each table in a database may have no more than one timestamp column. The `timestamp` value for a database can be read from the system global variable `@@dbts`.

To store a 1 or 0 value, and nothing else, use the `bit` data type. This type is good for simple flags or indicators and uses only 1 byte of storage.

The `uniqueidentifier` type stores a globally unique identification number (GUID) consisting of a 16-byte binary string.

GUIDs are unique values derived from network card identifiers, or random numbers in the absence of a network card, and various other machine information. They are used in database replication schemes for uniquely identifying rows of a table and in the world of the Component Object Model (COM) to identify components and interfaces.

A column of type `uniqueidentifier` may be assigned a value either through the `NEWID()` system function or as a hexadecimal string consisting of 32 hexadecimal digits and hyphens in the pattern `dddddddd-dddd-dddd-dddd-dddddddddddd` where each `d` is a hexadecimal digit.

Using the SQL Server-supplied data types, you can craft your own data type to fit your application needs.

Let's define a special account number made up of two characters to identify the initial account manager, followed by an eight digit number. Give this data type a name of `fundacct` for use in any table where the account number is needed.

We'll use the `sp_addtype` stored procedure to add the `fundacct` type to the `FundAccts` database:

```
sp_addtype fundacct, 'VARCHAR(10)', 'NOT NULL'
```

Since we need characters and numbers in our account number, we base the new type on SQL Server's `varchar` data type and give it enough characters to hold the special string. Any SQL Server data type can be specified here with the exception of the `timestamp` type.

We specify `NOT NULL` to indicate that `fundacct` types cannot accept `NULL` values as a default. If nullability is specified for a column of type `fundacct` in a `CREATE TABLE` or `ALTER TABLE` statement, the specified nullability overrides the default we specify in the `sp_addtype` stored procedure.

Unicode Data Types

`Unicode` data types enable storage of data defined by the Unicode Standard. Unlike characters stored in standard SQL Server data types, which are stored as characters of the character set specified during SQL Server installation, Unicode characters include characters defined in various character sets. The use of Unicode data types takes twice as much storage space as SQL Server's non-Unicode data types.

The SQL Server Unicode data types are nchar, nvarchar, and ntext. The nvarchar and nchar types can store up to 4,000 Unicode characters (8,000 bytes) while the ntext data type can store up to 1,073,741,823 Unicode characters (2,147,483,647 bytes).

To assign constant string values into these Unicode types, prefix the string with N, as in the following:

```
Declare @unicode_var nchar(10)
set @unicode_var = N'unicode string'

select @unicode_var
```

Comparing SQL Data Types and C++ Data Types

It would certainly make our job easier if there were a standard set of data types used across all programming languages and databases. That isn't the case, however, and we're forced to deal with mapping one data type to another.

This mapping chore comes up whenever you use a programming language, such as C++, C, or some other language to access SQL Server. Since SQL Server defines its own data types, you need to be aware of required conversions from SQL Server to your language data types and vice versa.

ODBC, used in Part III of this book, allows you to specify the SQL Server data type when referencing columns and parameters and C data types when referencing program variables.

Refer to Appendix I for a table that maps SQL Server data types to those found in ODBC and OLE DB. This is a very handy table to have when you come to Part III of this book and start programming with ODBC and OLE DB interfaces.

Creating and Deleting Databases

In Chapter 2 we used the SQL Server Enterprise Manager to create the FundAccts sample database. That action was equivalent to executing the following CREATE DATABASE statement, which we could have done in the SQL Server Query Analyzer:

```
USE master
GO
CREATE DATABASE FundAccts
ON PRIMARY
  (NAME=FundAccts_Data,FILENAME='d:\mssql7\data\FundAccts_Data.MDF',S
  IZE=4MB,MAXSIZE=UNLIMITED,FILEGROWTH=1MB)
```

The CREATE DATABASE statement above creates a database and names it FundAccts.

Specifying the Physical Files

The ON PRIMARY clause indicates to SQL Server that the file specified is the first file for the database. In this case, only one OS file is being used, but the statement does allow multiple files to be entered. Had the ON PRIMARY clause been omitted, the first file specified in the list would become the primary file. The primary file specifier is enclosed in parentheses.

The NAME clause of the file specifier provides a logical name for the file to be used by SQL Server. This name must be unique within the server.

The FILENAME clause designates the path and file name of the operating system file on which the database will be allocated. SIZE is the initial minimum file size and MAXSIZE designates the maximum allowed size for the file. FILEGROWTH provides an allocation amount for the file when space is needed. In our FundAccts example, we allow a maximum size of the available disk space and allocate an additional 1MB to the file each time space is needed.

Specifying the Log File

When we created the database we also specified a log file to be created for the database. The log can be specified in the CREATE statement by appending the following:

```
LOG ON
(NAME='FundAccts_Log',
 FILENAME='d:\mssql7\data\FundAccts_Log.Ldf',
 SIZE=2MB)
```

The log file will record transactions against the database for purposes of recovering from a failed transaction. Transactions will be covered in more detail in Chapter 16.

To view the database allocation, execute the stored procedure sp_helpdb FundAccts. The result is shown in Figure 5-1.

name	db_size	owner	dbid	created	status
FndAccts	6.00 MB	DEVELOP\amow	6	Jan 3 1998	select into/bulkcopy

(1 row(s) affected)

device_fragments	size	usage
FundAccts_Data	4.00 MB	data only
FundAccts_Log	2.00 MB	log only

(2 row(s) affected)

Figure 5-1: The results from executing sp_helpdb stored procedure

When you list the objects in the database with `sp_help`, you get something like that shown in Figure 5-2:

```
USE FundAccts
GO
sp_help
```

Name	Owner	Object_type
CHECK_CONSTRAINTS	INFORMATION_SCHEMA	view
COLUMN_DOMAIN_USAGE	INFORMATION_SCHEMA	view
COLUMN_PRIVILEGES	INFORMATION_SCHEMA	view
COLUMNS	INFORMATION_SCHEMA	view
CONSTRAINT_COLUMN_USAGE	INFORMATION_SCHEMA	view
CONSTRAINT_TABLE_USAGE	INFORMATION_SCHEMA	view
DOMAIN_CONSTRAINTS	INFORMATION_SCHEMA	view
DOMAINS	INFORMATION_SCHEMA	view
KEY_COLUMN_USAGE	INFORMATION_SCHEMA	view
REFERENTIAL_CONSTRAINTS	INFORMATION_SCHEMA	view
SCHEMATA	INFORMATION_SCHEMA	view
sysalternates	dbo	view
sysconstraints	dbo	view
syssegments	dbo	view
TABLE_CONSTRAINTS	INFORMATION_SCHEMA	view
TABLE_PRIVILEGES	INFORMATION_SCHEMA	view
TABLES	INFORMATION_SCHEMA	view
VIEW_COLUMN_USAGE	INFORMATION_SCHEMA	view
VIEW_TABLE_USAGE	INFORMATION_SCHEMA	view
VIEWS	INFORMATION_SCHEMA	view
Accounts	dbo	user table
dtproperties	dbo	user table
IX_Accounts	dbo	unique key cns
sysallocations	dbo	system table
syscolumns	dbo	system table
syscomments	dbo	system table
		system table
dt_verstamp003	dbo	stored procedure
dt_whocheckedout	dbo	stored procedure
help_index	dbo	stored procedure
pk_dtproperties	dbo	primary key cns
DF__dtproperties__version__08EA5793	dbo	default (maybe cns)
CK_Accounts	dbo	check cns

(70 row(s) affected)

Figure 5-2: The output from the sp_help stored procedure

When you issue the `CREATE DATABASE` statement, SQL Server creates your database from a copy of the Model database. The Model database contains the system objects required for managing the database and can be modified to contain custom applications or enterprise objects as well. Every database you create from this model will contain the same objects.

Removing Databases with the DROP DATABASE Statement

To delete a database and the os files it resides on, you can issue a DROP DATABASE statement:

```
DROP DATABASE FundAccts
```

The database being dropped must not be in use at the time you execute the statement or the DROP will fail.

Drop multiple databases with one DROP statement by specifying their names, separated by commas.

Attaching and Detaching Databases

At times, you may want to move an entire database – including all of its objects, data, and log files – to another SQL Server machine. To do this, SQL Server 7 enables attaching and detaching databases.

To detach a database from a server, you can use the sp_detach_db stored procedure.

```
sp_detach_db 'FundAccts'
```

The above statement detaches the FundAccts database from the current SQL Server, but leaves the database in tact within the files where the database is stored.

By adding a second argument and setting it to FALSE, you can have SQL Server run UPDATE STATISTICS on the database before the database is detached. Setting this argument to TRUE will skip the statistics update.

Before you detach the database, execute sp_helpfile to list the files associated with the database. You'll need these file names when you re-attach the database.

```
USE FundAccts
sp_helpfile
```

To attach a database to another SQL Server, or back to the same SQL Server, use the sp_attach_db stored procedure.

```
sp_attach_db 'FundAccts,
@filename1 = N'D:\MSSQL7\DATA\FundAccts_Data.MDF',
@filename2 = N'D:\MSSQL7\DATA\FundAccts_Log.LDF',
@filename3 = N'D:\MSSQL7\DATA\FundAccts_Data2.MDF'
```

This procedure re-attaches the database to a SQL Server installation using the file names supplied in the procedure.

Altering Existing Databases with ALTER DATABASE

Use `ALTER DATABASE` to change the files associated with a database.

If, for example, we need to add an os file to the `FundAccts` database, we would use an `ALTER DATABASE` statement like the following:

```
ALTER DATABASE FundAccts
 ADD FILE (NAME = 'FundAccts_Data2', FILENAME = '
 d:\mssql7\data\FundAccts_Data2.MDF',SIZE = 4MB)
```

You can add more than one file at a time by placing a comma at the end of the file specifier closing parenthesis and adding additional specifiers.

Adding a File Group and Log File

To add a log file, use `ADD LOG FILE` instead of `ADD FILE`. The file specifier is the same as that shown in the Specifying the log file section above.

In addition to adding data files and log files to a database, you can modify an existing file's `FILENAME`, `SIZE`, and `MAXSIZE` specifications by using a `MODIFY FILE` clause and using the `NAME` of an existing file allocated to the database.

File groups can be created for a database by using a `CREATE FILEGROUP` clause and providing a name for the file group. This clause is used for creating user-defined file groups where database files can be added and managed (for example, backup and restore operations) under a common name.

SQL Server allocates all database files not specifically added to a user-defined file group to the default file group. This default group is used for all system tables and for user-defined tables and indexes not directed to a user-defined file group.

Adding Files to a File Group

Once a user-defined file group is established with the `CREATE FILEGROUP` clause, you can add files to the file group with the `ALTER DATABASE` statement and an `ADD FILE` clause with `TO FILEGROUP filegroupname` specified after the file specifier closing parenthesis:

```
ALTER DATABASE FundAccts
 CREATE FILEGROUP AcctsGrp
Go
ALTER DATABASE FundAccts
 ADD FILE(NAME = 'FundAccts_Data2', FILENAME = '
 d:\mssql7\data\FundAccts_Data2.MDF',SIZE = 4MB) TO
FILEGROUP AcctsGrp
```

Executing the above `ALTER DATABASE` statement batches in the Query Analyzer yields the following results:

```
Extending database by 4 Mbytes on disk FundAccts_Data2
```

As we'll see in a moment, tables and indexes you create in a database can be directed to a specific user-defined file group to enable better management of disk space and performance.

Creating Tables with CREATE TABLE

During our exploration of the SQL Server Enterprise Manager in Chapter 2, we added two tables to the `FundAccts` sample database. The script from the creation of the Accounts table is shown in Figure 5-3 below.

```
BEGIN TRANSACTION
SET QUOTED_IDENTIFIER ON
GO
SET TRANSACTION ISOLATION LEVEL SERIALIZABLE
GO
COMMIT
BEGIN TRANSACTION
CREATE TABLE dbo.Accounts
        (
        acct_no varchar(10) NOT NULL,
        acct_lastname varchar(70) NOT NULL,
        acct_firstname varchar(50) NULL,
        last_contact datetime NULL,
        addr_line1 varchar(30) NULL,
        addr_line2 varchar(30) NULL,
        addr_line3 varchar(30) NULL,
        city varchar(30) NULL,
        state_abbr char(2) NOT NULL,
        zip varchar(10) NOT NULL,
        home_phone varchar(15) NULL,
        work_phone varchar(15) NULL,
        tot_assets money NOT NULL,
        fiscal_period char(2) NOT NULL,
        cycle tinyint NOT NULL,
        acct_type varchar(6) NOT NULL,
        acct_status varchar(8) NOT NULL,
        manager_num smallint NULL,
        acct_note text NULL
        ) ON [default]
    GO
    COMMIT
```

Figure 5-3: The T-SQL script generated in SQL Server Enterprise Manager for the Accounts CREATE TABLE

The CREATE TABLE statement names the table being created (Accounts) and then defines the columns the table is to have. Each column definition will contain a column name, a data type, an implicit or explicit size, and optional constraints.

The Accounts table CREATE TABLE statement shown above is very basic. All we have done here is define the table name, columns, data types, and nullability. The statement doesn't specify any constraints at all and uses the default file group we discussed earlier.

Specifying Constraints

Constraints tell SQL Server to apply certain rules to values being entered into a column and to reject records that don't satisfy the rules. The CREATE TABLE statement allows us to specify PRIMARY KEY or UNIQUE column constraints, FOREIGN KEY column constraints, DEFAULT, and CHECK COLUMN constraints. All of these constraints will be discussed shortly in the "Understanding Constraints" section.

In the above CREATE TABLE statement, we are using a NOT NULL constraint on some of the columns.

By specifying NOT NULL for state_abbr, for example, we are telling SQL Server not to allow a record with a NULL valued state_abbr. In other words, columns designated as NOT NULL are required whenever a new client is added to the table. What if our users don't enter a state_abbr when adding a new account? We can either allow SQL Server to fail the addition of the record and force the user to enter a state_abbr value or, as you'll see in the constraints discussion, we can fix the omission for them with a DEFAULT column constraint.

For the other columns in the table, we are defaulting to NULL, which says to allow NULL values in the column. We don't care if a value is supplied or not.

Using IDENTITY and ROWGUIDCOL

In addition to specifying constraints and nullability for a column, we can designate a column as an IDENTITY column or a ROWGUIDCOL column.

The IDENTITY keyword can be used once in the table definition and must be specified only on columns with data types of int, tinyint, or smallint, and decimal and numeric types with a scale of zero.,

An IDENTITY column is automatically assigned a unique value whenever a new row is added to the table. You can influence the values assigned by providing a seed and optional increment for the IDENTITY specification.

The seed is the value to be assigned to the initial row loaded into the table. If you don't specify a seed, SQL Server uses 1 as the seed.

If you don't specify an increment for the assigned value, SQL Server uses 1 to increment the seed for each additional record added. If this is not acceptable, you may specify an increment of your choice. Be sure that both seed and increment will accommodate the range of records you intend to add to the table for the data type of the IDENTITY column.

Since SQL Server automatically assigns a value to an IDENTITY column, the DEFAULT column constraint is not allowed.

The ROWGUIDCOL keyword is used to designate a column as the row global unique identifier for the table. As with IDENTITY, you can only specify ROWGUIDCOL once in a table definition. The data type of the ROWGUIDCOL column must be uniqueidentifier.

Specifying Computed Columns

Not all columns you define for a table are necessarily stored in the table. A computed column is one defined to be an expression that is executed whenever the column is retrieved.

Define the computed column with any valid expression. If we were to define the invest_gain column in the Statements table as a computed column, we could code it as follows:

```
[invest_gain] AS (([cur_value] - [invest_tot])/[invest_tot])
```

Any time we retrieve the invest_gain column, the difference between the cur_value column and the invest_tot column would be divided by the invest_tot column to give us a computed gain.

Considering Data Integrity

The integrity of a database is of utmost importance. Imagine what the clients would say if the fund accounts database lost records of their investments and gains, or if a client's portfolio were reported to another client on their quarterly statement. I doubt the money management firm would be in business for very long.

SQL Server defines four types of integrity: entity, domain, referential, and user-defined.

Entity integrity ensures that each row or record of a table defines a unique entity. This is enforced through the PRIMARY KEY constraint or UNIQUE constraint for each record.

Domain integrity defines a set of values that may exist in a column. This is usually enforced using the CHECK constraint. Rows that contain column values outside the range of the constraint are not allowed by SQL Server. This check ensures that our range of column values, or domain, is what we define it to be and nothing else.

Referential integrity ensures that every child or dependent row in a table is related to an existing parent row in another table. This is specified using FOREIGN KEY, PRIMARY KEY, or UNIQUE constraints.

Once established, referential integrity is maintained throughout such operations in the database as inserting rows, updating columns that play a role in referential integrity, and deleting rows. You must consider a specific order for these operations so as not to violate referential integrity rules.

The `FundAccts` Statements table defines `acct_no` with a `FOREIGN KEY` constraint referencing the `acct_no` column in the Accounts table, which was defined as a `PRIMARY KEY` via an `ALTER TABLE` statement. (Although not evident, we executed this `ALTER TABLE` statement in Chapter 2 when we set the `PRIMARY KEY` for Accounts in the database diagram.)

These constraints establish referential integrity, also known as declarative referential integrity (DRI), between the Accounts table (parent table) and the Statements table (child or dependent table). We now must ensure that any row added to the Statements table must contain an `acct_no` value that is already resident in a row in the Accounts table. If this rule is broken, the Statements row will not be allowed. Likewise, we cannot `DELETE` an Accounts row that has dependent rows in the Statements table, for this action would also break referential integrity.

User-defined integrity is dependent on the application. The business rules that govern the application must be implemented either through one or more of SQL Server's integrity schemes, stored procedures, or through your client application code.

Understanding Constraints

As noted above in the discussion of the `CREATE TABLE` statement, constraints are very useful things to have around. Without them, our applications would need to be much more complex. Let's summarize here the capabilities of constraints.

Constraints are rules that SQL Server will enforce when applying data to a table and can be defined in the `CREATE TABLE` statement or the `ALTER TABLE` statement. You can define a column-level constraint to any column in a table by placing the constraint condition within the column definition. A table-level constraint is placed after the last column definition in a `CREATE TABLE` statement and may reference multiple columns in the table. Using a table-level constraint is the only way to define a primary key on more than one column, as we did in the Statements table.

SQL Server provides the `CHECK`, `DEFAULT`, `UNIQUE`, `PRIMARY KEY`, and `FOREIGN KEY` constraints. Even though `NOT NULL` constrains a column to containing some value, `NOT NULL` is not considered a constraint. It pertains to the nullability attribute of a column.

Using a CHECK Constraint

A `CHECK` constraint specifies allowable data values or formats that are acceptable in one or more columns. We have specified a `CHECK` constraint on the Accounts table acct_type column as shown below:

```
CONSTRAINT [CK_Accounts] CHECK ([acct_type = 'Tax' or [acct_type] =
  'Nontax')
```

This constraint, applied to the `acct_type` column or to the table after the last column specification, defines the constraint named `CK_Accounts` as an expression that restricts the values entered into the `acct_type` column to the values of 'Tax' or 'Nontax'. Rows having `acct_type` values other than 'Tax' or 'Nontax' will not be accepted into the table.

As you can see from this example, a `CHECK` constraint condition can include multiple logical expressions. All expressions in a column constraint must, however, reference the constrained column only.

An alternative method to a `CHECK` constraint is to create a rule with the `CREATE RULE` statement and then bind the rule to a column. The preferred method is to use `CHECK` constraints as we've done in the sample database.

Using a DEFAULT Constraint

A `DEFAULT` constraint specifies a value to be applied to a column whenever a value is not supplied in an `INSERT`. The default value can be a constant literal of the column type or a SQL Server function. An example of a `DEFAULT` constraint is found in the Statements table where we defined a default value of zero for the invest_tot column as shown below:

```
CREATE TABLE Statements (
    . . .
invest_tot money NOT NULL CONSTRAINT
[DF_Statements_invest_tot] DEFAULT (0),
    . . .
)
```

The above `DEFAULT` constraint named `[DF_Statements_invest_tot]` defines a value of zero to be assigned to the column invest_tot whenever a value is not supplied in a row. This ensures that the `NOT NULL` nullability will not be violated.

Using a UNIQUE Constraint

A `UNIQUE` constraint ensures that values entered into a column are unique within the table. This constraint builds a unique index on the column containing the constraint.

To illustrate the `UNIQUE` constraint, we defined the `acct_no` column in the Accounts table to have this constraint and designated the resulting index as a `CLUSTERED` type. This results in the rows of the Accounts table being physically ordered by the `acct_no` values. Furthermore, the rows are actually the leaf nodes of the clustered index named `IX_Accounts`.

```
CONSTRAINT [IX_Accounts] UNIQUE CLUSTERED( [acct_no] )
```

You can define up to 249 unique constraints for a table.

Using a PRIMARY KEY Constraint

A PRIMARY KEY constraint ensures that the column contains unique values, that NULL is not a valid value, and that only one constraint of this type exists for a table. Defining this constraint also results in a unique index being built.

```
CONSTRAINT [PK_Accounts] PRIMARY KEY NONCLUSTERED ( [acct_no] )
```

This constraint is specified with the NONCLUSTERED keyword since we can have only one clustered index per table and the CLUSTERED keyword was already specified for the UNIQUE constraint defined above.

If you're confused as to why we have defined a UNIQUE constraint and a PRIMARY KEY constraint on the same column, your confusion is justified. We don't need to. It was done here only to illustrate the respective constraints and for no other reason. If you eliminate the UNIQUE constraint from the table, the referential integrity we established between the Accounts table and the Statements table would still work since PRIMARY KEY implies unique values.

The Statements table specifies two columns as the PRIMARY KEY:

```
CONSTRAINT [PK_Statements] PRIMARY KEY NONCLUSTERED (
[acct_no], [stmt_date] )
```

If you don't specify an index type for the PRIMARY KEY and there are no clustered indexes defined on the table, the index type defaults to CLUSTERED.

Using a FOREIGN KEY Constraint

A FOREIGN KEY constraint specifies that the column's value exists in another table's primary or unique column. As we've already seen, this constraint plays a role in referential integrity. The acct_no column of the Statements table has the following FOREIGN KEY constraint defined:

```
CONSTRAINT [FK_Statements_Accounts] FOREIGN KEY ( [acct_no] )
REFERENCES [dbo].[Accounts] ( [acct_no] )
```

The data types of the FOREIGN KEY column and the REFERENCES column must match.

You can specify up to 63 FOREIGN KEY constraints for a table.

Using Rule and Default Objects

In addition to or instead of using a CHECK constraint on a column, you can define a *rule* to be bound to a column. You can bind only one RULE object to a column but you can specify multiple CHECK constraints. It is more preferable to use CHECK constraints in a table definition since this nicely defines in one place the table's constraints.

Creating Rules

To define a rule object, use the `CREATE RULE` statement. Here, we use it to create a rule for the cycle column in the Accounts table:

```
CREATE RULE CycleCheck AS
@cyclerange >0 AND @cyclerange <4
```

Once we've defined the rule object in the database, we can bind it to the cycle using the `sp_bindrule` stored procedure:

```
sp_bindrule CycleCheck, 'Accounts.cycle'
```

In the case where we have a column with defined `CHECK` constraints and a bound rule, all are evaluated against column values.

Bound rules only apply to data added after the rule is bound. It does not apply to data already existing in a table. If you use the `CREATE RULE` statement with other Transact-SQL statements in a script file, be sure to include the `CREATE RULE` statement in a batch by itself using the `GO` statement as a delimiter.

Creating Defaults

Like rules, you can also create a *default* object to be applied to a column or `user-defined` data type. You might want to create one `DEFAULT` object and apply it to multiple columns or `user-defined` data types in the database. It is defined much the same as the `DEFAULT` constraint.

```
CREATE DEFAULT CycleDefault
 AS 3
```

The above default object will ensure that the column it is bound to will have a default value of 3 if a value is not provided for the column.

To bind a default object to a column, use the `sp_bindefault` store procedure:

```
sp_bindefault CycleDefault, 'Accounts.cycle'
```

Be sure that the data type of the default object matches that of the column it is being bound to.

Like rules, `CREATE DEFAULT` statements must appear by themselves in a batch. They cannot be grouped with other Transact-SQL statements.

Removing Rules and Defaults

To remove a rule object from a column, use the `sp_unbindrule` procedure. To remove a default object from a column, use the `sp_unbindefault` procedure.

To delete a RULE object, use DROP RULE, and to delete a default object, use DROP DEFAULT.

To remove the rule we just created, we would code as follows:

```
sp_unbindrule 'Accounts.cycle'
DROP RULE CycleCheck
```

To remove the default we created, we would code as follows:

```
sp_unbindefault 'Accounts.cycle'
DROP DEFAULT CycleDefault
```

Remember that as with CHECK constraints and DEFAULT constraints, a bound default object cannot conflict with a rule object bound to the same column or a CHECK constraint defined for the column.

Understanding Null Data

We saw in the Creating Tables with CREATE TABLE section that a column can be allowed to contain a NULL value. In doing this, we are saying that the value of the column is unknown.

Let's say you are developing a table to hold the responses of a survey. One of the survey questions asks for a Yes, No, or N/A response. How would you designate a column to hold this response in the table such that we know whether or not the respondent answered the question or skipped it?

By allowing a NULL value to be entered for the column containing the respondent's response to this question, you capture the fact that the respondent skipped the question. A NULL value in the column says, "this question was not answered," meaning we don't know the respondent's thoughts regarding this question. It is not the same as an N/A response and should not be treated as such. It should be treated as a skipped question. NULL comes to the rescue.

Now that we know that NULL values can be found in a table, we need to know how to handle them.

Using the ANSI_NULLS Option

When ANSI_NULLS is ON and a NULL is compared to another value, say in a WHERE condition of a SELECT statement, you will never get a TRUE result. This is because a NULL doesn't match anything. It doesn't even match another NULL. The value indicates "unknown" and therefore must always yield "unknown" when used in an expression.

So, if you can't use a comparison expression containing NULL, how do you go about finding records containing a NULL column? How would you find questions in a survey that were skipped?

One way is to set ANSI_NULLS OFF. This would enable the comparison against NULL values to behave as you expect. But this would mean that your application is not using SQL-92 standards. To meet the standard, leave ANSI_NULLS ON and use the keyword IS in conjunction with NULL to locate the NULL value records:

```
SELECT name, ssn FROM survey WHERE answer IS NULL
```

Testing for NULL

In our FundAccts database, we could use the IS NULL and IS NOT NULL to find all accounts with a NULL work_phone column and a non-NULL home_phone column, like this:

```
SELECT acct_no, home_phone FROM Accounts
WHERE work_phone IS NULL AND home_phone IS NOT NULL
```

You must also consider NULL values when you use aggregate functions or you join tables. In joining one table to another on a column that can contain NULL values, and using an equality join operator, you will never get a match on NULL values. The rows containing NULL values in the join columns will not be returned.

Aggregate functions ignore NULL values in calculating their results. Using the AVG() function, for example, to compute the average of a column will not include the NULL values in the resulting average.

Refer to Chapter 7 for more on aggregate functions and to Chapter 9 for more on joining tables.

Altering Existing Tables

If we need to change the definition of a table after creating it, we can use the ALTER TABLE statement.

You can use ALTER TABLE to add additional columns to a table, add and remove constraints, remove columns from the table, disable/enable constraints, and disable/enable triggers.

Adding Constraints

The Accounts table we built in Chapter 2 needed to have several constraints added to it after it was already created. For example, we added the PRIMARY KEY constraint with the following statement:

```
ALTER TABLE Accounts ADD CONSTRAINT
 PK_Accounts PRIMARY KEY NONCLUSTERED (acct_no) ON
 [default]
```

In this statement, we named the PRIMARY KEY constraint as PK_Accounts, designated it as a nonclustered index on the acct_no column, and told SQL Server to create the index on the default file group.

Likewise, after creating the Statements table, we added a FOREIGN KEY constraint to it to establish referential integrity between the Statements table and the Accounts table:

```
ALTER TABLE Statements ADD CONSTRAINT FK_Statements_Accounts
FOREIGN KEY (acct_no) REFERENCES Accounts (acct_no)
```

Using the ALTER TABLE statement, we can add or remove any column or table constraint. To remove the FOREIGN KEY constraint above, we would code as follows:

```
ALTER TABLE Statements DROP CONSTRAINT FK_Statements_Accounts
```

Columns can be removed from a table in a similar fashion. Use the keyword COLUMN in place of CONSTRAINT and the column name in place of the constraint name.

Using the NOCHECK Option

If you don't want to remove the constraint but temporarily disable it, use the NOCHECK keyword instead of DROP:

```
ALTER TABLE Statements NOCHECK CONSTRAINT FK_Statements_Accounts
```

NOCHECK tells SQL Server not to check the constraint on new values being inserted into the column. To enable the constraint again, use the CHECK keyword:

```
ALTER TABLE Statements CHECK CONSTRAINT FK_Statements_Accounts
```

Say you want to add a constraint to a column, but you know there are values in the column that violate the new constraint. To add the constraint and tell SQL Server to ignore existing values, use the WITH NOCHECK option:

```
ALTER TABLE Statements WITH NOCHECK
ADD CONSTRAINT CK_Invest_Tot CHECK ([invest_tot] > 0)
```

The above `WITH NOCHECK` option would ensure that existing values of zero would not be checked against the new constraint, but that all future values would be checked.

Adding and Altering Columns

Add a column to the Accounts table to store a Fee code we can use to determine the fee to be charged to the client for managing the account:

```
ALTER TABLE Accounts ADD fee_code char(2) NOT NULL
```

If we later determine that the fee code needs to be enlarged, we can alter the column with:

```
ALTER TABLE Accounts ALTER COLUMN fee_code char(4) NOT NULL
```

Any data already in the column that needs to be altered must be convertible to the data type you specify in the `ALTER COLUMN` specifier. You cannot specify `timestamp` as the data type. If you specify `IDENTITY` as the data type, the existing values must have valid identity values.

Using the DROP TABLE Statement

To remove a table from a database, use the `DROP TABLE` statement.

When you drop a table, you also drop the data in it, any indexes created on it, triggers created for it, and constraints defined for it:

```
DROP TABLE Statements
```

Here again you must be aware of referential integrity rules. You cannot drop a table if there is another table with a foreign key referencing the table being dropped. Had the Accounts table been named in the `DROP TABLE` statement above while we had the Statements table acct_no column defined as a foreign key referencing Accounts, the `DROP TABLE Accounts` would fail.

The drop of the Statements table would succeed since we currently don't have any other table dependent on it.

Creating Indexes

We now know that indexes are used by SQL Server to enhance the performance of data retrieval and to enforce `UNIQUE` or `PRIMARY KEY` constraints. We also know that SQL Server will build indexes for us whenever we define a PRIMARY KEY constraint or UNIQUE constraint in a table.

Now we'll find out how to create indexes as a standalone operation using the CREATE INDEX statement.

Understanding Index Types

In creating a *unique* index, the same rules apply to the column or columns involved as with the UNIQUE constraint in the CREATE TABLE statement. If data exists at the time you issue the CREATE INDEX, then there must be unique values in the index columns; otherwise, SQL Server will reject the index and issue an error.

Likewise, after the index is added, any values being inserted or updated must comply with the unique rules or the data will be rejected.

If an error does occur at the time you create the index, do a SELECT on the column or columns involved to determine which rows contain duplicates. Resolve the duplicate problem and then reissue the CREATE INDEX statement.

When we created the Accounts table, we specified the acct_no as the primary key nonclustered. This created a unique key index on acct_no.

In a CLUSTERED index, the physical order of the data rows in the table is the same as the key rows in the index. The leaf pages of the clustered index are the actual data pages. Because of this organization, you can have only one clustered index on a table. In contrast, in NONCLUSTERED indexes, the leaf pages of the index are separate and distinct from the data pages.

If NONCLUSTERED indexes exist on a table that also contains a clustered index, then SQL Server populates the leaf pages of the NONCLUSTERED index with cluster keys from the CLUSTERED index. These keys are then used to locate a row accessed through the NONCLUSTERED index.

If a CLUSTERED index is not present, then the NONCLUSTERED index uses the standard disk address to locate a row.

CLUSTERED indexes are generally good for applications that often make GROUP BY requests. You should always evaluate each application that will use the database before an indexing scheme can be selected, however.

With NONCLUSTERED indexes, the data rows are not ordered according to the index order as they are with clustered indexes.

Using the CREATE INDEX Statement

Let's create an index on the Accounts table. We'll make this index store values from the manager_num column. This will help us retrieve rows more efficiently given a specific manager number.

```
CREATE INDEX ManagerNum
 ON Accounts (manager_num)
```

Note that since this column is not unique across all rows and that it can contain NULL values, we have created a nonunique index for the column.

The PRIMARY KEY constraint we added to the Accounts table acct_no column earlier in this chapter resulted in a unique index being created. Since we already had a UNIQUE constraint on the acct_no column and specified its index as CLUS-TERED, we could only select NONCLUSTERED as the primary key index. Had we used the CREATE INDEX statement to build these indexes, we would have written code like this:

```
CREATE UNIQUE CLUSTERED INDEX IX_Accounts ON Accounts (acct_no)
CREATE UNIQUE NONCLUSTERED INDEX PK_Accounts ON Accounts
 (acct_no)
```

When you create a clustered index, you can reduce the overhead of creating the index by presorting the data. If you are rebuilding an index and index the same columns and keep the same index name as an existing index, you can specify the DROP_EXISTING clause to have SQL Server drop the existing index and rebuild it. In this case, SQL Server will not attempt to sort the rows prior to building the index. If different columns or name is used, the rows will be sorted.

```
CREATE UNIQUE CLUSTERED INDEX IX_Accounts ON Accounts
(acct_no) WITH DROP_EXISTING
```

Although sorting during index build does not occur with this option, SQL Server does verify that the indexed column contains sorted data as the index is being built. If SQL Server determines that the data is not sorted, the CREATE INDEX fails.

Summary

In this chapter we've learned about the SQL Server data types we can specify in a table definition.

We looked at how to create a database with the Transact-SQL CREATE DATABASE statement and how to modify the database definition with the ALTER DATABASE statement. We saw how file groups can be defined and used to manage the disk space our database uses.

Next, we looked at the various definitions of data integrity and how we can manage it using constraints. We learned about constraints, the types of constraints we can define, and how to specify those constraints in a table definition.

We took a brief look at NULL values and the implication of having NULL values in a table. We learned how to detect NULL values and how aggregate functions treat NULL values.

The CREATE TABLE statement was explored in this chapter. We learned how to define columns, column-level and table-level constraints, and how to relate tables with FOREIGN KEY constraints.

This chapter explored the `ALTER TABLE` statement and we saw how to use it to change column definitions, add and remove constraints, and enable or disable constraints.

Last, we looked at the `CREATE INDEX` statement. We found out what a clustered index was and how to create one. We saw the difference between a unique index and a nonunique index, and we learned how to improve the time it takes to build a clustered index.

Chapter 6

Using the Data Manipulation Language

IN THIS CHAPTER

- ◆ Learn how to insert data into a table with positional inserts

- ◆ Insert data into named columns

- ◆ Explore the basic SELECT statement to retrieve rows

- ◆ Learn how to use a WHERE clause to limit the number of rows returned

- ◆ Find out how to use aliases to reference columns and tables

- ◆ See how the rows of a result set can be sorted using an ORDER BY clause

- ◆ Learn how to create a table with SELECT INTO

- ◆ Discover how to update a table's rows using values from other tables

- ◆ Find out how to delete rows from a table

THE NEXT SET of statements we explore deal with getting data into the database you built in Chapter 5. To do this, we use the Data Manipulation Language (DML) of Transact-SQL, which encompasses INSERT, UPDATE, and DELETE statements.

As you saw in Chapter 2, you can use the BCP utility to load data into tables. As you'll see in this chapter, you can also use Transact-SQL statements to load data. Once data is loaded, you'll need a way to retrieve it, modify it, and remove it. Transact-SQL provides a number of statements categorized under the heading of DML to perform all of these tasks.

The Transact-SQL INSERT statement is used to insert new records into a table. The UPDATE statement is used to modify values already in a table's records, and DELETE is used to remove one or more records from a table.

Inserting Data with the INSERT Statement

A row can be appended to a table using the INSERT statement. There are two ways to use this statement when providing explicit values. You can supply values for the columns in a VALUES list, where the values are placed in column order, or you can prefix the value list with the column names that the values should target.

To provide the values for a row in the Statements table with implied column naming, you can use a statement that looks like this:

```
INSERT Statements VALUES('1003','12/31/97',37462.85,96294.53,
157.04,-183,171, 808.02, 1286.30,2767.57,1722.07,6583.96,832.98,
1742.45,2813.93,1737.37,7126.74)

(1 row(s) affected)
```

The values entered in the VALUES list must match the number of columns, the order of columns as defined in the Statements table, and the data types of the target columns.

Note in the above INSERT statement that no column names were provided. We merely gave a value for each column in the table without naming them.

Using Column Names

Another form of the INSERT statement specifies a column list listing the column names you are providing values for. Using this method, you can order the value however you want and you can skip columns:

```
INSERT Statements (acct_no,stmt_date,invest_tot,cur_value, invest_
gain, ytd_tot_return,tot_return) VALUES('1004','12/31/97',37462.85,
96294.53, 157.04,171,-183)

(1 row(s) affected)
```

Notice in the above statement that the ytd_tot_return and tot_return columns in the column list are not in the same order as they are in the Statements table. In this form of the INSERT statement, it doesn't matter. You can order the target columns however you want. You must only take care to provide the values in the values list according to the order of the columns in the columns list and provide the correct data types for those columns.

Not all columns of the Statements table have been named in the above INSERT statement. The columns not named are defined as having default values (DEFAULT constraints) or they accept NULL values. If a column does not meet either of these conditions, and it is not a `timestamp` data type and it is not an `IDENTITY` column, then you must name it in the columns list and provide a value for it in the values list.

Inserting Values Returned from a SELECT Statement

To illustrate the inserting of values selected from another table, let's create a table to hold current account values for each account and statement date. We'll call this table the AccountValues table.

After creating the AccountValues table, we'll use an `INSERT` statement that gets its values list from a `SELECT` statement that retrieves data from the Statements table. The values returned from the `SELECT` statement are inserted into the like-named columns in the AccountValues table. The statements to do this are shown below:

```
CREATE TABLE AccountValues (
  acct_no varchar(10) not null,
  stmt_date datetime not null,
  invest_tot money not null default 0,
  cur_value money not null default 0
)
INSERT AccountValues
SELECT acct_no, stmt_date,invest_tot,cur_value
FROM Statements
WHERE acct_no = '1003'
```

The above `INSERT` statement selects a column value from Statements for each column specified for AccountValues. Had the column names in AccountValues been different from the selected column names in the Statements table, we could have used aliases to designate the target AccountValues column. (See "Using Aliases" later in this chapter.)

Using the EXECUTE Keyword

The `INSERT` statement can also be coded with the `EXECUTE` keyword to execute a stored procedure or `SELECT` statement string.

If we had a procedure call `GetStmtValues` that returned the Statements columns as we did above, we could execute this procedure in an `INSERT` statement as follows:

```
INSERT AccountValues EXECUTE GetStmtValues
```

The same results can be achieved when we execute the `SELECT` statement as a string argument to `EXECUTE`:

```
INSERT AccountValues EXECUTE ("SELECT acct_no,
 stmt_date,invest_tot,cur_value
FROM Statements
WHERE acct_no = '1003'")
```

Using INSERT statements to load data into a table is an alternative to using the BCP utility. You most likely will use INSERT statements in your database applications to handle functions that require the addition of new rows in a table.

We've seen the use of SELECT statements in previous chapters and above in our discussion of the INSERT statement, but we've never taken the time to explore this frequently used statement in detail. We'll do that now in the next section.

Exploring Basic Queries Using the SELECT Statement

The SELECT statement is used to retrieve column values from the rows of one or more tables. The columns that are selected are placed into rows in a result set that is returned to the requestor.

A simple SELECT statement to return all columns from all rows in the Accounts table would look like this:

```
SELECT * FROM Accounts
```

When this statement is executed in the SQL Query Analyzer, you'll see all the column values for every row in the Accounts table. The * tells SQL Server that we want to see *all* columns from the data source named in the FROM clause.

On small tables, this form of SELECT is quick and easily coded, but on large tables holding hundreds of thousands of rows and possibly a large set of columns, it can become problematic for your application to deal with such large result sets.

Using the WHERE Clause

A general rule for database applications is to ask SQL Server only for the data necessary to perform a particular function. Let's say we only need to see accounts for clients with Connecticut addresses. We can limit the rows returned to only those clients with a state abbreviation of CT by using a WHERE clause in the SELECT statement.

The WHERE clause is used to specify the criteria that must be evaluated for each row in the data source, the Accounts table in this case, and yield a TRUE condition in order for the row to be selected into the result set:

```
SELECT * FROM Accounts
WHERE state_abbr = 'CT'
```

This is better. We get a smaller result set by limiting the rows to only those that have a `state_abbr = 'CT'`. Generally, we don't need to see all the columns for the selected rows. We usually know what data items we need to work with and select only those. This practice provides better performance and reduces the network overhead of transmitting data we don't need.

Using a Column List

We'll select the `acct_no`, `acct_lastname`, `last_contact`, `work_phone`, and `home_phone` for the Connecticut clients so that our money management firm can contact them with some new investment information. To tell SQL Server which columns to include in the result set, we provide the column names in a *column list* as follows:

```
SELECT acct_no,acct_lastname,last_contact,work_phone,home_phone
  FROM Accounts
WHERE state_abbr = 'CT'
```

If a client record doesn't contain a `work_phone` or a `home_phone` value, we would most likely be interested in knowing this and would certainly research these clients to obtain their phone numbers. The above query reports these clients to us, listing their phone numbers as `NULL`.

Using Expressions

For illustration, say we want to filter out of our result set the clients that don't have either a home phone number or a work phone number. In other words, we only want to see the clients in Connecticut with either a home phone number, a work phone number, or both. We use the following query to accomplish this:

```
SELECT acct_no,acct_lastname,last_contact,work_phone,home_phone
 FROM Accounts
WHERE state_abbr = 'CT' AND
  NOT (work_phone IS NULL AND home_phone IS NULL)
```

Notice, as pointed out in Chapter 5, that we use `IS NULL` to test rows for `NULL` values in the phone number columns.

These kinds of queries can be challenging and fun, but they can also be frustrating. You may be inclined to write the following:

```
SELECT acct_no,acct_lastname,last_contact,work_phone,home_phone
 FROM Accounts
WHERE state_abbr = 'CT' AND
  work_phone IS NOT NULL AND home_phone IS NOT NULL
```

Sounds good. Let's try it. Executing the above statement yields rows for Connecticut all right, but eliminates all rows that have a NULL work_phone or a NULL home_phone and returns only rows where both phone numbers are present.

Let's try this. Change the last AND operator to an OR operator and execute it.

This time we get Connecticut clients plus clients in every other state we have in the table. But the good news is, we have eliminated rows having both phone numbers equal to NULL.

To fix this, we put parentheses around the phone expressions. The resulting statement now returns the same rows as the first statement in this section. Reason? The two are logically equivalent. The first uses NOT to negate the AND expression of (NULL AND NULL) while the second statement uses an OR to combine two NOT expressions. They yield the same results.

Whenever you use expressions containing logical operators like this, the rule is to evaluate NOT first, then the AND operation, and lastly the OR operation. Using parentheses forces an evaluation of the expression inside the parentheses to be done first.

It helps to build yourself a truth table as shown in Figure 6-1. In the column header of the truth table you place the WHERE conditions you want to test and in the rows of the truth table you place combinations of column values for the columns listed in the header. Wherever you end up with a True value for the entire WHERE expression, those are the combinations of values your expression will select.

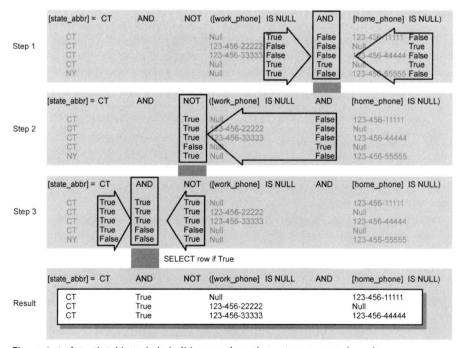

Figure 6-1: A truth table to help build expressions that return expected results

Refer to Appendix H for tables that show the results of applying the logical operators to operands containing TRUE, FALSE, and NULL values. These logical operator truth tables and your WHERE expression truth table will help ensure you get the results you expect.

As you can see from the SELECT statement example we've been exploring, the columns specified in the WHERE clause are not limited to those specified in the column list. The state_abbr column used in the WHERE expression is not one of the columns we wish to select into our result set, so state_abbr is not specified in the column list.

Keep in mind that you can specify columns to be selected in any order you wish. You are not limited to the order of the columns as they were defined in the CREATE TABLE statement.

Using Aliases

If you want to display a column name differently from the name of the column in the table, you can use one of the following column-naming techniques:

```
SELECT Client = acct_no,acct_lastname AS
 [Last Name],work_phone,home_phone
 FROM Accounts
WHERE state_abbr = 'CT'
```

In this case, the acct_no column will be labeled as Client and the acct_lastname column will be labeled as Last Name. The Client heading was applied using the heading = columnname syntax while the Last Name heading was applied using the AS syntax. Note, too, that if you want a column heading to contain one or more spaces, you need to use brackets as shown above.

When you select from more than one table, you can qualify column names with the names of their parent tables. This is especially necessary if the same column name appears in more than one table you are selecting from.

If you select the Accounts acct_no along with other columns from the Accounts table and the AccountValues table, you need to inform SQL Server which acct_no you want selected. To do this, qualify the acct_no column with the name of its parent table like this:

```
SELECT Accounts.acct_no,acct_lastname,last_contact,invest_tot
FROM Accounts,AccountValues
WHERE Accounts.acct_no = AccountValues.acct_no
```

Giving an alias to a table in the FROM clause, you can use that alias to qualify columns instead of using the full table name.

To do this, provide an alias for the Accounts table in the FROM clause and qualify the acct_no with the alias:

```
SELECT a.acct_no,acct_lastname,last_contact,invest_tot
FROM Accounts a,AccountValues b
WHERE a.acct_no = b.acct_no
```

When a column name is unique among the tables specified, SQL Server has no problem picking the right column. In the above statement, invest_tot is a column only in the AccountValues table, so it isn't necessary to qualify it. SQL Server knows it comes from the AccountValues table. If you like, however, you can qualify all columns with their respective table aliases without any complaints from SQL Server.

Notice that in the sample above, it really doesn't matter which acct_no we select — the one from Accounts or the one from AccountValues. Why? Because our WHERE clause is an equality expression on the acct_no column of both tables, the acct_no column returned will be equal in both tables. It doesn't matter which one we view.

In other circumstances, though, we could have two like-named columns from different tables where their values could be different. Qualifying the column we want with the parent table name will yield the correct results.

Sorting Results with ORDER BY

The next item we will explore is the ordering of the selected rows. You can sort the returned results on any column in the result and specify an ascending or descending sort order. To do this, you use the ORDER BY clause:

```
SELECT Client = acct_no,acct_lastname AS
 [Last Name],work_phone,home_phone
 FROM Accounts
WHERE state_abbr = 'CT'
  ORDER BY acct_no
```

In this statement, we are ordering the results by acct_no ascending, which is implied by default. To order the results in descending order, we would append the DESC specifier like this:

```
SELECT Client = acct_no,acct_lastname AS
 [Last Name],work_phone,home_phone
 FROM Accounts
WHERE state_abbr = 'CT'
  ORDER BY acct_no DESC
```

SQL Server would understand these statements just as well had we used the column alias of Client in place of acct_no in the ORDER BY clause:

```
SELECT Client = acct_no,acct_lastname AS
```

```
[Last Name],work_phone,home_phone
 FROM Accounts
WHERE state_abbr = 'CT'
  ORDER BY Client
```

You can specify multiple columns in the ORDER BY list and each can be either ascending or descending. This results in a nested sort order, the last column ordered within the next to last column and so on up to the first column in the ORDER BY list.

Using Expressions and Constants in a Column List

You aren't restricted to just specifying the names of columns in the SELECT statement column list. You can also specify literal constants and expressions as columns to be returned:

```
SELECT acct_no,stmt_date,
   InvestGain = (cur_value - invest_tot)/invest_tot
FROM AccountValues
```

In the above SELECT statement, we calculate the investment gain for each row in the AccountValues table and return the calculated result as a column named InvestGain.

You can use any valid expression in this manner. You'll see in Chapter 7 that these expressions can include SQL Server built-in functions as well.

At times, you may need to return a constant literal as a column. This comes in especially handy when combining two or more result sets with the UNION operator and you need to provide a column value for a result set to match the number of columns in another result set. As you'll see in Chapter 9, the UNION operator requires this.

To specify a constant, we again use a column alias and code a statement like the following:

```
SELECT acct_no,stmt_date,invest_tot,Source= 'stmt'
 FROM Statements
```

The above statement yields a result set containing the literal 'stmt' in every row returned.

Using BETWEEN to Search a Range

When the rows you want returned in the result set contain column values that lie in a range, you can use the BETWEEN keyword in a WHERE clause to specify the range you want selected.

The returned results are *inclusive* of the values given in the BETWEEN expression. If we select all accounts with account numbers between 1005 and 1018 for example, we would see rows for the beginning account number in the range (1005) and the ending account number in the range (1018) in the result set if those account numbers existed:

```
SELECT acct_no,acct_lastname
FROM Accounts
WHERE acct_no BETWEEN '1005' AND '1018'
acct_no    acct_lastname
---------- -------------
1005       Client5
1006       Client6
1007       Client7
1008       Client8
1009       Client9
1010       Client11
1011       Client12
1012       Client15
1013       Client16
1014       Client18
1015       Client19
1016       Client20
1017       Client21
1018       Client23

(14 row(s) affected)
```

To display accounts outside the range 1005 to 1018, we use NOT BETWEEN:

```
SELECT acct_no,acct_lastname
FROM Accounts
WHERE acct_no NOT BETWEEN '1005' AND '1018'
acct_no    acct_lastname
---------- -------------
1003       Client2
1004       Client3
1023       Client25
1024       Client26
1025       Client27
1027       Client29
1028       Client30
1029       Client31
1059       Client14
1060       Client4
1064       Client28
```

```
1066       Client24
1067       Client17
1068       Client13
1069       Client10
1070       Client22
1992       Client1
9847       Client32
(18 row(s) affected)
```

As you can see from the above results, using NOT BETWEEN gave us rows with account numbers below the start of the range and above the end of the range but NOT inclusive of the range. In other words, using NOT BETWEEN yields results that are *exclusive* of the stated range.

Using IN and Lists

The IN keyword can be used in a WHERE expression to match values in a list. The use of IN reduces the amount of coding we have to do when using AND and OR operators. For example, if we want to select accounts having state abbreviations of CA, NY, and FL, we could code as follows:

```
SELECT acct_no,state_abbr,zip
FROM Accounts
WHERE state_abbr = 'CA' OR state_abbr = 'NY' OR state_abbr = 'FL'
ORDER BY acct_no
acct_no    state_abbr zip
---------- ---------- -----
1009       CA         06473
1023       FL         33416
1024       NY         10533
1025       NY         12633
(4 row(s) affected)
```

An easier method to get the same results is to use a list of state abbreviations and the IN keyword, like this:

```
SELECT acct_no,state_abbr,zip
FROM Accounts
WHERE state_abbr IN ('CA','NY','FL')
ORDER BY acct_no
```

We can use NOT IN to return rows that don't have these state abbreviations:

```
SELECT acct_no,state_abbr,zip
FROM Accounts
WHERE state_Abbr NOT IN ('CA','NY','FL')
ORDER BY acct_no
acct_no    state_abbr zip
---------- ---------- -----
1003       CT         06510
```

```
1004        CT          06475
1005        CT          06511
1006        CT          06405
1007        CT          06511
1008        CT          06511
1010        CT          06514
...
1067        CT          06511
1068        TX          77015
1069        NC          28115
1070        CT          06880
1992        CT          06473
9847        CT          06109
(28 row(s) affected)
```

In Chapter 9, we explore the use of IN with a subquery as the source of the list instead of literal constants as used here.

Using the LIKE Keyword

Using WHERE expressions that match on datetime and character data type columns makes it possible to use the LIKE keyword and wildcards to match values against a pattern. Any row containing the pattern in the match column is selected into the result set.

Let's display rows from the Accounts table that have a 5 as the third digit of the ZIP code:

```
SELECT acct_no,state_abbr,zip
FROM Accounts
WHERE zip LIKE '__5%'
ORDER BY acct_no
acct_no     state_abbr zip
----------  ---------- -----
1003        CT          06510
1005        CT          06511
1007        CT          06511
1008        CT          06511
1010        CT          06514
1012        CT          06511
1016        CT          06515
1024        NY          10533
1029        CT          06503
1060        CT          06511
1067        CT          06511
(11 row(s) affected)
```

The underscore (_) character is a wildcard that matches any single character. In the above statement we used two underscores to inform SQL Server that we don't care what the first two characters of the ZIP code are.

The third character we place in the LIKE pattern is the number 5, indicating that this number must match exactly in this position of the ZIP code.

The last character in the pattern is the percent sign (%) that indicates any number of characters after the digit 5 are to be considered as a match, without regard for what those characters are or how many characters there are. This pattern will even match ZIPs with no digits after the 5 (but there are none in the table).

We can use NOT to display rows that are NOT LIKE the specified pattern:

```
SELECT acct_no,state_abbr,zip
FROM Accounts
WHERE zip NOT LIKE '__5%'
ORDER BY acct_no
acct_no      state_abbr zip
---------- ---------- -----
1004         CT         06475
1006         CT         06405
1009         CA         06473
1011         CT         06443
1013         CT         06798
1014         CT         06016
1015         CT         06118
1017         CT         06117
1018         CT         06472
1023         FL         33416
1025         NY         12633
1027         CT         06111
1028         CT         06489
1059         CT         06001
1064         CT         06066
1066         CT         06478
1068         TX         77015
1069         NC         28115
1070         CT         06880
1992         CT         06473
9847         CT         06109
(21 row(s) affected)
```

When matching a single character position, we can use more powerful wildcards than what we have used above. Say we want to match ZIP codes that have a 5 as the third digit but also have a 1 or 2 as the first digit. To do this, we use a set wildcard:

```
SELECT acct_no,state_abbr,zip
FROM Accounts
WHERE zip LIKE '[12]_5%'
ORDER BY acct_no
```

```
acct_no    state_abbr zip
---------- ---------- -----
1024       NY         10533
(1 row(s) affected)
```

The [] wildcard denotes any single character in the range or set within the brackets. To specify a range of values for the first character position, we use a dash in the brackets:

```
SELECT acct_no,state_abbr,zip
FROM Accounts
WHERE zip LIKE '_[1-3]%'
ORDER BY acct_no
acct_no    state_abbr zip
---------- ---------- -----
1023       FL         33416
1025       NY         12633
(2 row(s) affected)
```

The above statement uses a range wildcard specification to indicate that the ZIP code must have any of the digits 1 through 3 inclusive as the second digit to be included in the result set.

You can also mix the range and set specifications within the brackets like this:

```
SELECT acct_no,state_abbr,zip
FROM Accounts
WHERE zip LIKE '[1-3]_[13-56]%'
ORDER BY acct_no
acct_no    state_abbr zip
---------- ---------- -----
1023       FL         33416
1024       NY         10533
1025       NY         12633
1069       NC         28115
(4 row(s) affected)
```

The above pattern matches ZIP codes having a first digit between 1 and 3, any second digit, a third digit equal to 1, 3 through 5, or 6, and any digits thereafter.

You can use the caret (^) to negate a range or set in the brackets:

```
SELECT acct_no,state_abbr,zip
FROM Accounts
WHERE zip LIKE '[1-3]_[^6]%'
ORDER BY acct_no
acct_no    state_abbr zip
---------- ---------- -----
1023       FL         33416
1024       NY         10533
1069       NC         28115
(3 row(s) affected)
```

Here we use ^ to denote that any character *except* 6 in the third position of the ZIP code should be a match.

What if we want to match a string containing a wildcard character? How could we match last names containing the underscore character? To do this, we introduce the ESCAPE clause into the expression:

```
SELECT acct_no,acct_lastname
FROM Accounts
WHERE acct_lastname LIKE '%_%'
ESCAPE '_'
ORDER BY acct_no
acct_no     acct_lastname
----------  --------------------
1068        Way_Side Consultants
(1 row(s) affected)
```

The above statement matches any last name having any number of characters followed by an underscore (there are two in the pattern), followed by any number of characters. The ESCAPE clause specifies that the underscore is to be interpreted as a character in the last name column rather than a positional wildcard.

Selecting Rows with the TOP Predicate

You can limit the displayed rows in a result set to only the first *n* rows by using the TOP predicate in the SELECT statement. Let's select rows from the Statements table but display only the first ten rows from the result set:

```
SELECT TOP 10 acct_no,
CONVERT(varchar(15),stmt_date,102) StmtDate,cur_value
FROM Statements
WHERE cur_value > 100000 AND
DATEPART(yy,stmt_date) > '1993'
ORDER BY acct_no,stmt_date
acct_no     StmtDate          cur_value
----------  ----------------  -----------
1003        1994.03.31        192751.2500
1003        1994.06.30        191183.3700
1003        1994.09.30        202039.2200
1003        1994.12.31        202457.3500
1003        1996.03.31        202457.3500
1004        1994.03.31        192219.4700
1004        1994.06.30        192220.8400
1004        1994.09.30        201489.8600
1004        1994.12.31        164014.9700
1004        1996.03.31        164014.9700
(10 row(s) affected)
```

Without the predicate `TOP 10` in the `SELECT` statement, this statement would return 71 rows. Using `TOP` returns the number of rows specified with the predicate; here, only the first 10 out of 71 rows were returned.

You can specify that some percentage of rows be returned instead of the number of rows. To return the first 10 percent of rows in the result set, use the following:

```
SELECT TOP 10 PERCENT acct_no,CONVERT(varchar(15),stmt_date,102)
 StmtDate,cur_value
FROM Statements
WHERE cur_value > 100000 AND
DATEPART(yy,stmt_date) > '1993'
ORDER BY acct_no,stmt_date
acct_no    StmtDate           cur_value
---------- ----------------   -----------
1003       1994.03.31         192751.2500
1003       1994.06.30         191183.3700
1003       1994.09.30         202039.2200
1003       1994.12.31         202457.3500
1003       1996.03.31         202457.3500
1004       1994.03.31         192219.4700
1004       1994.06.30         192220.8400
1004       1994.09.30         201489.8600
(8 row(s) affected)
```

Using `TOP 10 PERCENT` returned about 10 percent of 71 rows, giving us 8 rows displayed rather than the 10 rows with `TOP 10`.

If the result set displayed with the `TOP` predicate contains qualifying rows beyond the `TOP` rows displayed, you can display those rows in addition to the `TOP` rows by using the `WITH TIES` clause.

To illustrate the `WITH TIES` clause, I'll modify the statement slightly to fit the data in the table. Without `WITH TIES`, we get the following:

```
SELECT TOP 9 acct_no,CONVERT(varchar(15),stmt_date,102)
 StmtDate,cur_value
FROM Statements
WHERE cur_value > 100000 AND
DATEPART(yy,stmt_date) > '1993'
ORDER BY acct_no
acct_no    StmtDate           cur_value
---------- ----------------   -----------
1003       1994.03.31         192751.2500
1003       1994.06.30         191183.3700
1003       1994.09.30         202039.2200
1003       1994.12.31         202457.3500
1003       1996.03.31         202457.3500
1004       1994.03.31         192219.4700
1004       1994.06.30         192220.8400
1004       1994.09.30         201489.8600
1004       1994.12.31         164014.9700
(9 row(s) affected)
```

When `WITH TIES` is introduced into the statement, we get the following:

```
SELECT TOP 9 WITH TIES acct_no,CONVERT(varchar(15),stmt_date,102)
 StmtDate,cur_value
FROM Statements
WHERE cur_value > 100000 AND
DATEPART(yy,stmt_date) > '1993'
ORDER BY acct_no
acct_no    StmtDate           cur_value
---------- ----------------   -----------
1003       1994.03.31         192751.2500
1003       1994.06.30         191183.3700
1003       1994.09.30         202039.2200
1003       1994.12.31         202457.3500
1003       1996.03.31         202457.3500
1004       1994.03.31         192219.4700
1004       1994.06.30         192220.8400
1004       1994.09.30         201489.8600
1004       1994.12.31         164014.9700
1004       1996.03.31         164014.9700
(10 row(s) affected)
```

The difference in the results is that `WITH TIES` gave us the `TOP 9` rows and other rows that match the last `ORDER BY` column of those `TOP 9` rows. Since `ORDER BY` specifies `acct_no`, `WITH TIES` returned rows beyond the `TOP 9` that match the last `acct_no` in the `TOP 9` (account number 1004).

Creating Tables with SELECT INTO

In Chapter 2 we went into the `FundAccts` database properties to set the select into/bulkcopy property on to enable loading tables with the BCP utility. This same property enables another operation as well. With `Select Into/Bulkcopy` on, we can use the `SELECT INTO` statement to create permanent tables.

Since the `SELECT INTO` is actually performing a `CREATE TABLE`, you must ensure that the user executing the `SELECT INTO` has permission to create a table. If they do, executing this statement creates the table named in the statement and then fills it with rows returned from the `SELECT` statement.

If you prefer to set the select into/bulkcopy property programmatically, you can use the `sp_dboption` stored procedure like this:

```
sp_dboption 'FundAccts','select into/bulkcopy','true'
```

Now, let's create a table named AcctAssets with the statement below.

```
SELECT acct_no,acct_lastname,city,state_abbr,tot_assets
INTO AcctAssets
FROM Accounts
WHERE acct_status = 'open'
ORDER BY state_abbr
```

If you execute an `sp_help` `AcctAssets` after creating the AcctAssets table, you'll find that the column properties are equal to those of the Accounts table columns we selected.

When you need to create a table but don't require it to be permanent, you can qualify the table name with a # sign to denote a temporary table:

```
SELECT acct_no,acct_lastname,city,state_abbr,tot_assets
INTO #AcctAssets
FROM Accounts
WHERE acct_status = 'open'
ORDER BY state_abbr
SELECT * FROM #AcctAssets
```

Temporary tables can be created without setting the select into/bulkcopy option. These tables are especially useful in stored procedures where you need to create a work table just for the purposes of the procedure processing. Temporary tables are dropped automatically at the end of the session.

Using the DISTINCT Keyword

The `DISTINCT` keyword can be used in a `SELECT` statement to ensure uniqueness of the rows returned.

The following statement selects distinct values of the combined city and `state_abbr` columns:

```
SELECT DISTINCT city,state_abbr FROM Accounts
city                              state_abbr
-----------------------------     ----------
A Town                            CT
Some City                         CT
Some City                         TX
Some Place                        CT
Some Place                        FL
Some Place                        NC
Some Town                         CT
Some Town                         NY
Some Village                      CT
Some Village                      NY
(10 row(s) affected)
```

We've only skimmed the surface of what you can do with the `SELECT` statement. You'll see the power of this statement explored further in later chapters. For now, let's put the `SELECT` statement on hold and find out how we can change values of rows already in a table.

Using Distributed Queries

SQL Server 7 supports queries against a remote data source through OLE DB providers. These queries are known as *distributed queries* and can be used to access heterogeneous data sources such as a Microsoft Excel spreadsheet, a Microsoft Jet database, a text file, an Oracle database, and any other data source for which an OLE DB provider or ODBC driver is available.

In this section, we'll look at a distributed query against a Microsoft Access 97 database holding price information for the various funds found in the FundAccts Funds table.

Before a distributed query can be executed, we must define the server we wish to access. To do this, we use the sp_addlinkedserver stored procedure.

The sp_addlinkedserver procedure takes six arguments to describe the server and the data source. The first argument is the name of the linked server as it will be referenced on the current server installation.

The second argument is the OLE DB data source product name. This argument has a default value of NULL if you don't specify it. The third argument is the name of the OLE DB provider as registered on the local machine.

The fourth, fifth, and sixth arguments specify the data source. The use and interpretation of these is dependent on the provider. The fourth argument is the name of the data source to be accessed by the provider specified in the third argument. The data source name therefore must conform to the format expected by the provider.

The fifth argument specifies the location of the database to be accessed and the sixth argument is the connection string used to connect to the data source.

If for example we needed to access a Jet database named Prices, we would add a linked server using the following:

```
sp_addlinkedserver 'FundPrices',
    'Access 97','Microsoft.Jet.OLEDB.4.0',
    'E:\Microsoft Office\OFFICE\DATA\prices.mdb'
```

To provide a login for the remote data source, we use sp_addlinkedsrvlogin to add the necessary login information.

```
sp_addlinkedsrvlogin 'FundPrices',false,'sa','Admin',NULL
```

The first parameter to sp_addlinkedsrvlogin is the local name of the linked server. The second parameter specifies whether or not SQL Server should use the current login information to login to the remote data source. If this parameter is false, SQL Server will not use the current login but instead use the login information provided in the fifth (remote login user ID) and sixth (remote login password) parameters of the call.

The third parameter specifies a local login that applies to this srvlogin entry. A value of NULL indicates that the entry applies to all logins that will access the remote server.

With the remote data source and login information successfully registered with the local SQL Server, we are ready to access the data source. To do this, we use the OPENQUERY() function.

The OPENQUERY() function executes a query, specified as the second argument, against a remote data source specified by the linked server name given as the first argument.

This function behaves like a native SQL Server table and can be placed in Transact-SQL statements anywhere that tables may appear. The capabilities of the OLE DB provider associated with the linked server determine what SQL operations can be applied to the remote data source.

```
SELECT *
 FROM OPENQUERY(FundPrices,'SELECT fund_cd, fund_name, price,
               price_date FROM Prices')
 WHERE fund_cd = 'BWINE'
```

OPENQUERY() passes the SQL statement, specified in the second argument, to the remote data source for execution. This query must conform to the syntax acceptable to the remote provider. SQL Server does not parse or compile this query string.

Of course a simple SELECT statement against the remote server can also be accomplished by using a four-part name as in the following:

```
SELECT * FROM FundPrices...Prices
```

Another method of accessing a remote data source is to use the OPENROWSET() function. This function is used in exactly the same way that OPENQUERY() is used, except the remote data source information is contained in the OPENROWSET() function arguments rather than referencing a linked server name.

SQL Server 7 ships with OLE DB providers for SQL Server 7, Jet, and ODBC. These providers, plus others that will undoubtedly soon be available from third-party vendors, can add tremendous value to your stored procedures and applications.

Updating Existing Data Using the UPDATE Statement

As time goes on, data within the database needs to change. Investors are adding to their accounts, mutual funds are distributing dividends to their shareholders, and clients may be moving and need to update their address information.

To apply these changes, we use T-SQL's UPDATE statement. UPDATE changes one or more column values in one or more rows.

Here's how we would update a specific client's work phone:

```
UPDATE Accounts
  SET work_phone = '563-5010'
  WHERE acct_no = '7336'
```

 Forget to specify the WHERE clause and you'll update the work phone of every client in the table to 563-5010.

Update with Values Selected from Other Tables

Instead of entering a constant literal as a value, we can select a value from another table, just as we did in the INSERT statement earlier. Let's say we store in the AccountValues table each account's current value as of the latest statement. We can update the AccountValues cur_value and stmt_date for a client by selecting these columns from the client's latest statement row:

```
UPDATE AccountValues
  SET AccountValues.stmt_date = b.stmt_date,
      AccountValues.cur_value = b.cur_value
  FROM AccountValues,Statements AS b
  WHERE  AccountValues.acct_no = '1003'

AND AccountValues.acct_no = b.acct_no
AND b.stmt_date = (SELECT MAX(stmt_date)
        FROM Statements
        WHERE acct_no = '1003')
```

The above statement is working with account number 1003, so we specify that account number in the WHERE clause.

We now need to find the latest statement row in the Statements table for this account and use the stmt_date and cur_value values to update the row in the AccountValues table for this account. The column assignments we want to make are specified in the SET clause.

In order to select the values from the correct row in the Statements table, we need to enhance the WHERE clause to ensure that the acct_no and stmt_date keys of both table match up.

The second line of the WHERE clause indicates that the Statements row must have an acct_no equal to the acct_no in the AccountValues table, which has already been qualified as '1003'.

The last line of the WHERE clause indicates that the Statements stmt_date must have a value that is equal to the latest date value in the Statements table for the acct_no '1003'. This enables us to choose the Statements row for acct_no 1003 for the latest statement and use that row for updating our AccountValues row.

Let's assume that the `stmt_date` in the 1003 row in the AccountValues table already equals the latest statement date in the Statements table and that we only need to update the cur_values column. We can do this with the following statement:

```
UPDATE AccountValues
  SET AccountValues.cur_value =
    (SELECT cur_value FROM Statements
      WHERE acct_no = AccountValues.acct_no
            AND stmt_date = AccountValues.stmt_date)
  FROM AccountValues,Statements
  WHERE AccountValues.acct_no='1003'
```

Be sure when you use a statement like the one above that the `SELECT` statement used to return a value for the update column returns only one value. An error will result if more than one value is returned. The best way to check for this, of course, is to test the `SELECT` statement by itself before incorporating it into the `UPDATE` statement.

You can see from these examples that T-SQL is quite flexible and that the `SELECT` statement has many applications. Later you'll discover that the `SELECT` statement can even be used in the `FROM` clause.

Deleting Data with the DELETE Statement

The `DELETE` statement is used to remove one or more rows from a table and free up the space used by those rows for new rows or objects in the database.

If you need to remove all rows from a table, you can issue a `DELETE` statement and merely name the table from which rows are to be removed:

```
DELETE AccountValues
```

The above statement then would remove all rows from the AccountValues table.

To delete only selected rows, you would use a `WHERE` clause in the `DELETE` statement to qualify the rows you want to delete. The statement below removes only the row where the `acct_no` is 1004 (one row):

```
DELETE FROM AccountValues
  WHERE acct_no = '1004'
```

Be careful to make sure the qualifier is unique to indicate what you want to delete. If you entered a statement like the following, you would delete all rows having a statement date of 1997-03-31:

```
DELETE FROM AccountValues
  WHERE stmt_date = '1997-03-31'
```

Since the same `stmt_date` can appear on more than one row in the AccountValues table, it is not enough to qualify the deletion of one row. It is enough of a qualification, however, if you intend to delete all rows for this date.

Now let's delete rows from the AccountValues table based on a selection from the Accounts table. If a client's row has a zero `tot_assets`, delete all AccountValues rows for the client:

```
DELETE AccountValues
  FROM Accounts a,AccountValues b
  WHERE a.tot_assets = 0 AND
  a.acct_no = b.acct_no
```

It's a good idea (and a good way to win the friendship of the database administrator) to check your `DELETE` statement out with a `SELECT` statement before executing the `DELETE`. By doing this, you can see which rows will be deleted.

Change the `DELETE AccountValues` part of the statement to `SELECT a.acct_no,a.tot_assets,b.cur_value` and run the query. The rows you get back are the ones targeted for deletion. If you don't see what you expect, your query needs some modifications.

Using the TRUNCATE TABLE Statement

When you have a table that is not referenced by a `FOREIGN KEY` constraint in another table, a faster method of deleting all rows of the table is to use `TRUNCATE TABLE`. To remove all rows from the AccountValues table, for example, using this method, you would code as follows:

```
TRUNCATE TABLE AccountValues
```

An advantage of using `TRUNCATE TABLE` over `DELETE` is that it does not record an entry for each deleted row in the transaction log.

Summary

In this chapter, we've explored the basics of the Data Manipulation Language.

We've seen how to load data into tables using the basic `INSERT` statement to specify column values. We've explored how to use the values of columns in other tables to insert into a table by joining an `INSERT` statement and `SELECT` statement together.

The basic clauses of the `SELECT` statement were explored in this chapter. We learned about the column list and that we can use literal constants and expressions there in addition to column names. We learned that result sets returned by a SELECT statement can be restricted by the use of a WHERE clause and sorted by using an ORDER BY clause.

The use of column and table aliases was illustrated, and we saw how to use the DISTINCT keyword to return unique rows.

A useful technique of creating tables by selecting columns from one or more tables with the SELECT INTO statement was explored, and you learned how to create permanent and temporary tables with this technique.

A couple of methods for updating tables were explored using the UPDATE statement. We covered the updating of columns coded as literals and as values selected from other tables.

Finally, we used the DELETE statement and the TRUNCATE TABLE statement to remove rows from a table.

We've used constant literal values throughout the discussion of DML in this chapter. Don't think that you are required to specify values in this fashion when working with your T-SQL statements. If we were, the language would fall far short of being very useful in database applications.

When you use DML in stored procedures in Chapter 15, and again in application programs in Part III of this book, you'll see that we can use variables as sources for WHERE clause expressions, INSERT values, UPDATE values, column list expressions, and constants.

The variables we use are parsed out to become literal values in the Transact-SQL statement sent to SQL Server, just as we've seen in this chapter. But from our program's perspective, we'll most often see variable names being used in our T-SQL statements or as parameters to stored procedures.

Chapter 7

Exploring Transact-SQL Functions

IN THIS CHAPTER

- ◆ Discover what functions are available in Transact-SQL
- ◆ Learn how to use functions in Transact-SQL expressions
- ◆ Learn about data type conversions using the `CONVERT()` function
- ◆ Explore commonly used functions in all function categories offered by SQL Server

IN DEVELOPING APPLICATIONS, we often come across a routine we need to call from multiple points in our program and even from multiple programs. These routines implement some process that behaves in a predictable way to produce a result. Generally, they return one value given a set of zero or more input arguments. We categorize these routines as *functions*.

In programming a Transact-SQL procedure or script, we have at our disposal a collection of functions we can include in statement expressions to help provide the results we require. Functions offered by Transact-SQL can be classified into six categories as shown in Table 7-1.

TABLE 7-1 THE TRANSACT-SQL FUNCTION CATEGORIES

Category	Description
Aggregate	Functions that operate on a set of values to return one numeric result
Date/Time	Functions that operate with date and time arguments
Mathematical	Functions that implement some mathematical calculations on the input values and return a numeric value
String	Functions that operate on `char` or `varchar` input parameters

Continued

TABLE 7-1 THE TRANSACT-SQL FUNCTION CATEGORIES *(Continued)*

Category	Description
System	Functions that are related to system objects and settings
Text/Image	Functions that operate on text and image input parameters

Due to the nature of the topic, the chapter is somewhat encyclopedic but illustrates many commonly used functions from each of the six categories.

Using Data Conversion Functions

SQL Server offers the `CONVERT()` function for explicitly converting an expression to a given data type. You can also use the `CAST()` function to convert data types, but it does not allow formatting of the result the way `CONVERT()` does.

These two functions are actually categorized as system functions, which we'll explore later in this chapter. However, since they are so widely used, sometimes in conjunction with other functions, we'll look at them first.

You've already seen the `CONVERT()` function in Chapter 4 to convert the Accounts table `tot_assets` column to a character string. The statement is shown again here:

```
SELECT (acct_firstname + acct_lastname) +
' Has a current value of ' + CONVERT(varchar(15),tot_assets)
FROM Accounts
-----------------------------------------
Client2 Has a current value of 202457.35
Client3 Has a current value of 0.00
Client5 Has a current value of 34738.64
Client6 Has a current value of 52693.81
Client7 Has a current value of 217219.64
Client8 Has a current value of 198314.47
```

In the above statement, we used `CONVERT()` to change a `money` data type to a `varchar` data type in order to use it in a string concatenation. We could have used the function `CAST()` in place of `CONVERT()`. A partial listing of the results are shown.

Here's how you can obtain the same results using `CAST()`:

```
SELECT (acct_firstname + acct_lastname) +
' Has a current value of ' +
```

```
CAST(tot_assets AS varchar(15))
FROM Accounts
```

SQL Server does handle some data type conversions for us. In comparison operations involving different data types, for example, SQL Server will change one data type to another in order to do the comparison. Although SQL Server is handling the conversion for you, you can and should specify the CONVERT() function to be more clear as to what is going on. This practice forces you to think about what you are actually doing and helps eliminate bugs.

Using the Style Parameter

A useful parameter to the CONVERT() function for formatting date/times and numeric values is the style parameter.

Style is used when you convert datetime or smalldatetime values to char or varchar and when converting numeric values such as float and money. This parameter specifies the format for the resulting string. Table 7-2 shows the values you can use for formatting date/time conversions.

TABLE 7-2 STYLE PARAMETERS FOR FORMATTING DATE/TIME VALUES
         IN THE CONVERT() FUNCTION

Without Century	With Century	Standard	Result
	0 or 100	Default	mon dd yyyy hh:miAM (or PM)
1	101	USA	mm/dd/yy mm/dd/yyyy
2	102	ANSI	yy.mm.dd yyyy.mm.dd
3	103	British/French	dd/mm/yy dd/mm/yyyy
4	104	German	dd.mm.yy dd.mm.yyyy
5	105	Italian	dd-mm-yy dd-mm-yyyy
6	106		dd mon yy dd mon yyyy

Continued

TABLE 7-2 STYLE PARAMETERS FOR FORMATTING DATE/TIME VALUES
IN THE CONVERT() FUNCTION (Continued)

Without Century	With Century	Standard	Result
7	107		mon dd,yy mon dd,yyyy
8	108		hh:mm:ss
9	109	Default + milliseconds	mon dd yyyy hh:mm:ss:mmm AM
10	110	USA	mm-dd-yy mm-dd-yyyy
11	111	JAPAN	yy/mm/dd yyyy/mm/dd
12	112	ISO	yymmdd yyyymmdd
13	113	Europe default milliseconds	dd mon yyyy + hh:mm:ss:mmm (24h)
14	114		hh:mm:ss:mmm (24h)
20	120	ODBC canonical	yyyy-mm-dd hh:mm:ss(24h)
21	121	ODBC canonical (with milliseconds)	yyyy-mm-dd- hh:mm:ss.mmm (24h)

Say we wanted to display the Statements stmt_date as a three-character month, two digits for day, and a four-digit year in the form "mon dd yyyy." We could code the following expression in the SELECT statement:

```
SELECT CONVERT(char,stmt_date,100) FROM Statements
```

The above statement displays a result that looks like this:

```
Dec 31 1997 12:00AM
```

To convert `real` and `float` data types to character, use the following styles:

Style	Result
0	A maximum of six digits in scientific notation(if appropriate)
1	Eight digits in scientific notation
2	Sixteen digits in scientific notation

For `money` and `smallmoney` conversions to character, use these styles:

Style	Result
0	No commas left of the decimal point, with two digits on the right of the decimal point
1	Commas every three digits to the left of the decimal point, with two digits on the right of the decimal point
2	No commas left of the decimal point, with four digits on the right of the decimal point.

Using a style argument of 1 to format the money conversion we used at the beginning of this section, we get these results:

```
SELECT (acct_firstname + acct_lastname) +
' Has a current value of ' + CONVERT(varchar(15),tot_assets,1)
FROM Accounts
-------------------------------------
Client2 Has a current value of 202,457.35
Client3 Has a current value of 0.00
Client5 Has a current value of 34,738.64
Client6 Has a current value of 52,693.81
Client7 Has a current value of 217,219.64
Client8 Has a current value of 198,314.47
```

Using Domain Aggregate Functions

Domain aggregate functions operate on a set of values to return a numeric result. These functions are most often found in statements implementing a GROUP BY clause. They can, however, be used in statements that don't implement the GROUP BY clause, as you'll see below.

The use of GROUP BY in Transact-SQL statements is explored in Chapter 8.

The AVG() function

The AVG() function returns the average of the numeric expression given as it's input argument.

To find the average total asset value across all of our open mutual fund accounts, we would use the following statement:

```
SELECT AVG(tot_assets) FROM Accounts
 WHERE acct_status = 'Open'
```

The DISTINCT keyword can be used to obtain the average over distinct values only. We could obtain the average total assets only for distinct values of total assets using the statement below:

```
SELECT AVG(DISTINCT tot_assets) FROM Accounts
 WHERE acct_status = 'Open'
```

If NULL values are allowed in the column expression, AVG() ignores them in calculating the average.

To obtain the average total assets for each account type, Tax or Nontax, we can use a GROUP BY clause in the SELECT statement:

```
SELECT acct_type,AVG(tot_assets)AS 'Avg Total Assets' FROM Accounts
 WHERE acct_status = 'Open'
 GROUP BY acct_type
```

The results of this statement are shown here:

```
acct_type Avg Total Assets
--------- ----------------
NonTax    216868.4100
Tax       121020.4538
(2 row(s) affected)
```

Since the expression argument to the AVG() function is data type money, the resulting average is also data type money. We can convert the result to a character string and format it with commas by using the CONVERT() function like this:

```
SELECT acct_type, CONVERT(varchar(12),AVG(tot_assets),1) AS 'Avg
 Total Assets' FROM Accounts WHERE acct_status = 'Open' GROUP BY
 acct_type
```

The result of this statement is as follows:

```
acct_type Avg Total Assets
--------- ----------------
NonTax    216,868.41
Tax       121,020.45
(2 row(s) affected)
```

Notice that we nested the AVG() function inside the CONVERT() function in order to format the resulting average with commas and convert it to a character string for display.

The COUNT() Function

The COUNT() function is used to return the number of values in argument that are non-NULL.

The most popular use of this function is to count the number of rows in a table, like this:

```
SELECT COUNT(*) FROM Accounts
```

This use of the COUNT() function merely counts the rows in the named table, without regard for duplicates or for NULL entries in columns.

You can use COUNT() to count distinct values in a column by coding as follows:

```
SELECT COUNT(DISTINCT zip) FROM Accounts
```

Keep in mind that COUNT() is an aggregate function. This means that you cannot ask SQL Server to return the count of some expression along with nonaggregated results. For example, you would get an error if you coded as follows:

```
SELECT acct_no,COUNT(DISTINCT zip), tot_assets FROM Accounts
```

The statement just doesn't make sense. The following statement, though, is perfectly valid:

```
SELECT COUNT(DISTINCT zip) as 'Zip Count',
 SUM(tot_assets) as 'Sum Tot Assets' FROM Accounts
```

The results are as follows:

```
Zip Count   Sum Tot Assets
----------- --------------
26          3996832.6955
(1 row(s) affected)
```

In the statement above, we are using two aggregate functions, COUNT() and SUM(). The Zip Count column in the results displays the number of distinct ZIP codes in the Accounts table and the Sum Tot Assets column displays the sum of the tot_assets from every row of the Accounts table.

If you need to count values from a subset of rows, use the WHERE clause to limit the rows selected and count those.

The SUM() Function

As you saw in the above discussion of the COUNT() function, the SUM() function is used to return the sum of an expression. Above, we summed the tot_assets column from every row in the Account table with the following simple statement:

```
SELECT SUM(tot_assets) FROM Accounts
```

Again, NULL values are ignored. To sum distinct expressions, use the DISTINCT keyword as you did with COUNT():

```
SELECT SUM(DISTINCT tot_assets) FROM Accounts
```

If any tot_assets values are the same, only one of them is included in the resulting sum with the above statement.

To filter out values you don't want in the sum, use the WHERE clause to select the values of interest as in the following statement:

```
SELECT SUM(tot_assets) FROM Accounts WHERE state_abbr = 'CT'
```

The MAX() and MIN() Functions

To find the minimum or maximum values of a numeric, datetime, or character expression, use the MIN() and MAX() functions:

```
SELECT MIN(tot_assets) AS 'Min Value', MAX(tot_assets) AS 'Max
 Value' FROM Accounts
GO

Min Value            Max Value
-------------------- --------------------
.0000                506296.0320
(1 row(s) affected)
```

We saw in Chapter 6 that functions can be used in WHERE clause expressions as well. The statement below returns the acct_no and lastname of the account with the largest tot_assets value:

```
SELECT acct_no, acct_lastname, tot_assets FROM Accounts
```

```
WHERE tot_assets = (SELECT MAX(tot_assets)
 FROM Accounts)
```

Working with Strings

String functions are used to work with character string data stored in `char` and `varchar` data types.

These functions are useful for interrogating strings for a particular pattern, choosing a substring out of a string, and for converting other data types to strings for display or further string processing.

You've already seen the use of string concatenation in previous chapters. The + sign placed between two string expressions results in the concatenation of those expressions to form one string:

```
SELECT 'Account last name is: ' + acct_lastname AS 'Title' FROM
 Accounts
WHERE acct_no = '1003'
```

The above `SELECT` statement results in the string below:

```
Title
-------------------------------
Account last name is: Client2
(1 row(s) affected)
```

The LEN() Function

Its often helpful to know the length of the string you are working with. To get the length of a string, use the `LEN()` function:

```
SELECT LEN(acct_lastname) FROM Accounts
WHERE acct_no = '1003'

-----------
7
(1 row(s) affected)
```

The use of `LEN()` above counts the number of characters in the acct_lastname column value for account 1003. It does not count trailing blanks, even if the column data type were defined as a fixed length `char` data type.

The UPPER() and LOWER() Functions

When you need to present data in lowercase or uppercase characters, you can use the LOWER() and UPPER() functions to convert the expressions. The following SELECT statement returns the account last name, first in all lowercase characters and then in all uppercase characters:

```
SELECT LOWER(acct_lastname) AS 'Lower Case', UPPER(acct_lastname) AS
 'Upper Case'
FROM Accounts
WHERE acct_no = '1003'

Lower Case          Upper Case
------------------  ----------
client2             CLIENT2
(1 row(s) affected)
```

The LTRIM() and RTRIM() Functions

If a string contains leading or trailing spaces that you want to omit from your display of the string, use either LTRIM() to remove leading spaces or RTRIM() to remove trailing spaces. The following SELECT statement shows the results of applying LTRIM() to a string:

```
SELECT LEN('   no leading spaces') AS 'Length before LTRIM',LTRIM('
 no leading spaces'),
LEN(LTRIM('   no leading spaces')) AS 'Length after LTRIM'

Length before LTRIM                         Length after LTRIM
------------------  ------------------  ------------------
20                  no leading spaces 17
(1 row(s) affected)
```

The next functions we'll look at are used to pull strings apart. Some of these are used to build substrings and some are used as helper functions to find a starting position in a string, where we might want to start collecting characters for our resultant substring.

The RIGHT() and LEFT() Functions

The RIGHT() and LEFT() functions return substrings consisting of some number of characters selected from either the right or left of a string expression:

```
SELECT RIGHT(acct_lastname,6)
 AS 'Right Six',LEFT(acct_lastname,6) AS 'Left Six'
 FROM Accounts WHERE acct_no = '1012'
Right Six Left Six
--------- --------
ient15    Client
```

(1 row(s) affected)

Specifying a number of characters greater than the results returned by LEN()
will return LEN() characters. Specifying zero characters returns NULL.

The SUBSTRING() Function

SUBSTRING() is used to extract a string from another string expression. This is a
very powerful string function that will come in handy quite often and can be used
on text, ntext, image, binary, and varbinary data types as well as char and
varchar types.

You need to specify a starting position in the string expression – where you wish
to start the substring extraction – and you need to specify the number of characters
you want to extract. For binary, varbinary, text, and image data type expressions, specify the number of bytes instead of the number of characters:

```
SELECT city,SUBSTRING(city,3,6) FROM Accounts
city
-------------------------------     ------
Some City                           me Cit
Some City                           me Cit
Some City                           me Cit
Some Village                        me Vil
Some Town                           me  Tow
Some Town                           me Tow
A Town                              Town
Some Town                           me Tow
Some City                           me Cit
Some Town                           me Tow
Some Village                        me Vil
Some City                           me Cit
Some City                           me Cit
Some Town                           me Tow
Some Place                          me Pla
Some City                           me Cit
Some Place                          me Pla
Some Town                           me Tow
Some Village                        me Vil
```

The SELECT statement above selects a substring from the city column in the
Accounts table. The substring starts in position 3 of city and extracts 6 characters.
The substring is displayed in column two of the result set.

As you can see from this example, the first character in the string expression is
specified as starting position 1.

Specifying zero as either the starting position or the length will cause NULL to be
returned.

The CHARINDEX() Function

So far we've been using numeric constants to specify the starting position for extracting substrings in LEFT(), RIGHT(), and SUBSTRING().

When we know something about the content of the substring we want to extract but don't know exactly where the substring starts, we can find the starting position with the CHARINDEX() function.

The CHARINDEX() function returns the starting position of a pattern string within a string expression:

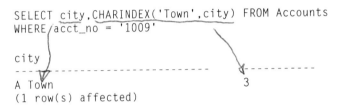

```
SELECT city,CHARINDEX('Town',city) FROM Accounts
WHERE acct_no = '1009'

city
---------------------------    -----------
A Town                          3
(1 row(s) affected)
```

Now we can use the CHARINDEX() function as a starting position specifier for other functions:

```
SELECT city,SUBSTRING(city,CHARINDEX('Town',city),LEN(city)) FROM
  Accounts
WHERE acct_no = '1009'

city
-----------------------------   ---------------------------
A Town                          Town
(1 row(s) affected)
```

You can supply a third argument to the CHARINDEX() function to give it a starting position in the string expression at which to start its search for the pattern string. The position returned in this case is still relative to the start of the string expression, 1, and not relative to the third argument. That is, if you specify 3 as a starting position and the pattern is found starting at that position, you get back 3 as the index and not 1.

The STR() Function

Use the STR() function to convert a float expression to a character string. A length can be used as the second argument to specify the total length of the resulting string, including the decimal point. A third argument specifies the number of decimal places to the right of the decimal point:

```
SELECT tot_assets,STR(tot_assets,6,2) AS 'STR Applied'
FROM Accounts WHERE acct_no = '1007'
```

```
tot_assets              STR Applied
--------------------    -----------
217219.6400             217220
(1 row(s) affected)
```

In the above use of STR(), the whole part of the tot_assets was rounded up to the next dollar since the length argument was not large enough to hold the whole number. Increasing the length to 8 yields the following results:

```
tot_assets              STR Applied
--------------------    -----------
217219.6400             217219.6
(1 row(s) affected)
```

This time we get one decimal place since the whole number plus the decimal point plus the first decimal digit takes up the eight characters specified for length.

Providing a length that is insufficient to hold the converted number will yield asterisks instead of the number.

The last two string functions we will explore before moving on to math functions deals with replacing parts of string expressions with other strings.

The STUFF() Function

STUFF() will delete a specified number of characters, starting at some point in a string, and replace the deleted string with another string:

```
SELECT city,STUFF(city,2,4,'********')
FROM Accounts WHERE acct_no = '1009'
```

```
city
--------------------    -----------------
A Town                  A********n
(1 row(s) affected)
```

The above statement deletes four characters from the city column's value starting at character position 2 and then stuffs the string argument into the result starting at position 2.

The REPLACE() Function

This function searches for a given string inside another string and replaces those characters with a replacement string:

```
SELECT city,REPLACE(city,'ow','oo')
FROM Accounts WHERE acct_no = '1009'
```

```
city
-------------------------------   -----------------------
A Town                            A Town
(1 row(s) affected
```

The third argument replacement string behaves like the STUFF() function. When you use a replacement string that is longer than the second argument search string, the replacement string is stuffed into the target string, starting at the position where the search string was found.

If the search string occurs multiple times in the target string, all occurrences are replaced:

```
SELECT REPLACE('abcowdefgowhjk','ow','***')
-----------------------------------
abc***defg***hjk
(1 row(s) affected)
```

Using the Math Functions

The mathematical functions provide a means to perform calculations on numeric expressions. The calculations supported by the mathematical function category include a means to round numbers, find the square of a number and take square roots, generate random numbers, and perform trigonometric calculations.

The ABS() Function

This function returns the absolute value of a numeric expression. The absolute value of a number is the number expressed as a positive number:

```
SELECT ABS(-123.4567890)
-----------
123.4567890
(1 row(s) affected)
```

The POWER() Function

POWER() is used to raise a numeric expression to some power specified as the second argument to the function:

```
SELECT POWER(-2.0,-3)
--------------------
-.1
(1 row(s) affected)
```

Raising an integer value to a negative power returns zero. The return value takes on the precision of the numeric first argument.

The SQUARE() and SQRT() Functions

The `SQUARE()` and `SQRT()` functions return the square and square root of a numeric expression, respectively:

```
SELECT SQUARE(6.2),SQRT(SQUARE(6.2))
-------------------- --------------------------------
38.440000000000005       6.2000000000000002
(1 row(s) affected)
```

The ROUND() Function

This function takes the numeric expression to be rounded as the first argument, a length specifier as the second argument, and an optional third argument used to interpret the length argument as either a precision or a length at which to truncate the numeric expression. Both the second and third arguments must be `int`, `small-int`, or `tinyint` data types.

When this function is called with a positive second argument, and either no third argument, a third argument that evaluates to zero, or you specify zero, the function returns the numeric expression rounded to the number of decimal places specified in the second argument:

```
SELECT ROUND(2517.47567,3)
----------
2517.47600
(1 row(s) affected)
```

Use a negative number as the second argument to round the expression to the number of digits specified:

```
SELECT ROUND(2517.47567,-3)
----------
3000.00000
(1 row(s) affected)
```

To truncate the expression to the length of the second argument, use a nonzero third argument:

```
SELECT ROUND(2517.47567,3,1)
----------
2517.47500
(1 row(s) affected)
```

Truncating with a negative length affects the digits to the left of the decimal point:

```
SELECT ROUND(2517.47567,-3,1)
```

```
- - - - - - - - - -
2000.00000
(1 row(s) affected)
```

The RAND() Function

RAND() returns a random number between 0 and 1. The function can take an optional argument for seeding the random number generator:

```
SELECT RAND(2.47567)
SELECT RAND()
SELECT RAND()
SELECT RAND(2.47567)
SELECT RAND()
0.7136106261841817
(1 row(s) affected)
- - - - - - - - - - - - - - - - - - - - - - - - - - - - - - - - - - - - - - - -
0.2178211392600386
(1 row(s) affected)
- - - - - - - - - - - - - - - - - - - - - - - - - - - - - - - - - - - - - - - -
0.570956802191051194
(1 row(s) affected)
- - - - - - - - - - - - - - - - - - - - - - - - - - - - - - - - - - - - - - - -
0.7136106261841817
(1 row(s) affected)
- - - - - - - - - - - - - - - - - - - - - - - - - - - - - - - - - - - - - - - -
0.2178211392600386
(1 row(s) affected)
```

Notice in the above set of statements that specifying the same seed starts the same random sequence of numbers over again.

Next, we'll explore some functions widely used in business database applications.

Working with Dates

The functions found in this category are used to perform date and time calculations.

These functions are useful in many business applications where date manipulation is common practice. Our mutual fund account sample application requires that we calculate previous dates given a current statement date in order to retrieve account values from statements issued a month or quarter previously.

We can also use date manipulation functions in processing transaction history entries and to retrieve fund prices from previous transactions.

The GETDATE() Function

The GETDATE() function returns the current date and time on the SQL Server machine:

```
SELECT GETDATE()
--------------------------
1998-02-24 20:00:56.873
(1 row(s) affected)
```

Pg 147-148

Format the result of GETDATE() using the CONVERT() function and an appropriate style:

```
SELECT CONVERT(char,GetDate(),101)
SELECT CONVERT(char,GetDate(),108)


-----------------------------------
02/24/1998
(1 row(s) affected)
-------------------
20:00:56
(1 row(s) affected)
```

The DATEADD() and DATEDIFF() Functions

The DATEADD() function increments a datetime argument by some specified datetime interval to yield another datetime value.

The DATEDIFF() function calculates the difference between two datetime arguments in a specified time interval.

Both of these functions use a time interval from Table 7-3 as the first argument.

TABLE 7-3 TIME INTERVAL ARGUMENTS
            (ABBREVIATIONS SHOWN IN PARENTHESES)

Interval	Range
day (dd)	1 – 31
dayofyear (dy)	1 – 366
hour (hh)	0 – 23
millisecond (ms)	0 – 999
minute (mi)	0 – 59

Continued

T<small>ABLE</small> **7-3 TIME INTERVAL ARGUMENTS**
        (ABBREVIATIONS SHOWN IN PARENTHESES) *(Continued)*

Interval	Range
month (mm)	1 – 12
quarter (qq)	1 – 4
second (ss)	0 – 59
week (wk)	1 – 53
weekday (dw)	1 – 7 representing Sunday through Saturday

DATEADD() adds some number of time intervals to the datetime values given as the third argument. Below is a series of DATEADD() function calls based on the return value from the GETDATE() function. The results have been edited to remove the "row(s) affected" message between statement result sets:

```
SELECT GetDate(),'GetDate value'
SELECT DATEADD(year,3,GetDate()),'time interval is year'
SELECT DATEADD(day,3,GetDate()),'time interval is day'
SELECT DATEADD(week,3,GetDate()),'time interval is week'
SELECT DATEADD(quarter,3,GetDate()),
'time interval is quarter'
SELECT DATEADD(month,3,GetDate()),
'time interval is month'
SELECT DATEADD(hour,3,GetDate()),'time interval is hour'
------------------------     ------------------------
1998-02-26 20:11:05.403     GetDate value
------------------------     ------------------------
2001-02-26 20:11:05.403     time interval is year
------------------------     ------------------------
1998-03-01 20:11:05.403     time interval is day
------------------------     ------------------------
1998-03-19 20:11:05.403     time interval is week
------------------------     ------------------------
1998-11-26 20:11:05.403     time interval is quarter
------------------------     ------------------------
1998-05-26 20:11:05.403     time interval is month
------------------------     ------------------------
1998-02-26 23:11:05.403     time interval is hour
```

The weekday time interval is not used with either the DATEADD() or DATEDIFF() functions, but will be used later in the DATENAME() function.

When you change the second argument in the above function calls from a 3 to a -3, you get the following results:

```
- - - - - - - - - - - - - - - - - - - - - - - - - -    - - - - - - - - - - - - -
1998-02-26 20:16:41.250     GetDate value
- - - - - - - - - - - - - - - - - - - - - - - - - -    - - - - - - - - - - - - - - - - - - - -
1995-02-26 20:16:41.250     time interval is year
- - - - - - - - - - - - - - - - - - - - - - - - - -    - - - - - - - - - - - - - - - - - - -
1998-02-23 20:16:41.250     time interval is day
- - - - - - - - - - - - - - - - - - - - - - - - - -    - - - - - - - - - - - - - - - - - - - - -
1998-02-05 20:16:41.250     time interval is week
- - - - - - - - - - - - - - - - - - - - - - - - - -    - - - - - - - - - - - - - - - - - - - - - - -   - -
1997-05-26 20:16:41.250     time interval is quarter
- - - - - - - . - - - - - - - - - - - - - - - -    - - - - - - - - - - - - - - - - - - - -
1997-11-26 20:16:41.250     time interval is month
- - - - - - - - - - - - - - - - - - - - - - - - - -    - - - - - - - - - - - - - - - - - - - -
1998-02-26 17:16:41.250     time interval is hour
```

The DATEDIFF() function returns the difference between the second and third datetime arguments as the number of time intervals specified as the first argument.

Below is a series of DATEDIFF() function calls to return the difference between the GETDATE() return value and the date constant '1997-02-26'. Again the "row(s) affected" messages have been removed:

```
SELECT GetDate(),'GetDate value'
SELECT DATEDIFF(year,'1997-02-26',GetDate()),
'time interval is year'
SELECT DATEDIFF(day,'1997-02-26',GetDate()),
'time interval is day'
SELECT DATEDIFF(week,'1997-02-26',GetDate()),
'time interval is week'
SELECT DATEDIFF(quarter,'1997-02-26',GetDate()),
'time interval is quarter'
SELECT DATEDIFF(month,'1997-02-26',GetDate()),
'time interval is month'
SELECT DATEDIFF(hour,'1997-02-26',GetDate()),
'time interval is hour'
- - - - - - - - - - - - - - - - - - - - - - - - - -    - - - - - - - - - - - - -
1998-02-26 20:23:55.293     GetDate value
- - - - - - - - - - -    - - - - - - - - - - - - - - - - - - - -
1           time interval is year
- - - - - - - - - - -    - - - - - - - - - - - - - - - - - - -
365         time interval is day
- - - - - - - - - - -    - - - - - - - - - - - - - - - - - - - -
52          time interval is week
- - - - - - - - - - -    - - - - - - - - - - - - - - - - - - - - -
4           time interval is quarter
- - - - - - - - - - -    - - - - - - - - - - - - - - - - - - -
12          time interval is month
- - - - - - - - - - -    - - - - - - - - - - - - - - - - - - -
8780        time interval is hour
```

Using the same value for second and third datetime arguments returns zero.

In both DATEADD() and DATEDIFF(), the datetime arguments can be a function that yields a datetime value, a literal datetime constant, or a column with datetime data type.

As we've seen with other functions, DATEADD() and DATEDIFF() can also be specified in WHERE clause expressions:

```
SELECT acct_no,CONVERT(char(11),stmt_date,101)
 AS Stmt_Date,invest_tot,DATEPART(month,GetDate())
 AS 'Current Month'
FROM Statements
WHERE DATEDIFF(month,stmt_date,GetDate()) = 2
acct_no    Stmt_Date   invest_tot        Current Month
---------- ----------- ------------------ -------------
1003       12/31/1997  37462.8500              2
(1 row(s) affected)
```

The DATENAME() Function

DATENAME() returns a string naming the time interval specified as the first argument of the datetime value given as the second argument.

The time intervals used in this function are those listed in Table 7-3.

```
SELECT DATENAME(year,GetDate())
SELECT DATENAME(month,GetDate())
SELECT DATENAME(weekday,GetDate())
SELECT DATENAME(day,GetDate())
SELECT DATENAME(hour,GetDate())
SELECT DATENAME(minute,GetDate())
-----------------------------
1998
-----------------------------
February
-----------------------------
Friday
-----------------------------
27
-----------------------------
19
-----------------------------
31
```

In some instances, this function behaves similar to the next function we'll explore, DATEPART(), in that a specific interval, such as year, day, and hour are extracted from the datetime argument. The difference between DATENAME() and DATEPART() in these cases is that DATENAME() returns a string whereas DATEPART() returns an integer.

The DATEPART() Function

The `DATEPART()` function returns the time interval specified as the first argument of the datetime value specified as the second argument. As mentioned above, the return data type is `integer`:

```
SELECT DATEPART(year,GetDate())
SELECT DATEPART(month,GetDate())
SELECT DATEPART(weekday,GetDate())
SELECT DATEPART(day,GetDate())
SELECT DATEPART(hour,GetDate())
SELECT DATEPART(minute,GetDate())
-----------
1998
-----------
2
-----------
6
-----------
27
-----------
19
-----------
40
```

Compare the results from the statements above with those from the `DATENAME()` function calls using the same intervals. You can easily see how these two functions differ.

Using ISDATE()

The `ISDATE()` function determines if a given character string represents a valid datetime value. If the string does represent a datetime value, the function returns 1; otherwise, it returns 0:

```
SELECT ISDATE('2-27-98')
SELECT ISDATE('2-30-98')
SELECT ISDATE('2-27-00')
SELECT ISDATE('2-@7-98')
SELECT ISDATE('2-27-98 21:00 PM')

-----------
1
-----------
0
-----------
1
-----------
0
-----------
1
```

This function is obviously useful for validating datetime values entered by a user of your application prior to attempting to commit them to a table.

Using the DAY(), MONTH() and YEAR() Functions

The DAY(), MONTH() and YEAR() functions are used to return these date components from the date expression passed into the function.

```
SELECT DAY(stmt_date) AS 'DAY',
 MONTH(stmt_date) AS 'MONTH',
 YEAR(stmt_date) AS YEAR
 FROM AccountValues
 WHERE acct_no = '1012'
DAY          MONTH          YEAR
-----------  -----------    -----------
31           12             1992
31           3              1993
31           12             1994
(3 row(s) affected)
```

These same results can be achieved by using the DATEPART function with the appropriate arguments.

Exploring the System Functions

The system category of functions return information stored in system tables, provide information about the current environment, or provide general methods for validating and converting data.

The CONVERT() and CAST() functions covered at the beginning of this chapter are system functions for converting data of one data type to another data type.

This section explores a few other system functions commonly found in applications.

Testing for a Numeric Expression

Prior to updating a numeric column, you will most likely want to validate the expression to be applied to the column to determine if the expression is numeric. To do this, use the ISNUMERIC() function:

```
SELECT ISNUMERIC(127.45)
SELECT ISNUMERIC('127.45')
SELECT ISNUMERIC(5 * 2.3672)
SELECT ISNUMERIC(GETDATE())
SELECT ISNUMERIC(DATENAME(weekday,GETDATE()))
-----------
1
-----------
```

```
1
- - - - - - - - - -
1
- - - - - - - - - -
0
- - - - - - - - - -
0
```

ISNUMERIC() returns TRUE if the expression is numeric or will convert to numeric and FALSE otherwise.

Using the COALESCE() Function

COALESCE() returns the first non-NULL expression in its argument list. This function is useful to obtain a non-NULL value from a list without the need to check each value separately.

For example, when we need to list a phone number for a client to contact them, we can use COALESCE() to return either the client's work phone or home phone, whichever is NOT NULL:

```
SELECT acct_no,acct_lastname,
COALESCE(home_phone,work_phone)
 AS 'Phone Number'
FROM Accounts
acct_no     acct_lastname               Phone Number
- - - - - - - - - - - - - - - - - - - - - - - - - - - - - - - - - - - - - -
1003        Client2                     NULL
1004        Client3                     999-9999
1005        Client5                     888-8888
1006        Client6                     222-3333
1007        Client7                     444-4444
1008        Client8                     444-7777
1009        Client9                     666-9999
1010        Client11                    666-6666
1011        Client12                    444-5555
1012        Client15                    777-6666
1013        Client16                    222-3344
1014        Client18                    787-7878
1015        Client19                    111-1111
1016        Client20                    111-1212
1017        Client21                    999-8989
1018        Client23                    666-5454
1023        Client25                    888-1818
1024        Client26                    222-2244
1025        Client27                    111-1155
1027        Client29                    545-4545
1028        Client30                    262-6262
1029        Client31                    010-1010
1059        Client14                    333-3333
1060        Client4                     777-7777
1064        Client28                    444-4455
```

```
1066        Client24                    333-3232
1067        Client17                    343-3434
1068        Client13                    888-8888
1069        Client10                    555-5555
1070        Client22                    444-1111
1992        Client1                     222-2222
9847        Client32                    555-5555
(32 row(s) affected)
```

As you can see from the results, account 1003 doesn't have a phone number in our Accounts table.

Using the DATALENGTH() Function

DATALENGTH() returns the actual length of the expression passed to it. It is particularly useful to determine the length of varying length data types, but it can be used on any data type:

```
SELECT acct_no,acct_lastname,
DATALENGTH(acct_lastname) AS 'Length of last name'
FROM Accounts
WHERE acct_no BETWEEN '1008' AND '1012'
acct_no     acct_lastname              Length of last name
----------  -------------------------  -------------------
1008        Client8                    7
1009        Client9                    7
1010        Client11                   8
1011        Client12                   8
1012        Client15                   8
(5 row(s) affected)
```

Although acct_lastname is defined as varchar(50), the DATALENGTH() function returns only the length of the data currently in the column, as shown above.

If we were to use DATALENGTH() on a fixed-length column such as state_abbr defined as char(2) or on a column with a money data type, we would see the actual length required to store the data type. In the case of char or nchar, the length returned would be the length specified when the column was defined rather than the length of the data in the column minus blank padding:

```
SELECT state_abbr AS 'State',tot_assets AS 'Assets',
DATALENGTH(state_abbr) AS 'Length state_abbr',
DATALENGTH(tot_assets) AS 'Length tot_assets'
FROM Accounts
WHERE acct_no BETWEEN '1008' AND '1012'
State Assets            Length state_abbr Length tot_assets
----- ------------      ----------------- -----------------
CT    198314.4680       2                 8
CA    186276.0425       2                 8
CT    56454.3980        2                 8
CT    141651.0260       2                 8
```

```
CT     134290.2660    2              8
(5 row(s) affected)
```

Retrieving Information About IDENTITY Columns

When you want to retrieve the seed and increment values for the identity column of a table, you can use the IDENT_SEED() and IDENT_INCR() functions. The information returned by these functions is the same as that returned by sp_help 'table_name' under the IDENTITY header.

IDENT_SEED() returns the seed of the identity column from the table named in the argument. If for example, we had defined the acct_no of AccountValues to be an IDENTITY column, the following function call would return the seed value we assigned to the column:

```
SELECT IDENT_SEED('AccountValues')
```

If the named table doesn't contain an IDENTITY column, NULL is returned.
The identity columns' increment value is returned by IDENT_INCR().

```
SELECT IDENT_INCR('AccountValues')
```

Like the IDENT_SEED() function, IDENT_INCR() returns NULL when the named table doesn't contain an identity column.

Retrieving Information About Objects

Data that describes other data is known as *metadata*. SQL Server offers a number of system functions that return metadata on various objects in a database. Some of these functions require an object ID as an argument to the function.

To obtain an object ID given an object name, you can use the OBJECT_ID() function. To return the object ID of the Accounts table, we would code as follows:

```
SELECT OBJECT_ID('Accounts')
---------
581577110
(1 row(s) affected)
```

The same result can be obtained by selecting the ID from the sysobjects system table:

```
SELECT id FROM sysobjects
WHERE name = 'Accounts'

id
---------
581577110
(1 row(s) affected)
```

We can use the OBJECT_ID() function call directly wherever we need an object ID as an argument rather than specifying the actual ID. One function where OBJECT_ID() can be used is the COLUMNPROPERTY() function to return metadata about a table column or a procedure parameter.

The COLUMNPROPERTY() function takes an object ID as the first argument, which is the object ID of a table or procedure, the name of a column or parameter as the second argument, and the name of the property you are interested in as the third argument.

To find out if the manager_num column in the Accounts table allows NULL values , we could code the following call to COLUMNPROPERTY():

```
SELECT COLUMNPROPERTY(OBJECT_ID('Accounts'),'manager_num',
'allowsnull')


-----------
1
(1 row(s) affected)
```

A TRUE return value from COLUMNPROPERTY() indicates that manager_num does allow NULL values. A FALSE return value would indicate manager_num does not allow NULL values and a NULL return value would indicate that the specified column or parameter name was not found in the object referred to by the object ID argument.

Other properties you can query with the COLUMNPROPERTY() function are listed in Table 7-4.

TABLE 7-4 PROPERTY NAMES FOR THE COLUMNPROPERTY() FUNCTION

Property	Description
allowsnull	Returns TRUE if column or parameter allows NULL values.
isidentity	TRUE if column is an identity column
isidnotforrepl	TRUE if IDENTITY-INSERT setting is checked for the column
isoutparam	TRUE if the parameter is an output parameter of the procedure
isrowguidcol	TRUE if the column has the uniqueidentifier type and the ROWGUIDCOL property
prccision	Returns the precision of the column
scale	Returns the scale of the column
usesansitrim	TRUE indicates ANSI padding was on when table was created

Note that some of the properties in Table 7-4 only apply to columns and some only to parameters.

Appendix D lists other system functions that are useful for returning metadata on a variety of database objects.

Using User Identification Functions

The functions explored here are useful for identifying the user logged in to a SQL Server session and database. A common application of these functions is to track changes to data by logging the user who made the changes in a table or special log file.

The following functions return the login ID of the database user executing this function:

```
SELECT USER
SELECT USER_NAME()
SELECT CURRENT_USER
------------------
Zachary
------------------
Zachary
------------------
Zachary
```

The USER_NAME() function can take a UID argument to return the user name with that ID in the sysusers system table. With no argument, the function returns the current user.

You can use these functions for DEFAULT values to be inserted into a table column to identify the user adding or updating the row. This is often paired with a timestamp column to indicate when the addition or change was made.

The column used for this purpose can have either a timestamp data type, which is automatically updated by SQL Server, or a datetime data type. If you use a datetime data type, you can use the CURRENT_TIMESTAMP() function as a DEFAULT or assign it yourself in your code:

```
SELECT CURRENT_TIMESTAMP
-----------------------
1998-02-28 14:44:32.793
(1 row(s) affected)
```

Using Text and Image Functions

We don't store any image data in the same mutual fund accounts database, and the only text data we store is for comments on each of the Accounts rows.

In Chapter 11, we explore the Transact-SQL statements necessary for working with these special data types.

In this section, we'll look at some of the functions you can use on text and image data types, a couple of which perform the same as they do for character strings.

Using the TEXTPTR() Function

The TEXTPTR() function returns the 16-byte pointer associated with a text or image column that points to the actual text and image data stored separately. Many of the statements and functions that work with text and image data require a valid TEXTPTR() to locate the data:

```
SELECT acct_no,TEXTPTR(acct_note)
FROM Accounts


acct_no
---------- ----------------------------------
1003       0xF3FFF92A00000000002701000001000100
1004       NULL
1005       NULL
1006       NULL
1007       NULL
1008       NULL
1009       NULL
1010       NULL
1011       NULL
1012       NULL
1013       NULL
...
1067       NULL
1068       NULL
1069       NULL
1070       NULL
1992       0xF3FF650000000000004101000001000000
9847       NULL
(32 row(s) affected)
```

You can see from the above SELECT statement that only two of the accounts have notes associated with them at the moment.

If we want to ensure that a TEXTPTR() is valid before using it, we can use the TEXTVALID() function and pass to it a TEXTPTR() to check. If the TEXTPTR() is valid, TEXTVALID() returns TRUE; otherwise, it returns FALSE:

```
SELECT acct_no,TEXTVALID('Accounts.acct_note',
   TEXTPTR(acct_note))
FROM Accounts
acct_no
---------- -----------
1003       1
1004       0
1005       0
1006       0
1007       0
1008       0
1009       0
1010       0
1011       0
1012       0
1013       0
...
1067       0
1068       0
1069       0
1070       0
1992       1
9847       0
(32 row(s) affected)
```

Using PATINDEX() to Locate a Substring

The PATINDEX() function returns the starting position of an expression within the text data.

If we wanted to locate the starting position of a known string stored within an account note, we would code the following:

```
SELECT PATINDEX('%discuss%',acct_note)
FROM Accounts
WHERE acct_no = '1003'
-----------
78
(1 row(s) affected)
```

The pattern expression can use wildcard characters (%) at either end of the pattern to represent any characters in the match expression. This behaves like the % wildcard used in the LIKE clause discussed in Chapter 6.

By itself, the position returned by PATINDEX() isn't of much value to us, but we can use it in functions like SUBSTRING() to specify a starting position in the text to extract a substring.

Using SUBSTRING() to Extract Strings from Text

We can use SUBSTRING() to extract a string from text data just as we did from character string data earlier in this chapter. The arguments are used the same here as they were for character strings:

```
SELECT SUBSTRING(acct_note,PATINDEX('%discuss%',acct_note),
DATALENGTH(acct_note))
FROM Accounts
WHERE acct_no = '1003'
-------------------------
discuss funds for college
(1 row(s) affected)
```

The return value from the PATINDEX() function discussed in the section above is used as the second argument to SUBSTRING() to specify the starting position at which to start extracting the substring. The third argument specifies the length to extract.

As you can see from these examples, working with text data is no harder than working with character data, and we can even use the same functions on both data types.

Summary

In this chapter we've explored some of the functions available from SQL Server. We've learned about the function categories offered by SQL Server and looked at some of the more commonly used functions in each category.

Further exploration on your own with these functions and the ones listed in Appendix D of this book will help a great deal in your programming projects. The more familiar you are with the available functions, the easier your job will become.

As we progress through the rest of the book, you'll find more examples of some of these functions. Although we used rather simple examples of function calls in this chapter to gain a fundamental understanding of how the functions work, remember that most functions can be nested in powerful ways to achieve required results with minimal coding.

Chapter 8

Grouping and Totaling

IN THIS CHAPTER

- ◆ Discover how to summarize data into groups
- ◆ Learn how to display summary information for nested groups
- ◆ See how to restrict results based on group information
- ◆ Learn how to display detail rows and summary rows in one result set
- ◆ Explore methods of displaying group breaks and totals
- ◆ Find out how to show a grand total across multiple groups

WITH THE EXCEPTION of the aggregate functions explored in Chapter 7, the SELECT statements we've been working with up to now have returned result sets containing one row for each set of columns we requested.

The aggregate functions section in Chapter 7 showed us that data can be summarized by SQL Server and returned as an aggregate result in one row. When we ask for an aggregate, we don't see the individual rows that make up the aggregate, but only the summary row that is returned.

How would we find the total assets under management by each account manager in the firm?

We'll learn in this chapter how to return summary data, along with the detail that goes into its makeup. First we'll explore how to return summary information by groups such as manager, ZIP, or some other column in our database that makes sense as a group.

Using the GROUP BY Clause

In Chapter 7 we discussed the following statement:

```
SELECT SUM(tot_assets) FROM Accounts
```

This statement returns the sum of the tot_assets column for every row in the Accounts table. SUM() is an aggregate function applied to the domain of tot_assets.

Using the above statement tells us the total assets under management by the firm, assuming all accounts are open, but says nothing about the assets under management by the individual managers in the firm.

To find out how much money each manager is managing, we can use the following statement:

```
SELECT manager_num,SUM(tot_assets) AS 'Assets Managed'
FROM Accounts
GROUP BY manager_num
ORDER BY 'Assets Managed'

manager_num Assets Managed
----------- --------------------
2877        472962.7980
2321        681603.7930
9277        1051153.3560
1647        1791112.7485
(4 row(s) affected)
```

The addition of the GROUP BY clause in our SELECT statement now applies the SUM() aggregate function to the rows in each manager_num group. This is the result equivalent to sorting the rows on manager_num, totaling the tot_assets to obtain a sum for each unique manager_num, and displaying these sums with their corresponding manager_num.

GROUP BY does not require that you include the GROUP BY column in the SELECT SELECTcolumn list. Omitting the manager_num from column list in the above SELECT statement would look like this:

```
SELECT SUM(tot_assets) AS 'Assets Managed'
FROM Accounts
GROUP BY manager_num
ORDER BY 'Assets Managed'

Assets Managed
--------------------
472962.7980
681603.7930
1051153.3560
1791112.7485
(4 row(s) affected)
```

You get the same sums as with the manager_num included, but you can't relate those sums to the manager_num they belong to. Nonetheless, it is valid to do this and may be useful in some applications.

If one of your grouping columns contains a NULL value, the NULL becomes a group in itself and all aggregate values, if any for that group, will be reported in the NULL group.

Selecting Nonaggregate Columns

Let's assume that each manager in the firm manages accounts only within one ZIP code area and we want to see this ZIP code along with their total assets managed. We would code the following:

```
SELECT manager_num,zip,SUM(tot_assets)
AS 'Assets Managed'
FROM Accounts
GROUP BY manager_num
ORDER BY 'Assets Managed'
```

SQL Server returns the results below:

```
Server: Msg 8120, Level 16, State 42000
Column 'Accounts.zip' is invalid in the select list because it is
not contained in either an aggregate
function or the GROUP BY clause.
```

What happened? We presume that each manager has only one ZIP code associated with him or her, so why can't SQL Server display it along with the man-ager_num?

The problem is that *we* presume the ZIP code is unique among managers, but SQL Server doesn't know that. As far as SQL Server is concerned, a zip column can contain any character string up to 10 characters long. Therefore, it doesn't make sense to display *one* zip value for the group when *multiple* zip values can be found within that group.

To fix this, we humor SQL Server and comply with its rules by including the zip column in the GROUP BY clause:

```
SELECT manager_num,zip,SUM(tot_assets)
 AS 'Assets Managed'
FROM Accounts
GROUP BY manager_num,zip
ORDER BY manager_num,zip
```

manager_num	zip	Assets Managed
1647	06016	68534.2680
1647	06473	186276.0425
1647	06478	82334.4720
1647	06489	69711.2900
1647	06510	202457.3540
1647	06511	113570.0940
1647	06880	248877.1340
1647	12633	313056.0620
1647	33416	506296.0320
2321	06001	67657.1720
2321	06109	34586.0000
2321	06472	69381.3120

```
2321        06473        218546.7170
2321        06511        134290.2660
2321        06514        56454.3980
2321        06798        100687.9280
2877        06066        17161.7160
2877        06111        120256.5100
2877        06118        70962.0120
2877        06443        141651.0260
2877        06475        .0000
2877        06511        10371.7900
2877        10533        111114.0800
2877        77015        1445.6640
9277        06117        31633.4040
9277        06405        52693.8060
9277        06503        283774.9860
9277        06511        415534.1080
9277        06515        36237.5860
9277        28115        231279.4660
(30 row(s) affected)
```

I guess our assumption was wrong! If each manager was associated with only one ZIP code, then we would expect to see the zip column contain the same zip value wherever the manager number was equal. Since we don't see those expected results, our assumption is not true.

What can we learn from this? The basic rule when using GROUP BY is to include in the GROUP BY list all nonaggregate columns found in the SELECT column list. In the case above, we are selecting manager_num and zip, so the rule states that these columns must be included in the GROUP BY list.

Including both manager_num and zip in the GROUP BY list gives us a grouping within a group. Here, we have the sum of tot_assets by zip within manager_num. In other words, the tot_assets are totaled from rows with unique combinations of zip and manager_num.

Here's another rule. Notice that in a previous example above we used an alias of 'Assets Managed' for the sum of the tot_assets and that we specified this alias as the column on which to order the results. It is perfectly valid to use an alias in an ORDER BY clause, but *not* in a GROUP BY clause. SQL Server requires that you use a column name in the GROUP BY clause and not an alias.

A note on the ORDER BY clause. You could also use the following syntax instead of using an alias:

```
ORDER BY SUM(tot_assets)
```

Using a WHERE Clause to Restrict Rows

You can restrict the rows that will participate in the aggregate groups to some condition by using the WHERE clause just as you do in a nongrouped query:

```
SELECT manager_num,SUM(tot_assets) AS 'Assets Managed'
```

```
FROM Accounts
WHERE state_abbr = 'CT'
GROUP BY manager_num
ORDER BY 'Assets Managed'

manager_num Assets Managed
----------- --------------------
2877           360403.0540
2321           681603.7930
1647           785484.6120
9277           819873.8900
(4 row(s) affected)
```

When we executed the above query without the WHERE clause, manager number 2877 had 472,962.7980 for a total. This sum was acquired from all rows having this manager number. Now that we are limiting the rows to only the state of Connecticut, manager number 2877 has a lower total of assets managed, indicating that this manager is managing accounts in other states. Manager 2321 however manages accounts with addresses solely in the state of Connecticut.

Using the ALL Keyword

When using a WHERE clause to restrict returned rows as we did above, we can lose some of the groups that were present when we don't restrict the results. If some of the managers managed accounts in New York and we restricted our results to that state, we would only see the manager groups with New York accounts, and other managers would not be listed:

```
SELECT manager_num,SUM(tot_assets) AS 'Assets Managed'
FROM Accounts
WHERE state_abbr = 'NY'
GROUP BY manager_num
ORDER BY 'Assets Managed'

manager_num Assets Managed
----------- --------------------
2877           111114.0800
1647           313056.0620
(2 row(s) affected)
```

Even though there are only two managers with New York accounts, we may want to see the other manager groups listed as well. We can use the ALL keyword in the GROUP BY clause to accomplish this:

```
SELECT manager_num,SUM(tot_assets) AS 'Assets Managed'
FROM Accounts
WHERE state_abbr = 'NY'
GROUP BY ALL manager_num
ORDER BY 'Assets Managed'
```

```
manager_num Assets Managed
----------- --------------------
2321        .0000
9277        .0000
2877        111114.0800
1647        313056.0620
(4 row(s) affected)
```

Using the ALL keyword caused all of the groups we requested in the GROUP BY clause to be returned even though those groups don't meet the WHERE clause criteria, indicated by the zero sum in the Assets Managed column.

Restricting Grouped Results

Using the WHERE clause in a SELECT statement restricts the result set to rows meeting the WHERE clause condition. In the previous section, we used a WHERE clause to restrict the rows that went into the SUM() function and then grouped them. Think of this as restriction *before* grouping. This same restriction process can be applied to select rows into a result set when using WHERE in a statement without GROUP BY.

How can we apply a condition to a group – that is, after the grouping has been completed but before the results are returned? To do this, we use a HAVING clause:

```
SELECT manager_num,SUM(tot_assets) AS 'Assets Managed'
FROM Accounts
GROUP BY manager_num
HAVING SUM(tot_assets) > 1000000
ORDER BY 'Assets Managed'

manager_num Assets Managed
----------- --------------------
9277        1051153.3560
1647        1791112.7485
(2 row(s) affected)
```

The above statement requests total assets managed by manager number as we've been doing, but this time we've asked SQL Server to restrict the returned results to groups having more than $1 million under management (for bonus purposes no doubt).

Using the HAVING clause restricts rows *after* grouping. The HAVING clause condition is applied to the group and not to the rows that make up the group, as a WHERE clause does.

Using WHERE and HAVING Together

We've seen that using WHERE can restrict rows that go into the grouping and aggregate calculations and that HAVING can restrict groups returned in a result set. Let's use them together:

```
SELECT manager_num,SUM(tot_assets) AS 'Assets Managed'
FROM Accounts
WHERE acct_status = 'open'
GROUP BY manager_num
HAVING SUM(tot_assets) > 1000000
ORDER BY 'Assets Managed'
manager_num Assets Managed
----------- --------------------
1647        1791112.7485
(1 row(s) affected)
```

Using a WHERE clause to restrict the rows that are summed to only those with Open accounts (acct_status column contains 'Open') and then asking for total assets greater than $1 million yields a different result from our previous query.

Without consideration for the account status, manager number 9277 was displayed as a manager with over $1 million under management. Taking account status into consideration, however, we see that only manager 1647 really manages assets that large (another bonus spoiled by a SQL Server query, darn!).

Interrogating Groups Without Using Aggregates

We can use HAVING to interrogate groups with some characteristics without regard for any summary information.

Say that we suspect that our state abbreviations for accounts with addresses in Connecticut are not accurate and we want to inspect our more trusted ZIP codes as a check against the state abbreviations. To do this, we code the following:

```
SELECT zip,state_abbr
FROM Accounts
GROUP BY zip,state_abbr
HAVING zip LIKE '06%'
ORDER BY zip

zip         state_abbr
----------  ----------
06001       CT
06016       CT
06066       CT
06109       CT
06111       CT
06117       CT
06118       CT
06405       CT
06443       CT
06472       CT
06473       CA
06473       CT
06475       CT
06478       CT
06489       CT
06503       CT
```

```
06510      CT
06511      CT
06514      CT
06515      CT
06798      CT
06880      CT
(22 row(s) affected)
```

Since our GROUP BY clause is asking for unique combinations of zip and state_abbr, a duplicate zip in the results would indicate that one or more accounts with Connecticut ZIP codes have a state_abbr other than CT. As we can see from the results above, ZIP code 06473 has found a problem.

Displaying the Number of Entries in a Group

We discovered above that ZIP code 06473 has one or more accounts with an improper state_abbr. Let's find out how many rows have this condition.

To list the number of rows with the displayed zip and state_abbr combination, we code the following:

```
SELECT zip,state_abbr,COUNT(*)
FROM Accounts
GROUP BY zip,state_abbr
HAVING zip LIKE '06%'
ORDER BY zip
```

```
zip          state_abbr
----------   ----------   ----------
06001        CT           1
06016        CT           1
06066        CT           1
06109        CT           1
06111        CT           1
06117        CT           1
06118        CT           1
06405        CT           1
06443        CT           1
06472        CT           1
06473        CA           1
06473        CT           1
06475        CT           1
06478        CT           1
06489        CT           1
06503        CT           1
06510        CT           1
06511        CT           6
06514        CT           1
06515        CT           1
06798        CT           1
06880        CT           1
(22 row(s) affected)
```

From the above, we discover that 06473 CA is found on only one row in the Accounts table. A simple UPDATE statement would correct the problem.

We can use functions in our HAVING clause, too. If we were interested in the most popular ZIP codes in the Accounts table, we could code something like this:

```
SELECT zip,COUNT(*)
FROM Accounts
GROUP BY zip
HAVING COUNT(*) > 1
ORDER BY zip

zip
---------- -----------
06473        2
06511        6
(2 row(s) affected)
```

A comparison of this result with the one above it indicates that the update to fix our 06473 problem row has not yet been applied.

Using COMPUTE and COMPUTE BY

Using the GROUP BY clause, we can display summary information on groups, as we've seen in the preceding sections. When we use GROUP BY, we only get the group summaries, we don't see the individual rows that make up the group. Transact-SQL does have a solution that lets us request the detail and the summary in one SELECT statement. That solution involves the use of the COMPUTE clause:

```
SELECT manager_num,tot_assets
FROM Accounts
ORDER BY manager_num
COMPUTE SUM(tot_assets) BY manager_num

manager_num tot_assets
----------- --------------------
1647        202457.3540
1647        34738.6380
1647        186276.0425
1647        68534.2680
1647        506296.0320
1647        313056.0620
1647        69711.2900
1647        82334.4720
1647        78831.4560
1647        248877.1340

(10 row(s) affected)
sum
```

```
--------------------
1791112.7485

(1 row(s) affected)
manager_num tot_assets
----------- --------------------
2321        56454.3980
2321        134290.2660
2321        100687.9280
2321        69381.3120
2321        67657.1720
2321        218546.7170
2321        34586.0000

(7 row(s) affected)
sum
--------------------
681603.7930

(1 row(s) affected)

manager_num tot_assets
----------- --------------------
2877        .0000
2877        141651.0260
2877        70962.0120
2877        111114.0800
2877        120256.5100
2877        10371.7900
2877        17161.7160
2877        1445.6640

(8 row(s) affected)

sum
--------------------
472962.7980

(1 row(s) affected)

manager_num tot_assets
----------- --------------------
9277        52693.8060
9277        217219.6400
9277        198314.4680
9277        36237.5860
9277        31633.4040
9277        283774.9860
9277        231279.4660

(7 row(s) affected)
```

```
sum
--------------------
1051153.3560

(1 row(s) affected)
```

Taking a look at the first set of rows in the result, we see that manager 1647 has 10 rows (accounts) that make up the total assets under management of 1,791,112.7485. This is the same total reported to us earlier when we used the GROUP BY statement.

The use of COMPUTE BY involves a sort on the BY column, which is required, a display of all rows with the same BY value and then finally, a group break and the row aggregate of those rows – in this case, the SUM() of total assets.

When using COMPUTE, the columns you list in the COMPUTE clause must be in the SELECT column list. If you use the BY keyword, you must also specify an ORDER BY clause and the columns in the BY clause must be a subset of the columns in the ORDER BY clause. If you use a subset of the ORDER BY columns in the BY clause, your subset must be specified from left to right without omission:

```
SELECT zip,manager_num,tot_assets
FROM Accounts
ORDER BY zip,manager_num
COMPUTE SUM(tot_assets) BY manager_num

Server: Msg 163, Level 15, State 42000
The COMPUTE BY list does not match the ORDER BY list.
```

In the above statement, we could use BY zip or BY zip, manager_num to correct the problem.

Using Multiple COMPUTE BY Clauses

To calculate a total for a subgroup and then a total for an outer group, you would use two COMPUTE BY clauses. This yields a break and the row aggregate reported for each of the COMPUTE BY clauses in order:

```
SELECT zip,manager_num,tot_assets
FROM Accounts
WHERE zip = '06511'
ORDER BY zip,manager_num
COMPUTE SUM(tot_assets) BY zip,manager_num
COMPUTE SUM(tot_assets) BY zip

zip        manager_num tot_assets
---------- ----------- --------------------
06511      1647        34738.6380
06511      1647        78831.4560

(2 row(s) affected)
```

```
sum
--------------------
113570.0940

(1 row(s) affected)

zip         manager_num tot_assets
----------- ----------- --------------------
06511       2321        134290.2660

(1 row(s) affected)

sum
--------------------
134290.2660

(1 row(s) affected)

zip         manager_num tot_assets
----------- ----------- --------------------
06511       2877        10371.7900
(1 row(s) affected)
sum
--------------------
10371.7900

(1 row(s) affected)

zip         manager_num tot_assets
----------- ----------- --------------------
06511       9277        217219.6400
06511       9277        198314.4680

(2 row(s) affected)
sum
--------------------
415534.1080

(1 row(s) affected)

sum
--------------------
673766.2580

(1 row(s) affected)
```

This statement displays results that break on unique combinations of `zip` and `manager_num` and shows the sum of the total assets at this break. The display then continues to show the next unique group of `zip` and `manager_num` and its total.

Finally, when the ZIP code value changes, we get another break and a total displayed for the entire ZIP code. This is shown as the last sum in the above display.

Displaying Multiple Aggregates

You are not restricted to using only one aggregate at a break. This next example shows the total assets for the `zip` and `manager_num` group along with the count of managers in the group:

```
SELECT zip,manager_num,tot_assets
FROM Accounts
WHERE zip = '06511'
ORDER BY zip,manager_num
COMPUTE SUM(tot_assets),COUNT(manager_num)
BY zip,manager_num
```

```
zip         manager_num tot_assets
----------  ----------- --------------------
06511       1647        34738.6380
06511       1647        78831.4560

(2 row(s) affected)

sum                      cnt
--------------------     -----------
113570.0940              2

(1 row(s) affected)

zip         manager_num tot_assets
----------  ----------- --------------------
06511       2321        134290.2660

(1 row(s) affected)

sum                      cnt
--------------------     -----------
134290.2660              1

(1 row(s) affected)

zip         manager_num tot_assets
----------  ----------- --------------------
06511       2877        10371.7900

(1 row(s) affected)

sum                      cnt
--------------------     -----------
10371.7900               1
```

```
(1 row(s) affected)

zip         manager_num tot_assets
----------  ----------- --------------------
06511       9277        217219.6400
06511       9277        198314.4680

(2 row(s) affected)

sum                  cnt
-------------------- -----------
415534.1080          2

(1 row(s) affected)
```

Not only can you use multiple row aggregate functions, but as you can see from the above example, the functions can be different.

Displaying a Grand Total

The COMPUTE clause can be used without the BY keyword to display a grand total across the entire result set. In the statement below, we show the sum of tot_assets at each zip break and at the very end of the result set we show the grand total of the tot_assets across all ZIP code displayed:

```
SELECT zip,manager_num,tot_assets
FROM Accounts
ORDER BY zip,manager_num
COMPUTE SUM(tot_assets),COUNT(manager_num) BY zip
COMPUTE SUM(tot_assets)
```

Here's a partial display of the result set:

```
...
zip         manager_num tot_assets
----------  ----------- --------------------
06511       1647        34738.6380
06511       1647        78831.4560
06511       2321        134290.2660
06511       2877        10371.7900
06511       9277        217219.6400
06511       9277        198314.4680

(6 row(s) affected)

sum                  cnt
-------------------- -----------
673766.2580          6

(1 row(s) affected)
```

```
zip        manager_num tot_assets
---------- ----------- --------------------
06514      2321        56454.3980

(1 row(s) affected)

sum                     cnt
--------------------    -----------
56454.3980              1

(1 row(s) affected)

zip        manager_num tot_assets
---------- ----------- --------------------
06515      9277        36237.5860

(1 row(s) affected)
...
sum
--------------------
3996832.6955

(1 row(s) affected)
```

Notice that the last sum displayed does not contain a count as we've requested for each `zip` code group break, but only the sum of the total assets across all ZIP codes.

Summary

This chapter has explored the use of the `GROUP BY` clause and the `COMPUTE BY` clause of the Transact-SQL `SELECT` statement.

You've seen how to create groups of information in a SELECT statement and how to restrict values that go into those groups using a `WHERE` clause.

You saw how the `ALL` keyword can be used in a `GROUP BY` expression to return groups that don't match a `WHERE` condition but should be displayed to form a complete listing of all groups in the `GROUP BY` columns.

To filter out rows based on the grouped results, you learned that in addition to the `GROUP BY` clause, you can use a `HAVING` clause with a condition that is evaluated after the groups are determined.

Using `COMPUTE` clauses, you learned how to display one or more summaries for a group comprised of one or more columns. You discovered how to display totals at subset breaks as well as at breaks for major groupings.

At the end of the chapter, you saw how to cause a grand total to appear in a result set that shows a row aggregate for all rows in the result.

Chapter 9

Exploring Joins, Subqueries, and Unions

IN THIS CHAPTER

♦ Learn how to select data from joined tables

♦ Learn about the join types and how to use them

♦ Explore the use of subqueries and learn how they can be put to use in a WHERE clause

♦ Learn about the ANY and ALL modifiers when used with subqueries and relational operators

♦ Find out how a UNION works and how to use it

THE POWER OF the relational database becomes evident when you are able to pull data from multiple tables in a single SELECT query.

We've already seen some examples that relate two tables through the use of a WHERE clause. We've used a WHERE clause to compare one or more columns in one table with one or more columns in another table and select columns from both tables where the rows match.

In this chapter, we discover another method of relating two or more tables by using a join expression in the FROM clause of a data manipulation statement. We'll discover how to code joins in such a way as to retrieve rows from multiple tables where a join condition is met and, in addition, return rows from one or both of the tables regardless of the join condition, all from the same query.

Beyond joins, we'll explore ways to enhance the power of the SELECT query by nesting other queries inside of queries. These are known as subqueries and can be a very powerful addition to your arsenal of Transact-SQL knowledge.

Subqueries can be used as a data source in a FROM clause, and they can be used in a WHERE clause to form some very complex expressions for selecting rows.

Finally, in this chapter, we'll look at a method for combining the result sets from two or more separate queries into one result set using the UNION operator.

Exploring Joins Between Tables

When we studied the use of column aliases in Chapter 6, we saw a SELECT query that pulled data from both the Accounts and AccountValues tables. In the WHERE clause of that SELECT statement, we used an expression like this:

```
WHERE Accounts.acct_no = AccountValues.acct_no
```

This statement is specifying an *equijoin* between the Accounts table and the AccountValues table on the acct_no column.

Internally, SQL Server must pair rows of these two tables where the acct_no values are equal and, from this pairing, select the columns specified in the column list. Some columns can come from the Accounts table side and other columns from the AccountValues side.

Although it is not required, it helps performance if you have an index on the join columns of both tables. This enables the query optimizer to build a plan of execution that will use the indexes to locate matching rows in both tables and return the results more quickly. Without an index, SQL Server needs to scan one of the tables for each row in the other table looking for matches and pairing rows for each one found.

All join operations in a SELECT statement can be specified in the WHERE clause as we've done above. The ANSI-style syntax for specifying joins uses join operators and expressions in the FROM clause and leaves the WHERE clause for restricting the rows to be included in the join operation.

In the following sections we'll explore the ANSI-style syntax for expressing joins, but make note of the non-ANSI syntax so you'll recognize joins when you see them in older code.

CROSS JOINS

When you specify multiple tables as sources for your select column list but omit a WHERE clause or join expression for SQL Server to match rows on, the result set contains a row for every combination of rows between the two tables.

This result is known as the *Cartesian product* of the two tables. Every row in one of the tables is paired with every row of the other table, producing a result set with (*number of rows in table 1*) times (*number of rows in table 2*) rows.

Although the results are of no use to us, the CROSS JOIN can be illustrated with the following SELECT statement:

```
SELECT a.acct_no,tot_assets,invest_tot
FROM Accounts AS a CROSS JOIN Statements

acct_no     tot_assets              invest_tot
-------     -----------             ----------
1003        202457.3540             37462.8500
1004        .0000                   37462.8500
```

```
1005      34738.6380        37462.8500
1006      52693.8060        37462.8500
1007      217219.6400       37462.8500
1008      198314.4680       37462.8500
1009      186276.0425       37462.8500
1010      56454.3980        37462.8500
1011      141651.0260       37462.8500
1012      134290.2660       37462.8500
...
9847      34586.0000        37462.8500
1003      202457.3540       47265.1800
1004      .0000             47265.1800
1005      34738.6380        47265.1800
1006      52693.8060        47265.1800
1007      217219.6400       47265.1800
1008      198314.4680       47265.1800
1009      186276.0425       47265.1800
1010      56454.3980        47265.1800
1011      141651.0260       47265.1800
1012      134290.2660       47265.1800
...
(64 row(s) affected)
```

The result pairs each of the two rows currently in the Statements table with each of the 32 rows currently in the Accounts table to yield (32) times (2) 64 rows in the result set. You can easily see the repetition of acct_no invest_tot pairs in the results.

The use of the keyword CROSS JOIN is the ANSI-style (and preferred) syntax. To specify this same query in non-ANSI syntax, you would code as follows:

```
SELECT a.acct_no,tot_assets,invest_tot
FROM Accounts AS a, Statements
```

The results are the same as above. In both the ANSI-style and non-ANSI-style cross join syntax, there is no WHERE clause or other condition on which to match rows.

Using INNER JOINS

When we want to return only the rows that satisfy some matching condition, we use an INNER JOIN in the FROM clause.

Inner joins are frequently stated with equal conditions for matching one or more columns of one table in the join with another table. This is an equijoin in ANSI-style syntax to match Accounts table rows with Statements table rows on the acct_no column:

```
SELECT a.acct_no,tot_assets,
CONVERT(varchar(15),stmt_date,102)AS StmtDate,
invest_tot
```

```
FROM Accounts AS a INNER JOIN Statements
ON a.acct_no = Statements.acct_no

acct_no    tot_assets    StmtDate      invest_tot
-------    -----------   ----------    ----------
1003       202457.3540   1997.12.31    37462.8500
1003       202457.3540   1998.01.31    47265.1800

(2 row(s) affected)
```

With the INNER JOIN and the match condition specified in the ON clause, we see only two rows returned in the result set. These are the rows that result from matching the acct_no in Accounts to acct_no in Statements and selecting the acct_no and tot_assets from the Accounts table side of the match and the stmt_date and invest_tot from the Statements side of the match.

When you include the match column from only one of the tables in the result set as we did above, instead of from both tables, the join is known as a *natural join.*

INNER JOINS can specify match conditions using operators other than the equal operator. To return rows from a join between the Statements table and the AccountValues table where the account numbers and statement dates are equal and the investment totals are not equal, we code as follows:

```
SELECT a.acct_no,
CONVERT(varchar(15),a.stmt_date,102) AS StmtDate,
a.invest_tot,b.invest_tot
FROM Statements AS a INNER JOIN AccountValues AS b
ON a.acct_no = b.acct_no AND
   a.stmt_date = b.stmt_date AND
   a.invest_tot <> b.invest_tot

acct_no    StmtDate      invest_tot    invest_tot
-------    ----------    ----------    ----------
1003       1998.01.31    47265.1800    37462.8500

(1 row(s) affected)
```

From this statement, we can see that the AccountValues table is out of sync with the Statements table in that matching accounts and statement date entries in both tables do not have the same investment totals.

Notice in the above statement's ON clause that we've used multiple conditions for matching rows. This is done to ensure that we include key values and don't match rows based only on investment totals not being equal. If we specified only the not equal condition, our result set would indicate multiple integrity problems when in fact we only have one.

In non-ANSI syntax, the above statement would look like this:

```
SELECT a.acct_no,
 CONVERT(varchar(15),a.stmt_date,102) AS StmtDate,
 a.invest_tot,b.invest_tot
FROM Statements AS a,AccountValues AS b
```

```
WHERE a.acct_no = b.acct_no AND
      a.stmt_date = b.stmt_date AND
      a.invest_tot <> b.invest_tot
```

The operators you can use in specifying the match conditions for the INNER
JOIN and the other JOIN types we'll explore next are found in Table 9-1.

TABLE 9-1 OPERATORS USED IN MATCH CONDITIONS

Operator	Description
=	Equal to
<	Less than
>	Greater than
<=	Less than or equal to
>=	Greater than or equal to
<>	Not equal to
!<	Not less than
!>	Not greater than

Using LEFT, RIGHT, and FULL OUTER JOIN Operations

Outer joins are used to return matching rows in addition to rows that don't match.
The rows that don't match are selected from either the left (first) table in the FROM
clause, the right (second) table in the FROM clause, or both tables.

When you specify the LEFT OUTER JOIN in the FROM clause, you are telling SQL
Server to return columns from matching rows and columns from the left table in the
FROM clause with NULL values replacing columns of the right table in the FROM clause.

Likewise, if you specify the RIGHT OUTER JOIN, you are asking for columns from
matching rows in addition to columns from the right table in the FROM clause with
NULL values replacing columns in the left table in the FROM clause.

If FULL OUTER JOIN is used, you get the combination of the LEFT OUTER JOIN
and the RIGHT OUTER JOIN in your result set.

The outer joins are useful for representing all rows of a table in the result set
whether or not a match is found in the joined table. Seeing NULL values in columns
from the joined table (selected columns cannot allow NULL values) indicates that no
match was found by SQL Server and you can process this according to your application requirements.

If, for example, we want to see all account numbers and the Statements cur_value column from matching account number and statement dates between the AccountValues and Statements tables regardless of the existence of a statement, we could code the following:

```
SELECT b.acct_no,
  CONVERT(varchar(15),b.stmt_date,102) AS StmtDate,
  a.cur_value
FROM Statements AS a RIGHT OUTER JOIN AccountValues AS b
ON a.acct_no = b.acct_no AND
   a.stmt_date = b.stmt_date
ORDER BY b.acct_no,StmtDate
```

```
acct_no   StmtDate       cur_value
-------   ----------     ---------
1001      1991.09.30     NULL
1001      1991.12.31     NULL
1001      1991.12.31     NULL
1001      1994.09.30     NULL
1001      1994.12.31     NULL
1001      1995.07.31     NULL
1001      1996.03.31     NULL
1003      1988.12.31     NULL
1003      1988.12.31     NULL
1003      1989.03.31     NULL
1003      1989.06.30     NULL
1003      1989.09.30     NULL
1003      1989.12.31     NULL
1003      1989.12.31     NULL
1003      1990.03.31     NULL
1003      1990.06.30     NULL
1003      1990.09.30     NULL
1003      1990.12.31     NULL
1003      1991.03.31     NULL
1003      1991.06.30     NULL
1003      1991.09.30     NULL
1003      1991.12.31     NULL
1003      1992.03.31     NULL
1003      1992.06.30     NULL
1003      1992.09.30     NULL
1003      1992.12.31     172786.4100
1003      1993.03.31     179836.8700
1003      1994.09.30     202039.2200
1003      1994.12.31     202457.3500
1003      1996.03.31     202457.3500
...
1992      1991.06.30     NULL
1992      1991.09.30     NULL
1992      1991.12.31     NULL
1992      1991.12.31     NULL
1992      1992.03.31     NULL
1992      1992.06.30     NULL
1992      1992.09.30     NULL
1992      1992.12.31     152463.3300
```

```
1992        1992.12.31        152463.3300
1992        1994.06.30        153698.9200
1992        1994.12.31        165785.6900
1992        1995.03.31        160230.2800
1992        1995.06.30        185442.8100
1992        1995.07.31        218546.7100
```

```
(211 row(s) affected)
```

The results tell us that for many of the AccountValues rows, there is no matching account number and statement date row in the Statements table. This is indicated by the NULL value returned in the cur_value column. Remember, the cur_value column in the Statements table is defined as NOT NULL, so a NULL returned in this result indicates a match could not be found for the specified match condition.

Since we originally defined the AccountValues table to hold the value of an account as of each of the statement dates in the Statements table, the above result set indicates a problem in the database. We'll solve this problem shortly by deleting all AccountValues rows that don't have matching Statements rows.

While we're on the subject of NULL values, note that a NULL value in a join column – that is a column used for matching – will not match to anything, even another NULL value.

The non-ANSI version of the above outer join would look like this: *not*

```
SELECT b.acct_no,
 CONVERT(varchar(15),b.stmt_date,102) AS StmtDate,
 a.cur_value
FROM Statements AS a,AccountValues AS b
WHERE a.acct_no =* b.acct_no AND
    a.stmt_date =* b.stmt_date
ORDER BY b.acct_no,StmtDate
```

Using SELF-JOINS

SQL Server allows you to join a table to itself. This is done when you need to pull information from relationships that exist within the same table.

For example, say we were asked to produce a report for each account as of the December 1992 statement showing all other accounts for the same statement period that have higher current values. All information relevant to the request is stored in either the Statements table or the AccountValues table. Since our AccountValues table is in question at the moment (as discovered from the above outer join exercise), we'll use the Statements table and code the following SELECT statement:

```
SELECT S1.acct_no,CONVERT(varchar(10),S1.stmt_date,102) AS
 StmtDate,S1.cur_value,S2.acct_no,S2.cur_value
FROM Statements S1 INNER JOIN Statements S2
ON S1.stmt_date = S2.stmt_date
WHERE S1.cur_value < S2.cur_value AND
```

```
    S1.stmt_date = '1992-12-31'
ORDER BY S1.acct_no,S1.stmt_date

acct_no    StmtDate    cur_value    acct_no    cur_value
-------    ----------  -----------  -------    -----------
1003       1992.12.31  172786.4100  1008       261368.6300
1003       1992.12.31  172786.4100  1023       222977.2000
1003       1992.12.31  172786.4100  1029       220206.1400
1003       1992.12.31  172786.4100  1012       247522.4900
1004       1992.12.31  162730.4400  1003       172786.4100
1004       1992.12.31  162730.4400  1008       261368.6300
1004       1992.12.31  162730.4400  1023       222977.2000
1004       1992.12.31  162730.4400  1029       220206.1400
1004       1992.12.31  162730.4400  1012       247522.4900
...
9847       1992.12.31  84714.4100   1992       152463.3300
9847       1992.12.31  84714.4100   1003       172786.4100
9847       1992.12.31  84714.4100   1004       162730.4400
9847       1992.12.31  84714.4100   1007       131161.4400
9847       1992.12.31  84714.4100   1008       261368.6300
9847       1992.12.31  84714.4100   1027       143694.3300
9847       1992.12.31  84714.4100   1024       109190.0400
9847       1992.12.31  84714.4100   1023       222977.2000
9847       1992.12.31  84714.4100   1018       85921.8800
9847       1992.12.31  84714.4100   1029       220206.1400
9847       1992.12.31  84714.4100   1012       247522.4900

(378 row(s) affected)
```

The result set displays each of the accounts found in the Statements table where the statement date is '1992.12.31' and shows every other account for the same statement having a higher current value than the account displayed at the left of the report.

You can run a quick visual check on this result. Since account 9847 has a lower current value than account 1003, we would not expect to find account number 9847 in the list for account number 1003. On the other hand, account number 1003 should appear in the list for account 9847 since the current value for 1003 is greater than the current value for 9847. The same relationship holds for account number 1004. Checking the above results verifies our expectations.

Self-joins can be confusing at times, and it helps to think of the one table as two separate (and identical) tables and design your joins with this vision in mind. The use of aliases in the self-join query, as done above, helps in this respect.

Joining More Than Two Tables

When we work with joined tables, we think in terms of just two tables being involved in the join operation. This is indeed the model we work with when performing a LEFT OUTER or RIGHT OUTER JOIN. These joins imply a two-table involvement.

Although two tables are considered in each join operation, we are not limited to specifying just two tables in the join. We can join much more than that.

Let's create a join between the Accounts table, the Statements table and the AccountValues table:

```
SELECT a1.acct_no, a1.home_phone,
  CONVERT(varchar(15),a2.stmt_date,102)StmtDate,
  a2.cur_value,s1.invest_tot
FROM Accounts a1 INNER JOIN AccountValues a2
 ON a1.acct_no = a2.acct_no INNER JOIN Statements s1
 ON a2.acct_no = s1.acct_no AND
    a2.stmt_date = s1.stmt_date
ORDER BY a1.acct_no,a2.stmt_date DESC
```

acct_no	home_phone	StmtDate	cur_value	invest_tot
1003	NULL	1996.03.31	202457.3500	125315.6300
1003	NULL	1994.12.31	202457.3500	125315.6300
1003	NULL	1994.09.30	202039.2200	125315.6300
1003	NULL	1992.12.31	172786.4100	125315.6300
1004	999-9999	1996.03.31	164014.9700	118900.6200
1004	999-9999	1994.12.31	164014.9700	118900.6200
1004	999-9999	1993.09.30	117208.7800	118900.6200
1004	999-9999	1993.03.31	177200.4700	118900.6200
1004	999-9999	1992.12.31	168184.3100	118900.6200
1005	888-8888	1994.12.31	34738.6300	19314.3300
1005	888-8888	1993.03.31	58749.8900	57000.0000
...				
1070	444-1111	1994.12.31	248877.1300	177604.9600
1992	222-2222	1995.07.31	218546.7100	129135.6800
1992	222-2222	1995.06.30	185442.8100	129135.6800
1992	222-2222	1995.03.31	160230.2800	129135.6800
1992	222-2222	1994.12.31	165785.6900	129135.6800
1992	222-2222	1994.06.30	153698.9200	129135.6800
1992	222-2222	1992.12.31	149103.9200	121093.5200
1992	222-2222	1992.12.31	149103.9200	121093.5200

```
(65 row(s) affected)
```

In this statement, we join the Accounts table to the AccountValues table on account number and then join AccountValues to Statements on account number and statement date — still working with two tables at a time.

You can join as many tables as you need up to the limit of 64 tables per SELECT statement.

Exploring Subqueries

Subqueries are SELECT statements nested within a data manipulation statement. Subqueries can return one or more values, depending on their use, from any table.

You've seen some subqueries in preceding examples where we've selected a value from a table for comparison in an outer query.

In Chapter 6, we find this statement:

```
UPDATE AccountValues
  SET AccountValues.stmt_date = b.stmt_date,
      AccountValues.cur_value = b.cur_value
  FROM AccountValues,Statements AS b
  WHERE  AccountValues.acct_no = '1003'
  AND AccountValues.acct_no = b.acct_no
  AND b.stmt_date = (SELECT MAX(stmt_date)
        FROM Statements
        WHERE acct_no = '1003')
```

The above UPDATE statement is using a subquery to select the maximum statement date from the Statements table to use as a comparison against the statement date in the WHERE condition of the UPDATE statement. When a subquery returns one value in this way, the subquery can be used wherever an expression can be used. In this case, we need to update the AccountValues with the current value of the latest statement for the same account. The subquery works nicely here to retrieve the latest statement date for account 1003.

In this example, the select statement of MAX(stmt_date) is the *inner* (sometimes called *nested*, as used in this chapter) subquery within the *outer* UPDATE statement. Nesting of subqueries is unlimited. If necessary, you can nest a subquery inside a subquery inside a ... inside an outer data manipulation statement.

Subqueries are enclosed in parentheses and can include all SELECT statement clauses with the exception of ORDER BY (if not using a TOP clause), INTO, and COMPUTE (COMPUTE BY).

In addition to using subqueries in a WHERE or HAVING clause, subqueries can also be used in a SELECT statement's FROM clause. In this context, the subquery acts as a data source just as a table or a join would and is permitted to return more than one value. When used in the FROM clause, subqueries are called *derived tables*.

```
SELECT acct_no,invest_tot,stmt_date
FROM (SELECT acct_no,stmt_date,invest_tot FROM Statements
WHERE DATEPART(yy,stmt_date) = '1992') AS S1      — required
ORDER BY acct_no
```

acct_no	invest_tot	stmt_date
1003	125315.6300	1992-12-31 00:00:00.000
1004	118900.6200	1992-12-31 00:00:00.000
1005	57000.0000	1992-12-31 00:00:00.000
1006	15000.0000	1992-12-31 00:00:00.000
1007	120000.0000	1992-12-31 00:00:00.000
1008	202221.5500	1992-12-31 00:00:00.000
1009	33000.0000	1992-12-31 00:00:00.000
...		
1064	6000.0000	1992-12-31 00:00:00.000

```
1067        44594.9200      1992-12-31 00:00:00.000
1070        15004.4700      1992-12-31 00:00:00.000
1992        121093.5200     1992-12-31 00:00:00.000
9847        62033.6400      1992-12-31 00:00:00.000

(28 row(s) affected)
```

You can include other tables along with the subquery in the FROM clause and even join the subquery derived table to the other tables. The alias for the subquery is required.

Using IN and NOT IN with a Subquery

In Chapter 6 we explored the use of the IN keyword with lists comprised of literal constants. Here, we'll develop a use of IN that uses a subquery as the source of the list items.

We want to select the account number and home phone number of accounts having a tot_assets value (which is derived from the accounts' latest statements) in the top 10 cur_values selected from statements in the range of years between 1994 and 1996 inclusive. We are not interested in the months these statements were produced.

```
SELECT TOP 10 cur_value FROM Statements WHERE
 DATEPART(yy,stmt_date) BETWEEN '1994' AND '1996' ORDER BY cur_value
 DESC

GO

SELECT a1.acct_no, a1.home_phone,a1.tot_assets
FROM Accounts a1
WHERE a1.tot_assets IN
(SELECT TOP 10 cur_value FROM Statements WHERE
 DATEPART(yy,stmt_date) BETWEEN '1994' AND '1996' ORDER
 BY cur_value DESC)
ORDER BY a1.tot_assets DESC

cur_value
-----------
506296.0300
339736.0400
333582.4200
333215.7400
313056.0600
306711.0600
305288.8700
299170.2200
283774.9800
280985.0100

(10 row(s) affected)
```

```
acct_no    home_phone    tot_assets
-------    ----------    -----------
1023       888-1818      506296.0300
1025       111-1155      313056.0600
1029       010-1010      283774.9800

(3 row(s) affected)
```

The first SELECT statement is for reference and selects the top 10 cur_values from statements between 1994 and 1996. These values are ordered descending from highest to lowest. This statement is the innermost subquery in the next SELECT statement in the batch file.

The second SELECT statement selects the account number, home phone number, and total assets value from accounts having a total assets value in the top 10 current values list derived from the nested subquery (equal to the first query).

The top 10 cur_values list from the first query is displayed first followed by the accounts that have tot_assets values in this list.

Correlated Subqueries

Take a closer look at the subquery we just executed in the section above. Notice that the subquery is totally independent from the outer query. The nested subquery selects cur_values from Statements without any relation to the Accounts table in the outer query. The subquery can execute once to retrieve the list of cur_values no matter how many rows from Accounts are compared to the list.

On the other hand, if we look at a subquery like the following, we discover a different situation:

```
SELECT a1.acct_no, tot_assets
FROM Accounts a1
WHERE a1.tot_assets IN
  (SELECT cur_value FROM Statements WHERE
   Statements.acct_no = a1.acct_no)
ORDER BY a1.tot_assets DESC

acct_no    tot_assets
-------    -----------
1023       506296.0300
1025       313056.0600
1029       283774.9800
1070       248877.1300
1069       231279.4600
1992       218546.7100
1007       217219.6400
1003       202457.3500
1008       198314.4600
1009       186276.0400
1004       164014.9700
1011       141651.0200
1012       134290.2600
```

```
1027        120256.5100
1024        111114.0800
1013        100687.9200
1066        82334.4700
9847        81240.8700
1067        78831.4500
1015        70962.0100
1028        69711.2900
1018        69381.3100
1014        68534.2600
1059        67657.1700
1010        56454.3900
1006        52693.8000
1016        36237.5800
1005        34738.6300
1017        31633.4000
1064        17161.7100
1060        10371.7900
1068        1445.6600

(32 row(s) affected)
```

The above query is checking each account's `tot_assets` to ensure it is found somewhere among the accounts' statements. Notice that the subquery used here requires a value from the outer query, the account number.

For each row evaluated by SQL Server in the outer query, the row's account number is used to evaluate the inner subquery to select rows from the Statements table where the Statements account number equals the Accounts account number.

The inner subquery is now dependent on the outer query for values it needs to perform the `SELECT` statement. This subquery is known as a *correlated* or *repeating* subquery. It cannot execute once for the entire outer query but must be executed repeatedly for each row of the outer query.

Using EXISTS and NOT EXISTS with a Subquery

Remember when we looked at outer joins earlier in this chapter, we discovered that we had rows in the AccountValues table that had no matching keys in the Statements table. The query is repeated here to show the mismatches:

```
SELECT b.acct_no,
 CONVERT(varchar(15),b.stmt_date,102) AS StmtDate,
 a.cur_value
 FROM Statements AS a RIGHT OUTER JOIN AccountValues AS b
 ON a.acct_no = b.acct_no AND
    a.stmt_date = b.stmt_date
 ORDER BY b.acct_no,StmtDate

acct_no     StmtDate          cur_value
-------     --------          ---------
1001        1991.09.30        NULL
1001        1991.12.31        NULL
```

```
1001        1991.12.31         NULL
1001        1994.09.30         NULL
1001        1994.12.31         NULL
1001        1995.07.31         NULL
1001        1996.03.31         NULL
1003        1988.12.31         NULL
1003        1988.12.31         NULL
1003        1989.03.31         NULL
1003        1989.06.30         NULL
1003        1989.09.30         NULL
1003        1989.12.31         NULL
1003        1989.12.31         NULL
1003        1990.03.31         NULL
1003        1990.06.30         NULL
1003        1990.09.30         NULL
1003        1990.12.31         NULL
1003        1991.03.31         NULL
1003        1991.06.30         NULL
1003        1991.09.30         NULL
1003        1991.12.31         NULL
1003        1992.03.31         NULL
1003        1992.06.30         NULL
1003        1992.09.30         NULL
1003        1992.12.31         172786.4100
1003        1993.03.31         179836.8700
1003        1994.09.30         202039.2200
1003        1994.12.31         202457.3500
1003        1996.03.31         202457.3500
...
1992        1991.06.30         NULL
1992        1991.09.30         NULL
1992        1991.12.31         NULL
1992        1991.12.31         NULL
1992        1992.03.31         NULL
1992        1992.06.30         NULL
1992        1992.09.30         NULL
1992        1992.12.31         152463.3300
1992        1992.12.31         152463.3300
1992        1994.06.30         153698.9200
1992        1994.12.31         165785.6900
1992        1995.03.31         160230.2800
1992        1995.06.30         185442.8100
1992        1995.07.31         218546.7100

(211 row(s) affected)
```

Every NULL in the cur_value column indicates a bad record in the AccountValues table, one that does not match on account number and statement date to the Statements table.

Let's remove those records from the AccountValues table. We want to delete AccountValues rows where the account number and statement date are not found in the Statements table. How do we do it?

We can test for the existence of a match between AccountValues and Statements by using the EXISTS keyword and a subquery to select rows where the account numbers and statement dates match. The EXISTS keyword used in front of the subquery causes the subquery to be evaluated for either a TRUE or FALSE condition. The subquery in this case does not return rows, but merely checks for their existence according to the statement coded in the subquery:

```
SELECT * FROM AccountValues
WHERE EXISTS
(SELECT *
 FROM Statements AS a
 WHERE a.acct_no = AccountValues.acct_no AND
    a.stmt_date = AccountValues.stmt_date)
```

The above statement selects rows from the AccountValues table where the AccountValues acct_no and stmt_date are matched to a row in the Statements table. The subquery (a correlated subquery) matches the rows and returns TRUE if a match is found and FALSE otherwise. If TRUE is returned, the current row of the AccountValues table is selected; otherwise, it is not.

Notice that the subquery specifies * as the column list. This is done to form a valid SELECT statement, but since the subquery doesn't return values, a column list other than * would be meaningless.

Using NOT EXISTS is useful in our situation. We want to delete AccountValues rows that do *not* have a matching key in the Statements table. If the above SELECT statement displays AccountValues rows that *do* match rows in the Statement table, introducing a NOT in front of EXISTS will produce AccountValues rows that do *not* match. We'll incorporate this technique into a DELETE statement to remove the bad rows:

```
DELETE FROM AccountValues
WHERE NOT EXISTS
(SELECT *
 FROM Statements AS a
 WHERE a.acct_no = AccountValues.acct_no AND
    a.stmt_date = AccountValues.stmt_date)
```

Now when we execute our original outer join to test the integrity of the two tables (although now we can do the check using EXISTS), we get the expected results:

```
SELECT b.acct_no,
 CONVERT(varchar(15),b.stmt_date,102) AS StmtDate,
 a.cur_value
 FROM Statements AS a RIGHT OUTER JOIN AccountValues AS b
 ON a.acct_no = b.acct_no AND
    a.stmt_date = b.stmt_date
 ORDER BY b.acct_no,StmtDate
```

```
acct_no   StmtDate      cur_value
-------   ----------    ----------
1003      1992.12.31    172786.4100
1003      1993.03.31    179836.8700
1003      1994.09.30    202039.2200
1003      1994.12.31    202457.3500
1003      1996.03.31    202457.3500
1004      1992.12.31    162730.4400
1004      1993.03.31    173174.4100
1004      1993.09.30    185645.6900
1004      1994.12.31    164014.9700
...
1992      1992.12.31    152463.3300
1992      1994.06.30    153698.9200
1992      1994.12.31    165785.6900
1992      1995.03.31    160230.2800
1992      1995.06.30    185442.8100
1992      1995.07.31    218546.7100

(66 row(s) affected)
```

The use of EXISTS and NOT EXISTS comes in handy whenever you need to check for the existence or absence of a particular condition but don't need the rows meeting that condition.

Using the ANY and ALL Operators

The keywords ANY and ALL are used to modify a comparison operator used with a subquery.

Using the keyword ANY in front of a subquery returns TRUE when any values retrieved in the subquery satisfy the condition in which ANY is placed. FALSE is returned if the condition is not satisfied for all values in the subquery or when the subquery returns no rows.

For illustration of ANY and ALL, we'll use the following subquery:

```
SELECT zip FROM accounts
WHERE zip LIKE '_65%'

zip
-----
06510
06511
06511
06511
06514
06511
06515
06503
06511
06511
```

```
(10 row(s) affected)
```

The use of ANY with the > comparison operator is equivalent to a comparison greater than the minimum value in the list returned by the subquery. In the case below, a comparison is made of zip > 06503:

```
SELECT acct_no,home_phone,zip FROM Accounts
WHERE zip > ANY (SELECT zip FROM accounts
   WHERE zip LIKE '_65%')

acct_no    home_phone      zip
-------    ----------      -----
1003       NULL            06510
1005       888-8888        06511
1007       444-4444        06511
1008       444-7777        06511
1010       666-6666        06514
1012       777-6666        06511
1013       222-3344        06798
1016       111-1212        06515
1023       888-1818        33416
1024       222-2244        10533
1025       111-1155        12633
1060       777-7777        06511
1067       343-3434        06511
1068       888-8888        77015
1069       555-5555        28115
1070       444-1111        06880

(16 row(s) affected)
```

The use of ANY with the < comparison operator is equivalent to a comparison less than the maximum value in the list returned by the subquery. In the case below, a comparison is made of zip < 06515:

```
SELECT acct_no,home_phone,zip FROM accounts
WHERE zip < ANY_(SELECT zip FROM accounts
WHERE zip LIKE '_65%')

acct_no    home_phone      zip
-------    ----------      -----
1003       NULL            06510
1004       999-9999        06475
1005       888-8888        06511
1006       222-3333        06405
1007       444-4444        06511
1008       444-7777        06511
1009       666-9999        06473
1010       666-6666        06514
1011       444-5555        06443
1012       777-6666        06511
1014       787-7878        06016
```

```
1015        111-1111        06118
1017        999-8989        06117
1018        666-5454        06472
1027        545-4545        06111
1028        262-6262        06489
1029        010-1010        06503
1059        333-3333        06001
1060        777-7777        06511
1064        444-4455        06066
1066        333-3232        06478
1067        343-3434        06511
1992        222-2222        06473
9847        555-5555        06109

(24 row(s) affected)
```

When you use ANY with the = comparison operator, it is equivalent to using the IN keyword as described earlier. Don't expect the use of <> ANY to behave like NOT IN, however. To write the equivalent of NOT IN, use <> ALL.

The ALL keyword returns TRUE when all values returned by the subquery meet the condition in which ALL is placed. FALSE is returned when the condition is not met or the subquery doesn't return rows.

The use of ALL with the > comparison operator is equivalent to a comparison greater than the maximum value in the list returned by the subquery. In the case below, a comparison is made of zip > 06515:

```
SELECT acct_no,home_phone,zip FROM accounts
WHERE zip > ALL (SELECT zip FROM accounts
WHERE zip LIKE '_65%')

acct_no     home_phone      zip
-------     ----------      -----
1013        222-3344        06798
1023        888-1818        33416
1024        222-2244        10533
1025        111-1155        12633
1068        888-8888        77015
1069        555-5555        28115
1070        444-1111        06880

(7 row(s) affected)
```

The use of ALL with the < comparison operator is equivalent to a comparison less than the minimum value in the list returned by the subquery. In the case below, a comparison is made of zip < 06503:

```
SELECT acct_no,home_phone,zip FROM accounts
WHERE zip < ALL (SELECT zip FROM accounts
WHERE zip LIKE '_65%')
```

```
acct_no    home_phone    zip
-------    ----------    -----
1004       999-9999      06475
1006       222-3333      06405
1009       666-9999      06473
1011       444-5555      06443
1014       787-7878      06016
1015       111-1111      06118
1017       999-8989      06117
1018       666-5454      06472
1027       545-4545      06111
1028       262-6262      06489
1059       333-3333      06001
1064       444-4455      06066
1066       333-3232      06478
1992       222-2222      06473
9847       555-5555      06109

(15 row(s) affected)
```

Note that the use of ALL with the = comparison operator will return zero rows whenever the subquery returns more than one value since a comparison value cannot equal ALL values in the list returned by the subquery. If the subquery returns only one value, then = ALL has a chance of finding a match.

Using Unions and the UNION Operator

How could we satisfy a request like this? Display the account numbers, account last names, and total assets from the Accounts table. If the total assets are greater than $100,000, label these accounts as 'Large'. If, on the other hand, the total assets are equal to or less than $100,000, label them as 'Small'. Order the results by 'Large' and 'Small' accounts with total assets in descending order.

One way to satisfy this request is to use two separate queries to obtain the 'Large' and 'Small' results, and then join them together into one result set using a UNION. The UNION query would look like this:

```
SELECT acct_no, acct_lastname,tot_assets,'Large' As type
FROM Accounts
WHERE tot_assets > 100000
UNION
SELECT acct_no, acct_lastname,tot_assets,'Small' As type
FROM Accounts
WHERE tot_assets <= 100000
ORDER BY type,tot_assets DESC
```

```
acct_no  acct_lastname        tot_assets        type
-------  -------------        -----------       -----
1023     Client25             506296.0300       Large
1025     Client27             313056.0600       Large
1029     Client31             283774.9800       Large
1070     Client22             248877.1300       Large
1069     Client10             231279.4600       Large
1992     Client1              218546.7100       Large
1007     Client7              217219.6400       Large
1003     Client2              202457.3500       Large
1008     Client8              198314.4600       Large
1009     Client9              186276.0400       Large
1004     Client3              164014.9700       Large
1011     Client12             141651.0200       Large
1012     Client15             134290.2600       Large
1027     Client29             120256.5100       Large
1024     Client26             111114.0800       Large
1013     Client16             100687.9200       Large
1066     Client24             82334.4700        Small
9847     Client32             81240.8700        Small
1067     Client17             78831.4500        Small
1015     Client19             70962.0100        Small
1028     Client30             69711.2900        Small
1018     Client23             69381.3100        Small
1014     Client18             68534.2600        Small
1059     Client14             67657.1700        Small
1010     Client11             56454.3900        Small
1006     Client6              52693.8000        Small
1016     Client20             36237.5800        Small
1005     Client5              34738.6300        Small
1017     Client21             31633.4000        Small
1064     Client28             17161.7100        Small
1060     Client4              10371.7900        Small
1068     Way_Side Consultants 1445.6600         Small

(32 row(s) affected)
```

When we use UNIONs, we have to follow a few rules. Notice that in both queries above, the same number of columns is returned by both queries. Also, in these queries, the data types of the selected columns are the same. UNION requires *compatible* data types in matched column positions, meaning that the columns have data types that can be implicitly converted to a common data type.

The SELECT statements you use in the UNION query can be any valid SELECT statement, but cannot use the ORDER BY and COMPUTE clauses. They may use GROUP BY and HAVING clauses to return grouped results as long as the results of both queries meet the other rules for UNION queries.

To order the results of the UNION, use an ORDER BY clause at the very end of the UNION as we did above.

You can insert the UNION result set into a new table by placing the INTO keyword within the first query only. To append the UNION result set into a table, place the UNION query in the SELECT clause of an INSERT statement.

A result of UNION queries that may not be so evident is that the use of UNION results in DISTINCT rows being returned. Duplicate rows are automatically removed.

If you want duplicate rows in the UNION result set, use the keyword ALL after UNION. For example, the following query without the ALL keyword returns 288 rows:

```
SELECT acct_no, cur_value,'Large' As type
FROM Statements
WHERE cur_value > 100000
UNION
SELECT acct_no, cur_value,'Small' As type
FROM Statements
WHERE cur_value <= 100000
ORDER BY acct_no,cur_value
```

Adding ALL after UNION forces duplicates to be returned, and we get 291 rows. The duplicates are due to the same cur_values value found on multiple statement dates for the same account number:

```
SELECT acct_no, cur_value,'Large' As type
FROM Statements
WHERE cur_value > 100000
UNION ALL
SELECT acct_no, cur_value,'Small' As type
FROM Statements
WHERE cur_value <= 100000
ORDER BY acct_no,cur_value
```

You can include UNION multiple times to merge multiple result sets, and you can use parentheses to control the use of UNION and UNION ALL among the queries and the control of which unions are created first. As with other statements, unions within parentheses are executed before other unions, enabling you to control which result sets are brought together and when.

Summary

We've explored the various methods of joining two or more tables in a FROM clause to create a data source for selecting columns.

The INNER JOIN was used to select rows from two or more tables where joined columns met the join expression.

We used the OUTER JOIN to select rows from two or more tables where the joined columns met the join condition, and additionally selected rows from the left table, right table, or both regardless of the join condition. These joins were expressed as LEFT OUTER, RIGHT OUTER, and FULL OUTER joins.

The subquery was defined and explored in this chapter. You discovered how to create a subquery and how to use it to specify some very complex expressions to control the selection of rows in a SELECT statement.

You saw how subqueries can be used as the source of a list for use with the IN keyword to select rows based on a value found in a list of values.

The EXISTS and NOT EXISTS conditions were covered here. You learned that subqueries used for existence checking don't return rows but only a TRUE or FALSE value based on the existence of rows satisfying the subquery selection criteria.

You also discovered in this chapter how to use the ANY and ALL comparison operator modifier when used with subqueries. These keywords can be used to select rows based on minimum and maximum values in a list and based on the existence of a value in a list, just as the IN keyword is used.

Finally, you saw what a UNION was, how they work, and how to create them. You learned the rules for defining unions and how the union result set can be inserted into new and existing tables.

Chapter 10

Building and Using Views

IN THIS CHAPTER

- ◆ Learn what views are and how to create them
- ◆ Find out how to restrict users to specific views of your database
- ◆ Learn about the restrictions for modifying data through a view
- ◆ See how views can be changed and deleted

IN PREVIOUS CHAPTERS, we've used numerous SELECT statements to retrieve rows from one or more tables. Some of these SELECT statements were simple queries from one table while other statements included multitable joins, WHERE clauses, or grouping and sorting clauses.

In this chapter, we'll take a look at a SQL Server object that uses a SELECT statement to produce an object your users and applications can name in their SELECT statements in place of table names. These objects are essentially virtual tables, called *views*.

Why do we call them virtual tables? Because the view only exists in a database as a definition. There are no data rows stored anywhere in the database associated with the view name. The rows returned through a view are dynamically selected from the base tables named in the view when the view name is referenced in a Transact-SQL statement.

Since no data exists for the view until the view is referenced, the base tables named in the view can change and even disappear from the database, providing the view is not being actively used. As long as the base tables named in the view are present when the view is referenced, SQL Server (and your users) will be happy.

Why Use Views?

In some organizations, views are created on each base table and users name these views in their SELECT statements instead of naming the base tables.

This is done for security and integrity reasons. After the views are created, users are granted permissions to read and modify the views, but are not given permissions on the base tables used by the views. This prevents users from accessing the base tables with any Transact-SQL statements from any software. They are forced to use the views to access data.

213

A Consistent View of Data

Another reason to use views is to create a buffer between the base tables and the users of the database. The view enables changes to underlying tables to take place while still presenting a consistent "view" to the user. When changes to the base tables are needed, the view can be modified, if necessary, to present the same data the user of the view is accustomed to. The end user need not be aware of any changes at all to the tables the view is based on.

Hiding Complexity

A third reason for using views is to simplify the user or application interface to data. Since views can hide the complexity of a query, or possibly multiple queries combined with a UNION, the result set can be returned with nothing more than a simple SELECT query, just as you would get when selecting columns from a table.

Creating and Using Views

A view is created with, you guessed it, a CREATE VIEW statement.

The CREATE VIEW specifies a name for the view, an optional column list, and the SELECT statement that will feed the column list.

Let's create a simple view on the Accounts table:

```
CREATE VIEW Accounts_vu
  (acct_no,acct_lastname,home_phone,tot_assets)
AS
  SELECT acct_no,acct_lastname,home_phone,tot_assets
   FROM Accounts
```

The name you give to your view can be any valid SQL Server identifier. Most organizations have standards for naming views as they do for other SQL server objects. We've named the above view after the table it is based on and appended an underscore and the letters "vu" at the end.

After the view name, we list the columns the view is to have. In this case, we've listed the same column names as the base table. These columns will be selected in the view's SELECT statement.

It is not mandatory to list column names as done above. When no column list is provided, the view's column names are taken from the SELECT statement. The SELECT statement can provide the base table column names, or aliases can be used to give unique names to the view columns. The alias names can also be placed in the view column list if you prefer to use this technique.

If you do use column names in the view, the SELECT statement provides the column values by position – first result set column mapped to first view column and so on. You can use as many as 1,024 columns in a view.

The SELECT statement used to create the view can be any valid SELECT statement. The only restrictions are that the SELECT statement cannot include an ORDER BY or COMPUTE (BY) clause, an INTO keyword, and cannot reference a temporary table

We explore temporary tables in Chapter 15.

The SELECT statement can be quite complex, referencing multiple tables and using inner and outer joins, subqueries, and unions.

If necessary, we can create multiple views on the same table. Let's create another view on the Accounts table:

```
CREATE VIEW Accounts_1647vu
AS
  SELECT *
  FROM Accounts
  WHERE manager_num = '1647'
```

In the Accounts_vu view, we limited the number of columns that could be seen through the view to just the acct_no, acct_lastname, home_phone, and tot_assets columns of the Accounts table.

In the Accounts_1647vu view, we made all of the Accounts table columns accessible to the view but limited the rows that could be seen to only those rows where the manager number was equal to 1647.

These two views illustrate a different slice of the Accounts table. The Accounts_vu shows all rows but only a subset of columns, whereas the Accounts_1647vu shows all columns but only a subset of rows.

If necessary, we could set permissions on the Accounts table and these views such that manager number 1647 could access the Accounts table only through the Accounts_1647vu view limiting him or her to accessing their own accounts and no one else's.

Once we've defined a view in a SQL Server database, we can use the sp_helptext stored procedure to retrieve the view's definition:

```
sp_helptext Accounts_1647vu
Text
----------------------------
CREATE VIEW Accounts_1647vu
AS
  SELECT *
  FROM Accounts
  WHERE manager_num = '1647'

(6 row(s) affected)
```

To see a report listing the columns of the base tables in the view and the objects in the database that depend on the view, use the `sp_depends` stored procedure naming the view as the procedure's argument.

Before we move on to using these views to select data, let's create one more view. This time, let's create a view on a view:

```
CREATE VIEW Accounts_1647_Subvu
 AS
   SELECT acct_no,acct_lastname,tot_assets
    FROM Accounts_1647vu
```

Notice that in the above view, we selected columns from a view rather than a base table. Nonetheless, the new view still has a base table, which the base table of the `Accounts_1647vu` view.

Selecting through the new `Accounts_1647_Subvu` view returns rows from accounts managed by manager number 1647, but only the `acct_no`, `acct_last-name` and `tot_assets` columns are displayed.

Using the View to Select Data

To retrieve data through the `Accounts_vu` view we created above, we name the view in a select query:

```
SELECT * FROM Accounts_vu
```

The results are the same as if we had selected * from Accounts. The only difference is, with the view, we only get the columns defined in the view:

Now, consider the following query:

```
SELECT a.acct_no,b.acct_type,a.tot_assets
FROM Accounts_vu a, Accounts_1647vu b
 WHERE a.acct_no = b.acct_no

acct_no    acct_type tot_assets
-------    --------- -----------
1003       NonTax    202457.3500
1005       Tax       34738.6300
1009       Tax       186276.0400
1014       Tax       68534.2600
1023       Tax       506296.0300
1025       Tax       313056.0600
1028       Tax       69711.2900
1066       Tax       82334.4700
1067       Tax       78831.4500
1070       Tax       248877.1300

(10 row(s) affected)
```

Since `Accounts_1647vu` limits the rows in its result set to those where the man-ager_num equals 1647 (only 10 accounts), the join between the two views above returns only manager 1647's accounts.

Notice that the `acct_type` is selected from the `Accounts_1647vu`. This is required due to the fact that this column is not found in the `Accounts_vu` view. Had we attempted to select `acct_type` from the `Accounts_vu` view, SQL Server would have given us this gentle reminder:

```
Server: Msg 207, Level 16, State 42S22
Invalid column name 'acct_type'.
```

Is the above query a self-join? To answer this question, consider the definitions of the two views and the following query:

```
SELECT a.acct_no,b.acct_type,a.tot_assets
   FROM Accounts a, Accounts b
WHERE a.acct_no = b.acct_no AND b.manager_num = '1647'
```

```
acct_no     acct_type tot_assets
-------     --------- -----------
1003        NonTax    202457.3500
1005        Tax        34738.6300
1009        Tax       186276.0400
1014        Tax        68534.2600
1023        Tax       506296.0300
1025        Tax       313056.0600
1028        Tax        69711.2900
1066        Tax        82334.4700
1067        Tax        78831.4500
1070        Tax       248877.1300

(10 row(s) affected)
```

Certainly the results are the same, and if you answered yes, you answered cor-rectly.

Modifying Data Through Views

Inserting or updating data through a view is allowed as long as you follow a few simple rules.

If the view you are attempting to modify data through defines multiple tables, your data modification statement can modify only one of the tables of the view.

If your view ignores columns that are defined as `NOT NULL` and those columns do not have default constraints, you cannot insert rows through the view since SQL Server cannot provide values for the missing base table columns.

Views containing computed columns cannot be used for inserting rows since you cannot insert a value into a base table column that doesn't exist. The computed column is derived at the time the view is referenced and does not represent a col-umn in a base table.

When a view contains aggregate functions, a GROUP BY clause or SQL Server built-in functions, the view cannot be used to modify data.

It is possible to insert or update data through a view such that the updated data is no longer visible through the view. Consider the following INSERT statement:

```
INSERT Accounts_1647vu
 (acct_no,acct_lastname,state_abbr,zip,tot_assets,
fiscal_period,cycle,acct_type,acct_status,manager_num)
 VALUES
('9848','Client 9848','NY','13647',10000,'12',3,'Tax',
'Open',2877)
```

We've inserted a row into the Accounts table, through the Accounts_1647vu view, for account number 9849 and assigned this account to manager number 2877.

Since the Accounts_1647vu view only selects rows where the manager_num equals 1647, the new row will not be visible through this view. The same would be true had we changed the manager_num for an account that belongs to 1647; once changed to a non-1647 manager_num, the row is no longer visible through the Accounts_1647vu view:.

```
UPDATE Accounts_1647vu
 SET manager_num = 2877
WHERE acct_no = '1003'
```

Now, when we select rows through the Accounts_1647vu view, we only get 9 rows returned instead of the 10 rows returned previous to the update:

```
SELECT acct_no,acct_type,tot_assets
FROM Accounts_1647vu

acct_no     acct_type  tot_assets
-------     ---------  -----------
1005        Tax        34738.6300
1009        Tax        186276.0400
1014        Tax        68534.2600
1023        Tax        506296.0300
1025        Tax        313056.0600
1028        Tax        69711.2900
1066        Tax        82334.4700
1067        Tax        78831.4500
1070        Tax        248877.1300

(9 row(s) affected)
```

There is a way to prevent modifications through a view from becoming invisible to the view. You can use the WITH CHECK OPTION after the SELECT statement defining the view.

The WITH CHECK OPTION tells SQL Server to check modifications through the view to ensure that the modified data will remain visible through the view. We can modify the view definition above to prevent the situation we encountered above:

```
ALTER VIEW Accounts_1647vu
AS
  SELECT *
  FROM Accounts
  WHERE manager_num = '1647'
WITH CHECK OPTION
```

We'll get to the ALTER VIEW statement shortly. The above statement is changing the definition of the Accounts_1647vu view to include the WITH CHECK OPTION. With this option set on the view, an attempt to update or insert a row such that the row would no longer be visible (that is, returned in the view's result set) through the view would result in the following:

```
UPDATE Accounts_1647vu
 SET manager_num = 2877
WHERE acct_no = '1005'
```

```
Server: Msg 550, Level 16, State 44000
The attempted insert or update failed because the target view either
  specifies WITH CHECK OPTION or spans a view which specifies WITH
  CHECK OPTION and one or more rows resulting from the operation did
  not qualify under the CHECK OPTION constraint.
Command has been aborted.
```

Account number 1005 is one that belongs to manager number 1647 and thus returned through the Accounts_1647vu view. Since we now have a WITH CHECK OPTION on the view, an attempt to change the manager for account 1005 to something other than 1647 results in an aborted update as indicated in the message.

Modifying and Removing Views from the Database

If we change our minds about what a particular view should return, or if the business requirements change forcing views to change, we can use the ALTER VIEW statement to redefine a view:

```
ALTER VIEW Accounts_vu
 (account_number,last_name,phone,total_assets,
 account_type,account_status)
AS
  SELECT acct_no,acct_lastname,home_phone,tot_assets,acct_type,
acct_status
    FROM Accounts
```

In the above ALTER VIEW statement, we changed the definition of the Accounts_vu view to give the view results more meaningful column names and we added two additional columns to the view. Now when we select from the `Accounts_vu` view, we get the following:

```
SELECT account_number,total_assets,account_status
 FROM Accounts_vu

account_number total_assets  account_status
-------------- ------------  --------------
1003           202457.3500   Open
1004           164014.9700   Open
1005           34738.6300    Open
1006           52693.8000    Open
1007           217219.6400   Closed
1008           198314.4600   Open
1009           186276.0400   Open
1010           56454.3900    Open
1011           141651.0200   Closed
1012           134290.2600   Open
1013           100687.9200   Closed
1014           68534.2600    Open
...
1068           1445.6600     Open
1069           231279.4600   Open
1070           248877.1300   Open
1992           218546.7100   Open
9847           81240.8700    Open
9848           10000.0000    Open

(33 row(s) affected)
```

If you only want to give a new name to a view, you can use the `sp_rename` stored procedure:

```
sp_rename 'Accounts_1647vu', 'Accounts_1647Managervu'
Caution: Changing any part of object names may break scripts and
 stored procedures.
The object was renamed to 'Accounts_1647Managervu'.
```

Be mindful of the caution issued above. Remember that we have another view named `Accounts_1647_Subvu` that is dependent on the `Accounts_1647vu` view. After this name change, an attempt to select from the `Accounts_1647_Subvu` view yields the following:

```
SELECT * FROM Accounts_1647_Subvu

Server: Msg 208, Level 16, State 42S02
Invalid object name 'Accounts_1647vu'.
View 'Accounts_1647_Subvu' cannot be used because of
previous binding errors.
```

The `Accounts_1647vu` view that `Accounts_1647_Subvu` view is dependent on no longer exists due to our rename and therefore the error message results. It's best to use the `sp_depends` procedure before renaming views to check for dependent views.

Summary

We started this chapter off with an overview of how views work in SQL Server. You learned that views are actually virtual tables that are created at the time of reference to the view name.

Next, we explored the question of why we would use a view. Views are used for security and integrity reasons, ease of base table maintenance, and to simplify the user or application interface to data.

You learned in this chapter how to create a view using the `CREATE VIEW` statement. You saw how powerful views can be under the covers, and you learned about some rules you need to follow in building views.

The selection and modification of data through views was explored, and you found out why some views can't be updated.

Finally, you saw how an existing view can be modified and how you can remove a view from a database and the ramifications of doing so.

Chapter 11

Working with Text and Images

IN THIS CHAPTER

- ◆ Learn how to use the `TEXTSIZE` option to control the maximum number of bytes returned from a text column

- ◆ Explore reading blocks of text or image data with `READTEXT` statements

- ◆ Use `UPDATETEXT` statements to delete, replace and insert substrings in place

- ◆ Replace entire text strings with `WRITETEXT` statements

UNLIKE `char` AND `varchar` data types that are stored within the data pages of a table, `text` and `image` data types are stored in pages of their own. The text or image column in a table row holds a 16-byte pointer to the text or image data stored in the separate set of text pages. A table containing one or more text or image columns has one set of text and image pages associated with it.

The set of text and image pages for a table can hold data from multiple rows and columns and can be a mixture of text and image data. Each text and image page can store up to 8KB of data. The data in these text and image pages is arranged in a B-tree structure similar to index structures.

SQL Server's use of the B-tree structure for management of `text` and `image` data greatly improves the performance of working with these data types and SQL Server's improved management of space for text and image data greatly reduces the disk space usage over previous versions of SQL Server.

Exploring Text and Image Statements

In this chapter, we look at some Transact-SQL statements you can use to work with text and image data in your databases. These statements, in addition to the text and image functions you learned about in Chapter 7, will enable you to manipulate text and image data with ease.

223

Using SET TEXTSIZE

When you select a text column from a table, the maximum number of bytes returned by default is 4,096 (4KB).

You can change the maximum number of bytes returned by using the TEXTSIZE option of the SET statement. To set the number of bytes to 8KB for example, you would code as follows:

```
SET TEXTSIZE 8192
```

The maximum size you can specify for TEXTSIZE is 2,147,483,647 (2GB), which is the maximum number of characters you can store in a text data type column.

To find out what the current textsize setting is, you can select it from the @@textsize global variable:

```
SELECT @@textsize
-------------------
8192

(1 row(s) affected)
```

Setting TEXTSIZE to zero returns the textsize setting to the default.

The READTEXT statement we'll explore next provides a way to override the textsize setting as long as the READTEXT size is less than the TEXTSIZE. If the READTEXT size is greater than TEXTSIZE, then only TEXTSIZE bytes will be read.

Reading Text Columns with READTEXT

The READTEXT statement provides a means of reading text and image data in blocks. The block of data to read is defined by an offset from the textptr and a size.

 Chapter 7 introduced the TEXTPTR( ) function for returning the pointer of a text or image column. This pointer holds the address within the text and image data page where the text or image data is stored.

To read the first block of an account note, we would use the following code:

```
DECLARE @noteptr varbinary(16)

SELECT @noteptr = TEXTPTR(acct_note)
  FROM Accounts WHERE acct_no = '1003'

READTEXT Accounts.acct_note @noteptr 0 0
GO
```

```
acct_note
-------------------------------------------------------------------
Contacted client on 10-24-97. He is interested in growth funds and
  want's to discuss funds for college

(1 row(s) affected)
```

To store the 16-byte text pointer in the batch, we declared a local variable named `@noteptr` as `varbinary(16)`.

Next we select the text pointer using the `TEXTPTR()` function into our local variable. We're selecting the pointer to the note for account number 1003.

Once we have the text pointer, we issue a `READTEXT` statement to read the text, starting at zero offset from the text pointer with a zero byte size. Specifying zero for the size (the last argument specified in the `READTEXT` statement above) tells SQL Server we want the default number of bytes returned. Since our account note holds fewer bytes than the default setting, the entire note was returned.

Let's read blocks of text from this note in 10-byte increments. To do this, we'll need to use the offset and size arguments:

```
DECLARE @noteptr varbinary(16)

SELECT @noteptr = TEXTPTR(acct_note)
  FROM Accounts WHERE acct_no = '1003'

READTEXT Accounts.acct_note @noteptr 0 10
READTEXT Accounts.acct_note @noteptr 10 10
READTEXT Accounts.acct_note @noteptr 20 10
GO

acct_note
-----------------------------------
Contacted

(1 row(s) affected)

acct_note
-----------------------------------
 client on

(1 row(s) affected)

acct_note
-----------------------------------
10-24-97.

(1 row(s) affected)
```

The offset values specify the number of bytes to skip before reading text. The first `READTEXT` statement read bytes 0 through 9, the second `READTEXT` statement read bytes 10 through 19, and the third `READTEXT` statement read bytes 20 through

29. Each of the blocks read was 10 bytes in size, as was specified by the last argument to READTEXT.

As with all of the text and image statements discussed in this chapter, you must qualify the column name argument with the name of the base table where the column resides.

Note that READTEXT is only one way of reading text data. The standard SELECT statement will also read text columns up to the maximum number of bytes in the TEXTSIZE setting. As you saw in Chapter 7, you can use the SUBSTRING() function to return the same results as above by specifying a starting position and length that equate to the READTEXT offset and size arguments.

Change a Part of a Text Column with UPDATETEXT

We can delete a portion of a text string, change a substring within a text string, or insert a new substring within a text string by using the UPDATETEXT statement.

Like the READTEXT statement, UPDATETEXT uses a text pointer and offset value to point to the start of the update. Let's change the contact date mentioned in the note for account 1003:

```
DECLARE @noteptr varbinary(16)

SELECT @noteptr = TEXTPTR(acct_note)
  FROM Accounts WHERE acct_no = '1003'

UPDATETEXT Accounts.acct_note @noteptr 20 9 '02-24-98.'
GO
```

We know the date in this account's note starts at position 20 and is 9 bytes long including the period at the end. We can therefore specify the offset from the text pointer to be 20 and the length of bytes to be deleted as 9. The last argument to UPDATETEXT is the string of data to be inserted in place of the substring that was deleted.

Our note for account number 1003 now reads as follows:

```
SELECT acct_note FROM Accounts WHERE acct_no = '1003'

acct_note
-------------------------------------------------------------
Contacted client on 02-24-98. He is interested in growth funds and
  want's to discuss funds for college

(1 row(s) affected)
```

In practice, we would most likely use a `PATINDEX()` function to locate the starting position of the date in the note:

```
DECLARE @noteptr varbinary(16)
DECLARE @substringpos integer

SELECT @noteptr = TEXTPTR(acct_note),
@substringpos = PATINDEX('%__-__-__%',acct_note) - 1
   FROM Accounts WHERE acct_no = '1003'

UPDATETEXT Accounts.acct_note @noteptr @substringpos 9 '03-24-98.'
GO
```

The use of `PATINDEX()` above assumes we use two-digit date parts in the date strings contained in the note and locates the starting position of the first character of that date. We adjust this starting position to account for the zero-based offset used in `UPDATETEXT`. We then use the resulting starting position to delete 9 bytes and replace them with the new date string.

We can delete a portion of the text by specifying an offset to start the deletion and a length of bytes to delete, and omitting the text to be inserted. Let's remove the end of the sentence that reads "and want's to discuss funds for college" to get rid of the misplaced apostrophe:

```
DECLARE @noteptr varbinary(16)
DECLARE @substringpos integer
DECLARE @strlength as integer

SELECT @noteptr = TEXTPTR(acct_note),
@substringpos = PATINDEX('%and%',acct_note) - 1,
@strlength = DATALENGTH(acct_note) - @substringpos
   FROM Accounts WHERE acct_no = '1003'

UPDATETEXT Accounts.acct_note @noteptr @substringpos @strlength
GO
```

Looking again at the account note for account 1003, we have the following:

```
SELECT acct_note FROM Accounts WHERE acct_no = '1003'

acct_note
------------------------------------------------------------
Contacted client on 03-24-98. He is interested in growth funds

(1 row(s) affected)
```

Now let's insert a sentence after the date and before the last sentence:

```
DECLARE @noteptr varbinary(16)
DECLARE @substringpos integer
```

```
SELECT @noteptr = TEXTPTR(acct_note),
@substringpos = PATINDEX('%.%',acct_note)+ 1
  FROM Accounts WHERE acct_no = '1003'

UPDATETEXT Accounts.acct_note @noteptr @substringpos 0 'He''s
  looking for info on college savings plans.'
GO
```

Notice in the text string that we've added two apostrophes to get one apostrophe in the final string. Also note that zero was used to specify the size for an INSERT operation.

Our account note now looks like this:

```
SELECT acct_note FROM Accounts WHERE acct_no = '1003'

acct_note
-------------------------------------------------------------
Contacted client on 03-24-98. He's looking for info on college
  savings plans. He is interested in growth funds

(1 row(s) affected)
```

UPDATETEXT and WRITETEXT work by default in nonlogged mode. This means that the modifications to text and image data made by these statements are not written to the database log file. Since no log is written, recovery of the column data to prechange condition is not possible. To write nonlogged text into the database, you must ensure that the Select Into/Bulkcopy database option is turned on.

You can log text changes if necessary by using the WITH LOG for both UPDATETEXT and WRITETEXT. This option will log the changes you make with these statements. Place the WITH LOG keywords into the statement before the data to be written.

Writing Text Columns with WRITETEXT

The WRITETEXT statement allows interactive updating of a text or image column just as UPDATETEXT does. The difference is that WRITETEXT replaces the entire contents of the column with the updated text. There is no provision for specifying an offset or size as there is in UPDATETEXT.

WRITETEXT writes up to 120KB of data into the column pointed to by the text pointer. The pointer used in the statement must be valid to begin with. To get a valid pointer, you must insert or update some text string into the column. This action initializes a text pointer to a data page.

Let's add a note to account 1004:

```
DECLARE @noteptr varbinary(16)

SELECT @noteptr = TEXTPTR(acct_note)
  FROM Accounts WHERE acct_no = '1004'
IF (TEXTVALID('Accounts.acct_note', @noteptr)) = 0
```

```
BEGIN
  UPDATE Accounts SET acct_note = ' '
    WHERE acct_no = '1004'
  SELECT @noteptr = TEXTPTR(acct_note)
    FROM Accounts WHERE acct_no = '1004'
END

WRITETEXT Accounts.acct_note @noteptr
 'Client is interested in income funds and funds with a foreign
 interest.'
GO
```

Before writing text with the text pointer returned by the TEXTPTR() function, we check for a valid pointer using the TEXTVALID() function. If this function returns 0, then we know we have a bad pointer and must initialize one by updating the acct_note with a space (or any text at all). After the update, we then reset the local pointer variable so that WRITETEXT will work properly.

Now if we select the acct_note from account 1004, we get the following:

```
SELECT acct_note FROM Accounts WHERE acct_no = '1004'

acct_note
-------------------------------------------------------------
Client is interested in income funds and funds with a foreign
  interest.

(1 row(s) affected)
```

Summary

This chapter discussed the use of Transact-SQL text and image statements for working with text and image columns in a database.

We saw how to set the maximum textsize for text data returned in a SELECT statement using the TEXTSIZE option of the SET statement. We found out how to read this size setting by selecting the @@textsize global variable.

The READTEXT statement was introduced for reading blocks of text data starting at any offset within the text column and reading any size block up to the size set by TEXTSIZE.

Next, we explored the UPDATETEXT statement to delete, replace, and insert substrings within a text column. This statement is quite flexible for working with substrings in place.

The last statement we used was the WRITETEXT statement for replacing text strings. This statement is less powerful than the UPDATETEXT statement in that it can only be used to replace text strings and cannot deal with substrings the way UPDATETEXT does.

Chapter 12

Using the CUBE and ROLLUP Operators

IN THIS CHAPTER

- ◆ Discover how to produce summaries using the CUBE and ROLLUP operators
- ◆ Learn the difference between the CUBE and ROLLUP results
- ◆ See how to use the GROUPING() function to detect aggregate rows
- ◆ Learn how to use a subquery as the source for a FROM clause

In Chapter 8, we saw how the GROUP BY and COMPUTE clauses can be used to summarize data by one or more groups and produce totals for those group summaries.

THIS CHAPTER LOOKS at another method of summarizing data. This method uses the CUBE and ROLLUP operators in a GROUP BY clause to produce summaries for the GROUP BY columns.

The CUBE operator produces a summary for each combination of GROUP BY columns such that every possible summary level is represented in the result set.

The ROLLUP operator also produces a summary, but only for each of the GROUP BY columns in order from right to left in the GROUP BY column list. The results obtained from the ROLLUP operator are a subset of the results obtained from the CUBE operator.

Both of these operators can be very useful in analyzing and reporting data, as we'll see from this chapter's examples.

Exploring the CUBE Operator

Use of the CUBE operator in a GROUP BY query causes new rows to be added to the result set. The new rows are created by cross-referencing the GROUP BY columns and applying an aggregate function to each resulting combination. This action gives us a summary row for each possible breakdown of the GROUP BY columns.

The number of additional rows added to the result set depends on the number of GROUP BY columns and the distinct values contained in those columns.

Let's look at a simple example to see how the CUBE operator works:

```
SELECT fund_cd,trantype,SUM(amount) AS total_amount
FROM tranhistory
GROUP BY fund_cd,trantype WITH CUBE
ORDER BY fund_cd
```

```
fund_cd trantype    total_amount
------- --------    ------------
NULL    NULL        3771062.9300
NULL    Cap G D     288069.8800
NULL    Cap G D (C  25525.3200
NULL    Fee         -465.0000
NULL    Inc Div     268492.1400
NULL    Inc Div (C  55021.9500
NULL    Invest      3777013.8300
NULL    Redempt     -765407.7900
NULL    ST CG D     113075.9900
NULL    ST CG D (C  9736.6100
1090Z   Cap G D     8376.3900
1090Z   Fee         -20.0000
1090Z   Inc Div     7528.8200
1090Z   Invest      19000.0000
1090Z   ST CG D     972.4200
1090Z   NULL        35857.6300
AMECX   Invest      34950.5100

...
VGRIX   Inc Div     339.0300
VGRIX   Invest      30000.0000
VGRIX   NULL        30339.0300
VWLTX   Cap G D     4079.3000
VWLTX   Inc Div     19996.7000
VWLTX   Invest      73406.2200
VWLTX   Redempt     -18377.6400
VWLTX   ST CG D     764.4600
VWLTX   NULL        79869.0400
WELLS   Cap G D     643.5900
WELLS   Inc Div     2054.1700
WELLS   Invest      35000.0000
WELLS   ST CG D     139.8600
WELLS   NULL        37837.6200
WINSR   Cap G D     2256.1100
WINSR   Fee         -40.0000
WINSR   Inc Div     4667.1900
WINSR   Invest      43672.1900
WINSR   Redempt     -28348.0000
WINSR   ST CG D     183.4300
WINSR   NULL        22390.9200

(250 row(s) affected)
```

Without using the CUBE operator, the above GROUP BY clause would result in 198 rows in the result set. With the CUBE operator, we get 250 rows – the original 198 plus 52 additional.

The additional rows are the aggregate sum rows that display totals for each of the group combinations. In the case of this query, there is a group aggregate for each fund code that represents all transaction types within the fund, another group aggregate for each of the transaction types that represents all funds within the transaction type, and an aggregate for all funds all transaction types.

Calculating the Row Count

We can compute the row count by knowing the row count without CUBE and the number of distinct values for each of the GROUP BY columns.

In this example, the number of distinct fund_cd values is 42 and the number of distinct trantype values is 9. We add 42 plus 9 plus 198 to get 249 rows. To this sum, we add one more row to represent the row for all fund codes and all transaction types, resulting in 250 rows in the CUBEd result set.

Remember that if you use COUNT(DISTINCT columnname) to obtain the number of distinct values for your GROUP BY columns (as I did here), NULL values are not counted. If NULL values are possible, you'll need to add a row for the NULL.

If we wanted to compute the absolute maximum number of rows that could possibly occur in the result set, we would assume that each of the 42 fund_cd values would have all of the 9 trantype values associated with them, which yields an absolute maximum of 378 (42 x 9) rows. To this product, we would account for the aggregate rows resulting from CUBE and add 52 (42 fund codes + 9 transaction types + 1 all fund codes all transaction types) to get 430 rows in the CUBEd result set.

This absolute maximum row count can be expressed as follows:
(distinct fund codes + 1 aggregate) * (distinct transaction types + 1 aggregate)

which in this example is
(42 + 1) * (9 + 1) = (43) * (10) = 430 rows

Our real result of only 250 rows indicates that all fund codes do not have all transaction types represented. This can easily be seen by scanning the result.

Using the GROUPING Function

Notice that the aggregate rows resulting from the CUBE operator are represented by the keyword NULL. For example, in the result set we just examined, the row representing fund code VGRIX, all transaction types looks like this:

```
VGRIX     NULL       30339.0300
```

This row is interpreted as "for the fund VGRIX, the SUM of all transaction types (NULL) is 30339.0300."

We can easily deduce in this example that the NULL means aggregate and not a NULL trantype since the trantype column is part of the primary key and cannot contain NULL values. But what would happen if we had a query that grouped a column that could contain NULL values? Let's look at one now:

```
SELECT manager_num,AVG(tot_assets)
FROM Accounts
GROUP BY manager_num WITH CUBE
manager_num
----        -----------
NULL        34738.6300
1647        194239.5912
2321        104036.9471
2877        84943.5100
9277        150164.7600
NULL        127803.1033

(6 row(s) affected)
```

If we assume that the NULL is an aggregate representing the average total assets managed by the firm (all managers), which number do we use – the 34,738.63 or the 127803.1033?

Our math teacher would be quite upset with us if we chose the 34,738.63 since a quick inspection of the magnitude of the other averages indicates this cannot be the overall average. But if our application program were to see this result, it would take some overhead code to detect the proper aggregate row to use. There must be a better way.

This is where the GROUPING() function comes into play. The GROUPING() function applied to the GROUP BY column will return a 1 when the aggregate row is displayed and a 0 otherwise. If we add this function to our query, we get the following:

```
SELECT manager_num,GROUPING(manager_num),AVG(tot_assets)
FROM Accounts
GROUP BY manager_num WITH CUBE

manager_num
----        ---         -----------
NULL        0           34738.6300
1647        0           194239.5912
2321        0           104036.9471
2877        0           84943.5100
9277        0           150164.7600
NULL        1           127803.1033

(6 row(s) affected)
```

Now we can easily see which row represents the aggregate "all managers" row since the GROUPING() function indicates this row with a 1. Our application won't have any problem picking this row out from the crowd. The first NULL is indeed one or more accounts with a NULL manager number.

Using the ROLLUP Operator

Like the CUBE operator, the ROLLUP operator also produces aggregate rows, but fewer of them.

ROLLUP is used to produce cumulative aggregates of the GROUP BY columns. These aggregates are displayed for each of the GROUP BY columns in order from right to left in the GROUP BY clause.

Let's look at the same TranHistory query we looked at above, but this time using the ROLLUP operator:

```
SELECT fund_cd,trantype,SUM(amount) AS total_amount
FROM tranhistory
GROUP BY fund_cd,trantype WITH ROLLUP
ORDER BY fund_cd
```

fund_cd	trantype	total_amount
NULL	NULL	3771062.9300
1090Z	Cap G D	8376.3900
1090Z	Fee	-20.0000
1090Z	Inc Div	7528.8200
1090Z	Invest	19000.0000
1090Z	ST CG D	972.4200
1090Z	NULL	35857.6300
AMECX	Invest	34950.5100
...		
VGRIX	Inc Div	339.0300
VGRIX	Invest	30000.0000
VGRIX	NULL	30339.0300
VWLTX	Cap G D	4079.3000
VWLTX	Inc Div	19996.7000
VWLTX	Invest	73406.2200
VWLTX	Redempt	-18377.6400
VWLTX	ST CG D	764.4600
VWLTX	NULL	79869.0400
WELLS	Cap G D	643.5900
WELLS	Inc Div	2054.1700
WELLS	Invest	35000.0000
WELLS	ST CG D	139.8600
WELLS	NULL	37837.6200
WINSR	Cap G D	2256.1100
WINSR	Fee	-40.0000
WINSR	Inc Div	4667.1900
WINSR	Invest	43672.1900

```
WINSR    Redempt    -28348.0000
WINSR    ST CG D    183.4300
WINSR    NULL       22390.9200

(241 row(s) affected)
```

Inspecting the Results

This time we get nine fewer rows than with CUBE. The nine that are missing are the rows representing each of the transaction types all fund codes aggregates. These are not displayed in the ROLLUP since there is no cross-reference done by ROLLUP on the GROUP BY columns. Only a right-to-left aggregate display results.

Interpreting the GROUP BY columns in right-to-left order, we would expect to see (and we do) an aggregate row representing all trantypes for each of the fund codes listed and an overall aggregate row representing all fund codes and all transaction types.

In this example, the fund code rollup row displays a running sum across all transaction types within the fund code. The overall row (NULL NULL) displays a running sum across all transaction types across all fund codes.

A comparison of the aggregate rows using the ROLLUP operator to the same rows using the CUBE operator indicates that the results are the same. The only difference between the two operators is the missing aggregates resulting from the CUBE operator's cross-referencing.

Just the NULLS and Nothing But the NULLS

When we're only interested in the aggregate rows and not the other summary rows, we can pull them out of the result set by creating a view on the query or by using the GROUP BY query as a subquery in the FROM clause. Using the subquery approach would look like this:

```
SELECT fund_cd,trantype,total_amount
FROM
(SELECT fund_cd,trantype,SUM(amount) AS total_amount
FROM tranhistory
GROUP BY fund_cd,trantype WITH ROLLUP) AS Aggs
WHERE fund_cd IS null OR trantype IS null

fund_cd trantype    total_amount
------- ---------   ------------
1090Z   NULL        35857.6300
AMECX   NULL        77627.0000
ANEFX   NULL        10000.0000
BEGRX   NULL        247796.0200
BWINE   NULL        52781.2900
...
```

```
THIRD   NULL        114793.1400
VANSP   NULL         35430.2800
VCAGX   NULL         36384.8100
VEIPX   NULL          -331.1700
VGRIX   NULL         30339.0300
VWLTX   NULL         79869.0400
WELLS   NULL         37837.6200
WINSR   NULL         22390.9200
NULL    NULL       3771062.9300

(43 row(s) affected)
```

Using a subquery as the source for the FROM clause in a query is a useful syntax that provides us with some powerful constructs without requiring us to create views.

The row count displayed for the result set indicates that we did get all expected aggregate rows, because we calculated the number of aggregate rows to be 42 distinct fund codes plus 1 row for the overall aggregate.

When working with results that could contain NULL values and knowing that NULL could be either an aggregate row or a NULL column value, it might be better to base the WHERE clause on the results of a GROUPING() function instead of NULL:

```
SELECT manager_num,grp,average
FROM
(SELECT manager_num,grp=GROUPING(manager_num),AVG(tot_assets) AS
  average
FROM Accounts
GROUP BY manager_num WITH CUBE) AS Aggs
WHERE grp = 1
manager_num grp   average
----        ---   -----------
NULL         1    127803.1033

(1 row(s) affected)
```

Summary

We started out this chapter by looking at the CUBE operator and learned how to calculate the number of aggregate rows we can expect from a query using this operator.

We saw that aggregate rows are displayed in a result set using a NULL and that we can detect a true aggregate row from a NULL column value by using the GROUPING() function. This function returns a 1 when an aggregate is displayed and a 0 otherwise. This helps an application program pick out the aggregates with ease.

The ROLLUP operator was compared to the CUBE operator, and the difference between the two was explored. We learned that the aggregate rows common between the two operators display the same results, but the ROLLUP operator displays fewer aggregate rows. This is due to the fact that ROLLUP only aggregates with the GROUP BY columns in a right-to-left order in the GROUP BY clause, whereas the CUBE operator provides an aggregate row for all combinations of the GROUP BY columns.

Finally, we looked at using a GROUP BY query as the source for the FROM clause of an outer query so that we could select out only the aggregate rows. We learned that this syntax is a powerful alternative to views that can be used with other types of queries as well.

Chapter 13

Introduction to Cursors

IN THIS CHAPTER

◆ Find out what a cursor is and how to work with one

◆ Learn about cursor types and their differences

◆ Explore working with Transact-SQL Server cursors in procedures and batch files

◆ See how your choice of a locking strategy can affect performance and how cursors can be populated asynchronously

◆ Learn how to perform absolute and relative fetches in a cursor and how to fetch cursor columns into variables

◆ Explore the use of cursor variables to hold a pointer to a cursor

◆ Find out how to apply an UPDATE to a row in a cursor

◆ See how global variables and system functions are used in working with cursors

◆ Learn how to use system stored procedures to describe cursor attributes

THE SELECT STATEMENTS WE'VE been working with up to this point have returned one or more rows into the results pane of the SQL Query Analyzer tool we've been using to execute the queries.

When we pressed the Execute button in the Query Analyzer's toolbar, the SELECT statement was sent to SQL Server, compiled by the optimizer and executed. The rows of the result set were then returned to the Query Analyzer.

The Query Analyzer had to fetch the rows returned by SQL Server and display them in the Results pane so we could see the results of our query.

To access the rows of the result set, the Query Analyzer went through a series of calls to the ODBC API to fetch rows and get the data columns making up those rows in order to display them in the Results pane. Prior to the actual data fetching activity, the Query Analyzer had to make calls to ODBC to retrieve information about the result set, such as the names of the columns being returned.

The result set returned by SQL Server in this manner is known as a *default* result set. The query is executed and all of the rows returned to the requestor (in this case, the Query Analyzer application) as fast as the network, call-level interface, and application can handle them.

With default result set processing, all components from the application to SQL Server remain busy reading and sending rows of the result set through the connection until all the rows have been read by the application. There is no caching of data on behalf of the application connection, either at the server or at the client. There may be data caching taking place within the application memory, but to the rest of the components in the system, no caching is taking place.

In this chapter, you're going to learn of another type of result set, one that is associated with a processing mechanism called a *cursor*. You'll discover that through the use of cursors, rows of a result set can be returned in ways different from that of a default result set and, if necessary, even visited multiple times before ending the processing of the result set. You'll learn, too, that you can apply updates through a cursor.

What Are Cursors?

A cursor is a special kind of result set. It is a named result set that resides on either the server or client machine. The behavior of a cursor is described in terms of the navigation ability exhibited by the cursor and the cursor's sensitivity to data changes made by other users.

Cursors can be defined either through the Transact-SQL language or through the database application programming interface such as ODBC, DB-Library, and ADO. Some of these cursor definition methods allow the cursor's behavior to be defined explicitly while others define the behavior implicitly by use of a cursor type. ODBC and Transact-SQL cursor definitions allow either method. DB-Library and ADO only use cursor types to define a cursor's behavior.

We'll take a look at what is meant by explicitly defining cursor behavior when we explore the Transact-SQL DECLARE CURSOR statement. Let's first find out what the cursor types are and what behaviors they imply.

Exploring Cursor Types

Transact-SQL, ODBC, DB-Library, OLE DB and ADO can define cursor behavior by use of a cursor type. There are four types of cursors; Forward-only, Static, Keyset-driven, and Dynamic.

The *Forward-only* cursor behaves similar to the default result set. It only allows forward navigation through the result set. SQL Server uses the "Forward-only" description as a scrolling option and not as a cursor type. As far as SQL Server is concerned, "Forward-only" can be applied to Static, Keyset-driven, and Dynamic cursors to force a forward navigation through these cursors' result sets. When an API cursor is defined as Forward-only, SQL Server supports that cursor as a Forward-only Dynamic cursor. This means that API Forward-only cursors behave like Dynamic cursors in that rows returned through the cursor reflect changes made by other users after the cursor has been opened.

The *Static* cursor provides a snapshot in time of a result set. Changes made by other users, and even by the owner of the Static cursor, after the cursor is opened are not visible in the cursor's result set. The Static cursor is a cache of the result set at the time the cursor is opened. Updates through this cursor are not supported. Static cursors allow scrolling backwards and forwards through the result set.

Keyset-driven cursors are a cache of unique identifiers (the keyset) for the rows of the cursor's result set. Fetching rows through this cursor implies fetching keys from the keyset and then retrieving the corresponding row for the fetched key from the database. Once the cursor is opened, the keyset of the cursor is fixed in the cache. Updates to rows pointed to by keys in the keyset are seen by the cursor when a row is fetched. Inserts by other users and by the cursor's owner, if done outside the cursor, are not visible through the cursor since the keys of those new rows are not resident in the keyset. This is true even if the rows would normally qualify for membership in the keyset. Deletes of rows that the keyset points to are seen as "holes" when the row is fetched through the cursor. This is due to the fact that the key remains in the cursor's keyset even though another user has deleted the key's corresponding row. Keyset-driven cursors can be scrolled backward and forward.

Inserts and deletes by other users to rows that qualify as members of the cursor are visible through the *Dynamic* cursor. When the Dynamic cursor is opened, the cursor is populated with qualifying rows. Each time the application fetches from the cursor, the cursor may contain a result set different from the previous fetch or open. Inserts made by other users are visible and rows deleted by other users are eliminated. Let's look at a brief example of a Dynamic cursor and a row inserted by another user.

Say we define a Dynamic cursor on a SELECT statement that selects the account number, last name, and total assets from the Accounts table:

```
SELECT acct_no, acct_lastname, tot_assets FROM Accounts
WHERE acct_no > '1016' AND acct_no < '1026'
ORDER BY acct_no
```

When we open the cursor, it contains these account numbers:

```
1017
1018
1023
1024
1025
```

While the application is positioned in this cursor, another user of the database inserts a row for account number 1019. Now, when the application next fetches a row from the cursor, the cursor then contains these account numbers:

```
1017
1018
1019
```

```
1023
1024
1025
```

The account numbers in this result set are different from the one built when the cursor was first opened. This current result set contains the newly inserted 1019 account number.

Different cursor types use resources like memory and disk space differently and are one of the factors you need to consider when choosing a cursor type for your application.

Keyset-driven and Static server cursors (I'll explain the difference between server and client cursors shortly) use SQL Server's tempdb database to store the cursor's keyset and result set, respectively. Due to this activity, these cursors open more slowly than Dynamic cursors. On the other hand, if the cursor's SELECT statement involves a join, the Keyset-driven and Static cursors might be a faster choice than the Dynamic cursor.

If you are dealing with a small result set, it might be faster for you to cache the result set in your application memory rather than use a cursor. This would require you to implement your own result set navigation, but would eliminate the cursor resource requirements.

Now, let's consider server cursors versus client cursors.

Where Do Cursors Live?

Cursors defined with the Transact-SQL DECLARE CURSOR statement result in server cursors. This means that the cursor resides at the server and all cursor fetching done by an application must be transmitted over the network.

By default, API cursors are implemented as server cursors. If you are using Forward-only or Static cursors, however, you can implement these on the client. Keyset-driven and Dynamic cursors are only implemented on the server.

Client cursors are not usually chosen unless the server cannot support the SELECT statement or procedure used to define the cursor. If the SELECT statement or procedure returns multiple result sets or uses a COMPUTE, COMPUTE BY, or INTO clause, then a server cursor cannot be used.

Server cursors are a good choice for other reasons as well. If you are only going to use a part of the cursor's result set — that is, FETCH a subset of the result set rows — then a server cursor is a better choice since a client cursor would need to retrieve all rows into the client cache. Server cursors also support more cursor functionality than client cursors. When updating through the cursor, for example, a server cursor supports direct positioned updates where client cursors must submit UPDATE statements that qualify the row to be updated.

How Are Cursors Used?

Although APIs may implement cursor statements differently, the basic steps in working with cursors are the same.

The first step an application must take is to define the cursor. This involves specifying the SELECT statement and setting the cursor behavior attributes to define the behavior needed for the application.

The second step is to send the cursor definition statement to the server to define and open the cursor.

In the third step, the application can start fetching rows from the cursor and retrieving column data from the row buffer.

Finally, after working with the cursor rows, the application can close the cursor and free the cursor resources.

The steps outlined above, as used in each of the APIs covered in this book, are summarized in Table 13-1.

TABLE 13-1 WORKING WITH API CURSORS

API	Step	Statements Used
ODBC	Define the cursor	SQLSetStmtAttr SQLBindCol SQLSetCursorName
	Open the cursor	SQLExecDirect
	Fetch Rows	SQLFetchScroll
	Close the cursor	SQLCloseCursor
ADO	Define the cursor Open the cursor	Command.Execute or Recordset.Open
	Fetch Rows	Recordset.Move... Recordset.Fields.GetItem
	Close the cursor	Recordset.Close
DB-Library	Define the cursor Open the cursor	dbcursoropen
	Fetch Rows	dbcursorbind dbcursorfetchex
	Close the cursor	dbcursorclose

Transact-SQL cursors have a similar life cycle, as shown in Table 13-2.

TABLE 13-2 WORKING WITH TRANSACT-SQL CURSORS

Step	Statements Used
Define the cursor	DECLARE cursorname CURSOR
Open the cursor	OPEN cursorname
Fetch Rows	FETCH ... FROM cursorname
Close the cursor	CLOSE cursorname
Free the resources	DEALLOCATE cursorname

Transact-SQL cursors cannot be accessed from application programs. These cursors are server-based cursors used in stored procedures. The API cursors are used by applications instead of the Transact-SQL cursors.

Part III of this book will illustrate the use of API cursors in an application program. As for Transact-SQL cursors, we'll take a look at those next.

The DECLARE CURSOR Statement

To define a Transact-SQL cursor, you use the DECLARE CURSOR statement. This statement defines the cursor and its behavior. The first cursor we'll look at is a simple STATIC cursor on the Accounts table:

```
DECLARE AcctCursor CURSOR
FORWARD_ONLY STATIC FOR
SELECT acct_no,acct_lastname,tot_assets,manager_num
FROM Accounts
```

Remember that the STATIC cursor type is a snapshot of the cursor result set at the time the cursor is opened. The rows of this cursor are read-only and do not reflect any modifications made by other users against the base tables.

Notice in the cursor above that we are specifying FORWARD ONLY as an option applied to the STATIC cursor. This restricts us to retrieving rows from the cursor in a forward navigation through the result set. In the API cursors, FORWARD-ONLY is a cursor *type* rather than a navigation option.

To enable forward and backward navigation through the cursor result set, we could specify SCROLL in place of FORWARD_ONLY. Both of these navigation options are available for all cursor types.

To declare a cursor that will allow us to see changes made by other users, we need to declare either a KEYSET or a DYNAMIC cursor. The choice between these cursor types depends on your application. The differences are discussed in the "Exploring cursor types" section earlier in this chapter.

```
DECLARE AcctCursor CURSOR
SCROLL KEYSET FOR
SELECT acct_no,acct_lastname,tot_assets,manager_num
FROM Accounts
```

In addition to being sensitive to changes made by other users to base tables, the KEYSET and DYNAMIC cursors can be updated. All columns of the cursor result set are updateable when declared like the cursor in the above example.

Using the FOR UPDATE OF Clause

To restrict the columns that can be updated through a cursor, you can specify the columns to be updateable in a FOR UPDATE OF clause:

```
DECLARE AcctCursor CURSOR
SCROLL KEYSET FOR
SELECT acct_no,acct_lastname,tot_assets,manager_num
FROM Accounts
FOR UPDATE OF manager_num
```

The above declaration uses a FOR UPDATE OF clause to restrict updates to the manager_num column. Attempting to UPDATE columns other than the manager_num column will result is the following message:

```
Server: Msg 16932, Level 16, State 42000
Cursor has a 'FOR UPDATE' list and the requested column to be
 updated is not in this list
Command has been aborted.
```

Applying updates to a row where the cursor is currently positioned is known as a *positioned update*. Examples of updating through a cursor will be explored in the "Updating through a cursor" section later in this chapter.

Choosing a Locking Strategy

Another clause you can add to KEYSET and DYNAMIC cursor declarations enables you to specify the type of locking strategy you want the cursor to perform.

Locking rows in a shared multiuser database is a concurrency mechanism for managing database integrity.

Whenever a row is updated by an application, SQL Server must lock the row to prevent it from being modified by other users while the UPDATE is applied to the table. If an application attempts to UPDATE a row that is locked by another application (user), SQL Server returns an error indicating the row is locked. If this occurs, the application can wait and attempt to reapply the UPDATE or turn the situation over to the user for a decision.

Note

In many cases, the application or user will need to refetch the row to be updated in order to see what values the row holds after being updated by the other user. If you attempt to apply an UPDATE to a row and SQL Server discovers that the row isn't locked but has been modified by another user since you fetched the row, an error will be returned.

So, you are faced with the possibilities that a row you are attempting to update will either be locked by another user, have had its values changed since you last fetched the row, or will be accepted. Your application must deal with the first two of these possibilities in the form of error-handling routines.

When you declare a cursor, you can also specify a locking strategy that may help your situation. You can use either the OPTIMISTIC or SCROLL_LOCKS keywords to do this:

```
DECLARE AcctCursor CURSOR
SCROLL KEYSET OPTIMISTIC FOR
SELECT acct_no,acct_lastname,tot_assets,manager_num
FROM Accounts
FOR UPDATE OF manager_num
```

The keyword OPTIMISTIC specifies that the positioned UPDATE or DELETE should fail if the row has changed since being fetched. In this case, SQL Server will check the row in the table to ensure it has not changed since you fetched the row, and if it has not, place a lock on the row on your behalf and apply your UPDATE. If the row has changed, the UPDATE will fail and an error message will be returned.

Specifying SCROLL_LOCKS in place of OPTIMISTIC causes SQL Server to lock the row when you FETCH it. This action guarantees that another user will not change the row and your UPDATE attempt will succeed. You still have the possibility, though, that the row will be locked by another user when you FETCH it.

Choose the locking strategy carefully, because locking impacts the performance of the database. As long as a lock is held by an application, another application or user must wait for the lock to be released before continuing their processing.

Specifying the Scope of the Cursor

The scope of the cursor name defaults to the setting of the *default to local cursor* database option. If default to local cursor is TRUE, then a cursor declared without a scope specification will result in a LOCAL scope; otherwise, a GLOBAL scope is given to the cursor. Either scope keyword can be specified explicitly in the DECLARE statement.

LOCAL scope is the stored procedure or batch where the cursor was declared. With this scope, the cursor is implicitly deallocated when the procedure terminates.

You can return a cursor to a calling procedure or batch as an OUTPUT parameter (OUTPUT parameters are discussed in Chapter 15 "Working with Stored Procedures and Triggers"). The calling procedure can then assign the cursor to a *cursor variable* and use the cursor even though the procedure declaring the cursor has terminated. In this case, the cursor is deallocated when the last reference to the cursor is terminated. OUTPUT cursor parameters cannot be used by API cursors and procedures containing OUTPUT cursor parameters cannot be executed with API calls.

To change the scope of the cursor name to be globally known in any procedure or batch executed in a SQL Server session, you can specify the GLOBAL keyword in the cursor declaration:

```
DECLARE AcctCursor CURSOR
GLOBAL SCROLL KEYSET FOR
SELECT acct_no,acct_lastname,tot_assets,manager_num
FROM Accounts
FOR UPDATE OF manager_num
```

Using GLOBAL scope, the cursor will be implicitly deallocated when the session is terminated unless, of course, it is explicitly deallocated during the session.

Declaring Cursors with SQL-92 Syntax

The cursor declarations used so far in this section have not been using SQL-92 syntax. The cursor declaration in SQL-92 syntax is much simpler. To declare a STATIC cursor, for example, with SQL-92 syntax, we would code as follows:

```
DECLARE AcctCursor INSENSITIVE CURSOR
FOR
SELECT acct_no,acct_lastname,tot_assets,manager_num
FROM Accounts
```

The keyword INSENSITIVE placed in front of the keyword CURSOR specifies a cursor that is not sensitive to changes made by other users. This cursor cannot be updated.

Replacing the keyword INSENSITIVE with the keyword SCROLL results in a cursor that is sensitive to changes made by other users. This cursor behaves like a *dynamic* DYNAMIC cursor type, and since it can be updated, you can specify the FOR UPDATE OF clause.

The navigation option of SCROLL can be specified in the SQL-92 syntax to enable forward and backward navigation through the cursor. Without the keyword SCROLL, only forward navigation is possible.

The OPEN Statement

Now that we know how to declare a cursor, let's look at how we would open one to populate it with rows.

A Transact-SQL cursor is opened with the OPEN statement:

```
OPEN AcctCursor
```

If you have declared a cursor with GLOBAL scope, then open the cursor using the GLOBAL keyword. Specifying the GLOBAL keyword is required since GLOBAL and LOCAL cursor names have separate name spaces:

```
OPEN GLOBAL AcctCursor
```

After the cursor is opened, you can check the number of rows in the cursor's result set by selecting the @@cursor_rows global variable:

```
OPEN GLOBAL AcctCursor
SELECT @@cursor_rows
-------------
33

(1 row(s) affected)
```

Asynchronous Population of the Cursor

If @@cursor_rows returns a negative number, it means that the cursor is being populated via asynchronous population. The absolute value of @@cursor_rows is the number of rows currently in the cursor, but not necessarily the total number of rows.

Asynchronous population of the cursor occurs if the *cursor threshold* configuration setting is zero or the number of expected rows for the cursor is greater than the cursor threshold setting. It is generally better to set the cursor threshold high to force synchronous population of the cursor, especially if you will be working with small result sets. Large result set cursors can benefit from asynchronous population since it allows the application to start fetching from the cursor before it is fully populated.

The FETCH Statement

The FETCH statement is used to retrieve a row from a Transact-SQL cursor. If the cursor has been declared with the SCROLL keyword, you can use FETCH NEXT, FETCH PRIOR, FETCH FIRST, or FETCH LAST.

The fetched row is considered the current position in the cursor. To retrieve the next row from the current position, FETCH NEXT is used. To retrieve the previous row from the current position, use FETCH PRIOR. To retrieve the first cursor row, use FETCH FIRST, and to retrieve the last cursor row, use FETCH LAST.

If the cursor was declared as FORWARD_ONLY, you can only use FETCH NEXT to retrieve the next rows from the current position:

```
DECLARE AcctCursor CURSOR
GLOBAL SCROLL KEYSET FOR
SELECT acct_no,acct_lastname,tot_assets,manager_num
FROM Accounts
FOR UPDATE OF manager_num

OPEN GLOBAL AcctCursor

FETCH NEXT FROM AcctCursor

acct_no     acct_lastname    tot_assets    manager_num
-------     -------------    ----------    -----------
1003        Client2          202457.3500   2877

(1 row(s) affected)

FETCH NEXT FROM AcctCursor

acct_no     acct_lastname    tot_assets    manager_num
-------     -------------    ----------    -----------
1004        Client3          164014.9700   2877

(1 row(s) affected)

FETCH PRIOR FROM AcctCursor

acct_no     acct_lastname    tot_assets    manager_num
-------     -------------    ----------    -----------
1003        Client2          202457.3500   2877

(1 row(s) affected)
```

Using ABSOLUTE and RELATIVE Fetches

If you have declared either a STATIC or KEYSET cursor, you can use an ABSOLUTE or RELATIVE FETCH instead of fetching NEXT or PRIOR from the current position.

The ABSOLUTE FETCH retrieves a row that is some number of rows from the beginning or end of the cursor. If you specify a positive number, the row that is that number of rows from the beginning of the cursor result set will be returned. If you specify a negative number, then the end of the result set is used as the starting point. In our AcctCursor, we know from our SELECT FROM @@cursor_rows that there are 33 rows in the cursor. Let's select the 14th row from the beginning of the cursor:

```
FETCH ABSOLUTE 14 FROM AcctCursor
acct_no     acct_lastname    tot_assets      manager_num
-------     -------------    ----------      -----------
1016        Client20         36237.5800      9277

(1 row(s) affected)
```

Now if we FETCH NEXT, we get the following:

```
FETCH NEXT FROM AcctCursor
acct_no     acct_lastname     tot_assets     manager_num
-------     -------------     ----------     -----------
1017        Client21          31633.4000     9277

(1 row(s) affected)
```

Let's use a negative number to move a specified number of rows from the end of the result set, to return to the 1016 account number:

```
FETCH ABSOLUTE -20 FROM AcctCursor

acct_no     acct_lastname     tot_assets     manager_num
-------     -------------     ----------     -----------
1016        Client20          36237.5800     9277
(1 row(s) affected)
```

To FETCH rows relative from the current position instead of from the ends of the result set, use FETCH RELATIVE:

```
FETCH RELATIVE 2 FROM AcctCursor

acct_no     acct_lastname     tot_assets     manager_num
-------     -------------     ----------     -----------
1018        Client23          69381.3100     2321
(1 row(s) affected)
```

Using a positive number retrieves the row that number of rows from the current position in a forward direction towards the end of the result set. Using a negative number retrieves the row that number of rows from the current position in a backward direction towards the beginning of the result set:

```
FETCH RELATIVE -2 FROM AcctCursor

acct_no     acct_lastname     tot_assets     manager_num
-------     -------------     ----------     -----------
1016        Client20          36237.5800     9277

(1 row(s) affected)
```

As you can see from the above examples, fetching within a cursor can be very flexible to support any processing you need to do on the cursor rows, providing you select the appropriate cursor type.

Fetching into Variables

In a stored procedure or batch, you will often want to FETCH columns of the cursor into local variables. To do this, you can use the INTO clause of the FETCH statement:

```
DECLARE @acct AS varchar(10),@name AS varchar(70)
DECLARE @assets AS money, @manager AS smallint

FETCH NEXT FROM AcctCursor
INTO @acct,@name,@assets,@manager

SELECT 'Account ' + @acct + ' has total assets of ' +
  CONVERT(char(15),@assets,102) + ' managed by ' +
  CONVERT(char(6),@manager)
-------------------------------------------------------------
Account 1017 has total assets of       31,633.40 managed by 9277

(1 row(s) affected)
```

When you use FETCH INTO, you must supply the same number of variables as there are columns returned and the variables must be of the same data type as those columns.

Detecting the Bounds of the Cursor

When fetching from a cursor, you need some way of detecting that there are no more rows to be fetched. SQL Server provides a global variable named @@fetch_status for this purpose.

After fetching a row, the @@fetch_status variable will be 0 if the fetch was successful or -1 if there are no more rows to be fetched in the direction specified.

In KEYSET cursors, attempting to FETCH a row that is in the cursor keyset but no longer resident in the table due to a deletion of the row will be indicated by a value of -2 in the @@fetch_status variable:

```
FETCH FIRST FROM AcctCursor
SELECT @@fetch_status

FETCH PRIOR FROM AcctCursor
SELECT @@fetch_status

acct_no    acct_lastname    tot_assets      manager_num
-------    -------------    ----------      -----------
1003       Client2          202457.3500     2877

(1 row(s) affected)
------
0
(1 row(s) affected)
------
acct_no    acct_lastname    tot_assets      manager_num
-------    -------------    ----------      -----------
(0 row(s) affected)
------
-1

(1 row(s) affected)
```

While fetching with Transact-SQL cursors is limited to one row at a time, API cursors can optionally fetch more than one row at a time. These types of fetches use cursors known as *block cursors*. Block cursors are standard cursors but defined with an attribute called the *rowset size*. This attribute sets the number of rows to return with each FETCH.

The common theme in all the API cursors for dealing with block cursors is to allocate an array of variables and FETCH rows into the array. Each row is then processed by addressing the index of the row in the array.

The CLOSE and DEALLOCATE Statements

When you no longer need the cursor, you can close it out and deallocate the resources it was using. To close the cursor, use the CLOSE statement:

```
CLOSE AcctCursor
```

The CLOSE statement releases any lock that might be held on a row and releases the result set associated with the cursor.

The cursor declaration is still available for reopening the cursor even after the cursor has been closed. If you decide to reopen the cursor at this point, you can execute the OPEN statement to repopulate the cursor result set.

Remember from our discussion on the scope of cursor names that a cursor can be passed back to a calling procedure through an OUTPUT parameter. The calling procedure can then use the cursor as it wishes. When a procedure deallocates the cursor name or cursor variable name by executing a DEALLOCATE statement, SQL Server removes the cursor reference and decrements the reference count. The cursor does not get deallocated unless the reference being removed is the last reference to the cursor (a reference count of zero).

To remove a cursor reference and possibly free the cursor declaration, issue a DEALLOCATE statement:

```
DEALLOCATE AcctCursor
```

If reallocating a cursor through a cursor variable, you can specify the cursor variable name in place of the cursor name in the above statement.

Using Cursor Variables

SQL Server supports the declaration of cursor variables to be used for referencing cursors instead of using cursor names. This method of referencing cursors would be useful in procedures where a cursor is returned from another procedure or you wish to create a reference to a cursor that is local to your procedure.

A cursor variable is declared using the CURSOR keyword in a DECLARE statement:

```
DECLARE @proccursor CURSOR
```

Once declared, the cursor variable can be assigned a value by assigning a cursor name or another cursor variable:

```
DECLARE AcctCursor CURSOR
SCROLL KEYSET FOR
SELECT acct_no,acct_lastname,tot_assets,manager_num
FROM Accounts
FOR UPDATE OF manager_num

DECLARE @proccursor CURSOR

SET @proccursor = AcctCursor
```

If you only need the cursor variable and don't care about using a cursor name, you can condense the above sequence of statements into a direct assignment of the cursor declaration into the cursor variable:

```
DECLARE @proccursor CURSOR

SET @proccursor = CURSOR KEYSET FOR
SELECT acct_no,acct_lastname,tot_assets,manager_num
FROM Accounts
FOR UPDATE OF manager_num
```

Whichever method you use to declare the cursor, the cursor variable can now be referenced in cursor statements instead of cursor names:

```
OPEN @proccursor

FETCH NEXT FROM @proccursor
```

When you are finished with the cursor variable, close it and deallocate it as you would when using cursor names.

```
CLOSE @proccursor
DEALLOCATE @proccursor
```

Updating Through a Cursor

As you navigate through a KEYSET or DYNAMIC cursor and FETCH rows, you can modify the row's columns by applying a positioned UPDATE. A positioned UPDATE is an UPDATE to the row where the cursor is currently positioned – the position in the result set as of the last FETCH.

You can modify any column viewable through the cursor unless the cursor was declared with the FOR UPDATE OF clause, in which case you can only modify the columns in this clause.

Let's open the AcctCursor as we've previously declared it and navigate to account number 1004 so we can UPDATE the manager number:

```
DECLARE AcctCursor CURSOR

SCROLL KEYSET FOR
SELECT acct_no,acct_lastname,tot_assets,manager_num
FROM Accounts
FOR UPDATE OF manager_num

OPEN AcctCursor

FETCH NEXT FROM AcctCursor
FETCH NEXT FROM AcctCursor

acct_no     acct_lastname     tot_assets     manager_num
-------     -------------     ----------     -----------
1003        Client2           202457.3500    2877

(1 row(s) affected)

acct_no     acct_lastname     tot_assets     manager_num
-------     -------------     ----------     -----------
1004        Client3           164014.9700    2877

(1 row(s) affected)
```

Now that we're positioned on the row for account number 1004, let's UPDATE the manager number:

```
UPDATE Accounts SET manager_num = '9277'
  WHERE CURRENT OF AcctCursor

(1 row(s) affected)
```

The above UPDATE statement changes the manager number for account 1004 through the current position of the cursor. This is done by specifying the clause WHERE CURRENT OF AcctCursor.

To see the new value of manager number for this account as it appears in the cursor, we'll refetch it:

```
FETCH RELATIVE 0 FROM AcctCursor

acct_no     acct_lastname     tot_assets     manager_num
-------     -------------     ----------     -----------
```

```
1004      Client3          164014.9700   9277
(1 row(s) affected)
```

We could have issued a FETCH PRIOR and then a FETCH NEXT to refetch the row for account number 1004, but using RELATIVE 0 works much nicer by fetching the row we are currently positioned on – the one we just updated.

Once again, you'll need to consider the locking strategy you're using for the cursor and be prepared to handle any errors that might arise during the UPDATE action. We'll take a look at error detection next.

Using the @@error Global Variable

The @@error global variable will be set to zero if the Transact-SQL statement last executed was successful. If the last statement resulted in an error, then @@error will contain the error number of that error.

If we attempt to UPDATE a column that is not in the FOR UPDATE OF column list, for example, @@error will indicate that we have raised an error condition. Let's replace the UPDATE statement we executed above with the following two statements:

```
UPDATE Accounts SET acct_lastname = 'Smith'
  WHERE CURRENT OF AcctCursor

SELECT @@error

Server: Msg 16932, Level 16, State 42000
Cursor has a 'FOR UPDATE' list and the requested column to be
  updated is not in this list
Command has been aborted.
---------
16932

(1 row(s) affected)
```

As expected, SQL Server aborts the UPDATE because we attempted to UPDATE a column that was not specified in the FOR UPDATE OF column list. The message that SQL Server returned to our Query Analyzer display was as follows:

```
Server: Msg 16932, Level 16, State 42000
```

The error code of 16932 matches the error code we retrieved from the @@error global variable.

If we execute the UPDATE in a stored procedure, we can return our own error message or retrieve SQL Server's message for this error from the sysmessages system table in the master database:

```
SELECT severity,description FROM master.dbo.sysmessages
WHERE error = 16932
```

```
severity description
-------- ------------------------------------------------------------
16       Cursor has a 'FOR UPDATE' list and the requested column to
  be updated is not in this list

(1 row(s) affected)
```

Execute a SELECT statement against the sysmessages table and review the error codes and descriptions to determine which of these errors you want to test for in your application.

Updating with positioned updates can also be done through API cursors, but not by using WHERE CURRENT OF. API cursors have functions that support a similar capability and we'll look at those when we explore Part III.

Using the CURSOR_STATUS Function

The CURSOR_STATUS() function can be used to determine if a cursor is open and if it contains rows.

This function can be used with both local and global cursor names and with cursor variables.

After opening a KEYSET or STATIC cursor, we could select the CURSOR_STATUS() to determine if the cursor contains rows. A zero return from this function indicates that no rows exist in the cursor. If the function returns 1, then the cursor has at least one row.

If you use this function on DYNAMIC cursors, a return value of 1 can indicate zero or more rows in the cursor, so a 1 return does not mean a FETCH against the cursor will return a row. In this case, it is best to check the @@cursor_rows global variable.

In a procedure where the cursor might have been closed, you can use CURSOR_STATUS() to determine if the cursor is closed or open. If the function returns a -1, the cursor is closed and if it returns a 0 or 1, the cursor is open and interpreted as discussed above.

Describing Cursors with Stored Procedures

The Cursor category of Appendix F lists four system stored procedures that can be used to describe various cursor attributes. This section will explore one of those procedures — the sp_describe_cursor_columns procedure, which returns a number of attributes for the columns of the named cursor.

All these procedures return their output as a cursor. You can then assign this cursor to a local cursor variable and FETCH the description rows just as you would from any cursor. The only difference is these cursor result sets contain meta data rows (data about data) rather than data rows.

Table 13-3 lists the columns returned by the first FETCH from the output cursor returned by `sp_describe_cursor_columns`. Here is the script for the AcctCursor:

```
DECLARE @describeCursor CURSOR

EXEC sp_describe_cursor_columns
  @describeCursor OUTPUT,'global','AcctCursor'

FETCH NEXT FROM @describeCursor
```

TABLE 13-3 THE OUTPUT COLUMNS FROM SP_DESCRIBE_CURSOR_COLUMNS

Column Name	Value	Description
column_name	acct_no	`varchar(128)`. The name of the column in the cursor.
ordinal_position	0	`int`. The position of the column relative to the first column in the result set.
column_characteristics_flags	4	`int`. 1 = Bookmark 2 = Fixed length 4 = Nullable 16 = Updateable
column_size	10	`int`. Maximum size of column value.
data_type_sql	167	`smallint`. The SQL Server data type of the column. See xtype column in systypes table.
column_precision	0	`int`. Maximum precision of the column.
column_scale	0	`int`. Number of digits to right of decimal.
order_position	0	`smallint`. Position of the column in the `ORDER BY` clause.
order_direction	NULL	`char(1)`. A = Asc in `ORDER BY`clause D = Desc in `ORDER BY` clause NULL = not in `ORDER BY` clause

TABLE 13-3 THE OUTPUT COLUMNS FROM SP_DESCRIBE_CURSOR_COLUMNS
(Continued)

Column Name	Value	Description
hidden_column	0	`smallint`. 0 = column is in select list 1 = reserved for future use
columnid	1	`int`. Column ID of the column in the base table. If an expression, this value is -1. See colid column in syscolumns table where `id = objectid`.
objectid	581577110	`int`. Object ID of base table the column was selected from. If column is an expression, this value is -1.
dbid	6	`int`. Database ID containing base table, the object identified by `objectid`.

Obviously, the cursor you are describing with these procedures must be declared but does not necessarily have to be open. Some items such as `status`, `fetch_status`, and `row_count` returned by `sp_describe_cursor` are only meaningful if the cursor is open.

When you are finished with the cursor pointed to by the cursor variable declared for the procedure output, you need to close and deallocate it:

```
CLOSE @describeCursor
DEALLOCATE @describeCursor
```

Summary

In this chapter, we've discovered what cursors are and how to define and use them. We learned about client cursors and server cursors and defined their differences.

We saw that there are different cursor types available for various processing requirements. We learned about Keyset-driven and Dynamic cursors that are sensitive to changes made by other users and can be updated through the cursor. We also learned about Static cursors that are only a snapshot of the data in time and are not sensitive to changes made by other users, and cannot be updated through the cursor. We saw, too, that we have control over how we navigate the cursor rows.

The Transact-SQL server cursor was explored in depth. We learned about the cursor's life cycle and how to work with this cursor in stored procedures and batch files.

We took a brief look at locking as it applies to cursors and found out that we have some control over how locking will be applied as we perform updates through a cursor.

This chapter explored the `@@cursor_rows`, `@@fetch_status`, and `@@error` global variables and the `CURSOR_STATUS()` function. We saw how these variables and this function can be used when working with cursors.

The last section of this chapter explored the use of the system stored procedures available for describing cursor attributes. We looked at the `sp_describe_cursor_columns` procedure and defined its output.

Chapter 14

Transact-SQL for Administrators

IN THIS CHAPTER

♦ Learn about server and database configuration parameters

♦ See how to use DBCC statements to monitor various aspects of a SQL Server installation

♦ Explore SQL Server jobs, jobsteps and schedules, and the SQL Server Agent that runs them

♦ Learn the options for backup and recovery of a database and how to perform these critical tasks

♦ Find out how to start SQL Server, pause it, and shut it down

THIS CHAPTER EXPLORES some Transact-SQL elements not typically used by application programmers but of interest to database administrators (DBAs).

We look at server and database configuration using `sp_configure` and `sp_dboption`. These procedures are used by the DBA to establish certain default behavior in the server for all logins and to establish defaults for a specific database. If allowed, users logging in to SQL Server to use a database can override these defaults.

Monitoring the server and its databases can be accomplished to some extent by using the Database Consistency Check statements (DBCC). The DBCC statements can be used to perform tasks such as checking database page allocations, checking the integrity of database objects, rebuilding indexes, and displaying SQL Server memory usage, to name a few.

In addition to monitoring databases, the administrator must be prepared to recover a database that may have become lost or corrupted. Transact-SQL provides backup and recovery statements to support the recovery of a database back to a healthy state.

The DBA must keep index statistics used by the SQL Server query optimizer up to date so that optimal plans can be achieved and application performance optimized. This chapter looks at index statistics and how to update them.

Jobs can be established in SQL Server to run repetitive tasks such as maintenance tasks and certain application processing. We'll look at how a job can be created and run in SQL Server, both manually and on a custom schedule.

At the end of the chapter, you'll see how a SQL Server can be started, paused, and shut down. You'll explore the effects different shutdown methods have on users of the server.

Server Configuration and Database Options

We've seen the use of SET statements throughout the book to set various options that affect a user session. There are also several options that can be set to control the behavior of a database and SQL Server itself.

To list the server options in effect for a server, execute the sp_configure procedure with no arguments. Likewise, to list database options in effect for a database, execute sp_helpdb with the name of the database as the argument. Executing sp_dboption with no arguments lists the available database options.

Changing Server Options

SQL Server behavior can be changed by setting a number of configuration options using the sp_configure stored procedure. This procedure can be used to display and set configuration options such as the maximum number of user connections that can occur simultaneously, the size of the packet sent over the network, the ability to nest triggers, and the maximum amount of time a query will wait before timing out.

When a server configuration option is changed, the change will normally take effect when SQL Server is restarted. If you want the change to take effect immediately, execute the RECONFIGURE statement.

For example, wanted to set the query wait time before timeout. We can use the option to set the amount of time a submitted query will wait to be executed before timing out and returning an error.

```
EXEC master..sp_configure 'show advanced options', '1'
EXEC master..sp_configure 'max query wait',30
RECONFIGURE
```

To set the option, it is required to first set the 'show advanced option' on.

After setting the query wait time to 30 seconds, we run the RECONFIGURE statement to put the option into effect immediately.

If we want users of the application to be able to override server options using `sp_configure`, we can specify the `WITH OVERRIDE` clause:

```
RECONFIGURE WITH OVERRIDE
```

As with many other Transact-SQL statements and procedures, you must have system administrator permissions to execute the `RECONFIGURE` statement.

Changing Database Options

Database behavior can be configured by using the `sp_dboption` procedure. This procedure can set a database to read-only mode, take a database offline, set a database to single-user mode and set a database for bulk copy operations.

Appendix K lists the settings you can use with `sp_configure` and `sp_dboption`.

When we declare a cursor, the cursor scope is `GLOBAL` by default. To change the cursor to a local cursor, we must specify `LOCAL` in the cursor declaration. We can change the default so that cursor declarations in the `FundAccts` database are local instead of global by setting the `'default to local cursor'` database option.

```
EXEC master..sp_dboption 'FundAccts',
    'default to local cursor', 'TRUE'
```

Setting the above option to `FALSE` reverts cursors back to `GLOBAL` scope.

Database option changes take effect immediately. To change database options, you need system administrator permission or you need to be the owner of the database.

Using the DBCC Statement

SQL Server resources and performance factors can be monitored through the use of DBCC statements and trace flags. We'll look at a few DBCC statements in this section and then tackle trace flags in the next section.

The DBCC statements provide a great deal of information about the performance and resource usage of SQL Server and databases. Furthermore, these statements can be used to check the structural integrity of a database's objects, including indexes.

Using DBCC MEMUSAGE

A popular DBCC statement that enables us to display the memory used by SQL Server's' data buffer and stored procedure cache is the DBCC MEMUSAGE statement:

```
DBCC MEMUSAGE('BUFFER','PROCEDURE')
```

The above statement syntax is default, so you can display both data buffer and procedure cache by specifying no arguments at all.

The buffer display shows the memory, in 8K pages, used by the 20 largest objects in SQL Server's' buffer cache (data cache).

The procedure display shows the memory used by the 12 largest procedures in the procedure cache.

Using DBCC USEROPTIONS

The SET options that are in effect for a user session can be listed using the DBCC USEROPTIONS statement:

```
DBCC USEROPTIONS

Set Option                      Value
-----------------               ----------
textsize                        64512
language                        us_english
dateformat                      mdy
datefirst                       7
ansi_null_dflt_on               SET
ansi_warnings                   SET
ansi_padding                    SET
ansi_nulls                      SET
(8 row(s) affected)
DBCC execution completed. If DBCC printed error messages, see your
  System Administrator.
```

Some of the option settings you see from this statement can be derived by querying the bit positions of the @@OPTIONS global variable.

Each user session has an @@OPTIONS global variable that holds the sp_configure 'user options' server settings. These settings are used by SQL Server to provide logins with a set of default options. These options can be overridden by using SET statements. The combination of default settings plus user override settings will be held in the @@OPTIONS variable.

To query the @@OPTIONS settings, you can use a routine similar to this one:

```
DECLARE @i AS int,@configval AS int
SET @i = 0
WHILE @i < 13
BEGIN
```

```
SET @configval = POWER(2,@i)
IF @@options & @configval > 0
    PRINT 'Configuration value ' + LTRIM(@configval) +
           ' is set'
SET @i = @i + 1
END

Configuration value 8 is set
Configuration value 16 is set
Configuration value 32 is set
Configuration value 1024 is set
```

Referring to the user options table in Appendix K tells us that the user options in effect for this user are as follows:

```
8       ANSI_WARNINGS
16      ANSI_PADDING
32      ANSI_NULLS
1024    ANSI_NULL_DFLT_ON
```

Keep in mind that settings such as textsize and language that are shown by the DBCC USEROPTIONS statement are settings not shown in @@OPTIONS since they are not part of the server user options configuration setting.

Using DBCC CHECKDB

The DBCC CHECKDB statement will check the allocation and integrity of the tables in a database.

Table indexes and data pages are checked to ensure the data is properly indexed and that indexes are in the correct order. Pointers and sizes of text, image, and ntext pages are also checked. In fact, every page in the database is checked by this statement.

The following statement will check our FundAccts sample database:

```
DBCC CHECKDB ('FundAccts')
Checking FundAccts
Checking sysobjects
There are 109 rows in 2 pages for object 'sysobjects'.
Checking sysindexes
There are 40 rows in 1 pages for object 'sysindexes'.
Checking syscolumns
There are 568 rows in 8 pages for object 'syscolumns'.
Checking systypes
There are 24 rows in 1 pages for object 'systypes'.
Checking syscomments
There are 162 rows in 46 pages for object 'syscomments'.
Checking sysfiles1
There are 3 rows in 1 pages for object 'sysfiles1'.
Checking syspermissions
There are 59 rows in 1 pages for object 'syspermissions'.
```

```
Checking sysusers
There are 14 rows in 1 pages for object 'sysusers'.
Checking sysdepends
There are 313 rows in 2 pages for object 'sysdepends'.
Checking sysreferences
There are 4 rows in 1 pages for object 'sysreferences'.
Checking sysfilegroups
There are 2 rows in 1 pages for object 'sysfilegroups'.
Checking sysallocations
There are 1 rows in 1 pages for object 'sysallocations'.
Checking dtproperties
There are 7 rows in 1 pages for object 'dtproperties'.
Checking Statements
There are 291 rows in 14 pages for object 'Statements'.
Checking Accounts
There are 33 rows in 1 pages for object 'Accounts'.
Checking AccountValues
There are 66 rows in 5 pages for object 'AccountValues'.
Checking FundAccounts
There are 172 rows in 3 pages for object 'FundAccounts'.
Checking TranHistory
There are 3412 rows in 71 pages for object 'TranHistory'.
Checking Funds
There are 77 rows in 4 pages for object 'Funds'.
CHECKDB found 0 errors in database FundAccts
DBCC execution completed. If DBCC printed error messages, see your
  System Administrator.
```

If you don't want CHECKDB to check nonclustered indexes on user tables to save time, use the NOINDEX option. System table indexes, however, will still be checked:

```
DBCC CHECKDB ('FundAccts',NOINDEX)
```

You can check tables and indexes that reside in a particular filegroup by executing the DBCC CHECKFILEGROUP statement. This statement runs the same checks as DBCC CHECKDB except that only tables and indexes in the specified filegroup are checked.

Running DBCC CHECKFILEGROUP on all filegroups in the database is equivalent to running DBCC CHECKDB. To run DBCC CHECKFILEGROUP, you can specify the filegroup to be checked by naming the filegroup or by specifying the filegroup ID:

```
USE FUNDACCTS
DBCC CHECKFILEGROUP ('primary')
```

or

```
USE FUNDACCTS
DBCC CHECKFILEGROUP (1)
```

One method of obtaining a filegroup ID is to select it from the sysfilegroups table:

```
SELECT * FROM sysfilegroups
groupid allocpolicy status     groupname
---     ---        ---         ----------
1       0          0           default
2       0          0           AcctsGrp

(2 row(s) affected)
```

Since all of the FundAccts tables and indexes are contained in the default file-group, running the above CHECKFILEGROUP statements will yield the same results we got from the CHECKDB statement.

Using DBCC DBREINDEX

A table's indexes can be rebuilt without the need to drop and re-create indexes or issue alter table statements to drop and re-create PRIMARY KEY and UNIQUE constraints:

```
DBCC DBREINDEX ('Fundaccts..Accounts')

Index (id = 1) is being rebuilt.
Index (id = 2) is being rebuilt.
DBCC execution completed. If DBCC printed error messages, see your
  System Administrator.
```

A specific index can be rebuilt by specifying the index name:

```
DBCC DBREINDEX ('Fundaccts..Accounts',PK_Accounts)

Index (id = 2) is being rebuilt.
DBCC execution completed. If DBCC printed error messages, see your
  System Administrator.
```

When the name of a clustered index is specified, all indexes are rebuilt just as they are when you don't specify any index name.

Using DBCC (FREE)

SQL Server supports special stored procedures called extended stored procedures. These procedures are implemented as functions in a Dynamic Link Library (DLL). When an extended procedure is called, SQL Server will load the corresponding DLL into its memory space if the DLL is not already loaded. When the procedure finishes, the DLL is left in memory for possible future use and is not unloaded until SQL Server is shut down or the memory is needed for some other purpose.

You can force a DLL out of memory by executing the DBCC (FREE) statement. If we had an extended stored procedure named 'xp_DownLoadPrices', we could force its DLL to be freed from memory with this statement:

```
DBCC xp_DownLoadPrices (FREE)
```

SQL Server knows the DLL name associated with the extended procedure by means of the sp_addextendedproc used to register the procedure.

Using DBCC SQLPERF (LOGSPACE)

This DBCC statement reports the amount of transaction log space allocated and used for each database in the SQL Server installation (results have been reformatted to fit the page):

```
DBCC SQLPERF (LOGSPACE)

Database     Log         Log
  Name       Size (MB)   Space Used (%)      Status
---------    ---------   ---------------     -------
FundAccts    1.9921875   21.985294                 0
pubs         2.4921875   13.793103                 0
msdb         1.9921875   33.89706                  0
tempdb       1.9921875   16.299019                 0
model        1.0         30.068897                 0
master       3.9921875   28.877201                 0

(6 row(s) affected)
```

Use this statement to periodically check the log space usage and take appropriate action.

Using DBCC PERFMON

This statement displays IO statistics, least recently used (LRU) statistics and network statistics for the server, and it is also used to monitor server performance in these areas:

```
DBCC PERFMON

Statistic                   Value
---------------------       -----
Log Flush Requests          0.0
Log Logical Page IO         0.0
Log Physical IO             0.0
Log Flush Average           0.0
Log Logical IO Average      0.0
Batch Writes                0.0
Batch Average Size          0.0
Batch Max Size              0.0
Page Reads                  724.0
Single Page Writes          82.0
Reads Outstanding           0.0
Writes Outstanding          0.0
Transactions                137.0
Transactions/Log Write      0.0

(14 row(s) affected)
```

```
Statistic                      Value
-----------------------        ---------
Cache Hit Ratio                98.608185
Cache Flushes                  0.0
Free Page Scan (Avg)           0.0
Free Page Scan (Max)           0.0
Min Free Buffers               331.0
Cache Size                     4362.0
Free Buffers                   118.0

(7 row(s) affected)

Statistic                      Value
-----------------------        ---------
Network Reads                  0.0
Network Writes                 2031.0
Command Queue Length           0.0
Max Command Queue Length       0.0
Worker Threads                 0.0
Max Worker Threads             0.0
Network Threads                0.0
Max Network Threads            0.0

(8 row(s) affected)

Statistic                      Value
-----------------------        ---------
RA Pages Found in Cache        0.0
RA Pages Placed in Cache       0.0
RA Physical IO                 0.0
Used Slots                     0.0

(4 row(s) affected)
```

In the data cache statistics section for example, the *Cache Hit Ratio* shows the percentage of time that a request for data could be satisfied from the *Data Cache*. In other words, the percentage of time shown here is the amount of time disk I/O was not necessary to meet the needs of the request. The value shown here should be as high as possible, but will depend on how the system is used. A consistently low number is an indication that your server is doing a great deal of I/O and is not gaining much benefit from the data cache. Remember that the unit being cached is an 8KB data page, which could satisfy multiple requests depending on the row density of the page.

Page Reads in the I/O section indicates the number of Page Reads per second. This number represents page reads across all databases in the installation. This is physical I/O it should be kept as low as possible to maximize performance.

Network Writes in the network section is the number of tabular data stream (TDS) packets written to the network per second. A high number indicates a high volume of network traffic. What "high" means for your installation needs to be discussed with your network engineers.

The RA section of the report is the statistics for the Read-Ahead Manager component of SQL Server. `RA Pages Placed in Cache`, for example, is the number of pages placed into the cache by the Read-Ahead Manager. This number indicates read-ahead activity when SQL Server detects sequential scans of a table. It can be compared with the `RA Pages Found in Cache` statistic to determine how effective the Read-Ahead Manager is. The `Pages Placed in Cache` number should be higher than the `Pages Found in Cache` number.

Descriptions of the other statistics shown in this report can be found in SQL Server Books Online.

Using DBCC SHOW_STATISTICS

The key distribution statistics for an index is an important factor for the query optimizer when creating a plan of execution for a query. These statistics can be viewed using the DBCC `SHOW_STATISTICS` statement:

```
DBCC SHOW_STATISTICS (Accounts, IX_Accounts)
```

This statement will show statistics on the IX_Accounts index on the Accounts table. The important statistic out of this statement is the density. A low key density means that the index has good selectivity since keys are more unique in the index. A high density would mean keys are less unique and would indicate lower selectivity. The optimizer would tend to choose the lower density index.

Using DBCC SHOWCONTIG

This statement scans the data pages of a table or index and reports the amount of fragmentation found. Fragmentation results from change activity on a table and can impact performance, especially when sequential reads are performed:

```
USE FundAccts
DECLARE @objid AS int
SELECT @objid = OBJECT_ID('TranHistory')
DBCC SHOWCONTIG (@objid)

DBCC SHOWCONTIG scanning 'TranHistory' table...
[SHOW_CONTIG - SCAN ANALYSIS]
---------------------------------------------------------
Table: 'TranHistory' (1470628282)  Indid: 0  dbid:6
TABLE level scan performed.
- Pages Scanned...........................: 71
- Extent Switches.........................: 10
- Avg. Pages per Extent...................: 6.5
- Scan Density [Best Count:Actual Count]..: 81.82% [9:11]
- Avg. Bytes free per page................: 419.2
- Avg. Page density (full)................: 94.82%

(8 row(s) affected)
```

If there were no fragmentation in the TranHistory table, the Scan Density number would show 100. Since it is less than 100, we know there is some fragmentation in the table's pages.

If a table has a clustered index and becomes fragmented, you can rebuild the index to remove the fragmentation.

Setting Up Jobs

An administrator can establish a collection of jobs in a SQL Server installation to run maintenance tasks such as backups and restores. Jobs can be used in applications to perform unattended processing such as special checks against a database, as we'll do in this section.

Jobs are composed of one or more job steps. A job step can be comprised of any of the following commands:

◆ Transact-SQL statement or call to a stored procedure or extended procedure

◆ CmdExec command that executes a .cmd or .exe program

◆ Replication command to manage some aspect of database replication

◆ Active Script containing VBScript or Java Script

Jobs are managed by SQL Server Agent, which is a service used to schedule and execute jobs, and process alerts and operator notifications. The Agent can manage the execution of jobs on a single server or multiple servers. Before continuing this section, be sure the SQL Server Agent is started using SQL Server Enterprise Manager or the command prompt.

Creating a Job

The principals of our money management firm want a weekly report from their manager tracking system that shows any client redemptions greater than $5,000. To satisfy this request, we need to feed the manager tracking system with a file containing all redemption transactions with amounts less than or equal to -5000.

Since we'll be doing this on a periodic basis, we'll create a job to pull the required information out of the FundAccts database and save it in a file that the manager tracking system can import.

First, we need to create the job and give it a meaningful name. Let's call this job "Redemptions."

```
USE msdb
GO
EXEC sp_add_job @job_name = 'Redemptions'
```

The use of the `sp_add_job` stored procedure above is quite basic. The only parameter we have supplied to it is the `job_name` parameter.

There are several defaults for the `sp_add_job`. The job is automatically enabled (`@enabled`) when the job is created. You can disable it by setting this parameter to zero.

If the job fails for some reason, an entry is written to the NT event log. If you want to have an event log entry written on something other than failure, or not at all, you can set the `@notify_level_eventlog` parameter (default value is 2):

◆ The value 0 will cause nothing to be written to the event log.

◆ The value 1 will write an entry when the job succeeds.

◆ The value 3 will write failure and success entries in the log.

The above values also have meaning for other types of notification. You can notify operators via e-mail (`@notify_email_operator_name`), **network message** (`@notify_netsend_operator_name`), **and pager** (`@notify_page_operator_name`).

Each of the operator notifications is controlled by a `@notify_level_xxxx` parameter where xxxx is either `'email'`, `'netsend'`, or `'page'`. The settings of these levels is the same as that used for `@notify_level_eventlog` listed above.

You can assign a job to a job category by setting the `@category_name` parameter. This is sometimes helpful to organize jobs in an installation. The category name can be up to 100 characters long.

An additional parameter that can be helpful in documenting the job is the job description parameter. A description for the job is entered with the `@description` parameter and can be up to 512 characters long.

Now let's add a jobstep to this job.

Adding jobsteps to a Job

For this request, we only need a single step, but you can specify multiple steps in a job if you need them. To add steps, we use the `sp_add_jobstep` procedure.

We provide the name of the job to add the step to using the `@job_name` parameter. Next, we name the job step using the `@step_name` parameter. In this example, we simply call it 'Step 1':

```
USE msdb
GO
EXEC sp add jobstep @job name = 'Redemptions',
                @step_name = 'Step 1',
                @command = 'SELECT
            acct_no,T.fund_cd,T.fundacctno,trandate,
  amount
                FROM TranHistory T INNER JOIN FundAccounts F
                ON T.fund_cd = F.fund_cd AND
                   T.fundacctno = F.fundacctno
                WHERE trantype = ''redempt'' AND
```

```
        amount <= -5000
ORDER BY trandate DESC',
    @database_name = 'FundAccts',
    @output_file_name = 'Redemptions.dat',
    @server='SECRETS'
```

To satisfy the requirements of the Redemptions report, we specify a command parameter for this step that contains a Transact-SQL statement. The statement simply queries transactions that have a `trantype` equal to `'redempt'` and an amount less than or equal to `-5000`. We join the TranHistory table to the FundAccounts table in order to retrieve the account number.

The `@database_name` parameter specifies the database to execute this query against and the `@server` parameter specifies the server where the database is installed.

The output from this jobstep command is directed to an external file using the `@output_file_name` parameter. Here, we use a file named `'Redemptions.dat'` to hold the query results.

The `sp_add_jobstep` procedure allows us to enter parameters that will dictate what action to take when the command succeeds or fails. These actions are based on the setting for `@cmdexec_success_code`, which specifies the success code for the command. In our example, if SQL Server returns zero, the default code, then the command is considered to have completed successfully. If any code other than zero is returned by SQL Server, the command is considered to have failed.

If no success or fail action is specified, as in this example, the job merely quits and returns success or failure. To override the default behavior, we can use the `@on_success_action` and `@on_fail_action` parameters to specify some other action to take on these events.

The `@on_success_action` dictates what action to take when the `@cmdexec_success_code` is returned. The `@on_success_action` can be any of these values:

- The value 1 causes a quit with success.

- The value 2 causes a quit with failure.

- The value 3 causes a branch to the next step in the job.

- The value 4 causes a branch to the jobstep specified in the `@on_success_step_id` parameter.

The `@on_fail_action` parameter uses these same values but value 4 is interpreted as a branch to the jobstep specified in the `@on_fail_step_id` parameter.

That's it for our Redemptions job. Let's try it out.

Running a Job Manually

We can test our job by running it with the `sp_start_job` procedure. Before we do this, however, we need to tell the SQL Server Agent which server should be used to run the job. We do this using the `sp_add_jobserver` procedure:

```
USE msdb
GO
EXEC sp_add_jobserver @job_name = 'Redemptions',
                      @server_name = 'Secrets'
```

All we need for this procedure is the name of the job and the name of the server to execute the job on.

Now we're ready to test our Redemptions job using sp_start_job:

```
USE msdb
GO
EXEC sp_start_job @job_name = 'Redemptions'
```

All we get from this statement is that the job was started (if we did everything correctly). To see the results, we can open the 'Redemptions.dat' file and look at the results of the query. Since we didn't provide a path for the file, it is found in the Windows\System directory.

This file can now be imported to the manager tracking system and used to produce the report for management. To run this job on a weekly basis, we can establish a schedule for the job. This way, the job will run unattended and provide the output to the tracking system when needed. We don't have to remember to execute sp_start_job every week.

Creating a Job Schedule

To set up a weekly schedule for the Redemptions job, we use sp_add_jobschedule. This procedure names the job for which the schedule is being created and then names the schedule using the @name parameter.

We specify the frequency type for the job by assigning one of the following values to the @freq_type parameter:

Value	Frequency Type
1	Once
4	Daily
8	Weekly
16	Monthly
32	Monthly relative to the value in @freq_interval
64	Run when the SQL Server Agent is started

The @freq_interval parameter designates which day the job is to be run:

Value	Interval
1	Sunday

2	Monday
3	Tuesday
4	Wednesday
5	Thursday
6	Friday
7	Saturday
8	day
9	weekdays
10	weekend days

The `@freq_subday_type` specifies the unit of time for the `@freq_subday_interval`:

Value	Unit of Time
1	At the time specified
2	Seconds
3	Minutes
4	Hours

The number of `@freq_subday_type` units that are to elapse between job runs is specified in the `@freq_subday_interval` parameter.

The `@active_start_time` designates when the job is to run on the day specified in the `@freq_interval`. This time uses a HHMMSS format. You can also specify an `@active_start_date`, `@active_end_date`, and `@active_end_time`. Dates use a YYYYMMDD format.

The `@freq_recurrence_factor` parameter designates the recurrence of `@freq_type`. In this example, we want the job to run every week, so we set a value of 1 here. If we wanted the job to run every two weeks, we would set a value of 2, and so on:

```
USE msdb
GO
EXEC sp_add_jobschedule @job_name = 'Redemptions',
                        @name = 'WeeklySchedule',
                        @freq_type = 8,
                        @freq_interval = 1,
                        @freq_subday_type = 1,
                        @active_start_time = '000000',
                        @freq_recurrence_factor = 1
```

The above `sp_add_jobschedule` statement sets up a schedule that runs the Redemptions job every Sunday at 12 A.M. If we want to change this start time to 5 P.M., we can execute an `sp_update_jobschedule` and set the desired start time with the `@active_start_time` parameter. The time entered in this parameter is in the form HHMMSS and uses the 24-hour clock:

```
USE msdb
GO
EXEC sp_update_jobschedule @job_name = 'Redemptions',
                           @name = 'WeeklySchedule',
                           @active_start_time = '170000'
```

All of the job properties can be displayed in SQL Server Enterprise Manager in the Jobs folder under the SQL Server Agent object. To list these properties with stored procedures, you can use the following procedures:

◆ `sp_help_job` to list the job properties

◆ `sp_help_jobstep` to list jobstep properties

◆ `sp_help_jobschedule` to list the schedule properties

If a job is running and you need to cancel it for some reason, you can use the `sp_stop_job` procedure to do so:

```
sp_stop_job @job_name = 'Redemptions'
```

Before stopping a running job, however, be sure to consider the ramifications of doing so. In the case of the Redemptions job, the effect of stopping the job would be an incomplete `redemptions.dat` file being fed into the tracking system.

Performing Backup and Recovery

Databases and transaction logs must be backed up periodically as insurance against a failure of a disk drive or a large-scale data integrity problem, or possibly the loss of an entire server machine.

When recovery is necessary, the administrator needs to go back to the latest backup of the database and recover the database to that point in time. From this starting point, the database is then brought up to date (or close to it) by applying the transactions from either the current transaction log, if possible, or the latest backup of the transaction log.

Every installation needs to develop a backup scheme that meets the needs of the organization. The choice depends on the frequency of transactions applied to the database, the criticality of the database (taking into account the availability requirements), and the required timeliness of the data. Volume of data and time required to backup and restore that data are other factors to consider.

Some organizations will do a full database backup on one schedule, an incremental backup to capture changes since the full backup on a more frequent schedule, and transaction log backups on an even more frequent schedule to enable recovery from the point of the last incremental backup.

SQL Server 7 enables backup and recovery to take place at the file and filegroup level as well so that parts of a database can be backed up and recovered. This type of backup/recovery process can be helpful in a large database installation where the database is spread across several files. For this type of backup/recovery to be successful, the use of the files and filegroups in the database must be well understood so that data integrity is preserved.

Backing Up the FundAccts Database

Here, we'll perform a simple backup of the entire FundAccts database, including the transaction log:

```
BACKUP DATABASE FundAccts
    TO DISK = 'J:\backups\dbbackup.dat'
Processed 688 pages for database 'FundAccts', file 'FundAccts_Data'
  on file <1>.
Processed 8 pages for database 'FundAccts', file 'FundAccts_Data2'
  on file <1>.
Processed 1 pages for database 'FundAccts', file 'FundAccts_Log' on
  file <1>.
Backup/restore operation successfully processed 697 pages in 15.919
  seconds (0.358 Mbytes/sec).
```

The above BACKUP statement performs a backup of the database to a DISK file named J:\backups\back.dat. This type of backup is usually a temporary backup applied to a network drive, with the intention of copying the file to tape or some other archive media.

A backup can be applied to tape directly by specifying TAPE instead of DISK. Backup file destinations can also be created with the sp_addumpdevice procedure. The file name created with this procedure is then specified after the TO keyword without a media type keyword.

Use the INIT keyword to overwrite the data already present in the backup file. If the backup file contains any backups that have not yet expired, specified with the EXPIREDATE or RETAINDAYS keywords, or the backup set name in the file does not match the name provided in the NAME keyword of the BACKUP statement, the backup data will not be overwritten. To bypass these checks, use the SKIP keyword.

To perform an incremental backup, supply the INCREMENTAL keyword.

Backing up files and filegroups is performed using this format:

```
BACKUP DATABASE FundAccts FILE = 'FundAccts_Data'
    TO ...
```

or

```
BACKUP DATABASE FundAccts FILEGROUP = 'AcctsGrp'
  TO ...
```

To back up the transaction log only, use the following:

```
BACKUP LOG FundAccts TO DISK 'J:\backups\logbackup.dat'
```

The log backup cannot be run when the `'truncate log on checkpoint'` database option is in effect.

Restoring the FundAccts Database

To restore the database from the BACKUP we made above, we would issue the following RESTORE statement:

```
RESTORE DATABASE FundAccts FROM
 DISK = 'J:\backups\back.dat'

Processed 688 pages for database 'FundAccts', file 'FundAccts_Data'
  on file <1>.
Processed 8 pages for database 'FundAccts', file 'FundAccts_Data2'
  on file <1>.
Processed 1 pages for database 'FundAccts', file 'FundAccts_Log' on
  file <1>.
Backup/restore operation successfully processed 697 pages in 31.594
  seconds (0.180 Mbytes/sec).
```

As mentioned in the BACKUP section, you can restore entire databases as we have just done with the FundAccts database, one or more files or filegroups, or just transaction logs. Database restores can be done from full and incremental backups. Before the RESTORE can proceed, the database must be in exclusive use by the system administrator.

If the backup media contains more than one backup set, you can point the RESTORE to the set you want restored using the FILE keyword followed by the number of the set you want. Use FILE = 1 to get the first backup set, FILE = 2 to get the second backup set, and so on.

If a MEDIANAME was specified during BACKUP, you can provide that name for RESTORE using the same keyword. The RESTORE will check this name against the backup set and fail if not found or matched.

The STATS keyword and a specified percentage cause RESTORE to print a message when another percentage of the restore operation has completed.

When restoring multiple transaction logs to a database, you should use the NORE-COVERY keyword. NORECOVERY prevents rollback of uncommitted transactions found in the log. When a change is made to a row during normal database use, an image of the row before and after the change is written to the log. When the RESTORE applies the log to the database, the after image is written. If at the end of the log, a commit of the change is not found, then RESTORE backs the change out of the database by writing the before image into the row. If all transaction logs to be restored have not been applied, then RESTORE should not attempt to roll back changes until the last log has been restored. NORECOVERY is used on all log restores except the last, in which RECOVERY is specified (or implied by the absence of NORECOVERY).

RECOVERY and NORECOVERY are not used when restoring files and filegroups.

When restoring a log, the STOPAT keyword can be used to specify the date and time for stopping the restore. Any transactions found in the log occurring on or after this date and time will not be applied to the database.

More Maintenance Tasks

Beyond the tasks discussed thus far, the administrator may be called upon to ensure that database statistics used by the SQL Server query optimizer are kept up to date, manage the availability of SQL Server, manage database growth, and monitor overall system and database performance.

In this section, we take a quick look at some of these tasks. Performance as measured by the SQL Server Profiler is discussed in Chapter 17.

Using the UPDATE STATISTICS Statement

When the SQL Server query optimizer is asked to create a query execution plan for a query, one of the pieces of information it uses to develop an optimal plan is the distribution of keys in indexes.

The index statistics need to be refreshed whenever activity in the associated table may impact the distribution of index entries. This can occur when there has been a heavy volume of UPDATE, INSERT, and DELETE activity on indexed columns.

Statistics will be updated automatically when an index is created or rebuilt. You can update the statistics manually by executing the UPDATE STATISTICS statement:

```
UPDATE STATISTICS Accounts
```

The above statement refreshes statistics for all indexes on the Accounts table. When SQL Server computes the statistics, it may create a sample distribution from the entire population of index entries. If you want to force SQL Server to use the entire index, specify the keyword FULLSCAN.

If you feel that a FULLSCAN is not necessary to yield meaningful statistics, you can still influence the sample by using the SAMPLE keyword:

```
UPDATE STATISTICS Accounts WITH SAMPLE 70 PERCENT
```

The sample can be specified as either PERCENT, as done here, or ROWS.

You can cause statistics to be updated for a specific index using the following syntax:

```
UPDATE STATISTICS Accounts IX_Accounts
```

If you prefer to control the refresh of statistics manually, you can turn off the automatic statistics calculation by specifying the keyword NORECOMPUTE in the UPDATE STATISTICS statement. To turn automatic calculation back on, issue an UPDATE STATISTICS statement without this keyword.

The last time statistics were updated for an index can be obtained from the STATS_DATE() function:

```
DECLARE @objid AS int,-xid as int
SELECT @objid = OBJECT_ID('Accounts')
SELECT -xid = indid FROM sysindexes
  WHERE name = 'IX_Accounts'
SELECT STATS_DATE (@objid,-xid)
------------------------
1998-06-01 12:14:43.327

(1 row(s) affected)
```

The above statement has selected the object ID of the Accounts table using the OBJECT_ID() function and then the index ID of the IX_Accounts index by selecting it out of the sysindexes system table.

Once these IDs are obtained, the STATS_DATE() function can be called to display the date and time the statistics for this index were updated.

Starting Up SQL Server

The SQL Server service (MSSQLServer) can be started using any of the following methods:

◆ SQL Server Service Manager

◆ SQL Server Enterprise Manager

◆ NT Services Control Panel

◆ Command prompt

The service can be set up to start at NT startup by setting the appropriate option in the NT Services Control Panel applet or in the SQL Server Enterprise Manager server properties Autostart options.

Use the following command line to start SQL Server from the command prompt:

```
net start mssqlserver
```

You can also start SQL Server outside of the NT Service Control Manager by executing `sqlservr` from the command prompt. Doing this, however, causes messages to be sent to the command prompt window, disables the ability to pause, stop, or continue SQL Server as you would when it runs as a service, and disables your ability to log off of NT without shutting down SQL Server first. To stop `sqlservr`, use CTRL-BREAK in the command prompt window to display the "Do you want to stop SQL Server? Y/N" message.

When SQL Server is installed, a default set of startup options is written into the system registry. You can override these startup options when starting SQL Server. You do this by providing command line flags. For example, to start SQL Server in single-user mode, you would code as follows:

```
sqlservr -m
```

The startup options are shown in Table 14-1.

TABLE 14-1 STARTUP OPTIONS

Option Flag	Description
`-dmaster_database_filename`	The master database to use.
`-eerror_log_filename`	The file to use for the error log.
`-f`	Starts SQL Server with minimal configuration options.
`-lmaster_database_log_filename`	The file to use as the master database log.
`-m`	Starts SQL Server in single-user mode.
`-n`	Does not write SQL Server events to the NT event log. Will log to the error log if -e provided.
`-pprecision`	Sets the precision for decimal and numeric data types to the value specified by precision.
`-sregistrykey`	Starts SQL Server using the Registry entries found under the `registrykey` entry.
`/Ttraceflag`	Sets the indicated trace flag number to alter the behavior of SQL Server.
`-x`	Disables CPU time and cache hit ratio statistics.

Using these options may be necessary for troubleshooting various problems in the server environment.

Starting the SQL Server Agent

The same options for starting SQL Server also apply to SQL Server Agent. The Agent must be running to schedule and execute jobs and to handle event notifications.

To start the SQL Server Agent service from a command prompt, type the following:

```
net start sqlserveragent
```

As with other services started in this manner, logging off of NT after starting the service does not stop the service.

Shutting Down and Pausing SQL Server

SQL Server can be stopped using the `net stop mssqlserver` command line or by any of the utilities used to start it.

When SQL Server is stopped, all users are disconnected, no new user connections are accepted, and all server processes are stopped. This is only used when you are sure there is no activity on the server or an immediate shutdown is necessary.

A more user-friendly method of shutdown is the pause method:

```
net pause mssqlserver
```

Pausing the server allows current connections and processes to continue but disallows any new connections. This gives the administrator time to notify current users that the server will be shut down and give them time to do a normal disconnect. After all users have disconnected and processes stopped, the server can be stopped.

If a server is paused, it can be resumed by executing the `continue` command:

```
net continue mssqlserver
```

The server can be shut down using Transact-SQL. To shut down the server immediately without waiting on users to disconnect, use the following statement:

```
SHUTDOWN WITH NOWAIT
```

This is similar to stopping the SQL Server service. No checkpoints are taken and all users are disconnected immediately. To issue the user-friendly shutdown, omit the `WITH NOWAIT` option:

```
SHUTDOWN
```

This method behaves like a pause. No new logins are accepted, current executing statements are allowed to finish, and database checkpoints are taken (updated pages in the data cache are written to disk).

Terminate a Process

When you execute the `sp_who` procedure, you will see a list of system process IDs (SPID) for a number of system processes, including an SPID for each user connection. The following `sp_who` example shows system processes and two user connections (the results have been reformatted to fit the page):

```
sp_who

sp  status    login   host    blk db
id            name    name        name      cmd
--  --------  ------  ------- --  --------- ----------------
1   runnable  sa              0   master    LOCK MONITOR
2   sleeping  sa              0   master    SIGNAL HANDLER
3   sleeping  sa              0   master    LAZY WRITER
4   sleeping  sa              0   master    LOG WRITER
5   sleeping  sa              0   master    CHECKPOINT SLEEP
6   runnable  sa      SECRETS 0   master    SELECT
7   sleeping  B25755  SECRETS 0   FundAccts AWAITING COMMAND

(7 row(s) affected)
```

The last two SPIDs on server `'SECRETS'` are user connections using the `master` and the `FundAccts` databases. If a process needs to be terminated for some reason, possibly hoarding resources such that other processes cannot run, you can issue a `KILL` statement on the SPID of the process:

```
KILL 7
```

System processes and those representing extended stored procedure executions cannot be `KILL`ed. To determine the SPID of your user connection, you can select it from the `@@spid` global variable.

Summary

In this chapter, we learned how to create default configuration parameters for the server using `sp_configure` and for the database using `sp_dboption`.

We saw the use of various DBCC statements for monitoring performance and resource statistics for the server and databases.

The creation of SQL Server jobs was explored. We learned what a job was, what it could be used for, and how to create it. Jobsteps were added to a job to carry out the processing of the job, and we learned how to run a job manually and by creating a job schedule to run the job on a recurring basis.

The Transact-SQL backup and recovery process was explored. Databases can be backed up by a full database backup, including all objects and the transaction log, an incremental database backup to include only changes since the last backup, file and filegroup backups to include specific parts of a database, and transaction log backups to include only the transaction log to be used for forward recovery of a previous database backup.

Finally, various methods of starting SQL Server were explored, along with methods for shutting it down. We saw the difference between a shutdown and a shutdown with nowait, and what impact these have on connected users.

Chapter 15

Working with Stored Procedures and Triggers

IN THIS CHAPTER

- ◆ Find out what a stored procedure is, why we should use them, and how they are put together

- ◆ Learn how the flow of execution within a batch or procedure can be controlled using Transact-SQL control-of-flow statements

- ◆ Discover how to write and implement your own stored procedures

- ◆ Explore special stored procedures called triggers that are run when specified events occur in a table

- ◆ Learn what extended procedures are, how to build them, and run them in SQL Server

THROUGHOUT THE PRECEDING chapters, we've used some of SQL Server's stored procedures for various tasks such as establishing database users and permissions, displaying database and table properties, setting database options, working with views, and describing cursors.

SQL Server provides a number of system stored procedures in several categories. Descriptions of these stored procedures are listed in Appendix F . You can list the stored procedures in a database by executing the `sp_stored_procedures` procedure.

In this chapter, we find out what a stored procedure looks like internally and we write some procedures for use in the Fund Accounts database.

Writing parts of your application as a stored procedure resident on the SQL Server machine and executed there can reduce network traffic, provide faster execution, and improve overall performance by reducing the processing load of the client machines.

We'll see that in addition to the Transact-SQL statements we've been using all along to manipulate data in the database, we can code statements in a procedure that enables us to control the flow of execution through the procedure. This group of statements in Transact-SQL is called the *control-of-flow* language.

Once we understand what a stored procedure is and how it functions, we'll go a step further and create some special procedures that can be executed based on some event in the database. These special procedures are called *triggers*.

Before leaving this chapter, we take a peek at *extended stored procedures*, find out what they are, and how to create them.

Using Global and Local Variables

When writing a procedure, it is often necessary to store a value for use later in the procedure. These stored values can be the results of a SELECT statement, a cursor variable, or the results of a calculation or an internal flag, indicator, or code. Anything we need to save for some purpose later in the procedures' processing can be saved in a variable.

We've already seen a few examples of variables being used in sample scripts of previous chapters. There are two types of variables: global variables and local variables.

Global variables are supplied by SQL Server and are indicated by preceding double at (@@) signs. The @@cursor_rows, @@fetch_status, and @@error are examples of global variables. Any procedure can reference these variables and they do not have to be declared before using them. SQL Server knows them by name. A list of global variables can be found in Appendix F .

Local variables are supplied by the procedure developer and consist of a name, starting with a single at (@) sign, and a SQL Server data type. Unlike global variables, local variables must be declared before use so that SQL Server knows how to work with the variables' contents.

In this section, we'll explore how to declare local variables, how to set values into them, and how to retrieve values out of them.

The DECLARE Statement

To enable SQL Server to work with local variables, we must provide SQL Server with a few pieces of information about the variable.

We must first of all give the variable a name that is distinguishable from other variables in the procedure and from global variables and keywords. We prefix the variable with one at sign (@).

Next, we need to give the variable a data type that SQL Server understands. The data type can be declared just as we would declare the data type for a column in a table.

To provide SQL Server with this information, we use the DECLARE statement like this:

```
DECLARE @my_local_acct_no varchar(10)
```

Each variable to be used in the procedure can be declared in this manner, or you can include multiple variables in one `DECLARE` statement like this:

```
DECLARE @my_acct_type varchar(6),
  @my_acct_name varchar(70)
```

A local variable can be declared with any SQL Server-defined data type except `image`.

The scope of the variable, where the variable can be referenced, is the batch or procedure where the variable was declared. You cannot declare a variable in one procedure and reference it in another procedure. As we'll soon see, however, there are ways to pass variable values from procedure to procedure.

Setting Variable Values

A value can be assigned to a local variable in two ways. The first method uses a `SELECT` statement to assign a literal constant, column value, or expression, as shown here:

```
/* Assign a literal constant */
SELECT @my_acct_type = 'Tax'
/* Or assign a column value */
SELECT @my_acct_type = acct_type FROM Accounts
  WHERE acct_no = '1003'
```

The second method of assigning a value to a variable uses a `SET` statement:

```
SET @my_acct_type = 'Nontax'
SELECT acct_no, tot_assets
FROM Accounts
WHERE acct_type = @my_acct_type
```

Reading Variable Values

To read the value stored in a variable, use a `SELECT` statement as shown below:

```
DECLARE @my_acct_type varchar(6)
/* Select the column into a variable */
SELECT @my_acct_type = acct_type FROM Accounts
  WHERE acct_no = '1003'
/* Now select the variable to the output buffer */
SELECT @my_acct_type
------
NonTax

(1 row(s) affected)
```

Using Control-of-Flow Statements

When we write a stored procedure or script, the language we use needs to satisfy a few requirements.

First of all, we need some method of communicating parameters into the procedure and a method for accepting returned results. Using input parameters, we can change the behavior of the procedure or refine its processing to a subset of the data in the database. Output parameters and return values are used for accessing the results of the procedure processing.

Second, we need to control the flow of execution through the procedure based on the outcome of various conditions. We may need to test input parameter values, program variables, or database values against one or more conditional values and branch to routines appropriate for the conditions found.

Third, it would be nice to be able to execute loops – that is, repeat a section of code some specified number of times or until a certain condition is met.

And last, we should probably have a means of handling errors that may arise in our procedure and be able to communicate these errors back to the user.

All these requirements are met with Transact-SQLs control-of-flow language. Let's take a closer look at the statements in this language.

IF...ELSE Statement

When you execute a batch of Transact-SQL statements, the statements are executed in sequential order from topmost statement to the last. The control-of-flow statements can be used to alter this normal flow of execution in various ways.

The first control-of-flow statement we'll look at is the IF...ELSE statement.

IF...ELSE is used to test a condition and branch the execution path according to the outcome of the test:

```
DECLARE @acct_type varchar(6)
SELECT @acct_type = acct_type
FROM Accounts
WHERE acct_no = '1003'

IF @acct_type = 'Nontax'
  SELECT 'Account 1003 is not taxable'
ELSE
  SELECT 'Account 1003 is taxable'


---------------------------
Account 1003 is not taxable
(1 row(s) affected)
```

We would expect the Transact-SQL IF...ELSE statement to behave like the If-Then-Else statement found in other languages like C++ and Visual Basic. Indeed, it does. The IF...ELSE statement above tests the local variable @acct_type, selected from the 1003 account, for the value of 'Nontax'. If the variable holds the value 'Nontax', then we select out the constant string 'Account 1003 is not taxable'.

If the local variable is not equal to 'Nontax', then we select out 'Account 1003 is taxable' since the account type is limited to either 'Tax' or 'Nontax'.

The expression being tested can be any expression that returns a TRUE or FALSE value. If a TRUE value is returned, the statement immediately following the IF is executed; otherwise, the statement following the ELSE is executed.

Simple so far, but what do we do if we want to execute more than one statement as a result of the test? This is where the next control-of-flow statement is used.

BEGIN...END Block

Multiple Transact-SQL statements can be nested within BEGIN...END delimiters to cause more than one statement to execute based on the outcome of an IF test.

Consider the following example:

```
IF (SELECT COUNT(*)
    FROM tranhistory t INNER JOIN fundaccounts f
  ON  t.fund_cd = f.fund_cd
  AND t.fundacctno = f.fundacctno
  WHERE f.acct_type = 'IRA') > 0
  BEGIN
    SELECT 'Accounts with IRA fund account transactions'
    SELECT acct_no,fund_cd,fundacctno
        FROM fundaccounts
        WHERE acct_type = 'IRA'
  END
ELSE
    SELECT 'No accounts with IRA fund account
            transactions'
-------------------------------------------
Accounts with IRA fund account transactions
(1 row(s) affected)
acct_no    fund_cd fundacctno
-------    ------- -------------------------
1013       1090Z   111111111-3
1013       BEGRX   76-333333111-2
1017       BEGRX   76-777777777-1
1011       FMAGX   21-9999999222
1059       GABGX   400-222111122-1
1023       JANSX   44-22228887-40
1028       JAVTX   35-22222222-12
1059       LDDVX   19995B
1014       LDDVX   22221A
1028       LDDVX   33334B
1028       LDNRX   111005
1059       MONTX   700-111-8888888883
1014       MONTX   700-111-8888888884
1010       MQIFX   99-2222222112
1016       MQIFX   99-2222222114
1016       MUTHX   98-3333333115
1067       NICSX   200-4444444-405
1014       NICSX   200-4444444-406
1015       PARTR   1444444003
```

```
1027      PARTR    1444444005
1027      PARTR    1444444006
1015      WINSR    55588855-5
1067      LDDVX    444444X
1067      BEGRX    44401010101-0
1070      JANSX    400-222299981
1018      MDISC    700-7777222211
1018      MERID    66600066
1005      MDISC    700-98989898110
1006      MDISC    700-98989898112
1067      THIRD    6666998
1017      VCAGX    90-888888-93
1059      THIRD    8005555599
1028      VCAGX    900-40000101
1011      JAMRX    480-997-55551
9847      ANEFX    147777777-089-01
```

```
(35 row(s) affected)
```

The IF condition is based on a SELECT statement that selects the count of rows from the TranHistory table for fund accounts that have the IRA account type.

If there is at least one tranhistory row for an IRA fund account, a message is selected to the output buffer followed by a list of the fund accounts that have IRA account types.

If there are no transaction history rows for these account types, we would get another message indicating this fact.

Note that in this example we have grouped two SELECT statements into a BEGIN...END block so that both statements will execute if more than zero transaction history rows are counted.

Using the PRINT Statement

In the above example, we used a SELECT statement to return a literal constant to the output buffer. This displays in the SQL Query Analyzer Results pane as a separate result set indicated by the presence of the '(1 row(s) affected)' message.

We can include the message with the result set that lists the IRA fund accounts by changing the SELECT statement to a PRINT statement. When executed, we get a result that looks like this:

```
IF (SELECT COUNT(*)
    FROM tranhistory t INNER JOIN fundaccounts f
    ON t.fund_cd = f.fund_cd
    AND t.fundacctno = f.fundacctno
    WHERE f.acct_type = 'IRA') > 0
  BEGIN
    PRINT 'Accounts with IRA fund account transactions'
    SELECT acct_no,fund_cd,fundacctno
      FROM fundaccounts
      WHERE acct_type = 'IRA'
  END
```

```
ELSE
    PRINT 'No accounts with IRA fund account
          transactions'

Accounts with IRA fund account transactions
acct_no     fund_cd fundacctno
-------     ------- -----------------------
1013        1090Z   111111111-3
1013        BEGRX   76-333333111-2
1017        BEGRX   76-777777777-1
1011        FMAGX   21-9999999222
...
1011        JAMRX   480-997-55551
9847        ANEFX   147777777-089-01

(35 row(s) affected)
```

Using the PRINT statement, we can return a string into the result set that is a literal constant, the contents of a variable, or the result of an expression. The string returned is limited to 1,024 characters.

Using a CASE Expression

The CASE expression can be used to test a variable or column against several values and return a result based on the outcome of the tests.

One application of the CASE expression is to translate the acct_type column in the FundAccounts table from its code to a human-readable string. Here's what it looks like:

```
SELECT fund_cd,fundacctno,acct_no,AccountType =
  CASE acct_type
      WHEN 'IRA' THEN 'IRA'
      WHEN 'TF' THEN 'Trust Fund'
      WHEN '401' THEN '401(k)'
      WHEN 'PP' THEN 'Pension Plan'
      ELSE 'No entry'
  END
FROM FundAccounts
ORDER BY AccountType

fund_cd fundacctno       acct_no   AccountType
------- --------------   ------    -----------
1090Z   111111111-3      1013      IRA
BEGRX   76-333333111-2   1013      IRA
BEGRX   76-777777777-1   1017      IRA
FMAGX   21-9999999222    1011      IRA
GABGX   400-222111122-1  1059      IRA
...
JAVLX   400-11111100-9   1003      Pension Plan
PRFHX   1444444008-1     1016      Trust Fund
VWLTX   55588855-3       1023      Trust Fund
(172 row(s) affected)
```

In this example, we embed the CASE expression in the SELECT statement to translate the acct_type column values. These translated results are returned in the column named AccountType, which is used to order the results.

Notice that in the CASE expression, the ELSE clause is used to catch any entry for which we did not include a WHEN test. In this example, the ELSE is filling in 'No entry' for NULL values in the acct_type column.

The above use of the CASE expression tests the acct_type column for equivalency to each of the WHEN values. If you need to test for other than equal conditions, you can use this form:

```
DECLARE @avgcurval AS money
SELECT @avgcurval = AVG(cur_value)
FROM accountvalues
SELECT CASE
    WHEN @avgcurval > 150000 THEN 'Avg current value is
          greater than $150,000. Avg is: '
    ELSE 'Average current value is below target. Average
          is: '
END,@avgcurval
```

```
--------------------------------------------- ----------
Avg current value is below target. Avg is: 132778.4560
(1 row(s) affected)
```

When using Boolean expressions in the WHEN clauses, you do not specify a column name after the CASE keyword as we did in the first example. The column or variable being tested is specified in the WHEN clause itself.

WHILE Statement

Another construct often used in programming applications is the loop. Loops allow us to repeat a set of code multiple times and are usually associated with some control variable that is used to control the number of times the loop is executed.

In the Transact-SQL control-of-flow language, we use the WHILE statement to implement a loop:

```
DECLARE @curval AS money,@investtot AS money
DECLARE @acct AS varchar(10),@stmtdate AS datetime
DECLARE val_cursor SCROLL CURSOR FOR
SELECT acct_no,stmt_date,cur_value,invest_tot
FROM accountvalues
ORDER BY cur_value

OPEN val_cursor
FETCH FIRST FROM val_cursor INTO
 @acct,@stmtdate,@curval,@investtot

PRINT 'Accounts with current values below investments as
       of displayed statement date'
```

```
PRINT ''
WHILE @@fetch_status = 0
  BEGIN
    IF @curval < @investtot
       PRINT @acct + '  ' +
            CONVERT(varchar(15),@stmtdate,101)
    FETCH NEXT FROM val_cursor INTO
     @acct,@stmtdate,@curval,@investtot
  END
CLOSE val_cursor
DEALLOCATE val_cursor
```

```
Accounts with current values below investments as of displayed
 statement date
1017   12/31/1994
1059   12/31/1994
1067   12/31/1994
1012   12/31/1994
```

To illustrate the WHERE statement, we'll open a cursor on the selection of rows from the AccountValues table. This table holds the account current value and investment total from the latest statement run for the account.

We use the WHERE statement to loop through the cursor rows one at a time and check the current value of the account against the investment total for the account. If the current value is less than the investment total, then we print the account number and statement date for investigation.

The WHILE statement executes as long as the @@fetch_status global variable is equal to zero, meaning that the FETCH from the val_cursor succeeded.

The statement that executes as a result of the WHILE condition is the statement immediately below the WHILE statement, which in this case is a BEGIN...END block.

When @@fetch_status is no longer zero, the WHILE loop stops executing and the statement below the BEGIN...END block is executed. In this example, we merely close the cursor and deallocate it.

Using CONTINUE and BREAK

There are two keywords that can be used in conjunction with the WHILE statement to alter the code execution inside the WHILE statement.

The CONTINUE keyword is used to cause the WHILE statement to start another iteration of the loop. It immediately evaluates the WHILE condition and, if TRUE, starts another iteration through the code.

The BREAK keyword is used to break out of the loop. When the BREAK is executed, a jump is made to the statement immediately following the WHILE statement.

Let's modify the preceding example WHILE statement to use these keywords. We'll add a counter to the loop to identify no more than two accounts with current values below investment totals. If the counter reaches 2, we'll exit the loop; otherwise, we'll continue the loop until either the counter reaches 2 or @@fetch_status is nonzero:

```
DECLARE @counter AS int
...
SET @counter = 0
WHILE @@fetch_status = 0
  BEGIN
   IF @curval < @investtot
     BEGIN
       PRINT @acct + ' ' +
         convert(varchar(15),@stmtdate,101)
       SET @counter = @counter + 1
     END
     FETCH NEXT FROM val_cursor INTO
       @acct,@stmtdate,@curval,@investtot
   IF @counter >= 2
     BREAK
   ELSE
     CONTINUE
END
```

It's obvious from this example that we can eliminate the CONTINUE statement
and the code will operate the same way. This is due to the fact that the loop condition is the next statement to be executed after the CONTINUE statement, so the CON-
TINUE is redundant code.

We can eliminate the test for @counter >= 2 and the subsequent BREAK statement by including the @counter test (with a slight twist) in the WHILE condition,
like this:

```
WHILE NOT (@counter >= 2) AND @@fetch_status = 0
  BEGIN
   IF @curval < @investtot
     BEGIN
       PRINT @acct + ' ' +
         convert(varchar(15),@stmtdate,101)
       SET @counter = @counter + 1
     END
     FETCH NEXT FROM val_cursor INTO
       @acct,@stmtdate,@curval,@investtot
END
```

Here, we move the @counter test as is to the WHILE condition and negate it so
that the WHILE statement executes while the counter is less than 2.

Branching with GOTO and RETURN Statements

Like the CONTINUE and BREAK statements in a WHILE statement, execution flow can
be altered by the use of the GOTO and RETURN statements.

GOTO causes execution to branch to a named label in the batch script or procedure and resume execution with the statement after this label.

The RETURN statement is used to cause an exit from the batch script or procedure
and return control to the caller.

We'll now build our own version of the WHILE loop illustrated above using a label and a GOTO statement:

```
...
SET @counter = 0
top_of_loop:
  BEGIN
    IF @curval < @investtot
      BEGIN
        PRINT @acct + ' ' +
          CONVERT(varchar(15),@stmtdate,101)
        SET @counter = @counter + 1
      END
    FETCH NEXT FROM val_cursor INTO
      @acct,@stmtdate,@curval,@investtot
  END
  IF NOT (@counter >= 2) AND @@fetch_status = 0
    GOTO top_of_loop
```

We've placed a label named "top_of_loop" where the WHILE statement used to be and moved the WHILE condition to the bottom of the WHILE statement. If the WHILE condition is TRUE, we branch to the top_of_loop label and continue executing. If the condition is FALSE, we stop executing the loop and close out the cursor. This is the same behavior exhibited by the WHILE statement.

The RETURN statement is usually used to communicate success or failure of the executing procedure back to the caller of the procedure. In this way, a caller can check for zero as meaning success and nonzero as meaning failure. The nonzero return value is treated as an error code.

We'll defer an example of the RETURN statement until we get into writing a stored procedure later in this chapter.

WAITFOR Statement

The WAITFOR statement is equivalent to a pause for some amount of time or until a specified time is reached.

WAITFOR can be used in a batch or procedure to control scheduled operations. However, since WAITFOR can only delay execution according to a specified time interval or until a specified time, you can only assume that a scheduled operation should start at the end of the delay. This is a rudimentary control scheme at best. We saw in Chapter 14 that there are better methods for controlling scheduled operations.

You can delay execution for up to 24 hours using the DELAY argument:

```
WAITFOR DELAY '1:00'
```

Executing the above statement would delay execution for one hour. At the end of the hour, execution would resume with the statement following the WAITFOR statement.

Instead of delaying execution for a specified period of time, you can specify a clock time at which execution should resume:

```
WAITFOR TIME '23:00'
```

This use of the WAITFOR statement resumes execution at 11 P.M.

By using local variables as DELAY or TIME arguments, you could create a schedule script that controls the calling of other batches or stored procedures according to execution time estimates or absolute clock time calculated into the local variables.

Using the RAISERROR Statement

When an error condition is detected in your stored procedure or batch, you can use the RAISERROR statement to return error information to the caller.

Errors may result from SQL Server itself or you may detect an application error such as a failed edit. Using RAISERROR, you can return an error code and enable the caller to look up the error message associated with the code in the sysmessages system table, or you can format and return a custom error message. There is also an option for writing the error to the server error log.

In its simplest form, RAISERROR can return error code, severity, and state information to the caller:

```
RAISERROR (50100, 15, 1)
```

The *error code* in the first argument can be any number greater than 50,000 and less than 2,147,483,648. This is the range of error codes SQL Server considers to be user-defined.

The second argument is the *severity code*. This is a user-defined number between 1 and 18 to represent the level of severity for the error code returned. Severity levels between 19 and 25 can be returned by the system administrator user and must be logged. When severity levels between 20 and 25 are returned, SQL Server treats the error as a fatal error and terminates the client connection after sending the error to the client.

The third argument is the *state code*. State is an integer between 1 and 127, and may be used to indicate additional information about the error.

Since this example is returning an error code, the caller will need to use this code to look up the associated error message. Error messages are stored in the sysmessages system table using the sp_addmessage system stored procedure.

Let's add a simple custom message for the 50100 error code we used above:

```
sp_addmessage 50100, 15,'Dividend transaction failed.'
```

Executing the above `sp_addmessage` procedure adds the error code and severity code to the sysmessages table and associates the error code with the error message provided as the third argument. In this case, error code 50100 in the Fund Accounts application indicates that a dividend transaction could not be applied to the database.

Now, when we execute the above `RAISERROR` statement in the SQL Query Analyzer, we get the following:

```
RAISERROR (50100, 15, 1)
Server: Msg 50100, Level 15, State 1 Dividend transaction failed.
```

We can cause the error to be written to the server error log and the NT event log by appending the clause `WITH LOG` to the end of the `RAISERROR` statement:

```
RAISERROR (50100, 15, 1) WITH LOG
```

After executing this statement, open the NT Server Event Log viewer, select Application from the Log menu, and then look for a Server category message from MSSQLServer. Double-click the event to display the error message, as shown in Figure 15-1 below.

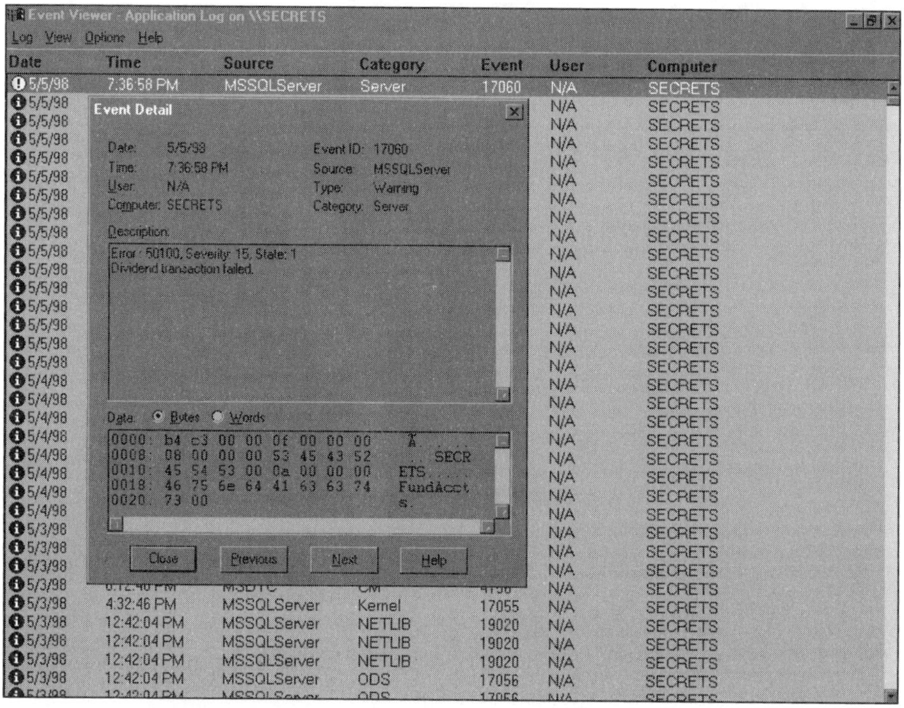

Figure 15-1: The RAISERROR message as shown in the NT application event log.

In the SQL Server error log, found in the Log folder under the SQL Server install directory, you should see two lines that look like this:

```
98/05/05 19:36:58.62 spid6    Error : 50100, Severity: 15, State: 1
98/05/05 19:36:58.62 spid6    Dividend transaction failed.
```

The error message you define, whether added to the sysmessages table or returned via RAISERROR, can be formatted with parameters that are replaced with arguments when the error is raised.

We drop the error message we added above and then define it to hold a parameter:

```
sp_dropmessage 50100
sp_addmessage 50100,15,
    'Dividend Transaction failed with reason: %d.'
```

With this error message stored in the sysmessages table, we can now pass a reason code (a term invented for this application) to SQL Server for insertion into the displayed message:

```
RAISERROR (50100, 15, 1, 147)

Server: Msg 50100, Level 15, State 42000
Dividend Transaction failed with reason: 147.
```

The types you can use as parameters are listed in Table 15-1.

TABLE 15-1 ERROR MESSAGE STRING PARAMETER TYPES

Type	Description
d	Signed integer
i	Signed integer
o	Unsigned octal
p	Pointer
s	String
u	Unsigned integer
x	Unsigned hexadecimal
X	Unsigned hexadecimal

The last option we look at for RAISERROR is the SETERROR option. You can use this option to cause your error code to be set into the @@error global variable:

```
RAISERROR (50100, 15, 1,147) WITH SETERROR
select @@error

Server: Msg 50100, Level 15, State 42000
Dividend Transaction failed with reason: 147.
-----------------
50100

(1 row(s) affected)
```

When you get a chance, browse through the sysmessages table in the master database and study the SQL Server error messages found there. It will give you a feel for the categories of errors found in SQL Server and some insight into what can go wrong. At the time of this writing, there were over 2,700 error messages in the sysmessages table, one of them being the 50100 message we just added.

Creating Temporary Tables

Stored procedures will often benefit from having a temporary workspace to hold data collected for processing over the course of the procedure's' execution.

SQL Server supports temporary tables for this purpose. Temporary tables are created like permanent tables, but are named differently and stored in memory. You can create either local or global temporary tables.

Local temporary table names are preceded by one number sign (#) and may have a length of up to 128 characters. These tables are accessible to the user session that created the table and are dropped automatically when the user session ends.

Global temporary tables have names preceded by two number signs (##). These tables are accessible to any user in the database and the tables are dropped when the last user disconnects.

You may create constraints for temporary tables but a FOREIGN KEY constraint will be ignored by SQL Server. In other words, temporary tables may not participate in referential integrity constraints.

Writing Your Own Stored Procedures

Now that we've seen the basic building blocks of a stored procedure, let's write a couple of procedures for the Fund Accounts application.

When you create a procedure, SQL Server parses the procedure statements and validates the syntax of these statements. If the procedure statements pass the validation, a normalized version of the procedure is created and stored for later execution by the query processor.

When the query processor executes the normalized procedure, the processor resolution step checks object names referenced in the procedure to ensure they exist. If referenced objects exist, the query optimizer creates a query plan of execution.

The query plan is dependent on statistics describing the current state of the database, such as the number of rows in tables, the existence of usable indexes, and the distribution of data in indexes.

The optimizer uses these statistics and various components of the procedure statements, such as WHERE clauses and JOINS, to create an optimal least-cost plan of execution.

After the plan is created, it is placed in the procedure cache for execution by the current call to the procedure and by subsequent calls to the procedure. The plan is freed from the cache only when SQL Server needs the memory occupied by the plan or SQL Server is shut down.

To start our exploration of procedures, we'll develop the BigAcct procedure we first saw in Chapter 4. The BigAcct procedure takes an input account type entered by the user and returns the maximum tot_assets for that account type and the corresponding account number.

After developing the BigAcct procedure, we'll try a more complicated procedure that we can use to calculate the total return for a portfolio. The ProcessFundAccount procedure will be useful when reporting a portfolio's' position on a client statement.

Creating a Procedure with CREATE PROCEDURE

The BigAcct stored procedure is to accept one input parameter to define the type of account the procedure is to operate on. The procedure finds the maximum total asset value in the Accounts table for accounts having the input account type and returns this value and the first account number having this value.

We define the procedure using the CREATE PROCEDURE statement. This statement names the procedure we are creating and defines the input and output parameters for the procedure:

```
CREATE PROCEDURE BigAcct @type varchar(6),
  @acct varchar(10) OUTPUT,
  @outtot money OUTPUT AS

/* %%%%%%%%%%%%%%%%%%%%%%%%%%%%%%%%%%%%
  Returns the maximum total asset value for the input
  account type (@type) and the first account number
  having the max total asset value.
  %%%%%%%%%%%%%%%%%%%%%%%%%%%%%%%%%%%% */
```

```
DECLARE @tot money
DECLARE @act varchar(10)

SELECT @tot = MAX(tot_assets)
   FROM Accounts WHERE acct_type = @type

SELECT @act = acct_no
   FROM Accounts
   WHERE acct_type = @type AND tot_assets = @tot
   ORDER BY acct_no

SELECT @acct = @act,@outtot = @tot
```

After naming the procedure and specifying its parameters, the keyword AS denotes the start of the procedure definition.

In the BigAcct procedure, we start by defining two local variables for internal use. These variables will hold the maximum total asset value and account number as the procedure's SELECT statements determine these values.

The first SELECT statement finds the maximum total asset for the account type input in the @type parameter. This maximum value is saved in the @tot local variable.

The second SELECT statement selects the first account number (the lowest account number) having the input account type and maximum asset value. The account number is saved in the @act local variable.

The last SELECT statement selects the two local variables into the output parameters for return to the caller of the procedure.

Although future enhancements to this procedure may take advantage of the two local variables used in this procedure, the procedure does not require them. They are unnecessary since the SELECT statements could have returned their output directly to the output parameters.

When procedures are created or altered, the current settings for QUOTED_IDENTI-FIER and ANSI_NULLS are saved and restored when the procedure is executed. If the procedure alters these settings during execution, the changes will not occur until the procedure ends. If the procedure does not make changes to these settings during execution, the settings that were in effect prior to execution are restored when the procedure ends.

Other settings can be set within a procedure execution, and they will take effect until the procedure ends. When the procedure ends, the settings in effect prior to procedure execution are restored.

To see a procedure definition as stored in the syscomments system table, use the sp_helptext stored procedure specifying the name of the procedure you want to display:

```
sp_helptext 'BigAcct'
```

Let's take a closer look at parameters and return values, and especially the parameters for BigAcct.

Parameters and Return Values

A parameter is declared in the CREATE PROCEDURE statement by name and data type. If the parameter is to be used for returning output values to the caller of the procedure, then the parameter requires the keyword OUTPUT to be a part of the parameter declaration. A procedure can have up to 1,024 parameters.

In the BigAcct procedure, the @type parameter is declared to be the same type as the Acct_type column of the Accounts table. This variable is used in the SELECT statement to qualify the rows to be considered.

The other two parameters have the OUTPUT keyword associated with them so that SQL Server knows the procedure will return values of these data types to the caller. The @acct is declared the same as acct_no and @outtot the same as tot_assets.

Parameters can be specified with default values to be used when a caller does not supply the parameters. For example, we could have coded the BigAcct procedure to default the @type parameter to 'Tax'. Doing this would cause the procedure to return data for the 'Tax' account type if a caller does not supply the type information:

```
CREATE PROCEDURE BigAcct @type varchar(6) = 'Tax',
```

Wildcard characters can be specified in the default constant as long as the procedure uses the parameter with the LIKE operator.

In addition to OUTPUT parameters, a procedure can return a value in a RETURN statement. Unlike OUTPUT parameters though, the return value must be a integer.

Many programmers use the return value to indicate success or failure of the procedure. SQL Server returns a zero to indicate success and a negative value to indicate the error code of an error. SQL Server uses –1 through –14, as shown in Table 15-2.

TABLE 15-2 STORED PROCEDURE ERROR CODES RETURNED BY SQL SERVER

Error code	Description
-1	Missing object
-2	Data type error
-3	Process involved in deadlock
-4	Permission error
-5	Syntax error
-6	User error
-7	Resource error

Continued

Error code	Description
-8	Internal problem (nonfatal)
-9	System limit reached
-10	Internal inconsistency (fatal)
-11	Internal inconsistency (fatal)
-12	Corrupt table or index
-13	Corrupt database
-14	Hardware error

Values outside the range shown in Table 15-2 can be used for user-defined error codes. In the BigAcct procedure, we could have returned a nonzero value to indicate a NULL return from the selection of the maximum total assets (indicating no records):

```
DECLARE @ret int
...
SELECT @tot = MAX(tot_assets)
    FROM Accounts WHERE acct_type = @type

IF @tot IS NULL
    RETURN (-20)
...
RETURN (0)
```

When you define a procedure that will return a cursor variable, you must specify the keyword VARYING in addition to the OUTPUT keyword:

```
CREATE PROCEDURE TaxAccts @taxacct_cursor CURSOR VARYING OUTPUT
AS
SET @taxacct_cursor = CURSOR SCROLL FOR
SELECT acct_no, state_abbr,zip,tot_assets,acct_status
FROM Accounts WHERE acct_type = 'Tax'

OPEN @taxacct_cursor
```

The above TaxAccts procedure does nothing more than declare a cursor on the Accounts table and open it. The cursor is defined to select only accounts that have the 'Tax' account type.

In just a moment, we'll look at how to call the TaxAccts procedure and use the returned cursor variable.

Granting Permission to Use Your Procedure

When you execute the CREATE PROCEDURE statement to define a stored procedure, your user ID becomes the owner of the procedure. In order for other users to execute the procedure, they must be granted execute permissions on the procedure name.

If, for example, Zachary logged in to SQL Server and the FundAccts database and attempted to execute the TaxAccts procedure at this time, he would get the following error:

```
Server: Msg 229, Level 14, State 42000
EXECUTE permission denied on object TaxAccts, database FundAccts,
 owner dbo
```

To enable Zachary to execute the TaxAccts procedure, the procedure owner must grant him EXECUTE permissions on the procedure, like this:

```
GRANT EXECUTE ON TaxAccts TO Zachary
```

Now when Zachary executes TaxAccts, he gets results rather than an error. We can grant execute permission in this manner to any user or group defined in the database.

Calling Stored Procedures

Calling a stored procedure without parameters is straightforward:

```
EXECUTE <procedure name>
```

This syntax works for procedures that do not define any parameters, or the required input parameters have defaults defined for them.

To call procedures with input parameters, you can pass the parameter value by position or by name. To call BigAcct by name, for example, and pass 'Tax' as the account type parameter, we would code the following (output parameters not shown):

```
EXECUTE BigAcct @type = 'Tax'
```

To pass the account type parameter by position, we would code as follows:

```
EXECUTE BigAcct 'Tax'
```

You cannot mix the two variations. If you use a parameter name for one parameter, you must use parameter names for all other parameters. Using names is more flexible since you can place the names in any order.

To pass OUTPUT parameters, you name the local variable and provide the keyword OUTPUT to indicate the variable is to receive a value from the procedure. Here is the complete call to the BigAcct procedure:

```
DECLARE @act varchar(10), @totasset money
EXECUTE BigAcct 'Tax', @act OUTPUT, @totasset OUTPUT
```

To execute the above statement using named parameters, we would code as follows:

```
DECLARE @act varchar(10),@totasset money
EXECUTE BigAcct  @type = 'Tax', @acct = @act OUTPUT, @outtot =
  @totasset OUTPUT
```

NAME AS IN CREATE

Now let's take a look at a call to the TaxAccts procedure and see how we would handle the cursor variable returned from that procedure:

```
DECLARE @cur CURSOR

EXECUTE TaxAccts @taxacct_cursor = @cur OUTPUT

WHILE @@fetch_status = 0
  FETCH NEXT FROM @cur

CLOSE @cur
DEALLOCATE @cur
```

As you can see from the above example, using a cursor variable returned from a procedure is quite simple. We declare a local variable as a cursor type and pass it to the procedure as an OUTPUT parameter. When the procedure returns, we use the returned cursor to fetch rows. When done with the cursor, we close and deallocate it.

Notice that in this example we assume the procedure did return a valid cursor. In practice, of course, you would check for a valid cursor using the CURSOR_STATUS() function before attempting to use it.

See Chapter 13 for more information on using CURSOR_STATUS().

Another Procedure Example

In this section, we build a more advanced example of a stored procedure. The ProcessFundAccount procedure is used in the calculation of the total return for a client's portfolio. We'll assume that in our sample money management firm portfolios are not valued daily, but, rather, on a monthly basis. To calculate the return for a portfolio, the company uses a method called the Modified Dietz method.

Modified Dietz calculates the time-weighted return for a portfolio by weighting each of the cash flows into and out of a portfolio by the amount of time the cash is held in the portfolio. The formula is

```
Return = (MVEnd - MVBegin - CFSum)/(MVBegin + WCFSum)
```

where:

```
MVEnd = market value at end of period
MVBegin = market value at begin of period
CFSum = sum of the cash flows within the period
WCFSum = sum of each cash flow times its weight
```

The weight of a cash flow is calculated as follows:

```
weight = (PD - CFD)/PD
```

where:

```
PD = total number of days in period
CFD = number of days since the beginning of the period in which the
 cash flow occurred
```

To calculate the return, it is necessary to process each fund account held by a client and evaluate the fund account's position at the beginning of the period and each transaction within the period.

Each transaction in the period is accumulated according to its type and weighted, if necessary, to obtain the weighted amounts for use in the total return calculation described above.

The procedure we look at here takes as input a fund code, fund account number, statement date, and fund price as of the statement date.

The procedure first obtains the value of the fund account one month back from the statement date. This is the value of the fund account at the beginning of the period.

After obtaining the beginning value, the procedure loops through the transaction history for the input fund account looking at transactions that fall between the statement date and one month back from the statement date. Each transaction amount is accumulated according to the transaction type and multiplied by the weight calculated, using the date of the transaction when the type indicates a cash flow into or out of the account.

When all transactions in the period have been evaluated, the fund account beginning value and transaction type sums are returned as output parameters.

Here's the code for the ProcessFundAccount procedure:

```
CREATE PROCEDURE ProcessFundAccount
@acct varchar(10),@fund char(5),
@fundacct char(35),@price money,
@stmtdate datetime,
@begincurvalue money OUTPUT,@totcurvalue money OUTPUT,
@totinvest money OUTPUT,@cash money OUTPUT,
@cfw money OUTPUT,@invest money OUTPUT,
@redempt money OUTPUT
AS

DECLARE @trandate datetime
DECLARE @begindate datetime
DECLARE @daysinperiod integer
DECLARE @trandays int
DECLARE @timeweight integer
DECLARE @trantype varchar(10)
DECLARE @amount money
DECLARE @shtot decimal(18,4),@invtot money

/* Get the beginning current value */
SET @begindate = DATEADD(mm,-1,@stmtdate)
SELECT @begincurvalue = ISNULL(cur_value,0)
 FROM Statements WHERE acct_no = @acct AND
 stmt_date = @begindate

/* Get the beginning date of the period */
SET @begindate = DATEADD(day,1,@begindate)

/* Calculate days in period */
SET @daysinperiod = DATEDIFF(day,@begindate,@stmtdate)

/* Get transaction history prior to stmt date */
DECLARE tranhistcursor SCROLL CURSOR FOR
SELECT sh_tot,inv_tot,trandate,trantype,amount
 FROM TranHistory
 WHERE fund_cd = @fund AND fundacctno = @fundacct AND
  trandate <= @stmtdate AND trandate >= @begindate
  ORDER BY trandate DESC,trantype DESC

OPEN tranhistcursor

/* Get current value as of latest transaction <= stmt date */

FETCH FIRST FROM tranhistcursor
 INTO @shtot,@invtot,@trandate,@trantype,@amount

SET @totcurvalue = (@shtot * @price)
SET @totinvest = @invtot

WHILE @@fetch_status = 0
 BEGIN /* Process transactions */

     BEGIN  /* Transaction in period */
```

```
SET @trandays = DATEDIFF(day,@trandate,@stmtdate)
SET @timeweight = @trandays/@daysinperiod
IF (PATINDEX('(C',@trantype) > 1)
  BEGIN   /* Cash transaction */
     SET @cash = @cash + @amount
     SET @cfw = @cfw + (@amount * @timeweight)
  END     /* Cash Transaction */
ELSE
  IF (@trantype = 'invest')
     BEGIN      /* Investment */
       SET @invest = @invest + @amount
       SET @cfw = @cfw + (@amount * @timeweight)
     END  /* Investment */
  ELSE
     IF (@trantype = 'redempt')
        BEGIN   /* Redemption */
           SET @redempt = @redempt + @amount
           SET @cfw = @cfw +
                     (@amount * @timeweight)
        END     /* Redemption */

  END     /* Transaction in period */

 FETCH NEXT FROM tranhistcursor
   INTO @shtot,@invtot,@trandate,@trantype,@amount

 END   /* Process transactions */

 CLOSE tranhistcursor
 DEALLOCATE tranhistcursor

 RETURN
 /* End of ProcessFundAccount */
```

To obtain the total return for a client's portfolio, a process would need to loop through all of the fund accounts for a client, calling the ProcessFundAccount procedure for each one, and accumulate the output values. Once all fund accounts are processed in this way, the accumulated values can be input to the Modified Dietz algorithm to obtain the total return for the client's statement.

Modifying and Removing Procedures

As an application evolves, requirements will change, raising the need to build new procedures and modify existing ones. We've already seen how new procedures can be created. To replace existing procedure definitions, Transact-SQL provides the ALTER PROCEDURE statement.

Likewise, new requirements or changes in processing may alleviate the need for one or more procedures already in place. We can delete these procedures using the Transact-SQL DROP PROCEDURE statement.

Using the ALTER PROCEDURE Statement

An existing procedure can be modified by using the ALTER PROCEDURE statement. The complete altered procedure must be specified since there is no provision for altering individual lines of code.

It would seem that since the entire procedure code, including parameters, must be provided with the ALTER PROCEDURE statement, we could just drop the procedure and reissue the CREATE PROCEDURE statement. This method can indeed be used; however, when you drop the procedure, all permissions set for the procedure are also dropped, forcing you to redefine them after the procedure has been re-created.

Using the ALTER PROCEDURE statement, any permissions that have been granted for the procedure remain active. Therefore, altering the BigAcct procedure using the statement below would not affect the execute permission we granted to Zachary earlier:

```
ALTER PROCEDURE BigAcct @type varchar(6),
  @acct varchar(10) OUTPUT,
  @outtot money OUTPUT AS

/* %%%%%%%%%%%%%%%%%%%%%%%%%%%%%%%%%%%%
   Returns the maximum total asset value for the input
   account type (@type) and the first account number
   having the max total asset value.
   %%%%%%%%%%%%%%%%%%%%%%%%%%%%%%%%%%%% */

  DECLARE @tot money
  DECLARE @act varchar(10)
  DECLARE @ret int

  SELECT @tot = MAX(tot_assets)
    FROM Accounts WHERE acct_type = @type

  IF @tot IS NULL
    RETURN(-20)

  SELECT @act = acct_no
    FROM Accounts
    WHERE acct_type = @type AND tot_assets = @tot
    ORDER BY acct_no

  SELECT @acct = @act,@outtot = @tot

  RETURN(0)
```

Deleting Procedures with DROP PROCEDURE

When a procedure is no longer needed, we can drop it from the database using DROP PROCEDURE. Multiple procedures can be dropped using one DROP PROCEDURE statement by listing the procedure names separated by commas.

Any permissions granted on the procedure are also dropped. Remember to check for dependencies using the sp_depends procedure before dropping any object in the database.

Exploring Triggers

Transact-SQL supports a special type of stored procedure that can be associated with a table and a data modification operation such as INSERT, UPDATE, or DELETE. These special procedures are called triggers.

Triggers can be used to cause some action to occur whenever a data change takes place on a table. For example, when a new account is inserted to the Accounts table, you could use a trigger to automatically run a query to report new business by account manager.

Another use of a trigger is to cascade changes from one table to another for enforcing referential integrity. SQL Server can ensure that referential integrity, defined through PRIMARY KEY and FOREIGN KEY check constraints, is not violated. However, there are no provisions for cascading key changes and deletion of child rows when a parent row is removed from a table. Triggers can be defined to fill this void.

A table can have multiple triggers defined on it, and each trigger can be defined for one or more data modification operations. This enables an application to trigger more than one action whenever an UPDATE, INSERT, or DELETE takes place on a table.

If check constraints are defined on a table and those constraints are violated, however, the triggers will not run. This means that if you have FOREIGN KEY check constraints defined on a table and expect to cascade UPDATE the FOREIGN KEY via a trigger when the referenced table key is changed, then you must disable the FOREIGN KEY constraint before changing the key. If you don't, the check constraint error will be raised when you change the PRIMARY KEY and the update trigger will not run. We'll see an example of this shortly.

Creating Triggers with the CREATE TRIGGER Statement

The money management firm wants to be able to change account numbers. This is easy enough to support—we simply write a procedure to UPDATE the Accounts acct_no column using an existing account number and a new account number as inputs.

Let's try a simple UPDATE to set the account number for account 1003 to 1995:

```
UPDATE Accounts SET acct_no = '1995'
  WHERE acct_no = '1003'

Server: Msg 547, Level 16, State 23000
UPDATE statement conflicted with COLUMN REFERENCE constraint
```

```
'FK_FundAccounts_Accounts'. The conflict occurred in database
'FundAccts', table 'Accounts', column 'acct_no'
Command has been aborted.
```

Reading the message that results, it looks as if this isn't going to be that simple after all. The FOREIGN KEY constraint defined on the FundAccounts table won't let us change a referenced column that would break the integrity of the database. Furthermore, we have another table – the Statements table – with a similar constraint defined on it.

With the constraints in place, we would need to INSERT a row for the new account number – that is, INSERT a copy of the 1003 row, but with the new account number – and then UPDATE the rows in the FundAccounts and Statements tables that reference the 1003 account to reference the newly inserted 1995 account. Using this method, the referential integrity constraints would not be violated and we wouldn't hear any complaints from SQL Server.

Another method would use a trigger to automatically update the FundAccounts, Statements and AccountValues (which has no FOREIGN KEY constraints defined) tables when the acct_no column in the Accounts table was changed. To do this, we need to define the trigger, drop the FOREIGN KEY constraints on the FundAccounts and Statements tables, run the UPDATE on the Accounts table, and then add the constraints back to the tables.

First, we define a trigger on the Accounts table that will UPDATE the related tables whenever the Account acct_no column is updated. Here's the CREATE TRIGGER statement to do that:

```
CREATE TRIGGER CascadeAcctChange
ON Accounts
FOR UPDATE
AS IF UPDATE(acct_no)
  BEGIN
    DECLARE @acct varchar(10)
    DECLARE @oldacct varchar(10)

    SELECT @acct = acct_no FROM inserted
    SELECT @oldacct = acct_no FROM deleted

    /* Update the AccountValues table */
    UPDATE AccountValues
      SET AccountValues.acct_no = @acct
      WHERE AccountValues.acct_no = @oldacct

  /* Update the Statements table */
  UPDATE Statements
    SET Statements.acct_no = @acct
     WHERE Statements.acct_no = @oldacct
  /* Update the FundAccounts table */
  UPDATE FundAccounts
    SET FundAccounts.acct_no = @acct
    WHERE FundAccounts.acct_no = @oldacct
END
```

We've named this trigger `CascadeAcctChange` and defined it on the Accounts table as an UPDATE event trigger. This trigger will be fired whenever an UPDATE occurs to an Accounts table row.

Next, we use a control-of-flow IF statement to test for UPDATE of the acct_no column since we are not interested in the UPDATE of other columns. If the acct_no column is being changed, we enter the BEGIN block of code.

To perform the required updates, we need to know what the old account number was and what the new account number is. We retrieve this information from two temporary trigger tables, called *inserted* and *deleted*.

The *inserted* table holds the updated or inserted values. We use this table to retrieve the new account number into a local variable called @acct.

The *deleted* table holds the old values that were deleted or existed before an UPDATE. We use this table to retrieve the old account number to refer to referenced rows in the tables related to the Accounts table. The old account number is saved in the @oldacct local variable.

Both the inserted and deleted tables have a structure like the table being modified. This is the table on which the trigger is defined. All old and new column values are accessible in these tables except text and image columns. If these columns are referenced, SQL Server returns NULL.

Now we can UPDATE the tables related to the Accounts table, those having an acct_no column referencing the Accounts acct_no column. Each UPDATE qualifies the rows to be updated with the value in @oldacct and sets the acct_no in these rows to the value in @acct.

That's it. After this trigger runs, the FundAccounts, Statements, and AccountValues rows that used to contain acct_no @oldacct now contain acct_no @acct.

Next, we have to drop our FOREIGN KEY constraints. The Statements table and the FundAccounts table are affected:

```
ALTER TABLE Statements DROP CONSTRAINT FK_Statements_Accounts
GO
ALTER TABLE FundAccounts DROP CONSTRAINT FK_FundAccounts_Accounts
```

Now we apply the UPDATE:

```
UPDATE ACCOUNTS SET acct_no = '1995'
 WHERE acct_no = '1003'
```

A check of the Accounts table and all related tables indicates that our `CascadeAcctChange` trigger worked as intended. Now we can put the FOREIGN KEY constraints back in place:

```
ALTER TABLE Statements ADD CONSTRAINT
 FK_Statements_Accounts FOREIGN KEY (acct_no)
 REFERENCES dbo.Accounts
```

```
ALTER TABLE FundAccounts ADD CONSTRAINT
FK_FundAccounts_Accounts FOREIGN KEY (acct_no)
REFERENCES dbo.Accounts
```

You be the judge. Use Declarative Referential Integrity (DRI) – that is, referential integrity declared as constraints in the table definitions – and have SQL Server enforce referential integrity for you. Or, don't use DRI and enforce referential integrity as part of your application (which, by the way, can also be done with triggers).

Using DRI, as you saw above, gets rather sticky when it comes to cascading updates and deletes. Not using DRI means you have much more work to do to manage referential integrity yourself.

You can use all Transact-SQL statements in a trigger *except* those listed in the following listing:

```
ALTER DATABASE          ALTER PROCEDURE
ALTER TABLE             ALTER TRIGGER
ALTER VIEW              CREATE DATABASE
CREATE DEFAULT          CREATE INDEX
CREATE PROCEDURE        CREATE RULE
CREATE SCHEMA           CREATE TABLE
CREATE TRIGGER          CREATE VIEW
DENY                    DISK INIT
DISK RESIZE             DROP DATABASE
DROP DEFAULT            DROP INDEX
DROP PROCEDURE          DROP RULE
DROP TABLE              DROP TRIGGER
DROP VIEW               GRANT
LOAD DATABASE           LOAD LOG
RESTORE DATABASE        RESTORE LOG
REVOKE                  RECONFIGURE
SELECT INTO             TRUNCATE TABLE
UPDATE STATISTICS
```

Modifying and Removing Triggers

Triggers are modified and dropped in the same way that stored procedures are. The ALTER TRIGGER statement is used to change a trigger definition and the DROP TRIGGER statement is used to DELETE a trigger from the database.

When altering a trigger, provide the trigger name and the full trigger definition in the ALTER TRIGGER statement:

```
ALTER TRIGGER CascadeAcctChange
ON Accounts
FOR UPDATE
AS ...
```

As was the case with procedures, you can specify multiple trigger names in one DROP TRIGGER statement:

```
DROP TRIGGER ChangeAcctValue, CascadeAcctChange
```

Let's now turn our attention to another kind of special stored procedure, called an extended stored procedure.

A Brief Look at Extended Stored Procedures

Extended stored procedures are procedures that live in DLLs and are loaded by SQL Server when a call to the procedure is detected.

SQL Server ships with several extended stored procedures that generally have names starting with xp_. Some extended procedure names are prefixed with sp_ and some stored procedure names are prefixed with xp_. A list of stored and extended procedures and their purpose can be found in Appendix F.

Extended procedure DLLs are loaded by SQL Server into SQL Server's process space and associated with the client connection thread for the client calling the procedure. The procedure execution is run under the security context of the SQL Server account. If running the xp_cmdshell procedure, the security context can be changed to the SQLAgentCmdExec account for nonadministrator users by checking the 'Non-administrators use SQLAgentCmdExec account when executing commands via xp_cmdshell' security setting in the SQL Server properties dialog.

Using SQL Server Extended Procedures

Let's try a couple of SQL Server's extended procedures. First we'll execute the xp_sscanf procedure, which enables us to parse a string according to a specified format. Here's a sample:

```
DECLARE @stmtdt AS varchar(12)
DECLARE @mo AS varchar(3),@da AS varchar(2),
 @yr AS varchar(4)
SET ROWCOUNT 1
SELECT @stmtdt = stmt_date FROM Statements
 WHERE acct_no='1003'
EXEC master..xp_sscanf @stmtdt,'%s %s %s',@mo OUTPUT,
  @da OUTPUT,@yr OUTPUT
SELECT @mo,@da,@yr
SET ROWCOUNT 0


------------------
Dec  31   1992

(1 row(s) affected)
```

The above script first declares the required variables and then sets the ROWCOUNT option to 1. This option specifies the number of rows SQL Server is to process and then stop. ROWCOUNT affects most of the Transact-SQL statements but does not limit dynamic cursors. In the example above, we want to stop processing the query after one row has been selected into the result set.

Once we have a date selected into the @stmtdt variable, we pass it into the xp_sscanf procedure to parse the string according to the format string passed as the second argument. Each %s in the format string represents a string value for xp_sscanf to parse into the OUTPUT parameter. The first %s value parsed will be put into the first OUTPUT parameter, the second %s into the second OUTPUT parameter, and so on. In this example, the format string white space is the delimiter character for parsing the input string.

After the xp_sscanf procedure has done its job, we select the OUTPUT variables to the result. Before leaving the script, we reset the ROWCOUNT to zero so that other SELECT statements executed in this session will return a normal result set.

To find out which DLL houses the xp_sscanf procedure, we can use the sp_helpextendedproc stored procedure:

```
sp_helpextendedproc xp_sscanf

name                      dll
-------------------       -----------
xp_sscanf                 xpsql70.dll

(1 row(s) affected)
```

Running the sp_helpextendedproc procedure without specifying a procedure name will yield a list of all extended procedures and their DLLs.

The next extended procedure we'll look at is the xp_printf procedure. This procedure inserts arguments into an OUTPUT parameter string according to a format string passed as the second argument:

```
DECLARE @stmtdt AS varchar(12)
DECLARE @outstring AS varchar(80)
SELECT @stmtdt = MAX(stmt_date) FROM Statements
  WHERE acct_no='1003'
exec master..xp_sprintf @outstring OUTPUT,
  'The latest statement for 1003 is %s',@stmtdt
SELECT @outstring


----------------------------------------------
The latest statement for 1003 is Mar 31 1996

(1 row(s) affected)
```

With xp_sprintf, we supply an OUTPUT string variable (@outstring) for the result, an input format string containing the %s placeholders, and the required arguments, which `xp_sprintf` will place into the `OUTPUT` parameter along with any literals from the format string.

In addition to the two simple procedures illustrated above, SQL Server supplies other extended procedures, mostly in the categories of SQL Mail and SQL Server Profiler. You may find that a special-purpose extended procedure can enhance your application. If so, you can develop your own extended procedure as discussed below.

Creating Your Own Extended Procedures

You can create your own extended stored procedure by creating a DLL and including in it one or more exported functions with names by which SQL Server will call them. You can name your procedures with the `xp_` prefix if you wish.

The function you write communicates its output and return values to SQL Server via Open Data Services (ODS) API calls. You learn about these calls in Chapter 21, where we write an ODS extended procedure.

Once your procedure DLL is created and stored at the server in the SQL Server DLL directory (`<SQLServer>\Binn`), you'll need to inform SQL Server about the procedure name and which DLL it is housed in. You do this by executing `sp_addextendedproc` and passing it the name of your procedure and the name of the DLL.

After registering the extended procedure with SQL Server, the procedure can be called just like any other procedure.

Writing your own extended procedure gives you full access to the operating system, the file system, and ODS. This enables you to implement functionality that cannot be implemented with Transact-SQL procedures alone.

In that extended procedures execute in SQL Server's memory space, a poorly tested procedure can cause SQL Server to crash or behave erratically. When developing your own procedures, be sure to thoroughly test them before implementing in the production server.

Summary

This chapter has explored stored procedures and triggers by taking a look inside at how these powerful database objects are created and used.

We saw how global and local variables are declared and used in a procedure or batch. These variables can accept values by either a `SET` or `SELECT` statement, and they can be used for passing values between caller and procedure parameters.

The Transact-SQL Control-of-Flow language was discussed, and we learned how this language can be used to control the flow of execution within a procedure. We looked at methods of branching with GOTO and RETURN, handling errors with RAIS-ERROR and PRINT, testing conditions with IF...ELSE, and looping with the WHILE statement.

Next, we found out how to create a stored procedure for our Fund Accounts application. We used the CREATE PROCEDURE statement to define a procedure to SQL Server and learned how to specify input and output parameters as well as return values.

We learned that we should use an ALTER PROCEDURE statement versus dropping a procedure with DROP PROCEDURE and then re-creating it so that we can preserve the permissions granted on the procedure.

We found out that triggers are special stored procedures that are executed when certain data change events occur on a table. We can create triggers that will be executed when a table has a row inserted, deleted, or updated. Multiple triggers can be defined for any event and a trigger can be defined to handle multiple events.

Last, we took a brief tour of extended stored procedures. These procedures are housed in DLLs that SQL Server loads when an internal procedure is called and the DLL is not resident in memory. We looked at a couple of SQL Server's extended procedures and how custom procedures can be built and implemented for an application.

Chapter 16

Exploring Transactions

IN THIS CHAPTER

◆ Learn what transactions are and how to use them

◆ Explore the Autocommit, implicit, and explicit transaction modes

◆ Learn how SQL Server handles nested transactions

◆ See how transactions can be managed across several machines using Microsoft Distributed Transaction Coordinator

◆ Find out what two-phase commit means in transaction processing

IF OUR APPLICATIONS had to account for every conceivable failure during database processing and manage the processing such that the database integrity was not jeopardized, our application code would be very complex and our development process very costly. Let's look at an example.

When we prepare a client's statement to report the earnings and current values for their portfolio, we need to perform the following steps:

1. Loop through each of the client's fund accounts and calculate returns for the reporting period. This requires us to scan the transaction history related to a fund account to calculate the cash flows into the account and out of the account.

2. Calculate the total portfolio return for the period, the year-to-date return, and taxable and nontaxable gains for the statement.

3. INSERT a statement to the Statements table.

4. UPDATE the current values and investment totals for the new statement in the AccountValues table.

5. UPDATE the total assets column in the Accounts table to show the latest valuation of the account.

Several questions can be raised about this process:

1. What if a transaction that falls within the reporting period is backed out or changed after we have accumulated the transaction into our calculations?

2. What if we UPDATE the AccountValues table with the latest Statement values but the Statement INSERT fails?

3. What if the AccountValues UPDATE fails?

4. What if the Account total assets cannot be updated?

Every database application of any significance faces issues like these. SQL Server helps in handling some of these issues by incorporating the concept of a *transaction* into the database change process.

A SQL Server transaction is a method by which an application can define a unit of change activity to be tracked by SQL Server such that the change activity can be reversed, leaving the database in the state it was in prior to the start of change activity.

The unit of change activity can consist of one or more updates, inserts, deletes, or creates. The transaction that defines this unit of change activity can be declared by SQL Server or by the database application.

When declared by SQL Server, the transaction is implied by any statement that makes a change to the database. Whenever you execute an UPDATE statement, an INSERT statement, or any other statement that changes the state of the database, SQL Server wraps a transaction around the statement. If the statement succeeds, the transaction is committed to the database. If the statement fails, the transaction is rolled back to the state of the database before the statement began executing. This mode of operation is known as *autocommit*.

Autocommit mode is always in effect until an explicit transaction is declared or implicit transaction mode is set on. Autocommit mode is also the default mode for the database APIs discussed in Part III of this book; DB-Library, ODBC, and ADO.

When a database application declares a transaction, it may use an implicit transaction mode or an explicit transaction mode.

Explicit transactions are declared by use of the BEGIN TRANSACTION or BEGIN DISTRIBUTED TRANSACTION statements. Once started, the application defines the change activity within the transaction and ends the transaction with a COMMIT TRANSACTION statement or a ROLLBACK TRANSACTION statement, depending on the outcome of the change activity.

An *implicit transaction* is established by setting IMPLICIT_TRANSACTIONS ON. This SET statement will automatically start a transaction with the next statement to be executed. When that transaction is completed by the application with either a COMMIT or ROLLBACK statement, the next statement executed starts another transaction.

An application may start transactions within transactions. This technique is known as *nesting* transactions. When nesting, any COMMIT or ROLLBACK statement executed refers to the previous BEGIN TRANSACTION statement. However, any COMMIT or ROLLBACK done at any level of nesting other than the outermost level is ignored by SQL Server. When the outermost level of nesting is committed, then all inner levels are committed. When a ROLLBACK is issued, all levels are rolled back.

Nesting is generally a consequence of application architecture and not an intentional technique. Why would we bother to explicitly nest transactions when any COMMIT or ROLLBACK at nested levels is ignored by SQL Server and only the outermost level matters?

The intent of nesting is to support the existence of transactions in procedures or scripts where the transaction may be implemented by itself. For example, if you include a transaction in a stored procedure, the transaction can be supported whether or not it is the only transaction active or part of a transaction initiated by the caller before the procedure was called.

If the procedure transaction is the only one active, then a procedure COMMIT or ROLLBACK can be honored. If on the other hand, it becomes a nested transaction by being called by a caller already involved in a transaction, then the procedure COMMIT or ROLLBACK is ignored by SQL Server in favor of the actions taken by the outer transaction.

Finally, in this chapter, we'll take a look at transactions distributed across several machines and how they are managed by the Microsoft Distributed Transaction Coordinator (MS DTC).

Using Transact-SQL Transactions

SQL Server's autocommit transaction mode results in a unit of change activity the size of one Transact-SQL statement. If the statement execution succeeds, the changes affected by the statement are committed to the database. If the statement execution fails, the changes are rolled back so that the state of the database is the way it was before the statement was executed.

We can declare larger units of change, to encompass several table changes or created objects, by using implicit and explicit transaction modes.

We'll explore these two modes in this section and see how they are started and ended using Transact-SQL statements.

Using BEGIN TRANSACTION

The BEGIN TRANSACTION statement starts a transaction on the local server installation. Any activity against the database after the start of the transaction is considered a part of the unit of change activity and is subject to being rolled back or undone by a ROLLBACK TRANSACTION statement.

While the transaction is active, SQL Server may take locks on database resources and hold those locks on behalf of the transaction user. Other users might experience errors when attempting to access the locked resources. These locks may be held until the transaction releases them with a COMMIT or ROLLBACK TRANSACTION.

If you want to provide a name for the transaction, specify the name after the BEGIN TRANSACTION keywords. This name can be specified when committing or rolling back the transaction. When nesting transactions, the name is only useful on the outer transaction since it is this outer transaction that controls the ROLLBACK or COMMIT of the inner transactions.

Using SET IMPLICIT_TRANSACTIONS

An application can use an implicit transaction mode by setting the IMPLICIT_TRANSACTIONS option ON. With this option set ON, a transaction is automatically started when a statement from the following list is executed:

ALTER TABLE

CREATE

DELETE

DROP

FETCH

GRANT

INSERT

OPEN

REVOKE

SELECT

TRUNCATE TABLE

UPDATE

Although the transaction is automatically started, the application is responsible for ending the transaction with either a COMMIT TRANSACTION or a ROLLBACK TRANSACTION. If the connection owning the transaction disconnects before the transaction is ended, a ROLLBACK is issued to roll back all changes.

When executing a trigger, SQL Server will start an implied transaction even when SQL Server is in autocommit mode.

To return SQL Server to autocommit mode, execute a SET IMPLICIT_TRANSACTION OFF statement.

Saving Changes with COMMIT

If the application decides that all processing of the unit of change activity has succeeded, the application can issue a COMMIT TRANSACTION statement to end the transaction, either explicit or implicit, and COMMIT the changes to the database.

If COMMIT is used within nested transactions, it has no effect on the database. Only a COMMIT at the outermost transaction level will actually COMMIT changes to the database and free any locks and other resources the transaction may have used.

Once changes are committed, they cannot be rolled back, because SQL Server has freed all tracking of the changes for ROLLBACK purposes.

To determine the nesting level of transactions, you can select the global variable @@trancount. This variable holds the number of transaction BEGIN statements still active. When an application issues a COMMIT, this variable is decremented by 1 since a transaction has been ended.

A synonym to COMMIT TRANSACTION is COMMIT WORK. This statement has the same effect as COMMIT TRANSACTION but cannot specify a transaction name to COMMIT as COMMIT TRANSACTION can.

Undoing Changes with ROLLBACK

When an application detects an error in the processing of the change activity, it should undo the changes made to put the database back into a consistent state (assuming the database was in a consistent state to begin with).

To undo the changes, an application executes a ROLLBACK TRANSACTION statement. This action will cause the changes made since the last BEGIN TRANSACTION to be rolled back.

If executed within a nested transaction (@@trancount > 1), the ROLLBACK goes beyond the last BEGIN TRANSACTION to roll back all levels of nested transactions up through the outermost transaction. The global variable @@trancount is then set to zero to indicate no active transaction.

Since a trigger is considered by SQL Server to be a nested transaction (this is automatic), a ROLLBACK executed in the trigger will roll back all changes in the trigger transaction and all changes in the transaction that caused the trigger to be executed. The batch that caused the trigger to be executed is then terminated.

Like the COMMIT TRANSACTION statement, the ROLLBACK TRANSACTION has a synonym called ROLLBACK WORK. This statement cannot accept a transaction or savepoint name (savepoints are discussed next) as the ROLLBACK TRANSACTION statement can.

Using SAVE TRANSACTION

During the processing of the change activity, an application can set a point in the processing where a ROLLBACK statement can roll back to without rolling back the entire transaction and without releasing acquired resources.

This point is known as a *savepoint* and is set with the SAVE TRANSACTION statement.

When the savepoint is named, a ROLLBACK TRANSACTION can refer to the savepoint name, causing a ROLLBACK of changes up to the savepoint. Resources are not released in this case. The application may then continue from the savepoint and eventually COMMIT or ROLLBACK the entire transaction.

Savepoints can be helpful in complex processing to enable partial changes to be saved while change activity beyond the savepoint may fail and need to be rolled back, or may be intended to be rolled back.

Using Distributed Transactions

Transactions started with the BEGIN TRANSACTION statement are local transactions; that is, they are run and managed on the local SQL Server. With local transactions, an application can process changes against databases managed by the local SQL Server installation only.

When an application wants to process changes against databases on remote machines and remote SQL Servers, it needs to start a distributed transaction, one that tracks change activity on all servers, not just the local server. Distributed transactions are started explicitly by executing a BEGIN DISTRIBUTED TRANSACTION.

We'll take a look at the BEGIN DISTRIBUTED TRANSACTION in a moment, but first let's see how distributed transactions are managed.

The Microsoft Distributed Transaction Coordinator

When an application starts a distributed transaction, SQL Server makes a call to the local Microsoft Distributed Transaction Coordinator (MS DTC) to obtain a transaction object and to enlist in the transaction.

The MS DTC on the machine starting the transaction becomes the transaction manager for the transaction and controls the COMMIT and ROLLBACK across all MS DTCs enlisted in the transaction through a two-phase COMMIT procedure. The SQL Server on the machine starting the transaction is called the originating server.

Local change activity is done in the context of the distributed transaction. If a call is made to a remote SQL Server via a remote procedure call or a distributed query, then the remote MS DTC is used by the remote SQL Server to enlist in the transaction passed by the originating SQL Server.

A *remote procedure call* is a call to a stored procedure on a remote SQL Server. The procedure name is qualified by the server and database names where the procedure is located. Assuming we had a second SQL Server installation in our firm called SECRETS2 and a database named Prices on that server, a call to a stored procedure named GetPrice would look like this:

```
Declare @retprice AS currency
EXECUTE @retprice = SECRETS2.Prices.dbo.GetPrice
```

If the application commits the transaction, then the transaction manager uses the two-phase COMMIT procedure to COMMIT changes on the remote server by communicating with the remote MS DTCs enlisted in the transaction.

The two-phase COMMIT first involves an announcement by the transaction manager to all enlisted coordinators that they should prepare for a COMMIT. If all enlisted coordinators successfully prepare, then the transaction manager issues a COMMIT to the coordinators to complete the transaction.

In the event of a ROLLBACK by the application, the transaction manager notifies all enlisted coordinators to undo the changes on their respective installations.

Distributed transaction activity can be monitored through the MS DTC entry in the SQL Server Enterprise Manager or in the MSDTC Admin Console.

Through the communication of the local SQL Server and the local MS DTC services, and the ability of MS DTC to communicate with remote MS DTC services, an application has a great deal of power to effect changes on servers and databases throughout the enterprise, with confidence that the integrity of those databases will be preserved.

Using BEGIN DISTRIBUTED TRANSACTION

An application starts a distributed transaction by executing a BEGIN DISTRIBUTED TRANSACTION statement.

This statement causes SQL Server to call the local MS DTC and start a transaction. The MS DTC returns a transaction object to SQL Server, which SQL Server can then pass to remote servers when the application makes a remote procedure call or executes a distributed query.

As remote servers are invoked, they enlist with their local MS DTC and participate in the transaction passed to them by the originating SQL Server. The remote server can in turn call another remote server, enlisting that server in the same transaction. All will communicate with the originating server MS DTC to coordinate the transaction outcome.

After the application finishes processing the transaction, it can COMMIT with a COMMIT TRANSACTION or roll back with a ROLLBACK TRANSACTION, just as it would for a local transaction. The local SQL Server and MS DTC then propagate the outcome to all enlisted servers.

Using Implicit Distributed Transactions

Distributed transactions can be started implicitly by promotion of a local transaction to a distributed transaction.

This occurs when an application starts a local transaction either implicitly or by a BEGIN TRANSACTION and then calls a remote stored procedure. If the sp_configure "remote proc trans" is ON in this case, or the REMOTE_PROC_TRANSACTIONS SET option is ON, then the local transaction will be promoted to a distributed transaction with the involvement of the local and remote MS DTC services.

If a distributed query is executed by the application involved in a local transaction, the local transaction is promoted if the OLE DB data source supports the ITransactionLocal interface. When ITransactionLocal is not supported, the query can only perform read-only processing.

Summary

In this chapter you've learned how to manage Transact-SQL transactions. You saw why we need transactions and the benefits of having SQL Server manage them.

We explored two methods of starting a local transaction. The BEGIN TRANSAC-TION statement is used to explicitly start a local transaction, and implicit transactions are started by setting the IMPLICIT_TRANSACTIONS option ON.

After an application has completed its processing within a transaction, it can COMMIT the work permanently to the database or ROLLBACK the work to the state the database was in before the transaction started.

At times, an application must make changes to databases on other SQL Servers. An application can make a remote procedure call or execute a distributed query to make a change on a remote server. These changes and the changes made to the local database can all be tracked in a distributed transaction.

You saw that a distributed transaction can be explicitly or implicitly started, just as a local transaction can be, and that distributed transactions are completed by the same means as local transaction — by COMMIT or ROLLBACK.

Distributed transactions use the Microsoft Distributed Transaction Coordinator to control the communication between the local originating SQL Server and the other SQL Servers enlisted in the transaction. Distributed transaction activity managed by MS DTC can be seen in SQL Server Enterprise Manager or by opening the MSDTC Administrative Console in the Microsoft SQL Server program folder.

Chapter 17

Monitoring SQL Server Events

IN THIS CHAPTER

◆ Learn what the SQL Server Profiler tool can do to help tune your application

◆ Learn about profiler events, queues, event criteria, and capture data

◆ Find out how to create a custom trace to monitor SQL Server activity

SQL SERVER PROFILER is a tool used to monitor a variety of events within a SQL Server installation.

This tool can monitor connection activity, Transact-SQL statements, resource usage, and a number of other events that can impact the overall performance of your database applications.

In this chapter, we go behind the scenes of this tool and explore the tracing of events through a set of extended stored procedures. These procedures enable us to create a custom profile for monitoring our application behavior in a SQL Server environment.

Exploring the SQL Server Profiler

The SQL Server Profiler utility can be used to monitor logins, connections, disconnections, and SELECT, INSERT, and UPDATE activity in addition to numerous other events in the SQL Server environment. The utility is used to monitor overall performance of the server or a database application.

Performance is monitored by creating a trace consisting of a collection of trace events to monitor and the data to be captured for these events. Trace events can be selected from lock events, stored procedure events, and transaction events, among others.

Application performance can be measured by specifying the application name and the process, object, and database IDs to be monitored.

Identify query performance by tracing Transact-SQL statements, indexes, databases, and execution time. The trace information collected can be used with the

Showplan setting or the with the Index Tuning Wizard to perform further analysis in an attempt to tune your queries to optimal performance.

The Profiler can be used directly through the tool's user interface or by using a number of extended stored procedures. This chapter will explore the Profiler through the use of extended stored procedures only.

Understanding Profiler Terminology

Server events are captured in a *trace queue*. The trace queue defines what is to be monitored through a collection of trace properties. *Producers* collect information on events in their respective event category and send that information to the trace queue in a first-in, first-out manner. The number of items being held in the queue is a function of the queue size, which can be specified when the queue is created.

When creating a trace, the key properties of the trace, which specify what is monitored, are the `Events` property, the `Trace Criteria` property and the `Capture data` property. A study of these three properties provides us with some insight as to what the profiler is capable of monitoring.

THE EVENTS PROPERTY

The *Events* property of a trace defines the events you wish to trace. The events you can select are shown in Table 17-1.

TABLE 17-1 EVENTS PROPERTY OPTIONS

Event	Description
Lock: Acquired	Display information on acquired locks
Lock: Cancel	Display lock requests that have been canceled
Lock: Deadlock	Display lock requests that require the same resources
Lock: Released	Display information on released locks
Lock: Timeout	Display locks that have timed out
Attention	Display attention events
Auto-UpdateStats	Display events for automatic UPDATE of index statistics
CursorOpen	Display cursor open information
ErrorLog	Display error events written to the SQL Server error log
EventLog	Display events written to the SQL Server event log
HashBail	Display information on hashing operations

Event	Description
LoginFailed	Display information on failed login attempts
Recompile(NoHints)	Display information on trigger and stored procedure recompilation
ServiceControl	Display server control events
Object: Closed	Display information on open objects that have closed
Object: Created	Display object create information
Object: Deleted	Display object deletion information
Object: Opened	Display information on object accesses
INSERT, DELETE, SELECT, UPDATE	Displays information on these statements and the degree of parallelism used
Scan: Started	Display information on table and index scans
Scan: Stopped	Display information on table and index scans that have stopped
Connect	Display events for connections to SQL Server
Disconnect	Display events for disconnects from SQL Server
ExistingConnection	Display information about pretrace connections
SP: CacheHit	Display information about procedures found in the procedure cache
SP: CacheInsert	Display information about procedures inserted into the procedure cache
SP: CacheMiss	Display information about procedures not found in the procedure cache
SP: CacheRemove	Display information about procedures removed from the procedure cache
SP: Completed	Display information on procedures that have ended
SP: ExecContext	Display context information on running procedures
SP: Recompile	Display information about procedure recompiles
SP: Starting	Display information about started procedures
SP: StmtStarting	Display information about started statements within procedures
RPC:Completed	Display information on completed remote procedure calls
RPC: Starting	Display information on remote procedure calls to be executed
RPC: BatchCompleted	Display information on Transact-SQL statements after execution

Continued

TABLE 17-1 EVENTS PROPERTY OPTIONS *(Continued)*

Event	Description
RPC: BatchStarting	Display information on Transact-SQL statements before execution
RPC: StmtStarting	Display information on Transact-SQL statements starting
DTCTransaction	Display tracking information on DTC coordinated transactions
SQLTransaction	Display tracking information on BEGIN, COMMIT, SAVE, and ROLLBACK transactions

THE TRACE CRITERIA PROPERTY

The *Trace Criteria* property is used to restrict the events chosen for monitoring. Some of these criteria specify a range of values to measure or whether to include or exclude the measurements specified. Table 17-2 lists the trace criteria you can use.

TABLE 17-2 TRACE CRITERIA PROPERTY OPTIONS

Trace Criteria	Description
Application name	The name of the application that fired the event
Connection ID	A unique connection ID
CPU	The CPU time in milliseconds
Database ID	A unique database ID
Duration	Execution time used for RPC and language statements
Event class	Events collections such as language events
Event text	Stored procedure SQL text
Host name	The name of the host that fired the event
Host process ID	A unique process ID for the host that fired the event
Index ID	A unique ID for the object being monitored
NT domain name	The name of the Windows NT domain of the client that fired the event
NT user name	The name of the user responsible for firing the event
Object ID	A unique ID for the object being monitored

Trace Criteria	Description
Owner ID	A unique ID for the object owner
Percent	The range for event completion
Reads	Number of disk reads
Server	The server name of the server performing the trace
Severity	The range of error severity levels
SPID	A unique process ID
SQL user name	The name of the user who fired the event
Writes	Number of synchronous disk writes

THE CAPTURE DATA PROPERTY

The *Capture Data* property specifies the actual data you want captured and sent to a specified destination such as the screen, a file, or a table. Internally, SQL Server captures data to a trace queue created specifically for the trace you are defining. Capture data options are listed in Table 17-3.

TABLE 17-3 CAPTURE DATA PROPERTY OPTIONS

Capture data	Description
Application	Capture one or more application names
Binary data	The binary data captured in the trace
Connection ID	The unique ID for the client. Select this when using the `Connect`, `Disconnect`, or `ExistingConnection` events
CPU usage	The amount of CPU time in milliseconds generated by an event
Database ID	The database ID monitored by the trace
Duration	The time in milliseconds required to complete an RPC or language statement
End	The completion time for language statement, RPC, connection, and session events
Event class	The event category in SQL Server Profiler

Continued

TABLE 17-3 CAPTURE DATA PROPERTY OPTIONS *(Continued)*

Capture data	Description
Host	The host name that generated the event
Host process ID	The host ID used to identify the process on a specific host
Index ID	The index ID used in the event
Integer data	The integer data captured in the trace
NT domain	The Windows NT domain of the user login
NT user	The Windows NT user login name
Object ID	The ID of the database object
Owner ID	The ID of the database object owner
Percentage	The percent completed
Reads	The number of disk reads
Server	The SQL Server name for the source of the trace
Severity	The error severity level range for the event
SPID	The ID of the system process that fired the event
SQL user	The SQL user that fired the event
Start	The begin execution time for the language statement or RPC that fired the event; or for session events, the time the user established the connection
Subclass	The type information for some event classes
Transaction ID	The unique ID for the transaction that fired the event
Text data	The language statement or RPC that fired the event
Writes	The number of synchronous disk writes generated by the event

Creating a Trace

To establish a trace, we first need to define a trace queue. To create a trace queue, we use the `xp_trace_addnewqueue` extended stored procedure. All of the `xp_trace` procedures discussed in this chapter must be executed from the master database.

Let's create a queue that monitors activity against the `FundAccts` database:

```
DECLARE @q_handle int,@cols int
SET @cols = 0
USE master
EXEC xp_trace_addnewqueue 1000,5,95,90,@cols,@q_handle OUTPUT
SELECT @q_handle
```

The first parameter designates the maximum number of items to hold in the queue and the next three are timeout, thread boost, and thread reduce, which are set to their default values.

The fifth parameter to the xp_trace_addnewqueue procedure defines the capture data we want to see in the trace. Setting this parameter to zero shows all columns. To set specific capture data columns, use the parameters shown in Table 17-4.

TABLE 17-4 CAPTURE DATA COLUMN PARAMETERS FOR
            XP_TRACE_ADDNEWQUEUE PROCEDURE

Parameter value	Description
1	String data
2	Binary data
4	Database ID
8	Transaction ID
16	User ID
32	NT user name
64	NT domain name
128	Host name
256	Host process ID
512	Application name
1024	Internal user name
2048	Internal process ID
4096	Duration
8192	Start time
16384	Stop time
32768	Number of reads

Continued

TABLE 17-4 CAPTURE DATA COLUMN PARAMETERS FOR
XP_TRACE_ADDNEWQUEUE PROCEDURE *(Continued)*

Parameter value	Description
65536	Number of writes
131072	CPU usage
262144	Percent complete
524288	Event severity
1048576	Event subclass
2097152	Object ID
4194304	Object owner ID
8388608	Index ID
16777216	Integer data
33554432	Server name

To specify multiple parameters, bitwise OR the values into the @cols variable like this:

```
SET @cols = 4|16|2097152
```

The last parameter to this procedure is the variable that will receive the queue handle. The queue handle will be needed for all subsequent procedures we'll be using.

After creating the trace queue, we can set the events we want to trace and the filters (criteria) for these events. We do this by using the xp_trace_setevent-classrequired and a number of xp_trace_set procedures specific to the filter we want to set:

```
—SQL:BatchCompleted
EXEC xp_trace_seteventclassrequired @q_handle,12,1
—Lock:Released
EXEC xp_trace_seteventclassrequired @q_handle,23,1
—Lock:Acquired
EXEC xp_trace_seteventclassrequired @q_handle,24,1
—EXEC xp_trace_setserverfilter @q_handle,'SECRETS',''
—EXEC xp_trace_setappfilter @q_handle,'FundMgr',''
```

The above `xp_trace_seteventclassrequired` procedures are setting our trace to monitor `SQL:BatchCompleted`, `Lock:Released`, and `Lock:Acquired` events. To see which events you can use here, execute the `xp_trace_geteventnames` procedure.

We are not setting any criteria for this trace queue, but you can set criteria by executing the procedure appropriate to the criteria you want set. The above code shows two commented out that can be set for the specific server and application you want to trace. See Appendix F and the Microsoft SQL Server Books Online for information on other procedures you can use.

Next, we need to set up a consumer for the trace queue output. You can specify the following values as the second parameter to `xp_trace_setqueuedestination`:

Value	Description
2	To a file
3	To the event log
4	To a table
5	To another server

We send the trace output to a table in the `FundAccts` database. This table, named Trace, will be created by the procedure and have a column for each of the Capture Data columns we have requested:

```
EXEC xp_trace_setqueuedestination @q_handle,
  4,1,'SECRETS','FundAccts.dbo.Trace'
```

The third parameter specifies 1 for an enabled destination and 0 for a disabled destination.

The fourth parameter specifies the server receiving the trace data and the last parameter specifies the destination name if writing to a file or table.

Now that we have a custom trace queue that we can use to monitor our application, we can save it for future use using the `xp_trace_savequeuedefinition`:

```
EXEC xp_trace_savequeuedefinition @q_handle,
  'FundAccountsTrace',1
```

This statement stores the trace queue definition in the system registry under the key:

```
HKEY_LOCAL_MACHINE\SOFTWARE\Microsoft\MSSQLServer\
  SQLServerProfiler\Server\Queues
```

In the case above, an entry named `'FundAccountsTrace'` would be stored under the Queues key.

To remove the key from the registry, execute the following procedure:

```
EXEC xp_trace_deletequeuedefinition 'FundAccountsTrace',1
```

Now we're ready to start the trace.

Starting and Stopping a Trace

To start collecting event data into the destination consumer, use the `xp_trace_startconsumer` procedure:

```
EXEC xp_trace_startconsumer @q_handle
```

We can list the active trace queue handles using the `xp_trace_enumqueuehandles` procedure as shown here:

```
EXEC xp_trace_enumqueuehandles
```

To pause queue handle 6, use the following statement:

```
EXEC xp_trace_pausequeue 6
```

This stops all trace events from being written to the queue and to the consumer. To restart the event monitoring, execute the following:

```
EXEC xp_trace_restartqueue 6
```

Finally, to stop the queue, use the following:

```
EXEC xp_trace_destroyqueue 6
```

To start this specific trace queue again after destroying it, execute another `xp_trace_addnewqueue` to obtain a queue handle, or use an active queue handle and then execute the `xp_trace_loadqueuedefinition` procedure:

```
EXEC xp_trace_loadqueuedefinition 5,'FundAccountsTrace',1
```

The above assumes we have an active queue handle 5 to associate our trace queue definition with. The last parameter specifies that this trace queue definition can be shared by all users.

Viewing the Trace Results

After you have executed the application code you are monitoring, pause the trace queue and open the destination you specified with `xp_trace_setqueuedestination`.

In the case above, we would select from the Trace table in the `FundAccts` database. We can select specific columns and event classes that interest us. For example, to look at lock activity, we would select rows that contain an EventClass equal to 23 or 24.

A word of caution when tracing your applications. The trace activity captured can be very voluminous, depending upon the trace events you have defined. A simple SELECT statement can generate hundreds of entries in the trace table or file. Design your trace queues carefully to ensure you obtain useful information.

Secondly, tracing takes resources away from applications. Be sure traces are on only for the duration necessary to capture your information, then turn them off.

Summary

You've seen that the SQL Server Profiler can be used to monitor application behavior in SQL Server as to the resources it uses and the duration of holding them.

Although you can use the Profiler's graphical user interface to define and monitor traces, you learned here that extended stored procedures can also be used for profiling.

The Profiler terminology was explained here, and you saw how the extended trace procedures are used to build and run a trace queue.

The trace procedures are a good choice for capturing information within a custom stored procedure or script file where the use of the Profiler tool would be impractical. Because of it's ease of use and the ability to view traces on screen, however, the Profiler tool will be the method you will use most often.

Part III

SQL Server Programming

Chapter 18

DB-Library

IN THIS CHAPTER

♦ Learn about the sample FundMgr application used in Part III

♦ See how rows are fetched through the default DB-Library cursor

♦ Find out how to bind columns in a DB-Library cursor to program variables

♦ Learn how to call stored procedures that use parameters

♦ Explore positioned updates through a DB-Library cursor

PART III PROVIDES SAMPLES of DB-Library, Open Database Connectivity (ODBC), ActiveX Data Objects (ADO), and Open Data Services (ODS) programs. These samples will show how these various application programming interfaces (APIs) are used to access a SQL Server database.

The samples, with the exception of the ODS sample, all have the same program architecture to implement a simple fund manager (FundMgr) application. FundMgr displays five Microsoft Foundation Class (MFC) views, two of which are updateable.

The difference between the samples of each chapter is found in the implementation of the DBObject class. This class uses one of the APIs to interface with the FundAccts database. Each of the views in the application uses a handle to the DBObject allocated to the view for all work with the database, including the fetching of rows to be displayed in the view and the updating of columns.

The overall FundMgr application behaves the same no matter which implementation of DBObject we are using. Unplug the ODBC version and plug in the ADO version. Unplug the ADO version and plug in the DB-Library version. The only difference is the API used.

Chapter 21 builds an extended stored procedure DLL to implement a custom application log that can be used to log messages. A message can be written to a log file as well as read from the log file to illustrate the use of extended procedures with parameters and a result set.

The Sample Program Architecture

When the FundMgr application opens, the first view a user sees is a list of accounts from the Accounts table. This view displays all columns of the table and all rows.

A user may click on one of the accounts in the list and click the Portfolio button. This brings up a list of the fund accounts from the FundAccounts table that belong to the selected account number.

From the Fund Accounts view, a fund account can be selected and the Transaction History button clicked to view the transactions for the selected fund account.

The DBObject Class

All these views are filled by the default cursor of the API implemented in the DBObject class. The cursor is opened on a simple SELECT statement and read in a forward direction from the first row to the last, fetching each row and returning the columns to the view for display in the view's list control. The interfacing between the application views and the DBObject is depicted in Figure 18-1.

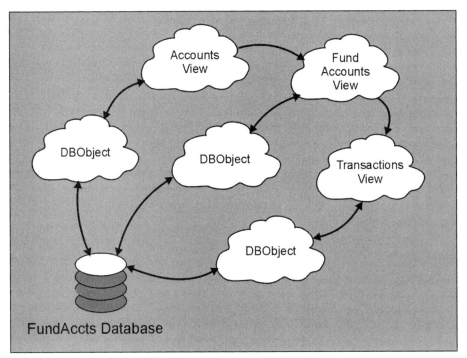

Figure 18-1: The FundMgr sample application's MFC view interfacing and the view/DBObject interaction for database access

The Accounts view enables an account to be updated through a simple `UPDATE` Transact-SQL statement. The account is selected in the list and the Edit button clicked to display a Form view in which some columns of the account are displayed for editing. The user may change values in this view and click OK to have the application `UPDATE` the account, or changes can be canceled by clicking the Cancel button.

Using a View on Results from a Stored Procedure

A user can display accounts for an account manager, one by one, in a Form view by selecting one of the accounts in the list and clicking the Manager Accounts button. The manager number comes from the selected account in the Accounts list. This number is passed to the DBObject, which in turn uses it as a parameter to the `ManagerAccounts` stored procedure to return accounts for that manager only.

The cursor opened on the result set from `ManagerAccounts` is a Keyset-driven scrollable cursor. This enables the single-account view to navigate forward and backward through the result set. When an account is to be updated, the Save button is clicked and DBObject performs a positioned `UPDATE` through the cursor.

All views are associated with the same document object. The document is used to allocate a DBObject object and return the pointer to that object back to the view. The view then uses its own DBObject to perform whatever tasks it is designed to do without affecting other views. The view/document/DBObject interaction is shown in Figure 18-2. This, of course, is only one among many designs you can use in an application.

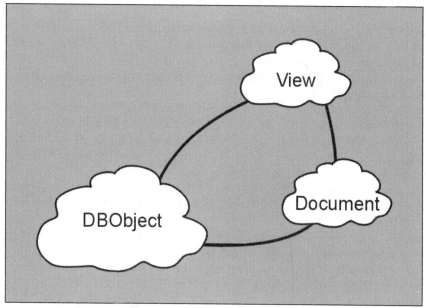

Figure 18-2: The interaction between the MFC view, its associated MFC document, and the custom DBObject

The DBObject class exposes the same functions in all implementations so that views can remain unchanged while database APIs can be switched within the functions themselves. The views don't care how the data is retrieved or how an UPDATE is applied; they just work with a common and familiar set of DBObject functions and the data returned from those functions.

Since the sample program architecture is the same throughout Part III, each chapter beyond this one will only discuss the DBObject implementation and provide an overview of the chapter API.

The remainder of this chapter will focus on the DB-Library API and its use in the DBObject class for the FundMgr application.

Using DB-Library

As was mentioned in Chapter 1, DB-Library has been around for quite awhile. It has grown from the days of 16-bit Windows to a 32-bit Windows version. This library has not been enhanced for SQL Server 7.

The sample we look at here can be found in the Ch18 directory on the CD-ROM that accompanies this book.

To use the DB-Library functions and constants, we first include the sqlfront.h and sqldb.h include files. These are found in the <SQL Server install directory>\DevTools\Include directory.

The first function we call in the DBObject code is the dbinit() function. This is used to initialize DB-Library.

Once the library has been initialized, we can proceed to open a connection with SQL Server. To do this, we first obtain a login record pointer by calling the dblogin() function. The login record pointer will be passed into a set of macros that will assign the user ID and password into the record structure. The record will then be passed into the open connection function.

The macro used to assign the user ID is DBSETLUSER and to set the password we use DBSETLPWD. Once these are set into the login record, we make a connection by calling the dbopen() function, passing it the login record pointer as the first argument and the name of the server we want to connect to as the second argument.

If the connection was successful, we get back a pointer to a DBPROCESS structure. This pointer will be used in all other calls made to DB-Library. If the pointer from dbopen() is NULL, then a connection could not be made and we return FAIL to the view.

The DBObject GetData() function has the task of opening a cursor on the Transact-SQL statement passed into the function. To do this, GetData() places the statement into the DBPROCESS structure with a call to the dbcmd() function.

To execute the statement, the dbsqlexec() function is called passing the DBPROCESS structure as the only argument. If the return from dbsqlexec() is SUCCESS, then the result set can be processed.

The first step in processing the result set is to call the dbresults() function, which enables access to the result set for the statement or statements executed with dbsqlexec(). In our example, there is only one result set to process, so dbresults() only needs to be called once. If, however, multiple statements were executed by dbsqlexec(), then dbresults() must be called for each statement in order to gain access to the statement result set. This is usually done in a WHILE loop that checks the return from dbresults() for NO_MORE_RESULTS.

Now that GetData() has set up the result set, DBObject is ready for the view to start fetching data from it. To begin this process, the view first calls GetNumberColumns() to determine how many columns it needs to process for the list. GetNumberColumns() obtains the number of columns by a call to dbnumcols.

The next step the view needs to perform is to retrieve the column names and data types for the list headers. GetColumnName() and GetColumnType() provide this meta data.

GetColumnName() uses dbcolname with the index of the column the view is interested in as the second argument. The resulting string is returned to the view.

GetColumnType() calls dbcoltype, also with the column index as the second argument, and returns the result to the view. The return types from dbcoltype are listed in Appendix I. Use the constants in the SQL Token column of the DB-Library table.

After the view fills the column headers for the result set, it begins fetching column data with calls to GetColumnData(). GetColumnData() accesses the indexed column with a call to dbdata. If the column contains NULL, then the string "NULL" is returned; otherwise, the column data is returned.

Once all columns indicated by column count are filled into the list, the view fetches the next row in the result set with a call to FetchData(). The FetchData() makes a call to dbnextrow and returns the return code from this call back to the view. When the return is NO_MORE_ROWS, the view stops fetching data for the list and the user is free to view the results.

Using Stored Procedures and Parameters

To support the Manager Accounts view, DBObject must open a scrollable Keyset-driven cursor on the result set returned from the ManagerAccounts stored procedure.

This procedure takes one input parameter, the manager number for which accounts are to be returned. The GetCursorData() function in DBObject is responsible for setting the procedure parameters and establishing the cursor.

GetCursorData() first calls dbrpcinit with the DBRPCCURSOR option to initialize the procedure. Once this is done, a call is made to dbrpcparam to set the input parameter for the ManagerAccounts procedure.

The third argument to dbrpcparam indicates the type of parameter we are specifying. The fourth argument to dbrpcparam specifies the data type of the parameter (see Appendix I for DB-Library data type constants).

The fifth and sixth arguments specify the maximum data length and actual data length. Since we are using a smallint data type, we set both of these arguments to -1. The last argument is the address of the variable that will hold the input parameter value.

For the input manager number parameter, we use SQLINT2 (smallint) as the data type argument and place the manager number passed from the view into the variable addressed by the last argument. The parameter type is specified as NULL to indicate an input parameter.

After setting the parameter for the procedure, GetCursorData() proceeds to open the cursor using dbcursoropen(). The scroll option for the cursor is specified as CUR_KEYSET since we are implementing a Keyset-driven cursor to support scrolling forward and backward through the result set.

If the cursor was opened successfully, dbcursoropen returns a cursor handle that we use for binding program variables to result set columns. We do this with the dbcursorbind() function, one call per column returned.

When the user scrolls to the next or previous row, the view calls FetchCursorData() with a navigation argument. FetchCursorData() in turn calls dbcursorfetch(), passing the cursor handle as the first argument and the appropriate navigation constant as the second argument. The navigation constants you can use in dbcursorfetch() are listed in Table 18-1.

TABLE 18-1 NAVIGATION CONSTANTS USED IN DBCURSORFETCH

Constant	Description
FETCH_FIRST	Fetch the first row or block of rows from the cursor
FETCH_NEXT	Fetch the next row or block of rows from current position
FETCH_PREV	Fetch the previous row or block of rows from the current position
FETCH_RANDOM	Fetch a row or block of rows from a keyset cursor
FETCH_RELATIVE	Fetch a row or block of rows which is before or after the current position by the number of rows specified as the third argument
FETCH_LAST	Fetch the last row or block of rows from the cursor.

Note that legal navigation arguments are dependent on the type of cursor being opened. In the case of CUR_KEYSET, we are allowed to use FETCH_FIRST, FETCH_NEXT, and FETCH_PREV.

Positioned Updates Through a Cursor

When a user makes changes to an account in the Manager Accounts Form view, the view calls UpdateCursorData() to perform a positioned UPDATE.

The UPDATE is done through a call to dbcursor passing the cursor handle as the first argument. The second argument specifies the type of operation we want to perform.

Since we are performing an UPDATE operation, we use CRS_UPDATE as the second argument. CRS_INSERT, CRS_DELETE, and CRS_REFRESH are among the other possibilities for this argument.

The third argument to dbcursor is used to indicate the row being operated on. The first row in the cursor is row number 1. The fourth argument specifies the name of the table the operation involves. Since our cursor was opened on a statement involving only one table, the Accounts table, we can specify NULL here.

We are using bound variables to hold the changes to the account columns, so we can specify NULL as the last argument as well. In some cases, you would need to specify a pointer to a string of values that will be inserted or updated to the table.

When the Manager Accounts view is closed, the cursor is closed with dbcursorclose(). This action will free all data and resources associated with the cursor.

Summary

In this chapter, we discussed the architecture of the sample FundMgr application used in this chapter and the two that follow. We saw that the application behaves the same in all sample programs, but the implementation of the database access in DBObject changes to illustrate the various APIs discussed.

We saw how the DB-Library implementation of DBObject works to support the various views of FundMgr. Default cursor fetching, stored procedures and parameters, and positioned updates were explored.

In the following chapters, you get an overview of ODBC and ADO and see how these APIs are used to perform the same functions that were implemented here with DB-Library. By the end of Part III, you'll be able to form your own opinions about which API you like to use for your applications. Although you won't gain an in-depth knowledge of an API from these samples, you will get enough of an understanding of these APIs to enable you to explore further on your own and learn more about processing a SQL Server database.

Chapter 19

Open Database Connectivity

IN THIS CHAPTER

- ◆ Learn how to use ODBC to fetch rows sequentially

- ◆ Discover how to use parameterized stored procedures

- ◆ Explore ODBC cursor types and how to define them

- ◆ See how to navigate a cursor's rows and perform positioned updates

OPEN DATABASE CONNECTIVITY (ODBC) is an application programming interface (API) that enables you to access and work with any data source for which an ODBC driver is available. ODBC is based on the X/Open and ISO/CAE Call-Level Interface (CLI) specification.

ODBC is composed of a driver manager and one or more drivers specifically built to access one or more data sources. SQL Server 7.0 ships with an ODBC 3.5 driver that you can use to build applications that access SQL Server.

The ODBC API function set is very powerful and can handle anything you will need to do with your SQL Server database (and other data sources as well). ODBC provides a heterogeneous data environment for your applications. All data sources, whether they be a relational database, a text file, or a Microsoft Excel spreadsheet, can be accessed through the same API function set.

ODBC is powerful, but trades this power for ease of use. Of course, "ease of use" has different meanings to different programmers. I'm sure there are many programmers out there who think DB-Library is very easy to use, while just as many would think that it is extremely difficult. Nonetheless, the ODBC API is quite extensive and will require some time before you become proficient in its use. In my opinion, it will be time well spent.

Let's look at how the ODBC version of the DBObject works.

Using the ODBC API

The DBObject source includes three header files that define functions and constants that we will use. The header files included are as follows:

SQL.H   Core ODBC functions

SQLEXT.H   ODBC Level 1 and 2 functions

SQLTYPES.H   Type definitions

To connect to SQL Server, the Connect() function first allocates an environment handle using the SQLAllocEnv() function. If this function returns success (SQL_SUCCESS), a connection handle is allocated using the environment handle and the SQLAllocConnect() function. The ODBC functions discussed in this chapter start with a prefix of SQL. Note that all environment, connect, and statement handles can be allocated with SQLAllocHandle() as well.

After obtaining a connection handle, a connection with SQL Server can be made. To do this, a call is made to the SQLDriverConnect() function, passing it the connection handle, the view pointer, a connection string, and a parameter coded as SQL_DRIVER_COMPLETE_REQUIRED.

The connection string specifies the data source information required to direct the driver manager to the right driver and the driver to the data source; in this case, the FundAccts database. The format of this string depends on whether or not you are using a data source name created with the ODBC Administrator applet in the Windows Control Panel and how much of the connection information you want to supply. If you don't supply all connection information required by the driver, the driver will prompt the user for the missing information before making the connection. Connection string keywords are listed in Table 19-1.

TABLE 19-1 CONNECTION STRING KEYWORDS

Keyword	Description
DSN=	The data source name created with the ODBC Administrator or any custom program that can write to the system registry
DRIVER=	The driver description
FILEDSN=	The name of a file data source from which data source information can be read
PWD=	The password for the UID

Keyword	Description
SAVEFILE=	The name of a file in which current connection string information will be saved as a file dsn
UID=	The user ID that will make the connection to the database

Most ODBC drivers also define specific connection string keywords such as Database= and Language=. See the driver help file for information on the use of these keywords.

The DBObject connection string specifies a DSN named FundAccts that was established with the ODBC Administrator and points to the SQL Server driver and FundAccts database. The UID uses the system administrator with a NULL PWD.

After a successful SQLDriverConnect(), the strConnOut argument will contain the full connection string information.

The SQL_DRIVER_COMPLETE_REQUIRED argument specifies that the driver or driver manager should prompt the user to complete required connection string information.

To execute a GetData() request, the function first allocates a statement handle using the SQLAllocStmt() function. This function uses the connection handle allocated above.

If the statement handle allocation is successful, the handle is passed to the SQLExecDirect() function along with the input request to be sent to SQL Server for execution.

The last task of GetData() is to call SQLNumResultCols to obtain the number of columns in the result set and save this value in a member variable for later access by the view.

After GetData() has created the result set, the view can retrieve data from it for display in the view's list control. To do this, the view has to obtain meta data on the column names and types for the list control column header and then FETCH the rows and columns of the result set and INSERT them into the list.

The GetNumberColumns() function in DBObject is called to obtain the number of columns in the result set. The function returns the m_numcols variable retrieved by SQLNumResultCols() in the GetData() function.

To get the column names and types, the view calls the GetColumnName() and GetColType() functions. Both of these functions call SQLDescribeCol() to get the column name and type of the indexed column.

Data from the record set is retrieved via the SQLFetch() function to fetch each row and the SQLGetData() function to get column values. When SQLFetch() returns SQL_NO_DATA indicating the end of the result set, the view stops retrieving data into the list control.

Using Stored Procedures

The single-account view of the FundMgr sample application uses a cursor defined on the result set from execution of the ManagerAccounts stored procedure. This procedure takes a manager number as an input parameter and retrieves all accounts for that manager.

Since the `ManagerAccounts` procedure takes one input parameter, we must first notify ODBC of this parameter and the addresses of the program variable for this parameter. We do this with `SQLBindParameter()`.

Parameters for the procedure to be executed are bound according to the order of the parameter starting with 1 for the leftmost parameter. The `GetCursorData()` function binds only one parameter on the statement handle that will open the cursor.

The `SQLBindParameter()` function specifies the parameter number as the second argument and the input-output type as the third argument. Input-output types are listed in Table 19-2 below.

TABLE 19-2 SQLBINDPARAMETER( ) INPUT-OUTPUT TYPES

Constant	Description
SQL_PARAM_INPUT	An input parameter to a procedure or marker for a Transact-SQL statement
SQL_PARAM_INPUT_OUTPUT	A parameter used for both input and output
SQL_PARAM_OUTPUT	Parameter used for return values and output parameters from stored procedures

The next two arguments specify the C data type of the parameter and the SQL data type of the parameter. See Appendix I for a listing of these data types.

The sixth and seventh arguments specify the column size and decimal digits for parameter markers. For the return parameter, we ignore both of these arguments. For the input manager number parameter, we set column size to the size of the manager_num column and set decimal digits to zero.

The next argument is a pointer to the program variable used for the parameter. The last two arguments specify the length of the variable buffer and the length of the value in the buffer for input parameters. This last argument is specified as SQL_NTS for the input parameter to indicate the value is a NULL-terminated string.

After binding the parameter to the program variable, we can then set the manager number that was passed into the GetCursorData() function into the input parameter variable and call the ManagerAccounts procedure. The format of the call in SQLExecDirect() is as follows:

```
{ call ManagerAccounts(?) }
```

The call specifies one parameter marker (?). The marker inside the parenthesis is parameter number one bound to the input variable holding the manager number we want to retrieve accounts for.

When the statement is no longer needed or we want to specify other parameters (or none at all), we execute the SQLFreeStmt() using the SQL_RESET_PARAMS option.

Now let's look at the cursor we'll open on the result set.

Using Cursors

To set up the cursor on the result set of the ManagerAccounts stored procedure execution, we use the SQLSetStmtAttr() API call. This function can be used to set various statement attributes before execution of the statement. We will set the SQL_ATTR_CURSOR_TYPE attribute to specify a Keyset-driven cursor. The cursor types we can use here are listed in Table 19-3.

TABLE 19-3 CURSOR TYPE STATEMENT ATTRIBUTE CONSTANTS

Constant	Description
SQL_CURSOR_DYNAMIC	Changes (inserts, deletes, updates) made by other users are visible in the cursor.
SQL_CURSOR_FORWARD_ONLY	A static cursor that only allows forward scrolling. Changes made by other users are not visible.
SQL_CURSOR_KEYSET_DRIVEN	Changes (deletes, updates) made by other users are visible but not inserts. Deletes are detected as a special ROW_STATUS in the statement attributes.
SQL_CURSOR_STATIC	A static cursor that allows forward and backward scrolling.

After setting the cursor type, we're ready to open the cursor by executing SQLExecDirect().

To navigate through the cursor, the view passes a navigation argument to FetchCursorData() that indicates the direction or position to FETCH. FetchCursorData() uses the SQLFetchScroll() function and one of the navigation constants listed in Table 19-4 as its second argument to navigate through the cursor.

TABLE 19-4 SQLFETCHSCROLL NAVIGATION CONSTANTS

Constant	Description
SQL_FETCH_NEXT	Fetches the next row in the cursor
SQL_FETCH_PRIOR	Fetches the prior row in the cursor
SQL_FETCH_FIRST	Fetches the first row in the cursor
SQL_FETCH_LAST	Fetches the last row in the cursor
SQL_FETCH_ABSOLUTE	Fetches the row indicated in the third argument of SQLFetchScroll()
SQL_FETCH_RELATIVE	Fetches the row which is x number of rows from the current row. The value x is the value in the third argument of SQLFetchScroll()
SQL_FETCH_BOOKMARK	Fetches the row that is x number of rows from the bookmark stored at the address indicated by the statement attribute SQL_ATTR_FETCH_BOOKMARK_PTR

The descriptions in Table 19-4 indicate that one row is fetched with the SQLFetchScroll() function when in reality it is possible to FETCH multiple rows. The number of rows fetched with one call to SQLFetchScroll() is set by the statement attribute SQL_ATTR_ROW_ARRAY_SIZE. Our sample fetches only one row at a time.

Note the similarity of these navigation options and those of the Transact-SQL FETCH statement.

Unlike the list view support where we did not bind any columns to program variables, the single-account view will use binding to illustrate its use and make life a little easier for updating.

We bind program variables to columns of the result set using SQLBindCol(). SQLBindCol() specifies a column number as the second argument. This column number starts at 1 if bookmarks are not being used on the statement. If bookmarks are being used, column zero is the bookmark column.

The third argument to SQLBindCol() is the C data type of the program variable the column is being bound to. The address of this variable is specified in the fourth argument. The fifth argument is the buffer length of the program variable while the sixth argument specifies the length of data returned into the variable by a FETCH. Each of the columns in the account view result set is bound to program variables for retrieval and updating of column data.

Updates in our ODBC sample use the SQLSetPos() function. This function can be used to position the current row pointer in a block of rows fetched with SQLFetchScroll() or to UPDATE or DELETE a row.

The third argument of SQLSetPos() dictates what action the function performs. To UPDATE the row, we use SQL_UPDATE as the third argument. The second argument designates the row number to UPDATE. Since we only have one row in the fetched row set, we set this argument to 1. Had we fetched a rowset size of 20, we could specify any number from 1 to 20. Using zero in the second argument would UPDATE all rows in the row set most recently fetched.

So, our basic string of events to implement updating in our sample application is as follows:

1. Set up the cursor and statement parameters and open the cursor with SQLExecDirect().

2. Scroll to the row we want to UPDATE.

3. Change the bound column values we wish to UPDATE.

4. Issue the UPDATE with SQLSetPos().

When we're done with the cursor and ready to exit the application, we can execute a SQLCloseCursor(), then free the statement with SQLFreeStmt() and the handles we allocated with SQLFreeHandle(). The first argument to this function specifies the handle to free, as shown in the program.

Summary

We saw in this chapter how ODBC can be used to access the FundAccts database to list a set of rows and to scroll through a cursor.

The basic steps of allocating handles and buffers, executing statements, and fetching rows and columns was illustrated in support of the multiple-account list view.

The single-account view based on a stored procedure requiring an input parameter was explored, and we discovered how to bind parameters to program variables and to specify the directional properties of statement parameters.

The use of a dynamic cursor was illustrated, and we learned how to use the SQLSetPos() function to perform a positioned UPDATE on the cursor.

Finally, we learned how to clean up the environment before exiting using the SQLFreeStmt() and SQLFreeHandle() functions.

Although we have seen some common ODBC processing in this sample application, there is plenty more we have not touched upon. There are numerous meta data functions you can call to access information about the database and the program environment. You should also look into the use of block cursors to improve program performance rather than the single-row fetches we did in this sample.

The study and use of ODBC provides a great deal of insight into how a database engine like SQL Server works and how you can enhance the performance and feature set of your application. ODBC is worth a more in-depth look.

Chapter 20

ActiveX Data Objects

IN THIS CHAPTER

- ◆ Explore the objects found in the ADO object model
- ◆ Learn about the OLE DB providers available for access to SQL Server
- ◆ See how to make a connection to a SQL Server database using the Connection object
- ◆ Find out how to use Parameter objects for stored procedure input and output parameters
- ◆ Learn about cursor options for the Recordset object

ACTIVEX DATA OBJECTS (ADO) is a component of the Microsoft Data Access Components. ADO provides a simple but powerful object model to the programmer and uses an OLE DB provider to access a data source such as SQL Server.

SQL Server 7.0 ships with an OLE DB provider that complies with the OLE DB 2.0 specification and an OLE DB for ODBC provider, both of which can be used by ADO to access a SQL Server 7.0 database. ADO can be used by applications written in Visual Basic, C, C++, and Java. It can even be used by Web-based applications using VBScript and JavaScript.

The ADO Object Model

ADO presents seven objects to enable a program to work with a data source, as shown in Figure 20-1.

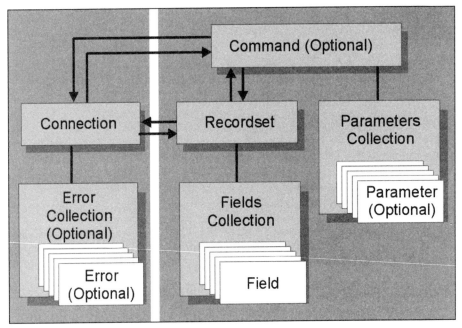

Figure 20-1: The ADO object model

The *Connection* object uses the OLE DB Data Source and Session objects to enable a program to connect to a data source and start a session with a data provider. The connection object provides a means of accessing meta data about the data source, accessing error information, and managing local transactions.

The *Command* object uses the OLE DB command object. The command is used to execute Transact-SQL statements against a database. Statement Property and Parameter objects can be created through this object and used to create Recordset objects.

The *Recordset* object uses the OLE DB Rowset object. The Recordset provides a means of establishing cursors and manipulating data in a result set. The columns of the rows in the Recordset are represented by Field objects, which in turn are described by Property objects.

The *Error* object depends on the Connection object and provides information on errors and warnings generated by the Connection, Command, or Recordset objects.

When a command to be executed requires parameters, such as a stored procedure that requires input and output parameters, a *Parameter* object can be created to define the parameter for the command.

A *Field* object is associated with a Recordset object and holds the meta information and data value for a column in the Recordset. It is accessed through the *Fields* collection of the Recordset.

A *Property* object and Properties collection is associated with the Connection, Command, Recordset, and Field objects. Properties provide information about the object they are associated with. A Property object associated with a Field object, for example, would hold information about the Field type — whether or not it is updateable, number of decimal places, and so on.

Let's take a look at how these objects are used in a program to access the FundAccts database.

Using the ADO Objects

 The `DBObject.cpp` code in the `Ch20` directory on the CD provides the functionality through ADO 1.5 to access the `FundAccts` database in the `FundMgr` sample application. In this section, we'll dissect some of that code to see how the ADO objects are put to use in a C++ program.

Before we get started, notice that DBObject in this example has included an `#import` directive. This directive imports the ADO typelib found in `msado15.dll` from the Microsoft Data Access Components available on the Microsoft Web site.

The `#import` directive brings in type definitions of ADO objects. The compiler converts these type definitions into typedefs, forward references, smart pointer definitions, and other declarations that describe these objects, their methods, and properties. The output of this conversion is written into the `msado15.tlh` and `msado15.tli` files found in the Release or Debug project directories. The definitions in these files enable the compiler to compile the ADO references in your program.

The first task the DBObject is called upon to perform is to connect to the FundAccts database. This code is found in, where else, the `Connect()` member function.

The `Connect()` function allocates a new COM smart pointer object (`_ConnectionPtr` class) and then calls that object's `CreateInstance()` function to create the actual ADO Connection object and obtain an interface pointer to it.

The next step in making a connection with SQL Server is to use the Connection's `Open()` function and pass it the Data Source name, user ID, and password. We're using the SQL Server system administrator (sa) account with a NULL password.

The components of the connection string argument are shown in Table 20-1.

TABLE 20-1 CONNECTIONSTRING KEYWORDS

Keyword	Description
Provider=	Name of the OLE DB provider
Driver=	Name of an ODBC driver
Data Source=	Name of the data source created with the ODBC Administrator
File Name= FileDSN=	Name of the File DSN containing DSN information
Database=	Name of the database to connect to
User ID= UID=	ID of the user making the connection
Password= PWD=	Password of the User ID

When using the OLE DB provider for ODBC, you can specify the Provider name and the ODBC driver or DSN name. The OLE DB provider for ODBC in SQL Server 7 is MSDASQL. The ODBC Driver is specified as {SQL Server}.

If not using the OLE DB provider for ODBC, but the native SQL Server provider, you specify the Provider name SQLOLEDB.

When a view in the application wants to retrieve data for display in a list, it calls the DBObject GetData() function. This function allocates a new smart pointer object for the Command object, creates the Command object, and then sets the Command object's ActiveConnection property equal to the Connection object.

Now that the command is aware of the connection to SQL Server, it can execute the data request passed into the GetData() function. This is done by setting the Command object's CommandText property equal to the request argument and then executing the statement with the Command's Execute method.

The Execute method returns a Recordset object that we will use to retrieve the results from the request execution.

The last task the GetData() function performs is to retrieve the number of rows in the resultset into a DBObject member variable. It does this by using the RecordCount property of the recordset.

Retrieving data from the recordset is implemented in the FetchData() and GetColumnData() functions. FetchData() is used to navigate to the next row in the recordset – it does a forward-only scroll through the recordset. GetColumnData() is used to retrieve the column values of the current row in the recordset.

Scrolling through the recordset is done with the `MoveNext` method of the Recordset object. `FetchData()` issues a `MoveNext` on the recordset and then checks for end of file (EOF) to notify the caller that the end of the recordset has been reached.

Prior to retrieving the column data for each row, the view calls the `GetNumberColumns()`, `GetColumnType()`, and `GetColumnName()` functions to retrieve column meta data.

`GetNumberColumns()` returns the value of the `Count` property of the recordset's Fields collection.

The `GetColumnType()` function returns the value of the `Type` property of the field object indexed in the recordset Fields collection by the input ndx argument. OLE DB data types and ADO constants for those types are listed in Appendix H.

`GetColumnName()` returns the `Name` property of the indexed field in the recordset.

At each row in the recordset, the `GetColumnData()` function is called and returns the `Value` property of the indexed field in the recordset. These values are placed in the view's list control by the view object.

When `FetchData()` returns `FALSE`, the view stops calling for data and the user can browse through the rows of the view's list control.

Next we'll look at the cursor used by the single-account Form view.

Using Stored Procedures

The cursor opened to support the single-account view is defined on the resultset from the execution of the ManagerAccounts stored procedure.

ManagerAccounts takes an input parameter that defines the manager number for selecting accounts.

Opening a cursor (recordset) on this procedure requires that we use a Parameter object for the input parameter. The `GetCursorData()` function in DBObject is responsible for setting up this parameter and opening the cursor.

After creating the command object, `GetCursorData()` sets the command's `CommandText` property equal to "ManagerAccounts."

Next the input parameter is created with the command object's `CreateParameter` method. After the parameter is created, it is appended to the command's Parameters collection.

The second argument to the `CreateParameter` method specifies the parameter type. These types are listed in Appendix I.

The third argument specifies the direction of the parameter. Valid constants for this argument are listed in Table 20-2.

TABLE 20-2 CREATEPARAMETER DIRECTION CONSTANTS

Constant	Description
adParamInput	An input parameter to the procedure
adParamOutput	An output parameter from the procedure
adParamInputOutput	A parameter that acts as both input and output
adParamReturnValue	A return value from the procedure

The fourth argument is used for the maximum size of the parameter value specified in the fifth argument or assigned to the Value property of the parameter.

The value of the manager number passed into GetCursorData() is set into the input parameter's Value property. With this parameter set, and the cursor type defined (which we'll discuss next), the command can be executed to create the recordset.

After executing the command, the function retrieves the return value from the return parameter and sends this back to the caller.

Using Cursors

To support the single-account view, we need a cursor that can be scrolled backward as well as forward, and it needs to be updateable.

We define cursors in ADO by setting a property of the Recordset object before opening it. In the GetCursorData() function, we use the CursorType property to set the type of cursor we want to use.

The default CursorType for a recordset is ForwardOnly, which means we get a recordset that is static and can be scrolled with MoveNext only. The types of cursor that can be set are described in Table 20-3.

TABLE 20-3 CURSORTYPE OPTIONS

Constant	Description
adOpenForwardOnly	A Forward-Only cursor. This is the default cursor type if none is specified when opening a recordset. It is a static cursor where only a MoveNext scroll can be used. The value of this constant is 0.

Constant	Description
adOpenDynamic	A Dynamic cursor. Any changes (inserts, updates, deletes) made by other users to the underlying tables of the recordset are visible in the recordset as you scroll to the record. Scrolling in the recordset can be both forward and backward. The value of this constant is 2.
adOpenKeyset	A Keyset cursor. Any changes (updates) made by other users to the underlying tables of the recordset are visible in the recordset as you scroll to the record. Scrolling to a record that has been deleted in the underlying table results in a status property setting indicating a deleted record. Inserts by other users into underlying tables are not visible in the recordset until the recordset is requeried. The value of this constant is 1.
adOpenStatic	A Static cursor. Changes (updates, inserts, deletes) made by other users to the underlying tables are not visible in the recordset. The data you see in this cursor is the data at the time the recordset was opened. To see new values, the recordset needs to be requeried. Both forward and backward scrolling is supported. The value of this constant is 3.

In `GetCursorData()` we use the `adOpenKeyset` cursor type since we need forward and backward scrolling and additions and deletions by other users that affect accounts for the specified manager number are not a concern. If we needed to see these changes, we would use adOpenDynamic.

Cursors can be either client-side or server-side. This is specified in the recordset's `CursorLocation` property as either `adUseClient` or `adUseServer`. We'll accept the default of `adUseServer`.

Prior to updating the record, the view sets changes into the record's columns by calling the `SetColumnData()` function. This function does nothing more than set the indexed field `Value` property to the input argument value and then return.

After all changes have been made, the view calls `UpdateCursorData()` to UPDATE the record in the database. Updating is applied at the current position of the cursor with the `Update` method of the recordset object.

The `Status` property of the recordset holds the sum of one or more constants that indicate the status of the current row. Some of these status constants are listed in Table 20-4.

TABLE **20-4** STATUS PROPERTY CONSTANTS FOR THE RECORDSET OBJECT

Constant	Description
adRecDBDeleted	The row was already deleted from the data source
adRecDeleted	The row has been deleted
adRecModified	The row has been changed
adRecNew	The row is new
adRecOK	The row was updated successfully
adRecUnmodified	The row has not been changed

Other status constants indicate some error with saving the row to the data source. These constants can be found in the ADO documentation in the Microsoft Data Access Components.

Summary

In this chapter we've taken a brief look at ActiveX Data Objects and how it can be used to access a SQL Server database.

We explored the objects that make up the ADO object model and how those objects interact to access a data source. Access through ADO to SQL Server can be established through the OLE DB provider for ODBC, MSDASQL, or through SQL Server 7's native OLE DB provider SQLOLEDB.

Connection strings required for specifying the method to use for data access, the database to connect to, and the server login information were discussed in the context of the ADO Connection object.

The creation of a cursor based on a stored procedure and the use of an input and return parameter for that procedure was explained, and you saw how the recordset object's status property can be used to check the status of the current row of the recordset.

There is plenty more to be learned about ADO and how you can use this powerful object model in your database applications, including Web-based applications. The methods and techniques used in this chapter, found on the accompanying CD in the Ch20 directory, illustrate only one way of using ADO. There are other techniques that you should explore.

Chapter 21

Open Data Services

IN THIS CHAPTER

- ◆ Learn what Open Data Services is and how you can use it in your applications
- ◆ See how to use the Open Data Services API
- ◆ Find out how to write an extended stored procedure

IN THE SQL SERVER architecture, Open Data Services (ODS) sits on the server between the network libraries and the SQL Server application and its extended stored procedures. SQL Server itself communicates with ODS via the ODS API.

ODS handles the Tabular Data Stream (TDS) communications between client and server and manages events such as client connections, Transact-SQL statements sent from a client application, and transmission of result set data from SQL Server back to the client.

SQL Server functionality can be extended by writing server-based applications using the same Open Data Services API that SQL Server uses. Using this API, you can write extended stored procedures that can be called in the same manner that SQL Server's extended procedures and system stored procedures are called.

ODS works with an event model. Each event involving ODS gets routed to an event handler adapted to work with that specific event. Events in ODS are classified as follows:

- ◆ Connection events, which are raised when a client connects or disconnects
- ◆ Language events, which are raised to process a Transact-SQL request
- ◆ Remote procedure events, which are raised when a remote procedure call is made by a server

In the case of an extended stored procedure, multiple event handlers can be implemented to process events in one or more of these event classifications. The procedure can use the Win32 API set and perform any processing it needs, just as it would as a standard application DLL. When the procedure needs to communicate with SQL Server or the client, it calls a function in the ODS API.

Extended stored procedures are registered with SQL Server using the `sp_addex-tendedproc` stored procedure. This procedure takes the name of an extended procedure as the first string argument and the name of the DLL the procedure is implemented in as the second string argument. The DLL can implement multiple extended procedures.

When an extended procedure is called, SQL Server looks up the DLL for the procedure and loads the DLL, if necessary, into the SQL Server address space. After loading, SQL Server then passes the call to the procedure.

Although you can use the ODS API to write an application similar to SQL Server that handles connections, language events, and so on, we'll concentrate in this chapter on building two extended procedures for use in the FundAccts database.

The source for this project is found in the Ch21 directory on the CD.

Let's get started.

Using the Open Data Services API

The extended procedures we'll create are used to log certain events in the FundAccts database. One procedure takes a string as an input parameter, write that string to the FundAccts log file, and return a fail or success return code. This procedure can be used to log any activity we wish, including messages, new accounts, redemptions, and account closings to name a few. The log this procedure writes is a simple text file readable by any utility that can read ASCII text.

The second procedure enables an application to read back any record in the log. In this procedure, the application passes a record number to the procedure and the procedure readies that record from the current log and returns it as a row back to the caller.

The include file for this project is srv.h, found in the <SQL Server install directory>\ DevTools\ Include directory. The import library required to resolve API function calls is opends70.lib found in the <SQL Server install directory>\ DevTools\ Lib directory. The Microsoft Visual C++ project type is a Win32 DLL.

All extended procedures you want to make available to clients must be declared as exported functions in the DLL. You can do this in a Def file using the EXPORTS statement or by declaring function prototypes with _declspec(dllexport).

All exported function (that is, extended procedures) have the following function prototype:

```
SRVRETCODE procedurename (SRV_PROC*)
```

The `SRVRETCODE` return value is defined in `srv.h` as a typedef `int`. The `SRV_PROC` is defined as typedef `struct srv_proc SRV_PROC` while `srv_proc` is defined as `struct srv_proc`; The definition of the `srv_proc` structure is not defined in this include file but the API includes a set of functions for reading and writing to this structure.

The `SRV_PROC` structure represents the client connection. This structure is used by ODS to manage the connection and to pass parameters and data between the ODS application and the client.

A Procedure to Log Messages

We'll name our first extended procedure `xp_AppLogMsgPut()` and expect that callers to this procedure will pass one input parameter, which is the string to be logged. We first obtain the count of the input parameters using the `srv_rpcparams()` function.

The `srv_rpcparams()` function passes the `SRV_PROC` pointer, which was input to our procedure, and accepts an integer as a return value. If this return value is other than 2, it is considered an error and the procedure returns an error message to the client.

If the number of input parameters is correct, the procedure next checks the type of the parameters to ensure they are correct. This is done using the `srv_paraminfo()` function.

The `srv_paraminfo()` function also takes, as the first argument, the pointer to the `SRV_PROC` structure. The second argument passed is the number of the parameter we want information on. We first call the function with parameter 1 to check the return parameter and then with 2 to check the input parameter.

The third argument is a pointer to `BYTE`, which is to receive the parameter data type information. These types are listed in Appendix I.

To get the direction of the parameter, we use the `srv_paramstatus()` function. The return value of this function is Anded with the `SRV_PARAMRETURN` constant defined in `srv.h`. If the result is `TRUE`, the parameter is an output or return parameter; otherwise, it is an input parameter.

If we find that the parameter is not of the expected direction or the data type of the parameter is not correct, we return an error message to the client.

To write the input string to the log file, the `xp_AppLogMsgPut()` procedure will open a file named FundAcctLog in the current directory for appending records. Once the file is open, the procedure will `fprintf` the string to the file along with the user ID for the connection and a `datetimestamp`. The format of the log record is:

```
User ID DateTimeStamp MessageString
```

The `datetimestamp` written to the log is obtained from the Win32 `GetLocalTime()` function while the user ID is obtained from the `srv_pfield()` function.

The srv_pfield() function is used to retrieve fields from the SRV_PROC structure. The fields you can specify as the second argument to this function are listed in Table 21-1.

TABLE 21-1 **THE FIELD CONSTANTS FOR THE SRV_PFIELD() FUNCTION**

Constant	Description
SRV_APPLNAME	Application name supplied during login
SRV_BCPFLAG	Equals TRUE if client is preparing for bulk copy; otherwise, it is FALSE
SRV_CLIB	The library name being used to communicate with the server
SRV_CPID	The process ID of the client process at the client machine
SRV_EVENT	The current srvproc event
SRV_HOST	The host name used for login to the ODS application
SRV_LIBVERS	The client library version
SRV_LSECURE	Equals TRUE if client connection is a trusted connection; otherwise, it is FALSE
SRV_NETWORK_MODULE	The Net-Library name used by the client connection
SRV_NETWORK_VERSION	The Net-Library version
SRV_NETWORK_CONNECTION	The connection string passed to the Net-Library
SRV_PIPEHANDLE	NULL if client connection is not using named pipes; otherwise, the handle of the named pipe used for the client connection
SRV_PWD	The user password used for login to the ODS application
SRV_RMTSERVER	The server at which the client is logged into; empty if login is from client directly
SRV_ROWSENT	The number of rows sent to client for the current resultset
SRV_SPID	The server thread ID of the srvproc
SRV_STATUS	The current srvproc status
SRV_TDS	The version of TDS used by the client

Constant	Description
SRV_TYPE	Equal to "server" if connection is from SQL Server; otherwise, it is "client," meaning connection from client library
SRV_USER	The username used to login to the ODS application

The user ID we write to the log is obtained from SRV_USER in the call to srv_pfield.

After writing the string to the log, the file is closed. The procedure has completed its job of logging the message and can now return to the client.

A return code is returned to the client by calling the srv_paramsetoutput() function. Again, the SRV_PROC pointer is passed as the first argument. The second argument is the number of the parameter to set. In our case, we pass a 1 for this argument.

The third argument is a pointer to an int where we will store the actual return value of 0 for success and 1 for failure. The fourth argument indicates the length of the return value if the data type of the return parameter is not a constant length. In the case of xp_AppLogMsgPut(), the return data type is int, so this argument is ignored.

If the return parameter can indicate a NULL value, the fifth argument should be set to TRUE; otherwise, it can be set to FALSE or not passed.

After setting the return parameter, the procedure notifies ODS that it is done processing by calling srv_senddone(). The second argument of this function indicates the status of the procedure and can be a combination of values ORed together. The values you can specify are listed in Table 21-2.

TABLE 21-2 THE STATUS FLAGS FOR THE SRV_SENDDONE( ) FUNCTION

Flag	Description
SRV_DONE_ERROR	The procedure resulted in an error
SRV_DONE_FINAL	The procedure has returned all results
SRV_DONE_MORE	The procedure has returned one of more results to the client
SRV_DONE_COUNT	The fourth argument to the function call holds the count of the result set (1 if only one result set)
SRV_DONE_RPC_IN_BATCH	The current results are the last for the remote procedure being executed

Our call to `srv_senddone()` uses `SRV_DONE_FINAL` since no results were returned from this procedure.

A Procedure to Read Messages

The second procedure we implement in this DLL is the `xp_AppLogMsgGet()`. This procedure takes an input parameter to designate the log record to read and the procedure sends back the corresponding record of the log as a one-record result set.

The processing done in this procedure is exactly the same as in `xp_AppLogMsgPut()` with the exceptions of the input parameter type, the result set, and the call to `srv_senddone()`.

We check the input parameter data type to ensure an `int` type has been specified for the record number. This number will be used to read the log file.

With all parameters checked, the procedure opens the log and reads the specified record. To return this record, a result row is built with `srv_describe()`, and optionally `srv_setcoldata()`, and sent to the client with `srv_sendrow()`.

The `srv_describe()` function is used to describe a column of the result set row. The second argument is the column number being described. Columns must be described in order from 1 to the number of columns in the row.

The third argument can be a column name, or `NULL` if no name is to be assigned. If a name is assigned, the length of that name is specified in the fourth argument.

The fifth argument specifies the data type of the column. These types can be found in Appendix I. If the data type indicates variable-length data, the maximum length of the data to be sent in this column must be specified in the sixth argument.

The seventh and eighth arguments specify the source data type and length, respectively. Again, if the type is `fixed-length`, then the length argument is ignored.

The last argument to `srv_describe()` is the address of the data to send in the column being described. You can optionally set this argument to `NULL` and specify the column data later with `srv_setcoldata()`. Since we are dealing with three predefined data variables for the return columns, we will specify the addresses of these variables in the `srv_describe()` function.

After all the result columns have been described and the column variables set with the columns of the log record read from the log file, the row is ready to be sent to the client.

The `srv_sendrow()` function specifies one argument, the `SRV_PROC` pointer. The function uses the column data addresses specified in `srv_describe()` (or `srv_setcoldata()`) to access the data and return it to the client represented by the `SRV_PROC` handle. This function returns a `SUCCEED` or `FAIL` return code.

After sending the result row, `xp_AppLogMsgGet()` closes the log file, sets the return parameter and then sends a `srv_senddone()` with `SRV_DONE_COUNT` ORed with `SRV_DONE_FINAL` and a count argument of 1 to indicate the first and only result set.

If the caller passes in a record number beyond the bounds of the file, a failure is returned as the return parameter and no count is specified in the `srv_senddone()` call.

Summary

We saw in this chapter what Open Data Services (ODS) is and how it can be used to enhance your database applications. These enhancements can be accomplished with either event-handling standalone server applications like SQL Server or as extended stored procedures as we have built here.

Some of the ODS API functions were explored here to implement two extended procedures we can use in the `FundAccts` database (or any other database) to write and read messages to/from an application log file.

The two extended procedures illustrated in this chapter can be augmented with other log procedures. You could, for example, build a procedure to clear the log file, another to accept a path and file name to start a new log, and still another to return all records in the log. Additionally, you could modify `xp_AppLogMsgGet()` and `xp_AppLogMsgPut()` to accept a parameter to specify the path to a log file you wanted to write to or read from.

The final word on extended procedures is that they can be very powerful features of your application, but you need to test them thoroughly before implementing them. If they do not behave in SQL Server's address space, SQL Server and the entire production environment can be adversely affected.

Part IV

Appendixes

Appendix A

What's on the CD-ROM

Files with .sql extensions contain scripts illustrating the statements explained in the corresponding chapter. The script files are not meant to be run as a complete script file. You should open the file in an ASCII editor or in Microsoft Query Analyzer and select the portion of the script you want to run or modify for your own purposes.

There is no installation program for the CD contents. Copy the CD files or directory you want to your hard drive. None of the files is compressed.

To compile the Part III sample programs found in Chapters 18, 19, 20, and 21, use Microsoft Visual C++ 5.0. The project files and workspace files for this compiler are included in the chapter directories.

The root directory of the CD contains a readme.txt file and a sources.html file. The sources.html file contains a few Internet Web sites of interest to database and C++ developers. You can open this file in your Internet browser and use the links (jumps) directly.

Ch2

BCP data and format files for loading the Mutual Fund Account sample database.

```
Directory of \CH2

03/03/98   07:46p                279 acctval.fmt
05/31/98   12:51p             11,524 fundacct.dat
03/13/98   11:35a                410 fundacct.fmt
03/13/98   06:56p                168 funds.fmt
03/02/98   07:15p              1,438 stmts.fmt
05/31/98   12:54p            553,595 tranhist.dat
03/13/98   11:42a              1,198 tranhist.fmt
05/31/98   12:53p             39,131 stmts.dat
05/31/98   12:52p              1,985 funds.dat
05/31/98   12:50p              3,500 acctval.dat
07/03/97   01:27p              1,292 accounts.fmt
05/31/98   12:49p              3,899 accounts.dat
05/02/98   08:52a                109 sample_bcpcmd.txt
             13 File(s)        618,528 bytes
```

Ch3

Script file containing Transact-SQL statements covered in Chapter 3.

```
Directory of \CH3

07/30/98  09:34p                    2,964 Ch3.sql
              1 File(s)             2,964 bytes
```

Ch4

Script file containing Transact-SQL statements covered in Chapter 4.

```
Directory of \CH4

07/30/98  09:34p                    3,772 Ch4.sql
              1 File(s)             3,772 bytes
```

Ch5

Script file containing Transact-SQL Data Definition Language statements explained in Chapter 5. FundAccts.sql is a script file generated by Microsoft SQL Server Enterprise Manager. This file defines all objects in the FundAccts sample database.

```
Directory of \CH5

07/30/98  09:35p                    6,017 Ch5.sql
05/31/98  12:57p                   58,448 FundAccts.sql
              2 File(s)            64,465 bytes
```

Ch6

Script files exploring Data Manipulation Language as covered in Chapter 6. The Prices.mdb file is a Microsoft Access 97 database used by the distributed query contained in the file distquery.sql. See Chapter 6 for an explanation of distributed queries.

```
Directory of \CH6

07/30/98  09:35p                    9,474 Ch6.sql
08/01/98  06:55p                  157,696 Prices.mdb
07/06/98  12:01p                      434 distquery.sql
08/02/98  04:11p                      791 Sample_Readme.txt
              4 File(s)           168,395 bytes
```

Ch7

Sample scripts illustrating the use of Transact-SQL functions.

```
Directory of \CH7

07/30/98  09:35p                    9,799 Ch7.sql
             1 File(s)              9,799 bytes
```

Ch8

Sample script files illustrating the use of grouping, sorting, and totaling.

```
Directory of \CH8

07/30/98  09:35p                    3,383 Ch8.sql
             1 File(s)              3,383 bytes
```

Ch9

Sample scripts exploring the use of joins, subqueries, and unions.

```
Directory of \CH9

07/30/98  09:36p                    5,363 Ch9.sql
             1 File(s)              5,363 bytes
```

Ch10

Sample scripts illustrating Transact-SQL views.

```
Directory of \CH10

07/30/98  09:33p                    2,130 Ch10.sql
             1 File(s)              2,130 bytes
```

Ch11

Scripts that explore working with Text and Image.

```
Directory of \CH11

07/30/98  09:33p                    3,368 ch11.sql
             1 File(s)              3,368 bytes
```

Ch12

Scripts illustrating the use of the Cube and Rollup operators.

```
Directory of \CH12

07/30/98  09:33p                1,979 ch12.sql
            1 File(s)           1,979 bytes
```

Ch13

Scripts that explore the use of Transact-SQL cursors.

```
Directory of \CH13

07/30/98  09:33p                5,364 ch13.sql
            1 File(s)           5,364 bytes
```

Ch14

Scripts for SQL Server administrators.

```
Directory of \CH14

07/08/98  10:32p                1,170 job2.sql
07/08/98  10:33p                  617 job1.sql
08/01/98  07:12p                6,187 ch14.sql
            3 File(s)           7,974 bytes
```

Ch15

Scripts that explore stored procedures and triggers.

```
Directory of \CH15

07/08/98  10:25p                2,708 ProcessFundAccount.sql
07/08/98  10:27p                  449 MgrAccts.sql
07/08/98  10:24p                  928 CascadeAcctChange.sql
07/08/98  10:22p                  737 BigAcct.sql
08/01/98  07:25p               11,642 ch15.sql
            5 File(s)          16,464 bytes
```

Ch16

Script files illustrating the use of transactions.

```
Directory of \CH16
```

```
08/01/98   11:05p                     1,255  ch16.sql
                      1 File(s)        1,255  bytes
```

Ch17

Script file containing profiling statements explained in Chapter 17.

```
Directory of \CH17

08/01/98   11:19p                     1,408  trace.sql
08/01/98   11:1?p                     1,979  ch17.sql
                      2 File(s)        3,387  bytes
```

Ch18

Sample program using 32-bit DB-Library to query SQL Server FundAccts database.
DBObject.cpp file contains the DB-Library code.

```
Directory of \ch18

07/04/98   12:43p                     2,324  FundMgrView.h
08/02/98   03:49p      <DIR>                 res
02/17/98   11:13a                     1,556  ChildFrm.cpp
02/15/98   06:55p                     1,403  ChildFrm.h
07/03/98   10:32a                       342  DBError.cpp
07/03/98   05:06p                     4,141  EditAcct.cpp
07/18/98   04:02p                     2,026  EditAcct.h
06/12/98   08:06a                     1,712  FundAcctsDoc.cpp
06/12/98   07:57a                     1,527  FundAcctsDoc.h
07/04/98   12:35p                     5,240  FundMgr.cpp
02/15/98   07:07p                       537  FundMgr.dsw
07/04/98   09:34a                     1,541  FundMgr.h
02/15/98   05:55p                     1,078  FundMgr.ico
02/15/98   05:55p                       399  FundMgr.rc2
02/19/98   05:45p                       818  FundMgrDB.cpp
02/19/98   05:52p                       430  FundMgrDB.h
07/04/98   10:47a                     1,985  FundMgrDoc.cpp
07/04/98   12:14p                     3,485  FundMgrDoc.h
02/15/98   05:55p                     1,078  FundMgrDoc.ico
07/04/98   12:46p                     8,571  FundMgrView.cpp
02/17/98   10:14a                     2,655  MainFrm.cpp
02/15/98   06:55p                     1,550  MainFrm.h
02/15/98   06:55p                     4,253  ReadMe.txt
07/04/98   12:43p                     2,015  Resource.h
07/04/98   12:43p                       236  resource.hm
02/15/98   06:55p                       205  StdAfx.cpp
02/15/98   06:55p                     1,213  StdAfx.h
02/15/98   05:55p                     1,078  Toolbar.bmp
02/18/98   08:52a                     1,372  TransDoc.cpp
02/18/98   08:52a                     1,380  TransDoc.h
06/15/98   10:41p                     3,895  TransHist.cpp
07/18/98   04:04p                     1,949  TransHist.h
```

```
07/26/98   08:26p                    1,655  DBObject.h
07/26/98   08:56p                    2,097  FundAccts.h
07/26/98   08:57p                    5,629  FundAccts.cpp
07/26/98   09:03p                    2,141  MgrAccts.h
07/26/98   09:03p                    4,484  MgrAccts.cpp
07/26/98   09:06p                    5,682  FundMgr.dsp
08/02/98   04:06p                    1,624  Sample_Readme.txt
08/02/98   03:22p                   19,095  FundMgr.rc
08/02/98   03:25p                   10,768  DBObject.cpp
                41 File(s)         115,169  bytes


Directory of \ch18\res

02/15/98   06:55p                      399  FundMgr.rc2
02/15/98   06:55p                    1,078  FundMgr.ico
02/15/98   06:55p                    1,078  FundMgrDoc.ico
02/15/98   06:55p                    1,078  Toolbar.bmp
                 4 File(s)           3,633  bytes
```

Ch19

Sample program illustrating the use of ODBC to work with the FundAccts sample database. The DBObject.cpp file contains the ODBC code.

```
Directory of \ch19

02/15/98   06:55p                    4,253  ReadMe.txt
02/15/98   06:55p                    1,213  StdAfx.h
02/15/98   06:55p                      205  StdAfx.cpp
02/15/98   06:55p                    1,550  MainFrm.h
02/17/98   10:14a                    2,655  MainFrm.cpp
02/15/98   06:55p                    1,403  ChildFrm.h
02/17/98   11:13a                    1,556  ChildFrm.cpp
07/04/98   12:43p                    2,324  FundMgrView.h
07/18/98   04:02p                    2,026  EditAcct.h
08/02/98   03:50p      <DIR>                res
07/04/98   12:43p                      236  resource.hm
08/02/98   01:51p                   19,095  FundMgr.rc
07/04/98   12:43p                    2,015  Resource.h
02/15/98   07:07p                      537  FundMgr.dsw
07/04/98   12:46p                    8,571  FundMgrView.cpp
07/18/98   03:12p                    1,955  DBObject.h
07/18/98   01:10p                    4,367  MgrAccts.cpp
02/18/98   08:52a                    1,380  TransDoc.h
02/18/98   08:52a                    1,372  TransDoc.cpp
02/19/98   05:52p                      430  FundMgrDB.h
02/19/98   05:45p                      818  FundMgrDB.cpp
06/12/98   07:57a                    1,527  FundAcctsDoc.h
06/12/98   08:06a                    1,712  FundAcctsDoc.cpp
07/18/98   04:03p                    2,097  FundAccts.h
07/18/98   04:04p                    1,949  TransHist.h
07/18/98   04:04p                    2,113  MgrAccts.h
```

```
08/02/98    02:41p              13,697 DBObject.cpp
08/02/98    04:06p               1,593 Sample_Readme.txt
02/15/98    05:55p               1,078 Toolbar.bmp
02/15/98    05:55p               1,078 FundMgrDoc.ico
02/15/98    05:55p                 399 FundMgr.rc2
02/15/98    05:55p               1,078 FundMgr.ico
06/15/98    10:41p               3,895 TransHist.cpp
06/15/98    10:42p               5,625 FundAccts.cpp
07/03/98    10:32a                 342 DBError.cpp
07/03/98    05:06p               4,141 EditAcct.cpp
07/04/98    09:34a               1,541 FundMgr.h
07/04/98    09:52a               5,707 FundMgr.dsp
07/04/98    10:47a               1,985 FundMgrDoc.cpp
07/04/98    12:14p               3,485 FundMgrDoc.h
07/04/98    12:35p               5,240 FundMgr.cpp
               41 File(s)      118,243 bytes

Directory of \ch19\res

02/15/98    06:55p                 399 FundMgr.rc2
02/15/98    06:55p               1,078 FundMgr.ico
02/15/98    06:55p               1,078 FundMgrDoc.ico
02/15/98    06:55p               1,078 Toolbar.bmp
                4 File(s)         3,633 bytes
```

Ch20

Sample program using ActiveX Data Objects to access the FundAccts sample database. The DBObject.cpp file contains the ADO code.

```
Directory of \ch20

07/04/98    10:47a               1,985 FundMgrDoc.cpp
02/15/98    06:55p               1,403 ChildFrm.h
07/03/98    10:32a                 342 DBError.cpp
07/03/98    05:06p               4,141 EditAcct.cpp
07/18/98    04:02p               2,026 EditAcct.h
07/26/98    08:57p               5,629 FundAccts.cpp
07/26/98    08:56p               2,097 FundAccts.h
06/12/98    08:06a               1,712 FundAcctsDoc.cpp
06/12/98    07:57a               1,527 FundAcctsDoc.h
07/04/98    12:35p               5,240 FundMgr.cpp
02/15/98    07:07p                 537 FundMgr.dsw
07/04/98    09:34a               1,541 FundMgr.h
02/15/98    05:55p               1,078 FundMgr.ico
02/15/98    05:55p                 399 FundMgr.rc2
02/19/98    05:45p                 818 FundMgrDB.cpp
02/19/98    05:52p                 430 FundMgrDB.h
02/17/98    11:13a               1,556 ChildFrm.cpp
07/04/98    12:14p               3,485 FundMgrDoc.h
02/15/98    05:55p               1,078 FundMgrDoc.ico
07/04/98    12:43p               2,324 FundMgrView.h
```

```
02/17/98  10:14a                     2,655 MainFrm.cpp
02/15/98  06:55p                     1,550 MainFrm.h
07/26/98  09:03p                     4,484 MgrAccts.cpp
07/26/98  09:03p                     2,141 MgrAccts.h
02/15/98  06:55p                     4,253 ReadMe.txt
07/04/98  12:43p                     2,015 Resource.h
07/04/98  12:43p                       236 resource.hm
02/15/98  06:55p                       205 StdAfx.cpp
07/29/98  11:36a                     1,219 StdAfx.h
02/15/98  05:55p                     1,078 Toolbar.bmp
02/18/98  08:52a                     1,372 TransDoc.cpp
02/18/98  08:52a                     1,380 TransDoc.h
06/15/98  10:41p                     3,895 TransHist.cpp
07/18/98  04:04p                     1,949 TransHist.h
08/02/98  03:50p         <DIR>             res
07/28/98  10:43p                    13,713 FundMgr.mak
07/29/98  08:48a                     5,814 FundMgr.dsp
07/30/98  09:01p                     8,759 FundMgrView.cpp
08/02/98  12:53p                     1,625 DBObject.h
08/02/98  01:10p                    19,096 FundMgr.rc
08/02/98  02:48p                    10,804 DBObject.cpp
08/02/98  04:07p                     1,586 Sample_Readme.txt
               42 File(s)          129,177 bytes

Directory of \ch20\res

02/15/98  06:55p                       399 FundMgr.rc2
02/15/98  06:55p                     1,078 FundMgr.ico
02/15/98  06:55p                     1,078 FundMgrDoc.ico
02/15/98  06:55p                     1,078 Toolbar.bmp
                4 File(s)            3,633 bytes
```

Ch21

A sample Open Data Services extended stored procedure.

```
Directory of \ch21

08/01/98  12:40p                       531 ch21.dsw
08/02/98  10:55a                       258 ch21.sql
08/01/98  02:12p                     3,820 ch21.dsp
08/01/98  02:38p                       140 ch21.def
08/02/98  11:04a                       150 FundAcctLog.Log
08/02/98  10:38a                     6,666 xp_applog.c
08/02/98  03:18p                     2,340 Sample_Readme.txt
                7 File(s)           13,905 bytes
```

Appendix B

The FundAccts Sample Database

THIS APPENDIX LISTS the table definitions, table relationships, and database options used for the samples in this book. Table definitions were obtained from the Generate Scripts facility in the Microsoft SQL Server Enterprise Manager.

Accounts Table

```
CREATE TABLE [dbo].[Accounts] (
    [acct_no] [varchar] (10) NOT NULL ,
    [acct_lastname] [varchar] (70) NOT NULL ,
    [acct_firstname] [varchar] (50) NULL ,
    [last_contact] [datetime] NULL ,
    [addr_line1] [varchar] (30) NULL ,
    [addr_line2] [varchar] (30) NULL ,
    [addr_line3] [varchar] (30) NULL ,
    [city] [varchar] (30) NULL ,
    [state_abbr] [char] (2) NOT NULL ,
    [zip] [varchar] (10) NOT NULL ,
    [home_phone] [varchar] (15) NULL ,
    [work_phone] [varchar] (15) NULL ,
    [tot_assets] [money] NOT NULL ,
    [fiscal_period] [char] (2) NOT NULL ,
    [cycle] [tinyint] NOT NULL ,
    [acct_type] [varchar] (6) NOT NULL ,
    [acct_status] [varchar] (8) NOT NULL ,
    [manager_num] [smallint] NULL ,
    [acct_note] [text] NULL ,
    CONSTRAINT [PK_Accounts] PRIMARY KEY  NONCLUSTERED
    (
        [acct_no]
    ),
    CONSTRAINT [IX_Accounts] UNIQUE  CLUSTERED
    (
        [acct_no]
    ),
CONSTRAINT [CK_Accounts] CHECK ([acct_type] = 'Tax' or [acct_type] =
 'Nontax')
)
```

AccountValues Table

```
CREATE TABLE [dbo].[AccountValues] (
  [acct_no] [varchar] (10) NOT NULL ,
  [stmt_date] [datetime] NOT NULL ,
  [invest_tot] [money] NOT NULL CONSTRAINT
 [DF__AccountValues__invest_tot__3BFFE745] DEFAULT (0),
  [cur_value] [money] NOT NULL CONSTRAINT
 [DF__AccountValues__cur_value__3CF40B7E] DEFAULT (0)
)
```

FundAccounts Table

```
CREATE TABLE [dbo].[FundAccounts] (
  [fund_cd] [char] (5) NOT NULL ,
  [fundacctno] [char] (35) NOT NULL ,
  [acct_no] [varchar] (10) NOT NULL ,
  [acct_name] [varchar] (70) NULL ,
  [acct_type] [char] (4) NULL ,
  CONSTRAINT [PK_FundAccounts] PRIMARY KEY  NONCLUSTERED
  (
      [fund_cd],
      [fundacctno]
  ),
  CONSTRAINT [FK_FundAccounts_Accounts] FOREIGN KEY
  (
      [acct_no]
  ) REFERENCES [dbo].[Accounts] (
      [acct_no]
  ),
  CONSTRAINT [FK_FundAccounts_Funds] FOREIGN KEY
  (
      [fund_cd]
  ) REFERENCES [dbo].[Funds] (
      [fund_cd]
  )
)
```

Funds Table

```
CREATE TABLE [dbo].[Funds] (
  [fund_cd] [char] (5) NOT NULL ,
  [fund_name] [varchar] (45) NOT NULL ,
  CONSTRAINT [PK_Funds] PRIMARY KEY  NONCLUSTERED
  (
      [fund_cd]
  )
)
```

Statements Table

```
CREATE TABLE [dbo].[Statements] (
  [acct_no] [varchar] (10) NOT NULL ,
  [stmt_date] [datetime] NOT NULL ,
  [invest_tot] [money] NOT NULL CONSTRAINT
[DF_Statements_invest_tot] DEFAULT (0),
  [cur_value] [money] NOT NULL CONSTRAINT [DF_Statements_cur_value]
DEFAULT (0),
  [invest_gain] [numeric](18, 0) NOT NULL CONSTRAINT
[DF_Statements_invest_gain] DEFAULT (0),
  [tot_return] [numeric](18, 0) NOT NULL CONSTRAINT
[DF_Statements_tot_return] DEFAULT (0),
  [ytd_tot_return] [numeric](18, 0) NOT NULL CONSTRAINT
[DF_Statements_ytd_tot_return] DEFAULT (0),
  [tax_income] [money] NOT NULL CONSTRAINT
[DF_Statements_tax_income] DEFAULT (0),
  [taxfree_income] [money] NOT NULL CONSTRAINT
[DF_Statements_taxfree_income] DEFAULT (0),
  [tax_cap_gain] [money] NOT NULL CONSTRAINT
[DF_Statements_tax_cap_gain] DEFAULT (0),
  [taxfree_cap_gain] [money] NOT NULL CONSTRAINT
[DF_Statements_taxfree_cap_gain] DEFAULT (0),
  [stmt_tot] [money] NOT NULL CONSTRAINT [DF_Statements_stmt_tot]
DEFAULT (0),
  [ytd_tax_income] [money] NOT NULL CONSTRAINT
[DF_Statements_ytd_tax_income] DEFAULT (0),
  [ytd_taxfree_income] [money] NOT NULL CONSTRAINT
[DF_Statements_ytd_taxfree_income] DEFAULT (0),
  [ytd_tax_cap_gain] [money] NOT NULL CONSTRAINT
[DF_Statements_ytd_tax_cap_gain] DEFAULT (0),
  [ytd_taxfree_cap_gain] [money] NOT NULL CONSTRAINT
[DF_Statements_ytd_taxfree_cap_gain] DEFAULT (0),
  [ytd_tot] [money] NOT NULL CONSTRAINT [DF_Statements_ytd_tot]
DEFAULT (0),
  CONSTRAINT [PK_Statements] PRIMARY KEY   NONCLUSTERED
  (
       [acct_no],
       [stmt_date]
  ),
  CONSTRAINT [FK_Statements_Accounts] FOREIGN KEY
  (
       [acct_no]
  ) REFERENCES [dbo].[Accounts] (
       [acct_no]
  )
)
```

TranHistory Table

```
CREATE TABLE [dbo].[TranHistory] (
  [fund_cd] [char] (5) NOT NULL ,
  [fundacctno] [char] (35) NOT NULL ,
  [trandate] [datetime] NOT NULL ,
  [trantype] [varchar] (10) NOT NULL ,
  [divamt] [money] NULL ,
  [amount] [money] NULL ,
  [sh_price] [money] NULL ,
  [sh_num] [decimal](18, 4) NULL ,
  [sh_tot] [decimal](18, 4) NULL ,
  [inv_tot] [money] NULL ,
  [inv_sh] [decimal](18, 4) NULL ,
  [cost_tot] [money] NULL ,
  [cost_sh] [money] NULL ,
  [tax_gain] [money] NULL ,
  [inv_gain] [money] NULL ,
CONSTRAINT [PK_TranHistory] PRIMARY KEY  NONCLUSTERED
(
     [fund_cd],
     [fundacctno],
     [trandate],
     [trantype]
),
CONSTRAINT [FK_TranHistory_FundAccounts] FOREIGN KEY
(
     [fund_cd],
     [fundacctno]
) REFERENCES [dbo].[FundAccounts] (
     [fund_cd],
     [fundacctno]
)
)
```

Figure B-1 shows the Fund Accounts Sample Database diagram. These diagrams can be accessed through the Database diagrams folder in the SQL Server Enterprise Manager.

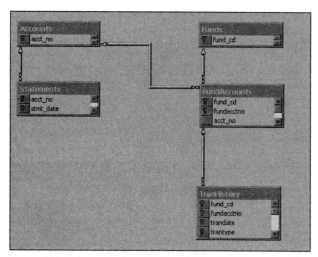

Figure B-1: Primary keys and table relationships in the FundAccts database

Figure B-2 shows the database options in effect for all samples used in the book. These options are SQL Server defaults but can be set with the sp_dboption stored procedure.

Figure B-2: The database options set for the samples in this book

Appendix C

SQL Server SET Statements

Setting	Description
SET ANSI_DEFAULTS ON SET ANSI_DEFAULTS OFF	Controls settings that specify SQL-92 standard behavior. These settings are set on or off: ANSI_NULLS ANSI_NULL_DFLT_ON ANSI_PADDING ANSI_WARNINGS CURSOR_CLOSE_ON_COMMIT IMPLICIT_TRANSACTIONS QUOTED_IDENTIFIER
SET ANSI_NULL_DFLT_OFF ON SET ANSI_NULL_DFLT_OFF OFF	When ANSI NULL DEFAULT option is FALSE, new columns will be NOT NULL if the nullability of the column is not specified. Setting ANSI_NULL_DFLT_OFF to ON will override the TRUE setting to cause new columns to be NULL when nullability is not specified.
SET ANSI_NULL_DFLT_ON ON SET ANSI_NULL_DFLT_ON OFF	When ANSI NULL DEFAULT option is FALSE, new columns will be NOT NULL if the nullability of the column is not specified. Setting ANSI_NULL_DFLT_ON to ON will override the FALSE setting to cause new columns to be NULL when nullability is not specified.
SET ANSI_NULLS ON SET ANSI_NULLS OFF	SQL-92 standard yields FALSE when a NULL value participates in an equality or inequality comparison. When ON: the SQL-92 standard is followed. When OFF: these NULL comparisons return TRUE.

Continued

Setting	Description
ANSI_PADDING=ON	When column is char(n): Pad the value with spaces to fill column size.
	When column is varchar(n): No padding with trailing spaces and keep any original trailing spaces.
	When column is varbinary(n): No padding with trailing zeroes, and keep original trailing zeroes.
ANSI_PADDING=OFF	When column is char(n): Trim trailing spaces from value and do not pad with trailing spaces.
	When column is varchar(n): Trim trailing spaces from value and do not pad with trailing spaces.
	When column is varbinary(n): Trim trailing zeroes and do not pad with zeroes.
SET ANSI_WARNINGS ON SET ANSI_WARNINGS OFF	When ON: A warning message is generated when NULL values appear in aggregate functions.
	Divide-by-zero and arithmetic overflow errors generate an error message and the rollback of the statement.
	Inserts and updates of values larger than the column size are aborted.
	When OFF: No warning is generated.
	Divide-by-zero and arithmetic overflow errors do not generate error messages and return nulls.
	Inserts and updates of values larger than the column size are truncated.
SET ARITHABORT ON SET ARITHABORT OFF	When ON: Divide-by-zero or overflow error terminates query and batch.
	When OFF: Message generated but does not terminate batch.
SET ARITHIGNORE ON SET ARITHIGNORE OFF	When ON: Divide-by-zero and overflow errors do not generate message.
	When OFF: These errors generate a message.

Setting	Description
SET CURSOR_CLOSE_ON_COMMIT ON	When ON: Cursor is closed when committed.
SET CURSOR_CLOSE_ON_COMMIT OFF	When OFF: Cursor is not closed on COMMIT.
SET DATEFIRST number	number can range from 1 through 7. Sets the last day of the week. The U.S. English default setting is 7, representing Saturday.
SET DATEFORMAT format	Sets the date parts order when entering datetime or smalldatetime data; format specifies the order of month/day/year.
SET DEADLOCK_PRIORITY LOW SET DEADLOCK_PRIORITY NORMAL	When LOW: The current process is the deadlock, cannot complete its transaction, and receives deadlock error.
SET DISABLE_DEF_CNST_CHK ON SET DISABLE_DEF_CNST_CHK OFF	When ON: SQL Server validates changes for foreign key and orphan record violations on a row-by-row basis rather than after all changes have taken place. Creation of work tables is prevented, but it may result in constraint violations that would not have occurred if SQL Server were to perform these checks after all updates completed.
SET FIPS_FLAGGER 'level' SET FIPS_FLAGGER OFF	level = ENTRY Checking for SQL-92 entry-level compliance.
	level = INTERMEDIATE Checking for SQL-92 intermediate-level compliance.
	level = FULL Checking for full SQL-92 compliance.
	When OFF: No standards checking is done.
SET FMTONLY ON SET FMTONLY OFF	When ON: No rows are processed or sent to the client. Only column meta data is returned.
SET FORCEPLAN ON SET FORCEPLAN OFF	When ON: Optimizer processes joins in the same order as the tables appear in the FROM clause rather than using optimizer-derived rules.

Continued

Setting	Description
SET IDENTITY_INSERT tablename ON	When ON: Explicit values can be inserted into the identity column of a table.
SET IDENTITY_INSERT tablename OFF	
SET IMPLICIT_TRANSACTIONS ON SET IMPLICIT_TRANSACTIONS OFF	When ON: Connection is set into implicit transaction mode.
	When OFF: Connection is set to autocommit transaction mode.
SET LANGUAGE language	language specifies the language for displaying system messages; language is one stored in syslanguages system table.
SET LOCK_TIMEOUT timeout_period	timeout_period is the number of seconds a statement will wait for a lock to be released. No timeout is specified as -1.
SET NOCOUNT ON SET NOCOUNT OFF	When ON: The "rows affected" message and the row count are not returned.
	When OFF: The message and row count are returned.
SET NOEXEC ON SET NOEXEC OFF	When ON: Batches of Transact-SQL statements are compiled but not executed.
	When OFF: Batches are executed after compilation.
SET NUMERIC_ROUNDABORT ON SET NUMERIC_ROUNDABORT OFF	When ON: Error message is generated when a loss of precision occurs in an expression.
	When OFF: No error messages are generated for losses of precision and the result is rounded to the precision of the column.
SET OFFSETS keyword_list	Returns the offset of keyword_list keywords in Transact-SQL statements.
	keyword_list is a comma-separated list of Transact-SQL keywords for which offsets are to be returned.

Setting	Description
SET PARSEONLY ON SET PARSEONLY OFF	When ON: SQL Server parses the statement but does not compile or execute it. When OFF: SQL Server compiles and executes the statement.
SET PROCID ON SET PROCID OFF	When ON: Returns the ID number of the stored procedure being executed to DB-Library applications before sending the result sets from the stored procedure.
SET QUOTED_IDENTIFIER ON SET QUOTED_IDENTIFIER OFF	When ON: Identifiers can be delimited by double quotes and literals must be delimited by single quotes.
SET REMOTE_PROC_TRANSACTIONS ON SET REMOTE_PROC_TRANSACTIONS OFF	When ON: A distributed transaction (managed by MS DTC) is started when a remote procedure call is made by a local transaction.
SET ROWCOUNT number	number is the number of rows to be returned by a query before stopping query processing.
SET SHOWPLAN_ALL ON SET SHOWPLAN_ALL OFF	When ON: Execution information for each statement is returned without executing the statement.
SET SHOWPLAN_TEXT ON SET SHOWPLAN_TEXT OFF	When ON: Returns readable information about execution plan without executing the plan.
SET STATISTICS IO ON STATISTICS IO OFF	When ON: Displays information about the SET amount of disk activity generated by Transact-SQL statements.
SET STATISTICS TIME ON STATISTICS TIME OFF	When ON: Displays time information for SET parsing, compiling, and executing each statement.
SET TEXTSIZE number	number is the size of text data returned with a SELECT statement.

Continued

Setting	Description
SET TRANSACTION ISOLATION LEVEL READ COMMITTED	Controls the default transaction locking behavior for all SQL Server SELECT statements executed by a connection.
SET TRANSACTION ISOLATION LEVEL READ UNCOMMITTED	READ COMMITTED: Shared locks are held while the data is being read.
SET TRANSACTION ISOLATION LEVEL REPEATABLE READ	READ UNCOMMITTED: shared locks are not issued and no exclusive locks are honored.
SET TRANSACTION ISOLATION LEVEL SERIALIZABLE	REPEATABLE READ: Locks are placed on all data used in a query, preventing other users from updating the data.
	SERIALIZABLE: Range lock is placed on the data preventing other users from updating or inserting rows until the transaction is complete.
SET XACT_ABORT ON SET XACT_ABORT OFF	When ON: Entire transaction is terminated and rolled back when runtime error occurs.
	When OFF: Only the Transact-SQL statement that raised the error is rolled back and the transaction processing continues.

Appendix D

Functions

Table D-1 AGGREGATE

Function	Description	Parameters	Syntax
AVG()	Calculates the average of the values in the specified expression	ALL: All values DISTINCT: Each unique value Expression: arithmetic, bitwise, and string operators	AVG(ALL expression) AVG(DISTINCT expression)
COUNT()	Retrieves the number of non-NULL values in the expression	See AVG()	COUNT(ALL expression) COUNT(DISTINCT expression) COUNT(*)
MAX()	Retrieves the maximum value in the expression	See AVG()	MAX(ALL expression) MAX(DISTINCT expression)
MIN()	Returns the minimum value in the expression	See AVG()	MIN(ALL expression) MIN(DISTINCT expression)
SUM()	Calculates the sum of the values in the expression	See AVG()	SUM(ALL expression) SUM(DISTINCT expression)

Continued

TABLE D-1 **AGGREGATE** *(Continued)*

Function	Description	Parameters	Syntax
STDEV()	Calculates the statistical standard deviation of all values in the specified expression	Expression: arithmetic, bitwise, and string operators	STDEV(expression)
STDEVP()	Calculates the statistical standard deviation for the population for all values in the specified expression	See STDEV() (expression)	STDEVP
VAR()	Calculates the statistical variance of all values in the given expression	See STDEV()	VAR(expression)
VARP()	Returns the statistical variance for the population for all values in the given expression	See STDEV()	VARP(expression)

TABLE D-2 **DATE AND TIME**

Function	Description	Parameters	Syntax
DATEADD()	Retrieves a new date/time value based on adding an interval to a supplied date	Date part: year, quarter, month, day, day of year, week, weekday, hour, minute, second, millisecond Number: year, 1753 – 9999 quarter, 1 – 4 month, 1 – 12 day, 1 – 31 day of year, 1 – 366 week, 1 – 52	DATEADD (datepart, number, date)

Function	Description	Parameters	Syntax
		weekday, 1 – 7 hour, 0 – 23 minute, 0 – 59 second, 0 – 59 millisecond, 0 – 999 Date: date format as character string, name of date/time column	
DATEDIFF()	Returns the number of datepart "boundaries" crossed between two specified dates	See DATEADD()	DATEDIFF (datepart, date, date)
DATENAME()	Retrieves a character string describing the specified date part (datepart) of the specified date (date)	See DATEADD()	DATENAME (datepart, date)
DATEPART()	Returns an integer representing the given date part (datepart) of the specified date (date)	See DATEADD()	DATEPART (datepart, date)
DAY	A number representing the day of the specified date	date: datetime expression	DAY(date)
MONTH	A number representing the month of the specified date	See DAY()	MONTH(date)
YEAR	A number representing the year of the specified date	See DAY()	YEAR(date)
GETDATE()	Retrieves the current system date and time in the Microsoft SQL Server standard internal format for date/time values		GETDATE()

TABLE D-3 MATH

Function	Description	Parameters	Syntax
ABS()	Gives the absolute, positive value of the specified numeric expression	Numeric expression: `decimal`, `float`, `int`, `money`, `numeric`, `real`, `smallint`, `smallmoney`, or `tinyint` data type	`ABS(numeric expression)`
ACOS()	Calculates the angle (in radians); also called arc cosine, whose cosine is the specified expression	Float expression: positive or negative floating point number	`ACOS(float expression)`
ASIN()	Calculates the angle (in radians); also called arc sine, for the specified expression	See ACOS()	`ASIN(float expression)`
ATAN()	Calculates the angle (in radians); also called arc tangent, whose tangent is the specified float expression	See ACOS()	`ATAN(float expression)`
ATN2()	Calculates the angle (in radians); also called arc tangent, whose tangent is between the two specified float expressions	See ACOS()	`ATN2(float expression, float expression)`
COS()	Calculates the trigonometric cosine of the given angle (in radians) in the specified expression	See ACOS()	`COS(float expression)`
COT()	Calculates the trigonometric cotangent of the specified angle (in radians) in the specified float expression	See ACOS()	`COT(float expression)`

Function	Description	Parameters	Syntax
CEILING()	Retrieves smallest integer greater than or equal to the expression	Numeric expression: decimal, float, int, money, numeric, real, smallint, smallmoney, or tinyint data type.	CEILING (numeric expression)
DEGREES()	Calculates a numeric expression from the stated number of radians	See CEILING()	DEGREES (numeric expression)
EXP()	Gives the exponential value of the specified float expression	Float expression: positive or negative floating-point number	EXP(float expression)
FLOOR()	Calculates the largest integer less than or equal to the stated numeric expression	Numeric expression: decimal, float, int, money, numeric, real, smallint, smallmoney, or tinyint data type	FLOOR(numeric expression)
LOG()	Calculates the natural logarithm of the stated float expression	Float expression: positive or negative floating-point number	LOG(float expression)
LOG10()	Calculates the base-10 logarithm of the specified float expression	See LOG()	LOG10(float expression)
PI()	Gives the constant value of pi		PI()
POWER()	Calculates the value of the specified numeric expression (numeric_expr) to the specified power (y); the result is the same data type as the given numeric_expr	Numeric expression: decimal, float, int, money, numeric, real, smallint, smallmoney, or tinyint y: power, can be a decimal, float, int, money, numeric, real, smallint, smallmoney, or tinyint	POWER(numeric expression, y)

Continued

TABLE D-3 MATH *(Continued)*

Function	Description	Parameters	Syntax
RADIANS()	Calculates radians for a numeric expression in degrees; The result of the RADIANS() function is the same data type as the given numeric_ expression	Numeric expression: decimal, float, int, money, numeric, real, smallint, smallmoney, or tinyint	RADIANS (numeric expression)
RAND()	Gives a random float value between 0 and 1 given some seed value of int, smallint, or tiny int data type	Seed: an integer as a starting value	RAND(seed) RAND()
ROUND()	Calculates the specified numeric expression rounded to the specified length or precision which must be of the tinyint, smallint, or int data types	Numeric expression: decimal, float, int, money, numeric, real, smallint, smallmoney, or tinyint

Length: precision, must be tinyint, small-int, or int

Function: function to round the given expression to tinyint, smallint, or int | ROUND(numeric expression, length, function) ROUND(numeric expression, length) |
| SIGN() | Gives the positive (+1), zero (0), or negative (-1) sign of the specified numeric expression | Numeric expression: decimal, float, int, money, numeric, real, smallint, smallmoney, or tinyint | SIGN(numeric expression) |
| SIN() | Gives the trigonometric sine of the given angle (in radians) | Float expression: positive or negative floating-point number | SIN(float expression) |

Function	Description	Parameters	Syntax
SQUARE()	Gives the square of the specified float expression	See SIN()	SQUARE(float expression)
SQRT()	Gives the square root of the specified float expression	See SIN()	SQRT(float expression)
TAN()	Gives the trigonometric tangent of the specified float expression; trigonometric tangent of the specified angle (measured in radians) in an approximate numeric (float) expression	See SIN()	TAN(float expression)

Table D-4 STRING

Function	Description	Parameters	Syntax
ASCII()	Gives the ASCII code value of the leftmost character of a character expression	Character expression: constant, variable, or column as an alphanumeric string	ASCII (character expression)
CHAR()	Converts a character from an ASCII code	Integer expression: positive whole number	CHAR(integer expression)
CHARINDEX()	Gives the starting position of the specified pattern	Pattern: character expression	CHARINDEX ('pattern', expression)
		Expression: char, varchar, or nchar column name	CHARINDEX ('pattern', expression, start_ location)
		start_location: position to start searching for the given pattern	

Continued

TABLE **D-4** **STRING** *(Continued)*

Function	Description	Parameters	Syntax
DIFFER-ENCE()	Calculates the difference between the values of two character expressions as returned by the SOUNDEX() function	Character expression: constant, variable, or column as an alphanumeric string Integer expression: positive whole number	DIFFERENCE (character expression, character expression)
LEFT()	Calculates the integer_ expression number of characters from the left of the specified character string	See DIFFERENCE()	LEFT (character expression, integer expression)
LEN()	Calculates the number of characters, rather than the number of bytes, of the specified string expression, excluding trailing blanks	String expression: the given string expression	LEN(string expression)
LOWER()	Converts uppercase character data to lowercase	Character expression: constant, variable, or column as an alphanumeric string	LOWER (character expression)
LTRIM()	Removes leading blanks	See LOWER()	LOWER (character expression)
NCHAR()	Gets the Unicode character for the given code	Integer expression: whole number 0 to 65535	NCHAR(integer expression)
PATINDEX()	Gives the starting position of the first occurrence of a pattern in a specified expression, or zeros if the pattern is not found	Pattern: nchar literal string, use % to indicate a wildcard Expression: string-valued expression	PATINDEX ('%pattern%', expression)

Function	Description	Parameters	Syntax
REPLACE()	In the first string expression, replaces all occurrences of the second specified string expression with a third expression	String expression: the given string expression	REPLACE ('string expression1', 'string expression2', 'string expression3')
REPLICATE()	Repeats a character expression a given number of times	Character expression: constant, variable, or column as an alphanumeric string Integer expression: positive whole number	REPLICATE (character expression, integer expression)
REVERSE()	Gives the reverse of a character expression	See REPLICATE()	REVERSE (character expression)
RIGHT()	Parses the part of a character string starting integer_expression characters from the right	See REPLICATE()	RIGHT (character expression, integer expression)
RTRIM()	Removes all trailing blanks	See REPLICATE()	RTRIM (character expression)
QUOTENAME()	Adds double quotation marks(") to make an input string a MS SQL Server quoted identifier, given as a Unicode string	Character expression: constant, variable, or column as an alphanumeric string quote_character: single character string, for example, ' or "	QUOTENAME ('character string') QUOTENAME ('character string', 'quote character')
SOUNDEX()	Gives a four-character (SOUNDEX) code to evaluate the similarity of two strings	Character expression: constant, variable, or column as an alphanumeric string	SOUNDEX character (expression)

Continued

TABLE **D-4** **STRING** *(Continued)*

Function	Description	Parameters	Syntax
SPACE()	Repeated spaces	Integer expression: positive whole number	SPACE (integer_ expression)
STR()	Converts character data to numeric data	Float expression: positive or negative floating-point number Length: length, including decimal point, sign, digits, and spaces Decimal: number of spaces to the right of the decimal point	STR(float expression) STR(float expression, length) STR(float expression, length, decimal)
STUFF()	Deletes length characters from the first character_ expression at start and then inserts the second character_expression into the first character_ expression at start	Character expression: constant, variable, or column as an alphanumeric string Start: starting location as integer Length: integer indicating number of characters to extract	STUFF (character expression, start, length, character expression)
SUBSTRING()	Part of a character, binary, text, or image expression		SUBSTRING (character expression, start, length)
UNICODE	Gives the Unicode integer code for the first character of expression	Ncharacter expression: nchar or nvarchar expression	UNICODE (ncharacter expression)
UPPER()	Converts lowercase character data to uppercase	Character expression: constant, variable, or column as an alphanumeric string	UPPER (character expression)

Table D-5 SYSTEM

Function	Description	Parameters	Syntax
APP_NAME()	Gets the program name for the current session		APP_NAME()
CAST() CONVERT()	Converts data type	Expression: any valid expression data_type: system data type to change expression into	CAST (expression AS data type)
COALESCE()	Gets the first non-NULL expression among its arguments	expression, any valid expression n: placeholder for multiple expressions; for example, constant, column name, function, subquery, or a combination of arithmetic, bitwise, and string operators	COALESCE (expression) COALESCE (expression, n...)
COL_ LENGTH()	Gets the defined length of a column	Table: name of table to calculate column length Column: name of column to calculate column length	COL_LENGTH ('table', 'column')
COL_NAME()	Gets the name of a database column from a given table ID number and column ID number	table_id: identification number of the table containing the specified column column_id: ID number of the column in the given table, int data type	COL_NAME (table id, column id)

Continued

TABLE D-5 SYSTEM *(Continued)*

Function	Description	Parameters	Syntax
COLUMN PROPERTY()	Gets information about a column or procedure parameter	ID: table or procedure identification number Column: column or parameter name Property: information about object with given ID	COLUMN PROPERTY (id, column, 'property')
CONVERT()	Converts an expression from one data type to another, compatible data type	data_type: system data type, for example, int Length: char, varchar, binary, or varbinary data types (optional) Expression: any valid expression Style: date, character, string format	CONVERT (data type, expression) CONVERT (data type(length), expression) CONVERT (data type(length), expression, style)
CURRENT_ TIME STAMP()	Inserts system-supplied current date/time		CURRENT_ TIMESTAMP
CURRENT_ USER()	Inserts system-supplied current user		CURRENT_USER
CURSOR_ STATUS()	Gets status of the cursor and result set for a given parameter for a procedure	Local: source of cursor is a local cursor name cursor_name: name of cursor, conforming to rules for identifiers Global: source of cursor is a global cursor name Variable: source of cursor is a local variable	CURSOR_STATUS ('variable', cursor_ variable) CURSOR_STATUS ('local', cursor name) CURSOR_STATUS ('global', cursor name)

Function	Description	Parameters	Syntax
		`cursor_variable:` name of cursor variable defined using cursor data type	
DATABASE PROPERTY()	Gets the named database property value of a specified database and property name	Database: name of database requesting property information Property: name of database property	DATABASE PROPERTY ('database', 'property')
DATA LENGTH()	Returns the actual length of any data type expression	Expression: constant, column name, function, subquery, or a combination of arithmetic, bitwise, and string operators	DATALENGTH (expression)
DB_ID()	Gets the database identification number	Database name: name of database requesting property information	DB_ID ('database name') DB_ID()
DB_NAME()	Gets the database name	Database ID: ID of database requested, `smallint` data type	DB_NAME (database_id) DB_NAME
FILE_ID()	Gets the file identification number (file ID) for a specified logical file name in the current database	File name: name of specified file	FILE_ID ('file name')
FILEGROUP _ID()	Gets the filegroup identification number (ID) for a specified filegroup name	Filegroup name: specified filegroup name	FILEGROUP_ID ('filegroup name')
FILE_ NAME()	Returns the logical file name for the given file identification number (ID)	File ID: file identifier number for requested file name	FILE_NAME (file id)
FILE PROPERTY()	Gets the file name property value for specified file and property	File name: name of the file Property: property name	FILEPROPERTY ('file name', 'property')

Continued

TABLE D-5 SYSTEM *(Continued)*

Function	Description	Parameters	Syntax
FILEGROUP PROPERTY	Returns specified filegroup property value	Filegroup name: a filegroup name Property: property name	FILEGROUP PROPERTY ('filegroup name', 'property')
FILEGROUP _NAME()	Returns the filegroup name for the given filegroup identification number (ID)	Filegroup ID: filegroup identifier number for requested file name	FILEGROUP_ NAME(file group id)
GETAN SINULL()	Gives the default nullability for the database	Database: name of database	GETANSINULL ('database') GETANSINULL()
HOST_ID()	Gets the workstation identification number		HOST_ID( )
HOST_ NAME()	Gets the workstation name		HOST_NAME( )
IDENT _INCR()	Retrieves the increment value (as numeric(@@ maxprecision,0)) specified during creation of an identity column of a table or a view that includes an identity column	Table or view: table or view to check for identity increment value; data type char or nchar	IDENT_INCR ('table or view')
IDENT_ SEED()	Gets the seed value (returned as numeric (@@maxprecision,0)) specified during creation of an identity column of a table or a view that includes an identity column	See IDENT_INCR()	IDENT_SEED ('table or view')
INDEX_ COL()	Gets the indexed column name	Table: table Index ID: index identification Key ID: key identification	INDEX_COL ('table', index id, key id)

Function	Description	Parameters	Syntax
IS_MEMBER()	Shows whether the current user is a member of the given Windows NT group or Microsoft SQL Server role	Group: name of Windows NT group in domain\group format Role: name of SQL Server role being verified	`IS_MEMBER ('group')` `IS_MEMBER ('role')`
IS_SRVROLE MEMBER()	Indicates whether the current user's login is a member of the specified server role	Role: name of SQL Server role being verified Login: option login name	`IS_SRVROLE MEMBER ('role')` `IS_SRVROLE MEMBER ('role', 'login')`
ISDATE()	Verifies a variable or column with `varchar` data type for valid date	Expression: variable or column; `varchar` data type	`ISDATE (expression)`
ISNULL()	Replaces NULL entries with the specified value	Expression: constant, column name, function, subquery, or a combination of arithmetic, bitwise, and string operators value: value to be used in NULL entry	`ISNULL (expression, value)`
ISNUMERIC()	Verifies a variable or column with `varchar` data type for valid numeric format	Expression: variable or column; `varchar` data type	`ISNUMERIC (expression)`
NEWID()	Makes a globally unique identification number		`NEWID()`
NULLIF()	Gets a NULL value if the two stated expressions are equivalent	Expression: constant, column name, function, subquery, or a combination of arithmetic, bitwise, and string operators	`NULLIF (expression, expression)`

Continued

TABLE D-5 SYSTEM *(Continued)*

Function	Description	Parameters	Syntax
OBJECT_ID()	Gets the database object identification number	Object: name of object to be used; char or nchar data type	OBJECT_ID ('object')
OBJECT_ NAME()	Gets the database object name	Object ID: identification number of object	OBJECT_NAME (object id)
OBJECT PROPERTY()	Returns information about objects in the database	ID: ID of object Property: information about given object	OBJECT PROPERTY (id, 'property')
PARSE NAME()	Shows the specified piece of an object name	Object name: name of object to retrieve requested piece Object piece: piece of object; int data type 1. Returns the object name 2. Returns the owner name 3. Returns the database name 4. Returns the server name	PARSENAME ('object name', object piece)
PERMIS SIONS()	Gets a value containing permissions for the current user	objectid: identifier of an object Column: column name (optional)	PERMISSIONS() PERMISSIONS (objectid) PERMISSIONS (objectid, 'column')
SESSION _USER()	Current session's user name		SESSION_USER
STATS_ DATE()	Gives the date that the statistics for the requested index (index_id) were last updated	Table ID: identifier of table being used Index ID: identifier of requested index	STATS_DATE (table id, index id)

Function	Description	Parameters	Syntax
SUSER_ID()	Gets the user's login identification number	Login: login name (optional)	SUSER_ID() SUSER_ID ('login')
SUSER_ NAME()	Gets the user's login identification name	server_user_id: user's login ID number	SUSER_NAME (server user id) SUSER_NAME()
SUSER_ SID()	Gets the user's security identification number (SID) from the login name	Login: login name (optional)	SUSER_SID ('login') SUSER_SID()
SUSER_ SNAME()	Gives the user's login identification name from a user's security identification number (SID)	Server user sid: user's security ID number (optional)	SUSER_SNAME (server user sid) SUSER_SNAME()
SYSTEM_ USER()	Current system user name		SYSTEM_USER
TYPE PROPERTY()	Gets information about a data type	Type: name of data type Property: information about data type	TYPEPROPERTY (type, property)
USER()	Current user's database username		USER
USER_ID()	Gets the user's database identification number		User: user name USER_ID ('user')USER_ ID()
USER_ NAME()	Give the user's database user name from a specified identification number	ID: user's identification number	USER_NAME(id USER_NAME()

TABLE D-6 TEXT

Function	Description	Parameters	Syntax
DATA LENGTH()	A system function that returns the actual length of any data type expression	Expression: constant, column name, function, subquery, or a combination of arithmetic, bitwise, and string operators	DATALENGTH (expression)
PATINDEX()	Gives the starting position of the first occurrence of a pattern in a specified expression, or zeros if the pattern is not found	Pattern: nchar literal string, use % to indicate a wildcard Expression: string-valued expression	PATINDEX ('%pattern%', expression)
SUB STRING()	Part of a character, binary, text, or image expression	Expression: char, varchar, or nchar column name Start: starting location as integer Length: integer indicating number of characters to extract	SUBSTRING (expression, start, length)
TEXTPTR()	Indicates the text-pointer value in varbinary format	Column: text or image column specified	TEXTPTR (column)
TEXT VALID()	A text or image function that checks whether a given text pointer is valid	Table: name of table Column: name of column Text ptr: specified text pointer	TEXTVALID ('table. column', text ptr)

Appendix E

Reserved Keywords

KEYWORDS USED BY SQL Server:

ADD	CURRENT	FROM
ALL	CURRENT_DATE	FULL
ALTER	CURRENT_TIME	GOTO
AND	CURRENT_TIMESTAMP	GRANT
ANY	CURRENT_USER	GROUP
AS	CURSOR	HAVING
ASC	DATABASE	HOLDLOCK
AUTHORIZATION	DBCC	IDENTITY
AVG	DEALLOCATE	IDENTITY_INSERT
BACKUP	DECLARE	IDENTITYCOL
BEGIN	DEFAULT	IF
BETWEEN	DELETE	IN
BREAK	DENY	INDEX
BROWSE	DESC	INNER
BULK	DISK	INSERT
BY	DISTINCT	INTERSECT
CASCADE	DISTRIBUTED	INTO
CASE	DOUBLE	IS
CHECK	DROP	ISOLATION
CHECKPOINT	DUMMY	JOIN
CLOSE	DUMP	KEY
CLUSTERED	ELSE	KILL
COALESCE	END	LEFT
COLUMN	ERRLVL	LEVEL
COMMIT	ERROREXIT	LIKE
COMMITTED	ESCAPE	LINENO
COMPUTE	EXCEPT	MAX
CONFIRM	EXECUTE	MIN
CONSTRAINT	EXIT	MIRROREXIT
CONTINUE	FETCH	NOCHECK
CONTROLROW	FILE	NONCLUSTERED
CONVERT	FILLFACTOR	NOT
COUNT	FLOPPY	NULL
CREATE	FOR	NULLIF
CROSS	FOREIGN	OF

OFF	READTEXT	TEMPORARY
OFFSETS	RECONFIGURE	TEXTSIZE
ON	REFERENCES	THEN
ONCE	REPEATABLE	TO
ONLY	REPLICATION	TOP
OPEN	RESTRICT	TRANSACTION
OPENQUERY	RETURN	TRIGGER
OPENROWSET	REVOKE	TRUNCATE
OPTION	RIGHT	TSEQUAL
OR	ROLLBACK	UNCOMMITTED
ORDER	ROWCOUNT	UNION
OUTER	ROWGUIDCOL	UNIQUE
OVER	RULE	UPDATE
PERCENT	SAVE	UPDATETEXT
PERMANENT	SCHEMA	USE
PIPE	SELECT	USER
PLAN	SERIALIZABLE	VALUES
PRECISION	SESSION_USER	VARYING
PREPARE	SET	VIEW
PRINT	SETUSER	WAITFOR
PRIVILEGES	SHUTDOWN	WHEN
PROCEDURE	STATISTICS	WHERE
PROCESSEXIT	SUM	WHILE
PUBLIC	SYSTEM_USER	WITH
RAISERROR	TABLE	WORK
READ	TAPE	WRITETEXT

Appendix F

System Stored Procedures

Catalog

Procedures	Description
sp_column_privileges	Returns privilege information for columns of a single table in the current environment
sp_columns	Returns column information for the specified tables or views
sp_databases	Produces a list of the databases in the Microsoft SQL Server installation or accessible through a database gateway
sp_fkeys	Reports logical foreign key information for the current environment
sp_pkeys	Reports primary key information for a single table in the current environment
sp_server_info	Produces a list of attribute names and matching values for SQL Server, a database gateway, and/or an underlying data source
sp_special_columns	Retrieves the set of columns that uniquely identify a row in the table and columns that are automatically updated when any value in the row is updated by a transaction
sp_sproc_columns	Retrieves column information for a stored procedure
sp_statistics	Produces a list of the indexes on a specified table
sp_stored_procedures	Retrieves a list of stored procedures in the installation
sp_table_privileges	Retrieves a list of tables and their privileges
sp_tables	Retrieves a list of objects that can be queried in the installation

Cursor

Procedures	Description
sp_cursor_list	Shows the attributes of open server cursors for a connection
sp_describe_cursor_tables	Shows the base tables referenced by a server cursor
sp_describe_cursor_columns	Shows the attributes of the columns in the result set of a server cursor

SQL Server Agent

Procedures	Description
sp_add_alert	Adds an alert
sp_add_category	Adds the specified category to the named server
sp_add_job	Adds a new job
sp_add_jobschedule	Adds a schedule for the specified job
sp_add_jobserver	Adds a server where the job can be run
sp_add_jobstep	Adds a step to the specified job
sp_add_notification	Adds a notification for an alert
sp_add_operator	Adds an operator (notification recipient) for use with alerts
sp_add_targetservergroup	Adds the specified server group name
sp_add_targertsvrgrp_member	Adds the specified group name
sp_addtask	Adds a scheduled task
sp_apply_job_to_targets	Deletes the specified job from servers where the job has already been applied or from servers where the job is not currently applied
sp_delete_alert	Deletes an alert that is used to respond to special conditions or events in Microsoft SQL Server

Procedures	Description
sp_delete_category	Deletes a category that is used to organize alerts, jobs, and operators
sp_delete_job	Deletes the specified job
sp_delete_jobschedule	Deletes a job schedule
sp_delete_jobserver	Deletes the specified server from processing jobs
sp_delete_jobstep	Deletes a job step from a job
sp_delete_notification	Deletes a notification used to send an alert to an operator
sp_delete_operator	Deletes an operator
sp_delete_targetserver	Deletes the specified server from the list of available job servers
sp_delete_targetservergroup	Deletes the specified server from the target server group
sp_delete_targetsvrgrp_member	Deletes the specified group name
sp_downloaded_row_limiter	Limits the number of rows in the sysdownloadlist system table that exist with a downloaded status of 1 for the specified server
sp_droptask	Deletes a scheduled task
sp_help_alert	Shows information alerts defined for the server
sp_help_category	Shows information about categories of jobs, operators, and alerts
sp_help_downloadlist	Shows rows in the sysdownloadlist system table for the supplied job, or all rows if no job is specified
sp_help_job	Displays information about jobs
sp_help_jobhistory	Displays the historical information about the execution of jobs
sp_help_jobschedule	Details the scheduling of jobs
sp_help_jobserver	Displays information about the named job
sp_help_jobstep	Details the job steps in a job

Continued

Procedures	Description
sp_help_notification	Displays a list of notifications
sp_help_operator	Displays information about operators
sp_helphistory	Shows history for those tasks owned by the user calling the procedure
sp_help_targetserver	Displays all target servers
sp_help_targetservergroup	Displays all target servers in the specified group
sp_helptask	Details one or more tasks that the user owns
sp_manage_jobs_by_login	Deletes or reassigns jobs belonging to the specified login
sp_msx_defect	Deletes the current server from multiserver operations
sp_msx_enlist	Puts the current server in the list of servers available for multiserver operations
sp_post_msx_operation	Puts rows into the sysdownloadlist system table for target servers to download job operations
sp_purge_jobhistory	Deletes the history records for jobs that have been executed
sp_purgehistory	Deletes history log information
sp_reassigntask	Reassigns the owner of a job or all jobs owned by a specified log
sp_remove_job_from_targets	Deletes the specified job from the given target servers or target server groups
sp_resync_targetserver	Resynchronizes the specified server in the multiserver domain
sp_start_job	Notifies SQL Server Agent to begin execution of a job
sp_stop_job	Notifies SQL Server Agent to cancel execution of a job
sp_update_alert	Updates information for an existing alert
sp_update_category	Updates information for an existing alert
sp_update_job	Updates the attributes of a job
sp_update_jobschedule	Updates the settings for a job schedule
sp_update_jobstep	Updates the setting for a step in a job
sp_update_notification	Updates the notification method of an alert notification

Procedures	Description
sp_update_operator	Updates statistics about an operator
sp_update_targetservergroup	Changes the designated server group name
sp_updatetask	Updates statistics about a task

Replication

Procedures	Description
sp_addarticle	Adds an article and adds it to a publication
sp_adddistpublisher	Adds a publisher that serves as its own distributor
sp_adddistributiondb	Adds a new distributor database and installs the distributor schema
sp_adddistributor	Adds a distributor
sp_addmergearticle	Adds an article to an existing merge publication
sp_addmergefilter	Adds a merge filter for creating partial data replicas
sp_addmergepublication	Adds a new merge publication
sp_addmergepullsubscription	Adds a merge pull type subscription
sp_addmergepullsubscription_agent	Adds an agent for merge pull subscription at the subscriber
sp_addmergesubscription	Adds a push or pull merge subscription
sp_addpublication	Adds a publication
sp_addpublication_snapshot	Adds a snapshot agent and sets the publication agent_id
sp_addsubscriber	Adds a subscriber and sets up a trusted remote login mapping from system administrator of the subscriber to the repl_subscriber login ID on the publisher (unless *sa* on the subscriber is already mapped to *sa* on the publisher).

Continued

Procedures	Description
sp_addsubscribersubscription	Adds a pull or anonymous subscription at the current database of the subscriber
sp_addsubscriber_schedule	Adds a schedule for the Distribution agent and Merge agent
sp_addsubscription	Adds a subscription to an article and sets the subscriber's status
sp_addsubsubscription_agent	Adds a new agent to the subscriber's database
sp_articlecolumn	Identifies columns used in an article
sp_articlefilter	Adds a filter-stored procedure to be used for horizontally partitioning data replicated from a published table
sp_articleview	Adds the synchronization object for an article when a table is filtered vertically and/or horizontally
sp_changearticle	Changes the properties of an article
sp_changedistpublisher	Changes the properties of a distributor publisher
sp_changedistributiondb	Changes the properties of a distributor database
sp_changedistributor_property	Changes the properties of the distributor
sp_changemergearticle	Changes the properties of a merge article
sp_changemergefilter	Changes merge filter properties
sp_changemergepublication	Changes merge publication properties
sp_changemergepullsubscription	Changes merge pull subscription properties
sp_changemergesubscription	Changes merge push or pull subscription
sp_changepublication	Changes publication's properties
sp_changesubscriber	Changes the options for a subscription server
sp_changesubscriber_schedule	Changes a subscriber's schedule for the distribution agent and merge agent
sp_changesubstatus	Changes the status of an existing subscriber
sp_distcounters	Shows the latest distribution information for all subscription servers

Procedures	Description
sp_droparticle	Deletes an article from a publication
sp_dropdistpublisher	Deletes a distributor publisher
sp_dropdistributiondb	Deletes a distributor database
sp_dropdistributor	Deletes the distributor designation from the registry of a registered server
sp_dropmergearticle	Deletes an article from a merge publication
sp_dropmergefilter	Deletes a merge filter
sp_dropmergepublication	Deletes a merge publication and its associated snapshot agent
sp_droppublisher	Deletes the publisher description from a server
sp_dropmergepullsubscription	Deletes a merge pull subscription
sp_dropmergesubscription	Deletes a subscription to a merge publication
sp_droppublication	Deletes a publication and its articles
sp_dropsubscriber	Deletes the subscriber designation from a registered server
sp_dropsubscribersubscription	Deletes a subscription at the current database of the subscriber
sp_dropsubscription	Deletes subscriptions to a particular article, publication, or set of subscriptions on the publisher
sp_enumcustomresolvers	Lists available custom resolvers
sp_enumfullsubscribers	Lists subscribers who have subscribed to all articles in a specified publication
sp_helparticle	Shows information about an article
sp_helparticlecolumns	Shows all columns in the underlying table of an article
sp_helpdistpublisher	Displays properties of the given distributor publisher
sp_helpdistributiondb	Displays properties of the specified distributor database

Continued

Procedures	Description
sp_helpdistributor	Display information about the distribution server, distribution database, working directory, and SQL Server Agent user account
sp_helpmergearticle	Shows information about an article
sp_helpmergefilter	Shows information about merge filter
sp_helpmergepublication	Shows information about a merge publication
sp_helpmergepullsubscription	Displays information about the pull subscription
sp_helpmergesubscription	Displays information about a push subscription
sp_helppublication	Shows information about a publication
sp_helpreplicationdb	Shows information about a specified database or a list of all publication databases on the server
sp_helpreplicationdboption	Displays the databases that have the replication option enabled
sp_helpreplicationoption	Lists the properties of the replication option
sp_helpsubscriberinfo	Returns information about a subscription server
sp_helpsubscribersubscription	Returns the information of one or more subscriptions at the subscriber
sp_helpsubscription	Lists subscription information associated with a particular publication, article, subscriber, or set of subscriptions
sp_MSdistribution_cleanup	Unsubscribes all subscribers who have not received distributions for the maximum retention period (max_distretention)
sp_MShistory_cleanup	Removes all history stored in the database for a time period greater than or equal to the history retention period
sp_refreshsubscriptions	Refresh subscriptions to new articles in a pull publication for all the existing subscribers to the publication
sp_replcmds	Designates the first client who runs sp_replcmds within a given database as the log reader

Procedures	Description
sp_replcounters	Shows replication statistics about latency, throughput, and transaction count for each published database
sp_repldone	Refreshes the record that identifies the server's last distributed transaction
sp_replflush	Flushes the article cache
sp_replicationdboption	Sets a replication database option for the current database
sp_repltrans	Displays a result set of all the transactions in the publication database transaction log that are marked for replication but have not been marked as distributed
sp_resyncmergesubscription	Forces the synchronization of designated subscriptions to a publication
sp_resyncsubscription	Resynchronizes the subscription

Security

Procedures	Description
sp_addalias	Adds a login to a user in a database
sp_addapprole	Adds a special type of role for application security
sp_addgroup	Adds a special type of role for application security
sp_addlogin	Adds a new Microsoft SQL Server login
sp_addremotelogin	Adds a new remote login ID to sysremotelogins in the master database
sp_addrole	Adds a new role in the database
sp_addrolemember	Assigns a security account as a member of a role
sp_addserver	Adds a remote server or the name of the local server

Continued

Procedures	Description
sp_addsrvrolemember	Assigns a login as a member of a server role
sp_adduser	Adds a security account to the current database
sp_addrolepassword	Changes the password of an application role
sp_change-users-login	Link a user in the current database with a different login
sp_changedbowner	Changes database owner
sp_changegroup	Changes the role membership for a user's security account
sp_changeobjectowner	Changes the object's owner in the current database
sp_dbfixedrolepermission	Shows the permissions for each fixed database role
sp_defaultdb	Changes the default database for a login
sp_defaultlanguage	Changes a user's default language
sp_denylogin	Prevents a Windows NT user from connecting with Microsoft SQL Server
sp_dropalias	Deletes an alias from a login to a user that was established by sp_addalias
sp_dropapprole	Deletes an application role from the current database
sp_dropgroup	Deletes a role from a database
sp_droplinkedsrvlogin	Deletes an existing Microsoft SQL Server login mapping to a linked server
sp_droplogin	Deletes a SQL Server login
sp_dropremotelogin	Deletes a remote user login
sp_droprole	Deletes a Microsoft SQL Server role
sp_droprolemember	Deletes a security account from a Microsoft SQL Server role
sp_dropserver	Deletes a server from the list of known servers in the master database sysservers table
sp_dropsrvrolemember	Deletes a Windows NT user or group, or a Microsoft SQL Server login from a server role
sp_dropuser	Deletes a user
sp_grantdbaccess	Adds a security account in a database for a login and enables it to be granted permissions to work with a database

Procedures	Description
sp_grantlogin	Grants permission for a Windows NT user account to connect with Microsoft SQL Server
sp_helpdbfixedrole	Lists the fixed database roles
sp_helpgroup	Returns information about a role or all roles in the current database
sp_helplogins	Shows information for logins and the associated users in each database
sp_helpntgoup	Shows information about Windows NT groups with accounts in the current database
sp_helpremotelogin	Shows information about a particular remote server's logins or about all remote servers' logins
sp_helprole	Shows information about the roles in the current database
sp_helprolemember	Shows information about the members of a role in the current database
sp_helpprotect	Shows on user permissions
sp_helpsrvrole	Shows a list of the fixed server roles
sp_helpsrvrolemember	Shows information about the members of a fixed server role
sp_helpuser	Returns information about users and roles in the current database
sp_password	Adds or changes a password for a Microsoft SQL Server login
sp_remoteoption	Shows or changes remote login options
sp_revokedbaccess	Deletes a security account from the current database
sp_revokelogin	Prevents login for a Windows NT user or group
sp_setapprole	Initiates the permissions associated with an application role
sp_srvrolepermission	Lists the permissions applied to a server role

System

Procedures	Description
sp_addextendedproc	Registers the name of an extended stored procedure with Microsoft SQL Server
sp_addmessage	Adds an error message to the sysmessages table
sp_addtype	Adds a user-defined data type
sp_addumpdevice	Adds a dump device to Microsoft SQL Server
sp_altermessage	Alters the state of a sysmessages error
sp_attach_db	Attaches database files to a server
sp_attach_single_file_db	Attaches a single file of a database to a server
sp_autostats	Immediately displays or changes the automatic UPDATE STATISTICS setting for one specific index or all indexes for a given table
sp_bindefault	Binds a default to a table column or to a user-defined data type
sp_bindrule	Binds a rule to a table column or to a user-defined data type
sp_bindsession	Binds or unbinds a connection to other connections
sp_certify_removable	Confirms that a database is properly configured for distribution on removable media
sp_configure	Displays or changes global configuration settings for the current server
sp_create_removable	Makes a removable media database
sp_createstats	Lists information about columns in the current database. Columns with bit, image, text, and timestamp data types are not included
sp_data_type_info	Displays information about the data types supported by the current environment
sp_dbcmptlevel	Restores the operation of certain features in a database to be compatible with previous versions of Microsoft SQL Server
sp_dboption	Displays or changes database options

Procedures	Description
sp_depends	Displays information about database object dependencies — the views and procedures that depend on the specified table or view, and the tables and views that are depended on by the specified view or procedure
sp_detach_db	Detaches a database from a server
sp_dropdevice	Deletes a Microsoft SQL Server database device or dump device
sp_dropextendedproc	Deletes an extended stored procedure
sp_droplanguage	Deletes an alternate language from the server and removes its row from syslogins table in the master database
sp_dropmessage	Deletes a specified error message from the sysmessages system table
sp_droptype	Deletes a user-defined data type from systypes
sp_dsninfo	Returns ODBC data source name (DSN) information from the replication distribution server that is associated with the current server if replication is installed
sp_enumdsn	Lists defined ODBC DSNs for a server running under a specific Windows NT user account
sp_executesql	Runs a Transact-SQL statement or batch
sp_fulltext_catalog	Makes and removes a full-text catalog
sp_fulltext_column	Indicates columns for full-text indexing
sp_fulltext_database	Begins full-text indexing of the current database
sp_fulltext_service	Changes properties of full-text search
sp_fulltext_table	Flags a table for full-text indexing
sp_getbindtoken	Makes a bound connection context and returns a unique identifier for the created context
sp_help	Displays information about a database object in the sysobjects table or about a SQL Server-supplied or user-defined data type

Continued

Procedures	Description
sp_helpconstraint	Lists information on all constraints defined in the database
sp_helpdb	Lists information about a specified database or all databases
sp_helpdevice	Lists information about Microsoft SQL Server database files
sp_helpextendedproc	Shows the currently defined extended stored procedures and the name of the DLL to which the function belongs
sp_helpfile	Lists names and attributes of database files
sp_helpfilegroup	Lists names and attributes of database filegroups
sp_help_fulltext_catalogs	Displays information about the full-text catalog
sp_help_fulltext_catalogs_cursor	Displays information about the full-text catalog via a cursor
sp_help_fulltext_columns	Lists columns that have been flagged for full-text indexing
sp_help_fulltext_columns_cursor	Lists columns that have been flagged for full-text indexing via a cursor
sp_help_fulltext_tables	Lists tables that are full-text indexed
sp_help_fulltext_tables_cursor	Lists tables that are full-text indexed via a cursor
sp_helpindex	Shows information about table indexes
sp_indexoption	Designates user-defined index option values
sp_helplanguage	Shows information about a specific alternate language or about all languages
sp_helpserver	Shows information about a remote or replication server or about all servers of both types
sp_helpsort	Shows the SQL Server sort order and character set
sp_helptext	Prints the text of a rule, a default, or an unencrypted stored procedure, trigger, or view
sp_helptrigger	Lists the type or types of triggers defined on the specified table in the current database

Procedures	Description
sp_lock	Displays lock information
sp_monitor	Displays statistics about Microsoft SQL Server
sp_processmail	Uses extended stored procedures xp_findnextmsg, xp_readmail, and xp_deletemail to process incoming mail messages from the inbox assigned to Microsoft SQL Server
sp_procoption	Sets procedure options for the specified procedure
sp_recompile	Recompiles each stored procedure and trigger that uses the specified table the next time the stored procedure and trigger are run
sp_refreshview	Refreshes metadata for the specified view
sp_rename	Updates the name of a user-created object (table, column, user data type) in the current database
sp_renamedb	Updates the name of a database
sp_serveroption	Sets server options
sp_setlangalias	Sets or changes the alias for an alternate language
sp_setnetname	Sets the network names in sysservers to their actual network machine names for remote computers running Microsoft SQL Server
sp_spaceused	Displays the number of rows, the reserved disk space, and the disk space used by a table in a database, or displays the reserved disk space and disk space used by an entire database
sp_tableoption	Sets option values for user-defined tables
sp_unbindefault	Unbinds a default from a column or from a user-defined data type in the current database
sp_unbindrule	Unbinds a rule from a column or a user-defined data type in the current database
sp_updatestats	Runs UPDATE STATISTICS against all user tables in the current database
sp_validname	Verifies valid SQL-Server identifier names
sp_who	Returns information about current SQL Server users and processes

Distributed Queries

Procedures	Description
sp_addlinkedserver	Adds a linked server that enables distributed, heterogeneous queries access to OLE DB data sources
sp_addlinkedsrvlogin	Adds a new SQL Server login mapping for a linked server
sp_catalogs	Lists the catalogs in the specified linked server, which is equivalent to databases in Microsoft SQL Server
sp_columns_ex	Displays the column information, one row per column, for the given linked server table
sp_column_privileges_ex	Gets column privileges for the specified linked server table
sp_droplinkedsrvlogin	Deletes an existing SQL Server login mapping to a linked server
sp_foreignkeys	Identifies the foreign keys defined on the remote table
sp_indexes	Shows index information for the specified remote table
sp_linkedservers	Shows a list of linked servers defined in the local server
sp_primarykeys	Displays the primary key columns for the specified table
sp_serveroption	Sets server options
sp_tables_ex	Retrieves table information on the tables from the specified linked server
sp_table_privileges_ex	Gets privilege information on specified linked server table

Web Assistant

Procedures	Description
sp_dropwebtask	Deletes a previously defined Web task
sp_enumcodepages	Lists the code pages supported by sp_makewebtask
sp_makewebtask	Adds a task that produces an HTML document
sp_runwebtask	Runs a previously defined Web task and generates the HTML document

General Extended

Procedures	Description
xp_cmdshell	Runs a given command string as an operating-system command shell and returns any output as rows of text
xp_enumgroups	Lists local Windows NT-based groups or groups defined in a specified Windows NT domain
xp_findnextmsg	Used to find messages for xp_processmail()
xp_grantlogin	Grants SQL Server access to a Windows NT-based group or user
xp_loginconfig	Returns the login security configuration of the server
xp_logevent	Puts a user-defined message into the NT event log or SQL Server log
xp_logininfo	Returns the login account information
xp_msver	Returns SQL Server version information
xp_revokelogin	Revokes SQL Server access from a Windows NT-based group or user
xp_snmp_getstate	Displays the state of the SQL Server Simple Network Management Protocol (SNMP) agent
xp_snmp_raisetrap	Allows a client to define and send an SNMP alert to an SNMP client
xp_sprintf	Formats and stores a series of characters and values in the string output parameter
xp_sqlinventory	Retrieves SQL Server configuration and inventory information into the specified database and table
xp_sqlmaint	Calls sqlmaint utility with a string of sqlmaint flags
xp_sscanf	Reads data from the string into the argument locations given by each format argument

SQL Mail Extended

Procedures	Description
xp_deletemail	Deletes a message from the SQL Server inbox
xp_findnextmsg	Accepts a message ID for input and returns the message ID of the next message
xp_readmail	Reads a mail message from the SQL Server mail inbox
xp_sendmail	Sends a message, query result set, and/or an attachment to the specified recipients
xp_startmail	Starts a SQL Server mail client session
xp_stopmail	Stops a SQL Server mail client session

SQL Profiler

Procedures	Description
xp_sqltrace	Monitor and record database activity
xp_trace_addnewqueue	Adds a new trace queue and sets queue configuration values
xp_trace_deletequeuedefinition	Removes all queue definition information for the given queue
xp_trace_destroyqueue	Deletes the specified queue
xp_trace_enumqueuedefname	Lists all defined queue names alphabetically
xp_trace_enumqueuehandles	Lists all currently defined queue handles
xp_trace_eventclassrequired	Retrieves whether or not an event class is being captured by the trace for the specified a queue handle
xp_trace_generate_event	Adds a user-defined event to all active queues
xp_trace_getappfilter	Retrieves one row for the current application filter for the given queue handle

Procedures	Description
xp_trace_getconnectionidfilter	Retrieves the current unique ID filter, created with xp_trace_setconnectionidfilter
xp_trace_getcpufilter	Retrieves the current cpu filter set with xp_trace_setcpufilter
xp_trace_getdbidfilter	Retrieves the current database filter, set by xp_trace_setdbidfiilter
xp_trace_getdurationfilter	Retrieves the current definition of the duration filter, created with xp_trace_setdurationfilter
xp_trace_geteventfilter	Retrieves the current event text filter definition for the queue, created with xp_trace_seteventfilter
xp_trace_geteventnames	Retrieves the names of the events currently available to trace
xp_trace_getevents	Deletes events from the event queue that were created with xp_trace_seteventclassrequired
xp_trace_gethostfilter	Retrieves the current host filter that was created with xp_trace_sethostfilter
xp_trace_gethpidfilter	Retrieves the host process ID filter associated with the queue that was created with xp_trace_sethpidfilter
xp_trace_getindidfilter	Retrieves the current index ID filter associated with this queue that was created with xp_trace_setindidfilter
xp_trace_getntdmfilter	Retrieves the current Windows NT domain name filter that was created with xp_setntdmfilter
xp_trace_getntnmfilter	Retrieves the current Windows NT machine name filter that was created with xp_trace_setntnmfilter
xp_trace_getobjidfilter	Retrieves the current object ID filter associated with the queue that was created by xp_trace_setobjidfilter
xp_trace_getowneridfilter	Retrieves the current owner ID filter associated with the queue that was created with xp_trace_setowneridfilter
xp_trace_getpercentfilter	Retrieves the current percent filter that was created with xp_trace_setpercentfilter

Continued

Procedures	Description
xp_trace_getqueueautostart	Retrieves the current queue's startup configuration information that was created with xp_setqueueautostart
xp_trace_getreadfilter	Retrieves the current read filter that was created with xp_trace_setreadfilter
xp_trace_getseverityfilter	Retrieves the current severity filter that was created with xp_trace_getseverityfilter
xp_trace_getspidfilter	Retrieves the current internal process ID filter associated with the queue that was created with xp_trace_setspidfilter
xp_trace_getuserfilter	Retrieves the current user filter that was created with xp_trace_setuserfilter
xp_trace_getwritefilter	Retrieves the current write filter that was created with xp_trace_setwritefilter
xp_trace_loadqueuedefinition	Loads a saved definition that was created with xp_trace_savequeuedefinition
xp_trace_pausequeue	Postpones new events from being added to the queue
xp_trace_restartqueue	Restarts a previously paused queue
xp_trace_savequeuedefinition	Defines the queue to save in the registry
xp_trace_setappfilter	Identifies the application filter so the only events captured are those that meet the given include filter, and exclude filter criteria
xp_trace_setconnectionidfilter	Identifies the unique connection ID filter so the only events captured are those that meet the given filter_value criteria
xp_trace_setcpufilter	Sets the cpu filter so the only events captured are those that meet the given minimum cpu, and maximum cpu criteria
xp_trace_setdbidfilter	Sets the database ID filter so the only events captured are those that meet the given filter_value criteria
xp_trace_setdurationfilter	Sets the duration filter so the only events captured are those that meet the given minimum duration, and maximum duration criteria

Procedures	Description
xp_trace_seteventclassrequired	Sets the event class criteria for the events to be captured by the given trace
xp_trace_seteventfilter	Sets the event description filter, entered as a text string, so the only events captured are those that meet the given event class, include filter, and exclude filter criteria
xp_trace_sethostfilter	Sets the host name filter so the only events captured are those that meet the given include filter, and exclude filter criteria
xp_trace_sethpidfilter	Sets the host process ID filter so the only events captured are those that meet the given filter value criteria
xp_trace_setindidfilter	Sets the index ID filter so the only events captured are those that meet the given filter value criteria
xp_trace_setntdmfilter	Sets the Windows NT domain name filter so that the only events captured are those that meet the given include filter, and exclude filter
xp_trace_setntnmfilter	Sets the Windows NT user name filter so the only events captured are those that meet the given include filter and exclude filter criteria
xp_trace_setobjidfilter	Sets the object ID filter so that the only events captured are those that meet the given filter value
xp_trace_setowneridfilter	Identifies the owner ID filter so the only events captured are those that meet the given filter value
xp_trace_setpercentfilter	Sets the percent use complete filter so the only transaction events captured are those that meet the given minimum percent and maximum percent criteria
xp_trace_setqueueautostart	Sets the queue for automatic startup
xp_trace_setqueuecreateinfo	Names trace queue properties for modification
xp_trace_setqueuedestination	Specifies the destination filter for the specified queue
xp_trace_setreadfilter	Sets the read filter so the only events captured are those that meet the given minimum read and maximum read criteria

Continued

Procedures	Description
xp_trace_setserverfilter	Sets the SQL Server name filter, or the SQL Server names to include and/or exclude for the events specified
xp_trace_setseverityfilter	Sets the severity filter so the only events captured are those that meet the given minimum severity and maximum severity criteria
xp_trace_setspidfilter	Sets the system process ID filter so the only events captured are those that meet the given filter value criteria
xp_trace_settextfilter	Specifies text filter for the specified queue
xp_trace_setuserfilter	Sets the user filter so the only events placed in the queue are those that meet the given include filter and exclude filter criteria
xp_trace_setwritefilter	Sets the write filter so the only events captured are those that meet the given minimum write and maximum write criteria

OLE Automation

Procedures	Description
sp_OACreate	Creates an OLE object on the SQL Server computer
sp_OADestroy	Destroys an OLE object
sp_OAGetErrorInfo	Retrieves OLE Automation error information
sp_OAGetProperty	Retrieves a property value of an OLE object
sp_OAMethod	Calls a method of an OLE object
sp_OASetProperty	Sets a property of an OLE object to a new value
sp_OAStop	Stops the server-wide OLE Automation stored procedure execution environment

Global Variables

Global Variable	Description
@@connections	Stores the number of logins or attempted logins since Microsoft SQL Server was last started
@@cpu_busy	Holds the number of ticks that the CPU spent doing SQL Server work since Microsoft SQL Server was last started
@@cursor_rows	Returns the number of qualifying rows in the last-opened cursor
@@datefirst	Retrieves the current value of the SET DATEFIRST parameter, which indicates the specified last day of each week: 1 for Sunday through 7 for Saturday
@@dbts	Stores the value of the current timestamp data type for the current database
@@error	Stores the error number for the last Transact-SQL statement executed
@@fetch_status	Stores the status of a cursor FETCH statement
@@identity	Stores the last-inserted IDENTITY value
@@idle	Retains the number of ticks that SQL Server has been idle since it was last started
@@io_busy	Retains the number of ticks that SQL Server spent doing input and output operations since it was last started
@@langid	Retains the local language ID of the language currently in use
@@language	Retains the name of the language currently in use
@@lock_timeout	Specifies the current lock time-out setting, in milliseconds, for the current session
@@max_connections	Specifies the maximum number of simultaneous connections that can be made with SQL Server in the current computer environment
@@max_precision	Specifies the level of precision currently set in the server for decimal and numeric data types

Continued

Global Variable	Description
@@nestlevel	Defines the transaction nesting level of the current execution (0-16)
@@options	Retains information about current SET options
@@pack_received	Specifies the number of input packets read by SQL Server since it was last started
@@pack_sent	Specifies the number of output packets written by SQL Server since it was last started
@@packet_errors	Retains the number of network packet errors on SQL Server connections that have occurred since the last time SQL Server was started
@@procid	Holds the stored procedure ID of the currently executing procedure
@@remserver	Holds the server name of the remote server as it appears in the login record
@@rowcount	Specifies the number of rows affected by the last statement
@@servername	Holds the name of the local SQL Server
@@servicename	Specifies the name of the registry key under which Microsoft SQL Server is running
@@spid	Holds the server process ID of the current user process
@@textsize	Holds the current value of the TEXTSIZE option of the SET statement, which specifies the maximum length, in bytes, of text or image data that a SELECT statement returns
@@timeticks	Specifies the number of microseconds per tick
@@total_errors	Displays the number of disk read/write errors encountered by SQL Server since it was last started
@@total_read	Displays the number of disk reads (but not cache reads) by SQL Server since it was last started
@@total_write	Holds the number of disk writes by SQL Server since it was last started
@@trancount	Specifies the number of active transactions for the current user
@@version	Holds the date, version, and processor type for the current installation of SQL Server

Appendix G

SQL Server Databases and Tables

Databases and Logs

Table G-1 SYSTEM DATABASES AND LOGS

Database File		File Name	Default Size
master	primary data	Master.mdf	7.5MB
master	log	Mastlog.ldf	1MB
tempdb	primary data	Tempdb.mdf	8MB
tempdb	log	Templog.ldf	.5MB
model	primary data	Model.mdf	.75MB
model	log	Modellog.ldf	.75MB
msdb	primary data	Msdbdata.mdf	3.5MB
msdb	log	Msdblog.ldf	.75MB

System Tables

TABLE G-2 MASTER DATABASE

Table	Description
sysarticles	Articles posted by the publishing server
syscharsets	Character sets defined for use by SQL Server
sysconfigures	Configuration options set by a user
syscurconfigs	Current values of configuration options
sysdatabases	Databases on the SQL Server installation
sysdevices	Disk dump devices, diskette dump devices, tape dump devices, and database devices
syslanguages	Languages present in the SQL Server installation
syslockinfo	Granted, converting, and waiting lock requests
syslogins	Login accounts
sysmessages	System error or warning messages that can be returned by SQL Server
sysobjects	Objects created within a database
sysoledbusers	User and password mappings for linked servers
sysperfinfo	SQL Server representation of the internal performance counters that can be displayed through the Windows NT Performance Monitor
sysprocesses	Processes running on the SQL Server
syspublications	Publications posted by the publishing server
sysremotelogins	Remote users who are permitted to call remote stored procedures on this SQL Server
sysservers	Remote servers that this SQL Server can access as an OLE DB data source
syssubscriptions	Correlates the IDs of published articles with the IDs of all subscribers expecting to receive data

TABLE G-3 EVERY DATABASE

Table	Description
syscolumns	Columns in every table and view, and parameters in a stored procedures
Syscomments	The text of views, rules, defaults, triggers, CHECK constraints, DEFAULT constraints, and stored procedures
Sysconstraints	Stores mappings of constraints to the objects that own the constraints
Sysdepends	Dependency information between objects and the objects contained in their definition
Sysfiles	Files in a database
Sysfilegroups	Filegroups in a database
Sysforeignkeys	Information regarding the FOREIGN KEY constraints that are in table definitions
Sysindexes	Indexes and tables in the database
Sysindexkeys	Keys or columns in an index
Sysmembers	Members of a role
Sysobjects	Objects created within a database
Syspermissions	Permissions that have been granted and denied to users, groups, and roles in the database
Sysprotects	Permissions that have been applied to security accounts with the GRANT and DENY statements
sysreferences	Mappings of FOREIGN KEY constraint definitions to the referenced columns
Systypes	System-supplied and user-defined data types
Sysusers	Windows NT users, Windows NT groups, SQL Server users, or SQL Server roles in the database

TABLE G-4 MSDB DATABASE

Table	Description
sysalerts	Alerts
syscategories	Categories used by SQL Server Enterprise Manager to organize jobs, alerts, and operators
sysdownloadlist	The queue of download instructions for all target servers
sysjobhistory	Holds information about the execution of scheduled jobs
sysjobs	The information for each scheduled job
sysjobservers	The association or relationship of a particular job with one or more target servers
sysjobsteps	The information for each step in a job
sysnotifications	Notifications
sysoperators	Operators
sysjobschedules	Schedule information for jobs
systargetservergroupmembers	Documents the target servers that are currently enlisted into this multiserver group
systargetservergroups	Documents the target server groups that are currently enlisted into this multiserver environment
systargetservers	Documents the target servers that are currently enlisted into this multiserver operation domain
systaskids	Mappings of tasks created in previous versions of Microsoft SQL Server to SQL Server Enterprise Manager jobs in the current version
sysvolumelabel	Incremental volume labels used for backups

Appendix H

Operators Reference

WHEN MULTIPLE LOGICAL operators appear in an expression, the NOT is evaluated first, followed by AND and then OR. If arithmetic and bitwise operators are present in the expression, they are handled before the logical operators. The following sections show this precedence.

Grouping by Parenthesis: ( )

Bitwise: ~

Multiplicative: * / %

Additive: + -

Other: + - ^ & |

NOT

AND

OR

Comparison Operators

>	(greater than)
<	(less than)
=	(equals)
<=	(less than or equal to)
>=	(greater than or equal to)
!=	(not equal to)
<>	(not equal to)
!<	(not less than)
!>	(not greater than)

Arithmetic Operators

+	(Add)
-	(Subtract)
*	(Multiply)
/	(Divide)
%	(Modulo)

Bitwise Operators

&	(Bitwise AND)
|	(Bitwise OR)
^	(Bitwise Exclusive OR)
~	(Bitwise NOT)

Logical Operator Tables

Figure H-1 shows the truth table for the logical AND operator. An expression having the value in the left-hand column ANDed with an expression having the value in the top row will yield the outcome at the intersection.

AND	True	False	Null
True	T	F	U
False	F	F	U
Null	U	U	U

T = True F = False U = Unknown

Figure H-1: Logical operator AND

Figure H-2 shows the truth table for the logical OR operator. An expression having the value in the left-hand column ORed with an expression having the value in the top row will yield the outcome at the intersection.

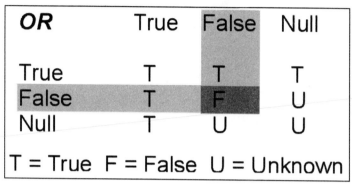

Figure H-2: Logical operator OR

Appendix 1

Data Types Reference

TABLE I-1 SQL SERVER DATA TYPES

SQL Server	Description
binary(n)	Fixed-length, *n* up to 8,000 bytes of binary data.
bit(n)	1-byte integer with value of 1 Or 0, with the *n* specifying number of bits determines storage required. Up to 8 bits uses 1 byte.
char(n), character, nchar(n)	Fixed-length, *n* maximum of 8,000 ANSI characters. nchar is used to store up to 4000 Unicode characters.
datetime	Date and time data between January 1, 1753 and December 31, 9999, with accuracy of 3.33 milliseconds and with 8 bytes of storage.
dec(p,s), decimal	Exact numeric data with values from $10^{38} - 1$ through $-10^{38} - 1$. Optional Precision (*p*) is maximum number of decimal digits to left and right of decimal point. Optional scale (*s*) is maximum number of decimal digits to the right of the decimal point.
double precision	Eight-byte float
float [(n)]	Positive or negative floating point numbers where the range of numbers. is from 2.23E - 308 through 1.79E + 308, negative values from –2.23E - 308 through –1.79E + 308. Zero can be stored. The *n* is the number of bits in mantissa and can be from 1 to 53. When *n* is 7 or less, storage is 4 bytes; otherwise, it is 8 bytes.
image	Variable-length data with maximum of 2,147,483,647 bytes of binary data.
int, integer	Four-byte whole numbers from -2^{31} through $2^{31} - 1$.

Continued

TABLE I-1 SQL SERVER DATA TYPES *(Continued)*

SQL Server	Description
money	Eight-byte currency values from –922,337,203,685,477.5807 through 922,337,203,685,477.5807, double precision integer.
numeric (p, s)	Exact numeric data with values from $10^{38} - 1$ through $-10^{38} - 1$. Optional Precision (*p*) is maximum number of decimal digits to left and right of decimal point. Optional scale (*s*) is maximum number of decimal digits to the right of the decimal point.
real	Floating point numbers. Seven-digit precision from 1.18E - 38 through 3.40E + 38, negative values from -1.18E - 38 through -3.40E + 38. Zero can be stored. 4 byte storage; float(1) through float(24).
smalldatetime	Date and time data between January 1, 1900 and June 6, 2079 with accuracy to 1 minute. Four bytes of storage.
smallint	Two-byte whole numbers from -2^{15} through $2^{15} - 1$.
smallmoney	Four-byte monetary values from –214,748.3648 through 214,748.3647, rounded up two places in display.
sysname	nvarchar(128), 128 Unicode characters
text, ntext	Variable-length data with maximum of 2,147,483,647 characters. ntext can store up to 1,073,741,823 2-byte Unicode characters.
timestamp	Binary or varbinary data to show sequence of activity on a row by date/time entry.
tinyint	One-byte whole numbers from 0 through 255.
uniqueidentifier	Sixteen-byte binary string for GUID (globally unique identifier) value.
varbinary(n)	Variable-length, *n* maximum of 8,000 bytes of binary data.
varchar(n), nvarchar(n)	Variable-length, *n* maximum of 8,000 characters. nvarchar is used to store up to 4,000 Unicode characters.

The following tables relate to mapping SQL to ODBC SQL, ODBC C, and OLE DB C.

TABLE I-2 SQL DATA TYPE MAPPING TO ODBC DATA TYPES

SQL Server	ODBC SQL	ODBC C
binary	SQL_BINARY	SQL_C_BINARY
bit	SQL_BIT	SQL_C_BIT
char	SQL_CHAR	SQL_C_CHAR
character	SQL_CHAR	SQL_C_CHAR
datetime	SQL_TIMESTAMP	SQL_C TIMESTAMP
decimal	SQL_DECIMAL	SQL_C_CHAR
dec	SQL_DECIMAL	SQL_C_CHAR
double precision	SQL_FLOAT	SQL_C_DOUBLE
float	SQL_FLOAT	SQL_C_DOUBLE
float(n)where n is 1 to 23	SQL_REAL	SQL_C_FLOAT
float(n) where n is 24 to 53	SQL_FLOAT	SQL_C_DOUBLE
image	SQL_LONG VARBINARY	SQL_C_BINARY
int	SQL_INTEGER	SQL_C_SLONG SQL_C_ULONG
integer	SQL_INTEGER	SQL_C_SLONG SQL_C_ULONG
money	SQL_DECIMAL	SQL_C_CHAR
numeric	SQL_NUMERIC	SQL_C_CHAR
real	SQL_REAL	SQL_C_FLOAT
smalldatetime	SQL_TIMESTAMP	SQL_C_ TIMESTAMP
smallint	SQL_SMALLINT	SQL_C_SSHORT SQL_C_USHORT
smallmoney	SQL_DECIMAL	SQL_C_CHAR

Continued

TABLE I-2 SQL DATA TYPE MAPPING TO ODBC DATA TYPES *(Continued)*

SQL Server	ODBC SQL	ODBC C
sysname	SQL_VARCHAR	SQL_C_CHAR
text	SQL_LONG VARCHAR	SQL_C_CHAR
timestamp	SQL_BINARY	SQL_C_BINARY
tinyint	SQL_TINYINT	SQL_C_SSHORT SQL_C_USHORT
varbinary	SQL_VARBINARY	SQL_C_BINARY
varchar	SQL_VARCHAR	SQL_C_CHAR

TABLE I-3 SQL SERVER DATA TYPE MAPPING TO OLE DB

SQL Server	ADO Constant	OLE DB
binary	adBinary	DBTYPE_ BYTES
bit	adBoolean	DBTYPE_BOOL
char	adChar	DBTYPE_STR
datetime	adDate	DBTYPE_DATE
decimal	adDecimal	DBTYPE_DECIMAL
double precision	adDouble	DBTYPE_R8
float	adDouble	DBTYPE_R8
float(n) **where** *n* is 1 to 23	adSingle	DBTYPE_R4
float(n) **where** *n* is 24 to 53	adDouble	DBTYPE_R8
image	adBinary	DBTYPE_ BYTES
integer	adInteger	DBTYPE_I4
money	adCurrency	DBTYPE_CY
numeric	adNumeric	DBTYPE_NUMERIC

SQL Server	ADO Constant	OLE DB
real	adSingle	DBTYPE_R4
smalldatetime	adDate	DBTYPE_DATE
smallint	adSmallInt	DBTYPE_I2
smallmoney	adCurrency	DBTYPE_CY
sysname	adWChar	DBTYPE_WSTR
text	adChar	DBTYPE_STR
timestamp	adDBTimeStamp	DBTYPE_ BYTES
tinyint	adUnsignedTinyInt	DBTYPE_UI1
varbinary	adBinary	DBTYPE_ BYTES
nchar	adWChar	DBTYPE_ WSTR
varchar	adChar	DBTYPE_STR
ntext	adWChar	DBTYPE_WSTR
nvarchar	adWChar	DBTYPE_WSTR

The following table relates to mapping SQL to Open Data Services data types.

TABLE I-4 SQL DATA TYPE MAPPING TO OPEN DATA SERVICES DATA TYPES

SQL Server Data Type	Data Type
varchar	SRVBIGBINARY
char	SRVBIGCHAR
varbinary	SRVBIGVARBINARY
varchar	SRVBIGVARCHAR
binary	SRVBINARY
bit	SRVBIT
bit null	SRVBITN

Continued

TABLE I-4 SQL DATA TYPE MAPPING TO OPEN DATA SERVICES DATA TYPES

SQL Server Data Type	Data Type
char	SRVCHAR
datetime	SRVDATETIME
smalldatetime	SRVDATETIM4
datetime null	SRVDATETIMN
decimal	SRVDECIMAL
decimal null	SRVDECIMALN
real	SRVFLT4
float	SRVFLT8
real|float null	SRVFLTN
image	SRVIMAGE
tinyint	SRVINT1
smallint	SRVINT2
int	SRVINT4
tinyint|small int|int null	SRVINTN
smallmoney	SRVMONEY4
money	SRVMONEY
money|smallmoney null	SRVMONEYN
nchar	SRVNCHAR
ntext	SRVNTEXT
numeric	SRVNUMERIC
numeric null	SRVNUMERICN
nvarchar	SRVNVARCHAR
text	SRVTEXT
varbinary	SRVVARBINARY
varchar	SRVVARCHAR

The following table relates to mapping SQL to DB_Library data types.

TABLE I-5 SQL DATA TYPE MAPPING TO DB_LIBRARY DATA TYPES

SQL Server Data Type	DB-Lib C Type	SQL Token Data Type
binary	DBBINARY	SQLBINARY
bit	DBBIT	SQLBIT
char	DBCHAR	SQLCHAR
smalldatetime	DBDATETIM4	SQLDATETIM4
datetime	DBDATETIME	SQLDATETIME
decimal	DBDECIMAL	SQLDECIMAL
float	DBFLT4	SQLFLT4
double	DBFLT8	SQLFLT8
image	DBBINARY	SQLIMAGE
tinyint	DBTINYINT	SQLINT1
smallint	DBSMALLINT	SQLINT2
int	DBINT	SQLINT4
smallmoney	DBMONEY4	SQLMONEY4
money	DBMONEY	SQLMONEY
numeric	DBNUMERIC	SQLNUMERIC
text	DBCHAR	SQLTEXT
varbinary	DBBINARY	SQLVARBINARY
varchar	DBCHAR	SQLVARCHAR

Appendix J

SQL Server 7.0 Technical Specifications

THE FOLLOWING LISTS the maximum sizes and quantity of objects specified in a Microsoft SQL Server database or referenced in Transact-SQL statements:

Category	Object	Size/Quantity
Batch	Batch size	65,536 times network packet size
Bytes	In a character or binary column	8,000
	In a text, ntext, or image column	2GB-2
	Allowed in GROUP BY, ORDER BY	8,060
	In an index	900
	In a foreign key	900
	In a primary key	900
	In a row	8060
	In source text of a stored procedure	the smaller of Batch size or 250MB
Columns	In GROUP BY, ORDER BY	Limited by the number of bytes
	Columns or expressions in a GROUP BY WITH CUBE or WITH ROLLUP statement	10
	In an index	16
	In a foreign key	16
	In a primary key	16
	In a base table	1,024
	In a SELECT statement	4,096
	In an INSERT statement	1,024

Continued

Category	Object	Size/Quantity
Files	Database size	1,048,516TB
	Files in a database	32,767
	Data file size	32TB
	Log file size	4TB
Indexes	Clustered indexes or constraints per table	1
	Nonclustered indexes or constraints per table	249
	Index key size (bytes)	900
Locks	In a connection	Max. value of locks configured up to 2,147,483,647
	Per server	2,147,483,647 static or 40% of SQL Server memory dynamic
Object	Connections per client	Maximum value of configured connections
	Characters in an identifier	128
	Nested subqueries	64
	Nested trigger levels	32
	Objects in a database	2,147,483,647
	Parameters in a stored procedure	1,024
String	SQL string length (batch size)	128 times the TDS packet size
Tables	FOREIGN KEY constraints	63
	PRIMARY KEY constraints	1
	UNIQUE constraint (indexes) in a table	249 Nonclustered 1 Clustered
	Foreign key table references	253
	Rows	Limited by available disk space
	Triggers per table	Limited by number of objects in a database

Category	Object	Size/Quantity
	Tables in a database	Limited by number of objects in a database
	Tables per SELECT statement	256
	References in a table	63

The following lists the allocated memory for objects in a SQL Server database:

Object	Bytes
Lock	96 per lock
Open database	2,880 per database
Open object	276 per object
User connection	24K per user

Appendix K

sp_configure and sp_dboption settings

Option	Value	Description if Value is TRUE...
autoclose	TRUE	Database shuts down when last user exits
autoshrink	TRUE	Database files marked for shrinking periodically
ANSI empty strings	TRUE	Enables empty strings; follows the SQL-92 rules
ANSI null default	TRUE	CREATE TABLE follows the SQL-92 rules to determine if a column allows NULL values
ANSI nulls	TRUE	Comparisons with NULL evaluate to NULL
ANSI nulls	FALSE	Comparison with NULL evaluates to TRUE
ANSI warnings	TRUE	Error messages generated for conditions such as divide by zero
concat null yields null	TRUE	Yields NULL if either operand in a concatenation is NULL
cursor close on commit	TRUE	Cursors are closed when transaction is committed
cursor close on commit	FALSE	Cursor remains open when transaction is committed
dbo use only	TRUE	Use restricted to database owner
default to local cursor	TRUE	Cursor declarations default to LOCAL

Continued

TABLE K-1 OPTIONS SET BY SP_DBOPTION

Option	Value	Description if Value is TRUE...
merge publish	TRUE	Database can be published for a merge replication
offline	TRUE	Database is offline
published	TRUE	Database can be published for replication
quoted identifier	TRUE	Identifiers enclosed in quotation marks or brackets
read only	TRUE	Database is read-only; users cannot modify it
recursive triggers	TRUE	Enables recursive firing of triggers
select into/bulkcopy	TRUE	Allows SELECT INTO statement and fast bulk copies
single user	TRUE	Database can be accessed by one user at a time
subscribed	TRUE	Database can be subscribed for publication
torn page detection	TRUE	Detects incomplete pages
trunc. log on chkpt.	TRUE	Database is checkpointed whenever the log becomes 70% full; the log is automatically truncated

---

TABLE K-2 SERVER OPTIONS WITH SP_CONFIGURE

Configuration Option	Advanced	Server Restart Required	Self-Configuring	Minimum Setting	Maximum Setting	Default Setting
Affinity mask	*	*		0	2,147,483,647	0
Allow updates				0	1	0

Configuration Option	Advanced	Server Restart Required	Self-Configuring	Minimum Setting	Maximum Setting	Default Setting
Cost threshold for parallelism				0	32,767	5
Cursor threshold	*			-1	2,147,483,647	-1
Default language				0	9,999	0
Default sortorder ID	*	*		0	255	52
Fill factor		*		0	100	0
Index create memory	*			704	1,600,000	1,216
Language in cache		*		3	100	3
Lightweight pooling	*			0	1	0
Locks	*	*	*	5,000	2,147,483,647	0
Max. async IO		*		1	255	8
Max. degree of parallelism	*			0	32	0
Max. server memory	*		*	0	2,147,483,647	2,147,483,647
Max. query wait				0	2,147,483,647	600
Max. text repl size				0	2147483647	65,536
Max. worker threads				10	1,024	255

Continued

TABLE **K-2** SERVER OPTIONS WITH SP_CONFIGURE *(Continued)*

Config-uration Option	Advanced	Server Restart Required	Self-Config-uring	Min-imum Setting	Maximum Setting	Default Setting
Media retention	*	*		0	365	0
Min. memory per query	*			0	2,147,483,647	1,024
Min. server memory	*		*	0	2,147,483,647	0
Nested triggers				0	1	1
Network packet size				512	32767	4,096
Open objects	*	*	*	0	2,147,483,647	500
Priority boost	*	*		0	1	0
Query governor cost limit	*	*		0	2,147,483,647	0
Recovery interval			*	1	32,767	5
Remote access		*		0	1	1
Remote login timeout	*			0	2,147,483,647	5
Remote proc trans		*		0	1	0
Remote query timeout	*			0	2,147,483,647	0

Config- uration Option	Advanced	Server Restart Required	Self- Config- uring	Min- imum Setting	Maximum Setting	Default Setting
Resource timeout	*			5	2,147,483,647	10
Scan for startup procs	*	*		0	1	0
Set working set size	*	*		0	1	0
Show advanced options				0	1	1
Spin counter	*	*		1	2,147,483,647	0, 10 000
Time slice	*	*		50	1,000	100
Unicode comparison style	*	*		0	2,147,483,647	0
Unicode locale id	*	*		0	2,147,483,647	1,033
User connections	*	*	*	0	32,767	0
User options (see User Options below)	*	*	*	0	4,095	0
VLM size				0	2,147,483,647	0

TABLE **K-3** USER OPTIONS

Configuration Value	Option	Controls
1	DISABLE_DEF_CNST_CHK	Interim/deferred constraint checking
2	IMPLICIT_TRANSACTIONS	A transaction is started implicitly when a statement is executed
4	CURSOR_CLOSE_ON_COMMIT	Closes cursors once a commit has been performed
8	ANSI_WARNINGS	Truncation and NULL in aggregate warnings
16	ANSI_PADDING	Padding of fixed-length variables
32	ANSI_NULLS	NULL handling when using equality operators
64	ARITHABORT	Termination of a query when an overflow or divide-by-zero error occurs during query execution
128	ARITHIGNORE	Returns NULL when an overflow or divide-by-zero error occurs during a query
256	QUOTED_IDENTIFIER	Differentiation between single and double quotation marks when evaluating an expression
512	NOCOUNT	Message at the end of each statement that gives the number of rows affected by the statement
1024	ANSI_NULL_DFLT_ON	Session use of ANSI compatibility for nullability to allow NULL values for new columns where nullability is not explicitly stated
2048	ANSI_NULL_DFLT_OFF	Session use of ANSI compatibility for nullability not to allow NULL values for new columns where nullability is not explicitly stated

Appendix L

Files and File Locations

THE DEFAULT SQL SERVER installation directory is `Mssql7`. If you specify a different location for the program files during setup, `<SQL Server Directory>` is the directory where you installed SQL Server 7 client.

TABLE L-1 SQL SERVER FILE LOCATIONS

Directory	Files
<SQL Server Directory>\Backup	Backup files
<SQL Server Directory>\Binn	Windows-based client and server executable files. Extended stored procedure DLLs and online help system
<SQL Server Directory>\Books	Files supporting SQL Server Books Online
<SQL Server Directory>\Data	Files for system and sample databases
<SQL Server Directory>\Ftdata	Files for full-text catalog
<SQL Server Directory>\HTML	HTML help and documentation files for Microsoft Management Console and SQL Server
<SQL Server Directory>\Install	Installation scripts and output files
<SQL Server Directory>\Jobs	Temporary job output storage
<SQL Server Directory>\Log	Files for error log
<SQL Server Directory>\Repldata	Replication tasks working directory
<SQL Server Directory>\Upgrade	Version upgrade from SQL Server 6.x to SQL Server 7.0

Continued

TABLE L-1 SQL SERVER FILE LOCATIONS *(Continued)*

Directory	Files	
<SQL Server Directory>\DevTools\Include	Include files (*.h)	Used to create ODBC, DB-Library, Open Data Services (ODS), SQL-DMO, Embedded SQL for C, and Microsoft Distributed Transaction Coordinator (MS DTC)
<SQL Server Directory>\DevTools\Lib	Library files (*.lib)	
<SQL Server Directory>\DevTools\Samples	Files and ODBC, DB-Library, Open Data Services, SQL-DMO, Embedded SQL for C, and MS DTC examples	
<SQL Server Directory>\Upgrade	Files used for version upgrade from SQL Server 6.x to SQL Server 7.0	

TABLE L-2 DB-LIBRARY FOR C FILE LOCATIONS

Directory	File Name	DB-Library Descriptions
<SQL Server Directory>\DevTools\Include	Sqldb.h	DB-Library function prototypes
	Sqlfront.h	DB-Library type and macro definitions
<SQL Server Directory>\Lib	Bldblib.lib	Borland large-model DB-Library static library for MS-DOS
	Bmdblib.lib	Borland medium-model DB-Library static library for MS-DOS
	Msdblib3.lib	DB-Library import library for Windows
	Ntwdblib.lib	DB-Library import library for Win32
	Rldblib.lib	Large-model DB-Library static library for MS-DOS

Directory	File Name	DB–Library Descriptions
	Rmdblib.lib	Medium-model DB-Library static library for MS-DOS
	W3dblib.lib	No longer used
\<SQL Server Directory> \DevTools\ Samples\ Dblib\C\	Readme.txt	DB-Library sample programs

TABLE L-3 ODE DB FILES

Directory	File	Description
C:\Program Files\ Common Files\ System\ Ole DB	Sqloledb.dll	DLL that implements the SQLOLEDB provider
\<SQL Server Directory> \DevTools\Include	Oledb.h	OLE DB header file for OLE DB providers and consumers
	Sqloledb.h	Header file for SQLOLEDB consumers
\<SQL Server Directory>\DevTools\Lib	Oledb.lib	Library file used for developing SQLOLEDB consumers

Appendix M

Using the Data Transformation Services Wizards

SQL SERVER 7.0 SHIPS with a set of tools called the Data Transformation Services (DTS). These services enable the movement of data between different data sources with or without conversions to the data and/or the schema.

Any OLE DB provider, ODBC data source, or ASCII text file can participate in the transformation as either a source or destination. To use the services, you will use tools such as the DTS Import Wizard, the DTS Export Wizard, and the DTS Package Designer.

This appendix will illustrate the use of the DTS Import and Export Wizards to export the Accounts table from the FundAccts database and then import that data back to a new table but with a slight change in the schema.

The DTS Import and Export Wizards can be run from within the SQL Server Enterprise Manager or from the command line. We'll use the command line to first run the export and then the import of the same data.

First, we'll use the wizard to export the Accounts table in the FundAccts database to a comma-delimited file named accts.txt.

To start the wizard, we enter the following command line:

```
dtswiz /x /usa /p /sSecrets /dFundAccts
```

This command line launches the Export Wizard (/x) and displays its first dialog page. Click *Next* to advance to the second page, where we will choose the data source to export from. See Figure M-1.

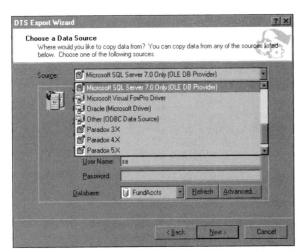

Figure M-1: The Data Transformation Export Wizard Data Source dialog

To export from the `FundAccts` database, already selected in the Database drop-down list, we will choose Microsoft SQL Server 7.0 Only (OLE DB Provider) from the Source drop-down list.

The next page of the Export Wizard asks for a destination. Here, we'll choose a Text file as the destination and enter the path and file name (`accts.txt`) where we want to save the exported data.

Next we specify a table copy or a query copy. Here, we'll select table copy to get the contents of the entire Accounts table. If we had selected query copy, we could select a query from which to export data.

The next page asks us to specify the destination file format, as shown in Figure M-2.

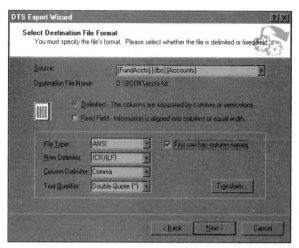

Figure M-2: The Destination File Format page in the Data Transformation Export Wizard

On this page, we'll click the *First row has column names* check box to obtain the column names from the Accounts table as the first row in our output acct.txt file. We will leave the default selections of Delimited columns, ANSI File Type, carriage return/line feed for Row Delimiter, comma as the Column Delimiter, and double quotes for Text Qualifiers.

Click the *Transform...* button to display the *Column Mappings and Transformations* dialog box. This dialog box is shown in Figure M-3.

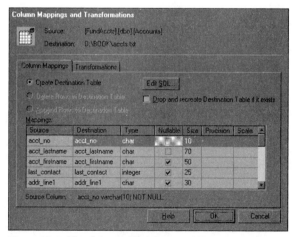

Figure M-3: The Column Mappings and Transformations dialog box enables you to specify how columns appear in the destination file.

The Column Mappings and Transformations dialog box enables us to choose how to handle the destination table – in this case, the creation of the `accts.txt` file – and which columns we want to map from the source to the destination. You have the option of ignoring columns, renaming columns, and changing data types and sizes. We'll look at how we can ignore columns when we import this table back into the `FundAccts` database.

If you want to see or change the `CREATE TABLE` statement for the destination, click the *Edit SQL...* button. If the destination exists and is to be deleted and re-created, check the *Drop and recreate Destination Table if it exits* check box.

Click the *Transformations* tab to display the dialog box in Figure M-4.

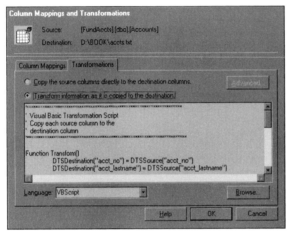

Figure M-4: The Transformation tab enabling you to specify conversions in VBScript, JScript, or PerlScript

On the Transformations tab you can specify that you want the source columns copied to the destination directly or you can use VBScript, JScript, or PerlScript to code data conversions that will take place during the transformation. We'll copy columns without any transformations.

If you copy columns directly, you can click the *Advanced...* button to specify options. The *Advanced* dialog box allows us to specify that all conversions on data be allowed, that the data between the source and destination be an exact match, or we can promote and demote data between 16-bit and 32-bit representations. Nullability can also be changed on the Advanced dialog box page.

The next dialog box page enables saving the specifications we just made to a DTS package, which will be stored in the `msdb` database and/or to run the package immediately.

The last page of the wizard shows a summary of your selections and specifications. From here, you can go back and change your selections or click the *Finish* button to run and/or save the package.

As the package runs, a Transferring Data dialog box is displayed showing the progress of the transformation. At the end of the transformation, you'll get either a successful message or an error message. If you receive an error, you can go to the step where the error occurred in the Transfer Status list box and double-click the error to get more information. From here, you can go back to correct the error or exit the wizard.

Now, we'll import the `accts.txt` file to a new table in the `FundAccts` database. To start the Import Wizard, enter the following command line:

```
dtswiz /i /usa /p /sSecrets /dFundAccts
```

The selections you'll make on the Import Wizard pages are pretty much the same as you made when exporting the data. Select the `accts.txt` file as the source and accept the default `accts` table as the destination.

This time, we're going to change the schema for the destination table. We'll eliminate the `addr_line3` column from the `accts` table. To do this, click the ... button in the Transform column on the *Source/Destination* page. This will display the *Column Mappings and Transformations* dialog box shown in Figure M-5.

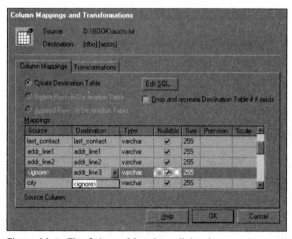

Figure M-5: The Column Mappings dialog box can be used to change the schema of the destination table

To remove the `addr_line3` column from the destination accts table, place the caret in the `addr_line3` source column in the Mappings table and choose `<ignore>` from the drop-down list box. Now, move to the destination column on the same row and do the same. This will cause the SQL `CREATE TABLE` script to regenerate without the `addr_line3` column specified. It will also cause the default transformation script to change. If the table already exists in the database, either check the *Drop and re-create Destination table if it exists* check box or choose the

Delete Rows in Destination Table or *Append Rows to Destination Table* radio but-tons.

Now you can proceed to the end of the wizard dialog box pages and click *Finish* to start importing data from `accts.txt` to the new accts table.

The Data Transformation Import and Export Wizards are great tools for obtain-ing quick results with easy to use point-and-click methods. With these tools, you can create data marts, subsets for testing, move files, and more without hassle. It's a great alternative to using BCP.

Index

Numbers and Symbols

@ sign
   at beginning of identifier, 75
   in local variable names, 286
@@ sign, in global variable names, 286
[] (brackets)
   as wildcard with LIKE keyword, 134
   using to make keywords identifiers, 79
^ (caret) character, using to negate a range or set in wildcard brackets, 134
_ (underscore) character
   as wildcard with LIKE keyword, 133–135
   in identifiers, 75
– character sequence, use of in comments, 74
*/ character sequence, ending comments with, 73
/* character sequence, beginning a comment with, 73
> comparison operator
   using ALL operator with in a subquery, 208
   using ANY operator with in a subquery, 207
< comparison operator
   using ALL operator with in a subquery, 208
   using ANY operator with in a subquery, 207–208
= comparison operator
   using ALL operator with in a subquery, 209
   using ANY operator with in a subquery, 208
<> ALL, as equivalent for NOT IN, 208

sign
   in identifiers, 75
   in local table names, 299
   in SELECT statements, 138
signs, in global table names, 299
* symbol
   for multiplication, 79, 80
   in SELECT statements, 124
$ symbol, in identifiers, 75
/ (division) symbol, 80
+ (plus) symbol, use of in expressions, 76, 79, 80
- (subtraction) symbol, 80
   (Modolo) symbol, 80
   (percent sign)
   with LIKE keyword in SELECT statements, 133
   with pattern expressions, 173

A

@@cursor_rows global variable, checking the number of rows in a result set with, 248
@@error global variable, 255–256
@@fetch_status global variable
   detecting the bounds of the cursor with, 251
   in WHILE statements, 293
@@OPTIONS settings, querying, 264–265
@active_start_time parameter, changing job start time with, 276
@category_name parameter, setting to assign a job to a job category, 272
@cmdexec_success_code, 273
@database_name parameter, specifying for a query, 273

475

G

continued

4. Restrictions on Use of Individual Programs. You must follow the individual requirements and restrictions detailed for each individual program in Appendix A "What's on the CD-ROM." These limitations are also contained in the individual license agreements recorded on the Software Media. These limitations may include a requirement that after using the program for a specified period of time, the user must pay a registration fee or discontinue use. By opening the Software packet(s), you will be agreeing to abide by the licenses and restrictions for these individual programs that are detailed in Appendix A "What's on the CD-ROM" and on the Software Media. None of the material on this Software Media or listed in this Book may ever be redistributed, in original or modified form, for commercial purposes.

5. Limited Warranty.

   (a) IDGB warrants that the Software and Software Media are free from defects in materials and workmanship under normal use for a period of sixty (60) days from the date of purchase of this Book. If IDGB receives notification within the warranty period of defects in materials or workmanship, IDGB will replace the defective Software Media.

   (b) IDGB AND THE AUTHOR OF THE BOOK DISCLAIM ALL OTHER WARRANTIES, EXPRESS OR IMPLIED, INCLUDING WITHOUT LIMITATION IMPLIED WARRANTIES OF MERCHANTABILITY AND FITNESS FOR A PARTICULAR PURPOSE, WITH RESPECT TO THE SOFTWARE, THE PROGRAMS, THE SOURCE CODE CONTAINED THEREIN, AND/OR THE TECHNIQUES DESCRIBED IN THIS BOOK. IDGB DOES NOT WARRANT THAT THE FUNCTIONS CONTAINED IN THE SOFTWARE WILL MEET YOUR REQUIREMENTS OR THAT THE OPERATION OF THE SOFTWARE WILL BE ERROR FREE.

   (c) This limited warranty gives you specific legal rights, and you may have other rights that vary from jurisdiction to jurisdiction.

6. Remedies.

   (a) IDGB's entire liability and your exclusive remedy for defects in materials and workmanship shall be limited to replacement of the Software Media, which may be returned to IDGB with a copy of your receipt at the following address: Software Media Fulfillment Department, Attn.: *Transact-SQL,* IDG Books Worldwide, Inc., 7260 Shadeland Station, Ste. 100, Indianapolis, IN 46256, or call 1-800-762-2974. Please allow three to four weeks for delivery. This Limited Warranty is void if failure of the Software Media has resulted from accident, abuse, or misapplication. Any replacement Software Media will be warranted for the remainder of the original warranty period or thirty (30) days, whichever is longer.

(b) In no event shall IDGB or the author be liable for any damages whatsoever (including without limitation damages for loss of business profits, business interruption, loss of business information, or any other pecuniary loss) arising from the use of or inability to use the Book or the Software, even if IDGB has been advised of the possibility of such damages.

(c) Because some jurisdictions do not allow the exclusion or limitation of liability for consequential or incidental damages, the above limitation or exclusion may not apply to you.

7. <u>U.S. Government Restricted Rights</u>. Use, duplication, or disclosure of the Software by the U.S. Government is subject to restrictions stated in paragraph (c)(1)(ii) of the Rights in Technical Data and Computer Software clause of DFARS 252.227-7013, and in subparagraphs (a) through (d) of the Commercial Computer – Restricted Rights clause at FAR 52.227-19, and in similar clauses in the NASA FAR supplement, when applicable.

8. <u>General</u>. This Agreement constitutes the entire understanding of the parties and revokes and supersedes all prior agreements, oral or written, between them and may not be modified or amended except in a writing signed by both parties hereto that specifically refers to this Agreement. This Agreement shall take precedence over any other documents that may be in conflict herewith. If any one or more provisions contained in this Agreement are held by any court or tribunal to be invalid, illegal, or otherwise unenforceable, each and every other provision shall remain in full force and effect.

my2cents.idgbooks.com

Register This Book — And Win!

Visit **http://my2cents.idgbooks.com** to register this book and we'll automatically enter you in our fantastic monthly prize giveaway. It's also your opportunity to give us feedback: let us know what you thought of this book and how you would like to see other topics covered.

Discover IDG Books Online!

The IDG Books Online Web site is your online resource for tackling technology — at home and at the office. Frequently updated, the IDG Books Online Web site features exclusive software, insider information, online books, and live events!

10 Productive & Career-Enhancing Things You Can Do at www.idgbooks.com

- Nab source code for your own programming projects.

- Download software.

- Read Web exclusives: special articles and book excerpts by IDG Books Worldwide authors.

- Take advantage of resources to help you advance your career as a Novell or Microsoft professional.

- Buy IDG Books Worldwide titles or find a convenient bookstore that carries them.

- Register your book and win a prize.

- Chat live online with authors.

- Sign up for regular e-mail updates about our latest books.

- Suggest a book you'd like to read or write.

- Give us your 2¢ about our books and about our Web site.

You say you're not on the Web yet? It's easy to get started with IDG Books' *Discover the Internet,* available at local retailers everywhere.

Installation Instructions

Programs

Place the disc in your CD-ROM drive, copy the files in the Part III chapter folders (ch18 through ch21) to your hard drive. All source files and the Microsoft Visual C++ 5.0 project make files included.

After compiling the ch19 ODBC sample, set up an ODBC data source using the ODBC control panel Administrator, pointing to your FundAccts sample database. Name the data source FundAccts.

Scripts and Sample Databases

The scripts and sample databases are contained in files named for the corresponding chapter. To access these files, open the appropriate chapter directory and copy the files onto your hard drive. For example, to use the files associated with Chapter 2, open the ch2 folder.